MW00612057

 booksonline

Read this book online today:

With SAP PRESS BooksOnline we offer you online access to knowledge from the leading SAP experts. Whether you use it as a beneficial supplement or as an alternative to the printed book, with SAP PRESS BooksOnline you can:

- Access your book anywhere, at any time. All you need is an Internet connection.
- Perform full text searches on your book and on the entire SAP PRESS library.
- Build your own personalized SAP library.

The SAP PRESS customer advantage:

Register this book today at *www.sap-press.com* and obtain exclusive free trial access to its online version. If you like it (and we think you will), you can choose to purchase permanent, unrestricted access to the online edition at a very special price!

Here's how to get started:

1. Visit *www.sap-press.com*.
2. Click on the link for SAP PRESS BooksOnline and login (or create an account).
3. Enter your free trial license key, shown below in the corner of the page.
4. Try out your online book with full, unrestricted access for a limited time!

Your personal free trial **license key**
for this online book is:

524k-9gyu-djan-8wtp

BRFplus—Business Rule Management for ABAP™ Applications

 PRESS

SAP PRESS is a joint initiative of SAP and Galileo Press. The know-how offered by SAP specialists combined with the expertise of the Galileo Press publishing house offers the reader expert books in the field. SAP PRESS features first-hand information and expert advice, and provides useful skills for professional decision-making.

SAP PRESS offers a variety of books on technical and business related topics for the SAP user. For further information, please visit our website: *www.sap-press.com*.

Chase, Omar, Taylor, Rosenberg, von Rosing
Applying Real-World BPM in an SAP Environment
2011, approx. 650 pp., hardcover
ISBN 978-1-59229-343-8

Jan Rauscher, Volker Stiehl
The Developer's Guide to the
SAP NetWeaver Composition Environment
2008, 365 pp., hardcover, with DVD
ISBN 978-1-59229-171-7

Snabe, Rosenberg, Møller, Scavillo
Business Process Management – the SAP Roadmap
2009, 411 pp., hardcover
ISBN 978-1-59229-231-8

Günther Färber, Julia Kirchner
ABAP Basics
2nd ed. 2010, approx. 520 pp., hardcover
ISBN 978-1-59229-369-8

Carsten Ziegler and Thomas Albrecht

BRFplus — Business Rule Management for ABAP™ Applications

Galileo Press

Bonn • Boston

Galileo Press is named after the Italian physicist, mathematician and philosopher Galileo Galilei (1564–1642). He is known as one of the founders of modern science and an advocate of our contemporary, heliocentric worldview. His words *Eppur si muove* (And yet it moves) have become legendary. The Galileo Press logo depicts Jupiter orbited by the four Galilean moons, which were discovered by Galileo in 1610.

Editor Florian Zimniak
Copyeditor Pamela Siska
Cover Design Nadine Kohl, Graham Geary
Photo Credit Getty Images/RF/Dorling Kindersley
Layout Design Vera Brauner
Production Manager Kelly O'Callaghan
Assistant Production Editor Graham Geary
Typesetting Publishers' Design and Production Services, Inc.
Printed and bound in Canada

ISBN 978-1-59229-293-6

© 2011 by Galileo Press Inc., Boston (MA)

1st Edition 2011

Library of Congress Cataloging-in-Publication Data
Albrecht, Thomas.
  BRFplus : business rule management for ABAP applications / Thomas Albrecht, Carsten Ziegler. — 1st ed.
    p. cm.
  Includes index.
  ISBN-13: 978-1-59229-293-6
  ISBN-10: 1-59229-293-3
  1. ABAP/4 (Computer program language) 2. Management information systems.
  3. SAP ERP. I. Ziegler, Carsten. II. Title.
  QA76.73.A12A43 2011
  658'.05—dc22
2010043166

All rights reserved. Neither this publication nor any part of it may be copied or reproduced in any form or by any means or translated into another language, without the prior consent of Galileo Press GmbH, Rheinwerkallee 4, 53227 Bonn, Germany.

Galileo Press makes no warranties or representations with respect to the content hereof and specifically disclaims any implied warranties of merchantability or fitness for any particular purpose. Galileo Press assumes no responsibility for any errors that may appear in this publication.

"Galileo Press" and the Galileo Press logo are registered trademarks of Galileo Press GmbH, Bonn, Germany. SAP PRESS is an imprint of Galileo Press.

All of the screenshots and graphics reproduced in this book are subject to copyright © SAP AG, Dietmar-Hopp-Allee 16, 69190 Walldorf, Germany.

SAP, the SAP-Logo, mySAP, mySAP.com, mySAP Business Suite, SAP NetWeaver, SAP R/3, SAP R/2, SAP B2B, SAPtronic, SAPscript, SAP BW, SAP CRM, SAP Early Watch, SAP ArchiveLink, SAP GUI, SAP Business Workflow, SAP Business Engineer, SAP Business Navigator, SAP Business Framework, SAP Business Information Warehouse, SAP inter-enterprise solutions, SAP APO, AcceleratedSAP, InterSAP, SAPoffice, SAPfind, SAPfile, SAPtime, SAPmail, SAPaccess, SAP-EDI, R/3 Retail, Accelerated HR, Accelerated HiTech, Accelerated Consumer Products, ABAP, ABAP/4, ALE/WEB, Alloy, BAPI, Business Framework, BW Explorer, Duet, Enjoy-SAP, mySAP.com e-business platform, mySAP Enterprise Portals, RIVA, SAPPHIRE, TeamSAP, Webflow and SAP PRESS are registered or unregistered trademarks of SAP AG, Walldorf, Germany.

All other products mentioned in this book are registered or unregistered trademarks of their respective companies.

Contents at a Glance

Dear Reader,

When Carsten Ziegler and Thomas Albrecht of SAP AG approached me almost two years ago with an idea of writing a book on BRFplus, they saw me frowning with doubt. Though I consider myself being quite up-to-date in regards to SAP's product portfolio, I had never heard of BRFplus before.

However, the motto that the authors chose for the introduction to this book, "There is nothing so stable as change," is very applicable to SAP product development and to the customer demand for new technology. Over the last two years, SAP has heavily invested in their strategy and tools for Business Process Management. Along with SAP NetWeaver BPM and SAP NetWeaver Business Rules Management, BRF-plus became one of the hottest new components that shipped with the latest SAP NetWeaver releases. I am very pleased that we are now able to provide you with the complete technical reference to BRFplus, just in time for the release of its new version in Application Server 7.02.

We appreciate your business, and welcome your feedback. Your comments and suggestions are the most useful tools to help us improve our books for you, the reader. We encourage you to visit our website at *www.sap-press.com* and share your feedback about this work.

Thank you for purchasing a book from SAP PRESS!

Florian Zimniak
Publishing Director, SAP PRESS

Galileo Press
100 Grossman Drive, Suite 205
Braintree, MA 02184

florian.zimniak@galileo-press.com
www.sap-press.com

Contents

7   Advanced 337

8   Deployment 399

Foreword

I first met Carsten at SAP TechEd in 2009 when he presented BRFplus. I was impressed then by the capability of both Carsten and his product. I have spent the last eight years promoting business rules and helping companies use business rules technology, like BRFplus, to automate and improve business decisions. When we met, I was writing a white paper for SAP customers on business rules and decisioning for process experts. Carsten's introduction of BRFplus made it clear to me that SAP has a robust, effective, ABAP-based business rules technology that is suitable as the foundation for effective Decision Management.

Decision Management is an approach that focuses on automating and improving operational business decisions, including the many micro-decisions that impact a single customer or a single claim. In the years since Neil Raden and I published *Smart (Enough) Systems*, the first book on Decision Management, the approach has become increasingly known and adopted. It requires a solid platform for managing decision-making logic which is a business rules management system. Such a system allows business rules—individual elements of business logic that are atomic, readable, and manageable—to be captured, updated, deployed, and analyzed. The combination of business rules management system and a Decision Management approach results in systems and processes that are simpler, more agile, more aligned with the business, and fundamentally smarter.

Take one company that I came across while I was writing a chapter on Decision Management and business rules for the book *Applying Real-World BPM in an SAP Environment*. This company realized that they needed to automate the decision to identify the failure implied by a set of reported symptoms. Using BRFplus to answer the question "What failure do the symptoms imply?" they were able to automate a previously manual decision. The use of BRFplus meant that they could change the rules behind this decision independent of their systems and processes. Because BRFplus let them add rules about new product models quickly and easily, it clearly increased their agility.

Many companies make the mistake of assuming that decision management and business rules are only relevant in a business process management context. In fact, they are also highly relevant to those who build and manage enterprise applications. Decision Management represents the last stage of decomposition for a monolithic application. Best practices already call for developers to separate the data, user interface, and process definitions from applications. Decision Management takes this one step further and separates decision-making logic from the remainder of the technical implementation. Extracting decision-making logic as business rules and putting them into BRFplus functions allows you to create coherent components for decision-making that are part of your enterprise backbone.

I have seen that such a separation makes systems more agile, because you can rapidly deploy changes to decision-making logic, change decision-making logic independent of the rest of your application, and encapsulate these changes behind a well-defined interface so that the main application remains stable even as decision-making logic changes. The use of business rules for managing the logic in decision-making components has also allowed the companies I work with to empower business users and analysts to collaborate effectively with their IT teams and even to control some of the logic themselves. Effective management of the decision logic has improved decision accuracy, compliance, and consistency.

This book on BRFplus is very timely. SAP is already adopting business rules and BRFplus in its applications. In everything from determining eligibility for social benefits to pricing and loyalty programs, SAP is using BRFplus to bring agility, accuracy, and consistency to the decisions that drive enterprise applications. This commitment to business rules at the core of the SAP Business Suite is significant and represents a milestone in development and technology. SAP is the first major enterprise application vendor to do so. This shows how the approach has become mainstream and provides further evidence that it works.

Many people talk about business rules as a "must" in the context of business process management. SAP supports such an approach with the NetWeaver Business Rules Management product (SAP NetWeaver BRM), but BRFplus extends the promise of business rules to your enterprise applications as well. It allows those applications direct access to business rules and decision making components. A crucial factor is that BRFplus executes natively on the ABAP stack, allowing it to take full advantage of your investments in tuning and managing your ABAP environment.

BRFplus is a not a lightweight product. It is a complete business rules management system that allows you to create, manage, and deploy simple and complex rules in an ABAP environment. With its web-based editor, hierarchical catalogs, robust access control, release management, simulation capabilities, testing tools, and multiple metaphors for writing rules (decision tables, decision trees, expression builder) it is extremely powerful. Because it integrates seamlessly with the rest of the SAP environment, it is an ideal choice for SAP customers to get started with business rules.

With SAP NetWeaver 7.0 Enhancement Package 2 the vision for BRFplus is complete. It is time for SAP customers to follow SAP's lead and adopt business rules technology to manage their decisions. You should stop writing decision-making logic in code but bring agility, accuracy, and consistency to the way your systems make decisions. When it comes to business rules on an ABAP foundation, BRFplus is the tool to use.

With this book, Carsten and Thomas have written a detailed yet readable description of BRFplus. It covers everything from the web-based user interface for non-technical users to the technical details of the APIs. If you plan to use business rules to extend and manage your SAP Business Suite applications, which I highly recommend, this book will show you how to do so.

James Taylor
CEO and Principal Consultant
Decision Management Solutions
Palo Alto, CA

"It is not the strongest of species that survives, nor the most intelligent, but rather the one most responsive to change." —Charles Darwin

"There is nothing so stable as change." —Bob Dylan

Introduction

Rules are an integral part of our everyday life. In general they can be characterized as directives that tell what should be done or what is expected in a specific situation, for example: "The size of an email must not exceed 10 megabytes," "If the traffic light is red, you have to stop," and "If you buy three items, you get one for free." Business-related rules can be formulated, for example, due to legal requirements, for policies and processes, for the collection of expert knowledge, and for many more reasons. Such rules are often simply written on paper, entered into spreadsheets, or even exist only in people's minds. The integration of arbitrary rules into business software therefore used to be a difficult task. In the past it often required either costly custom development or complex processes to integrate manual decision making.

With a Business Rule Management System (BRMS) the rules can be implemented, accessed, and managed in one central place. The rule logic is decoupled from the general application logic and can independently be adapted any time to changed requirements. At SAP many different tools exist that allow one to define only very specific types of rules for similar specific use cases. BRFplus is a relatively new Business Rule Management System that can replace all those tools. The first functional release of BRFplus was shipped in 2008 with Enhancement Package 1 of SAP NetWeaver 7.0. Due to several limitations it has been used either internally at SAP or by selected customers only. With Enhancement Package 2 of SAP NetWeaver 7.0, the first unrestricted release becomes available. Even though BRFplus has attracted considerable attention, it is not yet known by many customers because the available information materials are still scarce.

With this book we intend to remedy this drawback and help BRFplus to literally become a general rule for business rules in the SAP ABAP stack. As the architect and developer of BRFplus, we have not only collected and condensed existing information from different sources, such as the standard documentation and papers in the SAP developer network or training material: We also have gathered first-hand expert know-how directly from the development team members, which has not been documented so far. Combined with our own knowledge, you will find no better source of information.

Without the help of many contributors, the book could not have been realized. We therefore first of all want to thank the whole BRFplus team for its enduring contributions to the product itself and the information provided for this book. Particularly worthy of mention here are Nitesh Lohiya, Venu Janardhanan, Michael Aakolk, Piyush Deora, Joydeep Paul, Marco Wüst, Hans-Georg Beuter, Claus Horn, Christian Auth, Thomas Salm and Michael Bär. We want to thank of course also all other involved current or former colleagues and participants as well.

BRFplus would not have been possible without the support of Martin Deggelmann and Andrea Rösinger. They gave us the freedom and created the atmosphere for innovation, although there were tough times, especially at the beginning. Therefore they deserve our gratitude. Similarly, Heinz Ulrich Roggenkember and Ralf Ehret were great supporters. They promoted BRFplus and helped to identify and set live the first two pilot customers. This was a major milestone for BRFplus in terms of acceptance and architecture verification. And finally, we also want to thank Lars Biewald and Matthias Jordan. Their BRF experience and the numerous discussions with them helped a lot to bypass some of the many pitfalls on the way to the final architecture of BRFplus.

A big thank you goes to our editors and primary contacts Florian Zimniak and Maike Lübbers at Galileo Press for their patience and valuable help. Also, we would like to thank Pamela Siska who did the copyediting for this book, as well as Kelly O'Callaghan at Galileo Press who took care for a timely production.

Last but not least, we want to thank all our friends and family members for their motivation and understanding that we had to devote so much time to writing this book.

Overview

In case of *BRFplus – Business Rule Management for ABAP Applications*, the question "who will be the readers?" is not easy to answer, because the interested people can be manifold:

▸ Business analysts and consultants might want to get an overview of the capabilities and features of BRFplus.

▸ Business experts typically need to know how a specific rule or parts of a rule can be expressed and maintained with the Web-enabled user interface provided by BRFplus.

▶ Business rule administrators also require further technical knowledge for the general setup and management of the rules.

▶ Software developers need to know how BRFplus rules can be accessed programmatically. They may also want to use the provided programming interface (API) to create rules dynamically or to develop arbitrary user interfaces.

To satisfy these needs, the book will begin with the most generic parts, which should be of interest for all readers. The chapters become more and more specific and thus in part also more technical. The description of the API has, however, been moved into separate sections where feasible. These sections usually follow directly after the general description of the corresponding topic. If you are not interested in the API, you can simply skip these parts.

In detail, the structure of the book is the following.

▶ **Chapter 1** is intended for all readers interested in business rules in general. Here you will find the fundamental concepts and benefits of Business Rule Management Systems.

▶ **Chapter 2** contains a short walk through the basic concepts and usage of BRF-plus. You will first become acquainted with the provided user interface, the BRFplus Workbench. You will then learn how a business rule is typically realized. By way of a simple example, the various objects involved in the definition of a BRFplus rule are introduced

▶ **Chapter 3** provides a tutorial to get more familiar with BRFplus. The object types that already were mentioned in chapter 2 are characterized in more detail here. The tutorial describes the creation of a rule in the workbench step by step and with many screenshots. It should thus be easy to reproduce the example in your own system. For developers, the creation of the same rule is explained again, but this time with the usage of the relevant API.

▶ **Chapter 4** is of importance if you want to dive deeper into BRFplus. Here you find information with respect to the management of BRFplus objects in general. The chapter describes the lifecycle, distribution, and common characteristics of all BRFplus objects in detail. For developers, this chapter also outlines the basic architecture of the API.

▶ **Chapter 5** continues with the detailed description of BRFplus objects, this time with the focus on the characteristics of the different object types. They determine the functional scope of BRFplus with regard to rules. It is thus recommended that you read this chapter before you start defining your own rules with BRFplus. The embedded API sections are, however, optional.

- ► **Chapter 6** offers insight into additional tools that are available in the BRFplus workbench. The first tool, which allows simulation of BRFplus rules, is intended for all users. The other tools are relevant for administrative tasks and thus possibly not of interest to everyone.

- ► **Chapter 7** handles advanced features of BRFplus, such as performance optimization, tracing, extensibility and, last but not least, the integration of the user interface into custom applications. Programming skills are essential to understanding all parts of this chapter.

- ► **Chapter 8** presents deployment scenarios for BRFplus rules with respect to storage types and system landscapes. A fundamental understanding of the SAP change and transport system is expected.

- ► **Chapter 9** finally offers a methodology for how to set up a larger BRFplus project with the involvement of technical and business experts. The chapter also provides a rough estimate of the required efforts and costs.

This chapter provides an introduction to the business rules approach and business rule management systems in general. Afterwards, the business rule strategy at SAP will be explained.

1   About Business Rules

Companies have always had policies and rules in place to define what should or should not be done. Such rules can be found coded in software systems or in handbooks. Often, they even exist only as the expertise of a small group of employees in a department.

1.1   Definition

According to the Business Rules Group, an independent organization with the mission of formulating statements and supporting standards about business rules, a business rule is "a statement that defines or constrains some aspect of the business. It is intended to assert business structure or to control or influence the behavior of the business."[1] Business rules describe the operations, definitions, and constraints that apply to an organization. They can apply to people, processes, corporate behaviors, and computing systems in an organization, and are put in place to help the organization achieve its goals.

Barbara von Halle formulated a similar definition: "Business rules are a formal expression of knowledge or preference, a guidance system for steering behavior (a transaction) in a desired direction. On the grand scale, business rules, then, are the guidance system that influences the collective behavior of an organization's people and information systems."[2]

These are very general definitions of business rules that include any number of and various different types of rules. The rule "Smoking is prohibited inside all com-

---

1   David Hay and Keri Anderson Healy: *Defining Business Rules – What Are They Really?* Technical report, The Business Rules Group, *http://www.businessrulesgroup.org/first_paper/br01c0.htm*, 2000.

2   Barbara von Halle: *What is a Business Rules Approach?* The Data Administration Newsletter – *http://www.tdan.com/view-articles/4983*, January 2002.

pany buildings" is a valid rule adhering to the definitions. Not all business rules are relevant to business operations and the scope of the rules in total needs to be narrowed to the relevant rules to better deal with them. This fact leads to another important constraint that is typically used when defining business rules: a "business rule expresses specific constraints on the creation, updating, and removal of persistent data in an information system."[3]

Using this definition of business rules makes management of business rules in an information system possible because business rules are concerned only with the data in an information system. This is the definition of business rules that will be used in this book.

1.2 Ubiquity of Business Rules

Business rules exist in each and every organization around the world. This, however, says nothing about an organization's awareness of its business rules. Before business rules are analyzed and formalized, they exist in a multitude of forms: company policies, guidelines, industry standards, computer code, or as knowledge in the minds of employees. The first step toward the effective management of business rules is the creating awareness and compiling these different kinds of policies.

Figure 1.1 shows a simplified diagram of a mortgage process containing three major steps. For each of the steps, the business rules are depicted. For example, there are business rules that define whether the application is valid, whether all relevant data has been supplied, and whether the data is within expected ranges. Next a credit score can be determined with business rules, and special terms or conditions may become active or even mandatory. Finally, the approval decision is again based on business rules and a risk and compliance analysis for the complete process may be subject to a set of business rules as well. It becomes obvious that the quality and efficiency of the management of the rules becomes crucial for the organization's success.

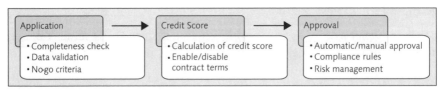

Figure 1.1 Business Rules in Mortgage Processing

3   David Hay and Keri Anderson Healy: *Defining Business Rules – What Are They Really?* Technical report, The Business Rules Group, *http://www.businessrulesgroup.org/first_paper/br01c0.htm*, 2000.

In general, business rules can be assumed whenever data has to be checked for errors or invalid states need to be detected. Another category of business rules deals with mapping or classification of data, including the derivation of new facts from existing facts. In addition, calculations are done based on business rules and, of course, all kinds of business decisions. Figure 1.2 shows various examples of the use of business rules.

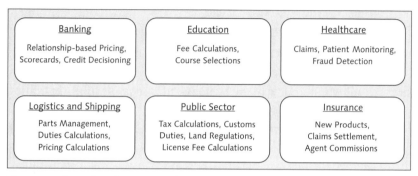

Figure 1.2 Examples of Business Rules

1.3 Business Rule Management Systems

Business rules can be as simple as adding the value added tax to the retail price of a good. However, they can be also very complex, such as those involved in the organization and optimization of commodity flow. Unforeseen contingencies in such mission-critical applications require real-time amendment because every moment of failure produces high costs. No matter how simple or complex the business rules are, being able to create, maintain, and track the business rules that are governing the operational processes of an organization is critical to its success.

An effective way of managing business rules is a Business Rule Management System (BRMS). A BRMS is a software system used to define, deploy, execute, monitor, and maintain the variety and complexity of decision logic in the form of business rules that are used by operational systems within an organization. The purpose of a BRMS is to ease the identification and authoring of business rules, and to enable the management and execution of the right rules at the right time and in the correct order, without making changes in the application code that implements the processes.

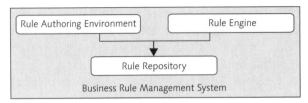

Figure 1.3 Components of a Business Rule Management System

Figure 1.3 shows the components a BRMS:

- An authoring environment for the definition and maintenance of the business rules
- A repository to allow the storage of the business rules separate from application code
- A rules engine to execute the business rules upon invocation by application code

1.3.1 Rule Authoring Environment

The rule authoring environment is a set of user interface tools that target technical as well as non-technical users. IT professionals should not make business decisions in the form of business rules but instead help the business experts responsible for running a business area. The business experts have all the required business expertise to make the best decisions. The BRMS aims at empowerment of business users to enable them to change and to organize the business rules directly. Therefore, a BRMS has to provide different rule expression and representation formats, such as natural language-like text rules (`IF condition THEN action`) and rulesets, rule flows, decision tables, or decision trees.

For consistent and complete business rules, the BRMS has to provide tools for detecting contradictions or value combinations that are not yet covered in the rules. Also, tools for impact and dependency analysis are very important because the rules base can become very large. Related to the analysis of the rules is the question of rule testing. The authoring environment must provide simulation capabilities that allow tests to be performed with predefined sets of input data. Rule authors need to verify that the results are as expected, and they should be able to understand the decision path, that is, the involved business rules artifacts and how they have influenced the final results.

Besides plain rule authoring, the user interface of a BRMS also has to provide a means of rules organization and management as well as related tools for the management of the rules lifecycle and the access and release control. In an organization there can be easily several thousands of business rules in various representation formats. To make the work efficient, a BRMS needs to provide simple and transparent capabilities for organizing the rules for many projects. Business rules are often grouped by high-level content areas, which are further broken down into specific tasks, also called decision services. Without grouping mechanisms, such as rule catalogs, the business rules would become unmanageable. Business rules must be easy to find, and only the business rules relevant to a business domain should be presented to experts in this domain. User roles may have further impact on the features made available in the BRMS. Although both user groups, technical and functional, may work on the same business rules, the IT professionals will be presented with more technical details, such as those involved in connecting business processes with business rules.

1.3.2 Rule Repository

The rule repository captures the business rules and the business vocabulary created in the rules authoring environment. It may also contain additional data that steers how the business processes make use of the business rules approach. The repository is kept separate from the rule engine in order to facilitate implementation and maintenance of the business rules. Typically, rule repositories provide change management with versioning support and access control, for multi-user business rules authoring. The rule repository contains the rules with their full lifecycle, from initial creation to the deployment of specific versions of the rules, and finally to rules archiving and deletion.

The rules repository is the backbone of the rules authoring environment. It needs to provide all the services that are made available by the authoring environment, such as grouping, powerful search capabilities, or change and execution logs for legal compliance and rules execution reporting and analytics. The repository is further used by the rules engine to retrieve the rule definitions for execution. Often, the business rules are pre-compiled or optimized in another way prior to execution.

Some rule repositories can tightly integrate with other technologies, such as Business Process Management (BPM) or Enterprise Resource Planning (ERP) applications, to reduce integration complexity, costs, and time-to-value. Linking to ERP applications also allows for jumpstart business vocabularies by using already existing data definitions from these applications.

1.3.3 Rule Engine

The business rule engine (BRE) is often seen as the heart of a BRMS. The purpose of the rule engine is to execute the rule based logic built with the rule authoring environment. For the invocation of rules, BREs expose APIs or provide Web services. Some applications, such as those for pricing or risk and compliance controls, call into the BRE extremely frequently. In such scenarios, high performance and the ability to run multiple instances in parallel are the key assets of a BRE. To meet those requirements, some BREs provide pre-compilation or code generators and optimized APIs to improve the rules execution runtime and reduce memory consumption. Some BREs also support dynamic rule changes so that rules can be changed without any downtime of the applications using the rules.

1.4 Rule Representation

Separating the business rules lifecycle from the application development cycle enables more timely responses to business changes. For transparency to non-technical users and to enable them to perform changes themselves, the BRMS needs to provide a collection of rule representations that can be understood by all user groups and that provide the best fit with specific business rules challenges. The most common approaches are:

- Rules and Rulesets
- Rule Flows
- Decision Tables
- Decision Trees
- Formulas
- Scorecards

1.4.1 Rules and Rulesets

Plain rules are also called IF-THEN rules. They are sets of textual statements. They contain a condition part, introduced by the IF term, and an action part, connected to the THEN term. When the condition is true the action is executed.

Often the rules of an organization contribute to a particular decision in a process. Those rules do not affect other decisions and processes and can be managed independently. Rulesets allow the grouping of rules for better organization, structuring, and management. Listing 1.1 shows an example of a ruleset with three rules that determines shipping costs based on the customer status.

```
IF     customer status is "Gold"
THEN   shipping costs are 0$


IF     customer status is "Silver"
THEN   shipping costs are 10$


IF     customer status is neither "Silver" nor "Gold"
THEN   shipping costs are 20$
```

Listing 1.1 Ruleset Example—Determination of Shipping Costs

1.4.2 Rule Flows

Rule flows define the graphically maintained sequence of execution steps in a decision process, using tasks, branching, and iterations. Tasks hold collections of rules or other representation formats, such as decision tables and decision trees. Figure 1.4 shows a rule flow that first computes the shopping cart and then adds shipping costs when the sum is less or equal to US $1,000.

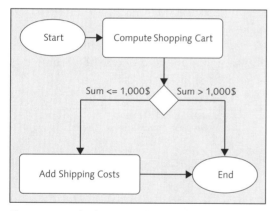

Figure 1.4   Rule Flow Example—Finalization of Purchase

1.4.3 Decision Tables

Many organizations implement a major part of their business rules with decision tables. Decision tables provide a very structured and organized view of interrelated business rules. They define condition columns with each cell in the column being a particular condition. If all conditions for a row match, the result from the corresponding result column cells are returned or actions are performed. Decision tables are very popular because of their spreadsheet-like nature and the ability they offer to exchange data easily with office applications such as Microsoft Excel. Capturing rules in a decision table provides a good overview, which leads to excellent capabilities in terms of analyzing gaps or contradictions in the defined rules. Table 1.1 shows a decision table that derives shipping costs from the customer status and the purchase amount.

Customer Status	Purchase Amount	Shipping Costs
Gold		$0
Silver	>$1,000	$0
Silver	<=$1,000	$10
not Silver, not Gold	>$1,000	$0
not Silver, not Gold	<=$1,000	$20

Table 1.1 Decision Table Example—Determination of Shipping Costs

1.4.4 Decision Trees

Decision trees graphically depict chains of dependent conditions leading to return values or to an action. Similar to decision tables, decision trees provide a mechanism to easily structure interrelated business rules. Making explicit the chain of conditions for specific results or actions provides a good overview of completeness and required inputs. Figure 1.5 shows how the decision table for the shipping cost determination can be converted into a decision tree. For a compact representation, the tree starts with a condition on purchase amount, and only when required is the customer status included to determine the shipping costs.

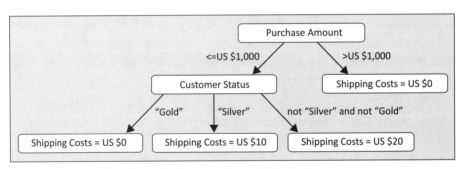

Figure 1.5 Decision Tree Example—Determination of Shipping Costs

1.4.5 Formulas

Formulas are business rules that produce a value according to a specified mathematical algorithm. Formulas access the business vocabulary as input for the calculation step and return the result. A BRMS usually provides a set of built-in functions for usage in formulas, such as for financial mathematics. The following is a simple formula for calculating the invoice amount:

Invoice Amount = Purchase Amount + Shipping Costs

1.4.6   Scorecards

A scorecard is a special form of table that examines different properties or characteristics of an object or transaction and assigns weights based on the values. All underlying weights are added to arrive at an overall score, which can be compared to other scores for a rank-based decision.

1.5   Application Architecture

Once the benefits of the business rule approach becomes obvious, organizational enthusiasm is likely to increase. Business rules define the manner in which organizations conduct their business. It is therefore imperative that they keep changing in accordance with market requirements. Business users are the first to understand why, how, and when rules should be changed. Consequently, they demand alterations of existing applications to include decisioning and business rules in the operations of the organization.

1.5.1   Traditional Application Design

Traditional application design moved business rules into software code, scripts, or even the database layers, using, for example, stored procedures and triggers. The advantage of automation and enforcement of the business rules was accompanied by the disadvantage of lack of transparency and poor organization agility. Business areas dodge the drawbacks of inscrutable system behavior and inflexible software architecture by moving decision logic out of the system into documents or by establishing expert teams. Subsequently, there are high costs for the education of experts and the required manual process steps. Another important problem is the consistency of business practice: it becomes very difficult to ensure compliance and to control risk when decisions are not reflected in the system. Figure 1.6 visualizes the conflict inherent in the traditional approaches.

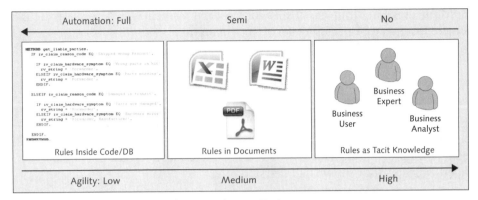

Figure 1.6 Automation Versus Agility in Application Design

1.5.2 Application Design with Business Rules Management

To solve this conflict of automation versus agility, business rules need to be considered in the architecture of the applications at an early stage. It is a widely accepted practice to separate data and application logic. This separation is achieved by putting an application's data into a database managed by a database management system (DBMS). Similarly, business rules should be put into a BRMS and business processes into a Business Process Management System (BPMS). Separating business logic in the form of decisions from other application logic allows users to apply the best tools for the specific segments. Programmers continue to develop the remaining application logic, while business experts are empowered to create and maintain the business rules using the BRMS. Figure 1.7 shows the evolution of application architecture with database, rules and processes being separated from the business application code.

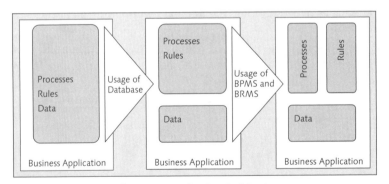

Figure 1.7 Evolution of Business Application Architecture

Managing business rules in an environment built especially for this particular task makes it easy to tailor optimized user interfaces. Natural language text, used in rules or decision tables, creates transparency for business experts. Once the connection between application code and BRMS is established, programming skills and code changes for updating the business rules are not required. The costly and time-consuming processes of requirements gathering, communication, implementation, and testing can be minimized. Instead, the business experts can conduct most of the changes directly in the BRMS.

With a BRMS, business rules can be centrally managed, readily found, and easily compared. Transparency not only increases the flexibility and time-to-market of new practice and products. As inefficiencies become visible, transparency also becomes the basis for higher business process quality, continuous improvement, and consistent decision making. The life cycle of business rules is naturally different from that of business processes and application code. Using a BRMS, business rules are updated with a much higher frequency, thus making business processes flexible. No matter whether the processes are hard coded or composed in a BPM tool, they do not need to change. Figure 1.8 illustrates the typical update frequency of business rules, business process, and the remaining application code.[4]

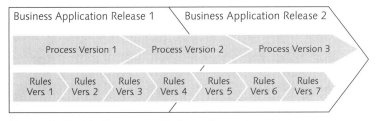

Figure 1.8 Update Frequency of Software Segments

1.5.3 Usage Patterns

Because the rules are defined external to the application code, the BRMS allows users to make explicit the decisions within processes. A decision service with a set of input and output (result) parameters is therefore best defined in the BRMS. The application calls the decision service providing the inputs according to the decision service interface. After execution of the rules in the rules engine, the results are returned to the application. Based on the received results, actions may be performed. The service-like connection between the application code and the

---

4   James Taylor, Neil Raden: *Smart Enough Systems: How to Deliver Competitive Advantage by Automating Hidden Decisions*, Prentice Hall, 2007.

business rules is often referred to as a decision service pattern.[5] This pattern makes it easy to automate many decisions and to iteratively improve the service quality, independent of the application code.

In addition to the plain decision service, some BRMSs provide powerful capabilities for accommodating direct action calls external to the BRE. It is a very smart concept to raise events, to cause alerts, or to write log entries from within the rule definition in case of extraordinary incidents. In use cases where the BRMS is tightly embedded into the surrounding application, more powerful actions to manage application entities may be defined in the rules. This approach requires at least a basic understanding of transaction and session management (Commit, Rollback) and error handling. The pattern therefore may be unsuitable for application by business experts, although they still benefit from the transparency of the business logic being exposed in a BRMS.

1.6   Business Rules at SAP

Software from SAP always allowed customers to implement business processes in a flexible way. In simple cases, customizing tables were used. Complex configuration was often done with code exits such as Business Add-Ins (BAdIs). In between these two extremes, a variety of tools, engines, and frameworks have emerged over the past 20 years. Although most of them do not claim to be a Business Rules Management System (BRMS), to some degree they offer functionality that is comparable to that of a BRMS. Some of these tools and frameworks were created with a focus on a specific application; some were also meant to be reused by multiple applications and processes. The most notable products are:

- Business Rule Framework (BRF)
- Condition Technique
- Derivation Tool
- Formula Builder (Fobu)
- Hierarchical Derivation Service (HDS)
- Internet Pricing Configurator (IPC)
- Rule Modeler

---

5 James Taylor, Neil Raden: *Smart Enough Systems: How to Deliver Competitive Advantage by Automating Hidden Decisions*, Prentice Hall, 2007.

▶ Validation, Substitution, Rules (VSR)

▶ Workflow Rules

1.6.1 The Origin of BRFplus

In 2005 SAP investigated the usage of business rules in the new technology platform for SAP Business ByDesign. There was consensus about the importance of business rules and the advantage of highly flexible and code-free customization. The existing tools and concepts were either limited in scope or required development skills and thus locked out business experts. Consequently, there began the development of a general purpose BRMS, what is known today as Business Rule Framework plus (BRFplus).

It was clear that the existing products reflected an impressive wealth of experience and expertise. Those approaches and features that turned out to work were preserved in the architecture of BRFplus and those that created problems were left out. Even though BRFplus is a completely new code line, its name indicates the major architectural influence of BRF. BRF turned out to be the best existing framework with respect to modular extensibility. This was an important factor because a generic component is never able to serve all possible use cases equally well.

BRFplus has been designed to integrate perfectly with the ABAP stack and support ABAP-based applications in the best possible way. Further, it was important to preserve the functionality of the existing tools as far as possible so that a migration from use case to BRFplus was possible. Today, BRFplus serves more than 100 usages in virtually all SAP solutions. Consolidating and migrating usages from the other BRMS-like tools towards BRFplus is the cornerstone of a bigger strategy to remove complexity and reduce total cost of ownership.

1.6.2 BRFplus Rules Authoring—Features

BRFplus provides its user interface, the BRFplus Workbench, in Web Dynpro ABAP technology. The Workbench encapsulates collaborative functionality for modeling, editing, and managing business rules and related artifacts:

▶ Because the Workbench runs completely in the browser, no installation is needed on client side.

▶ The Workbench or parts of it can be embedded into application UIs or used standalone.

▶ Full support of data dictionary artifacts in the BRFplus authoring environment provides data element description and documentation as well as dynamic value help based on domain value lists and data base table entries.

▶ An extensibility concept allows users to add custom action and expression editors.

▶ Several settings allow users to configure the Workbench according to user groups or personal preferences.

▶ Catalogs help to organize the rules artifacts in an arbitrary manner.

▶ The building blocks for modeling of business logic have their individual, business user friendly user interfaces.

▶ A full-blown public maintenance API for custom UIs is provided.

▶ The simulation tool allows business users to test rules before releasing them.

▶ Additional tools and views are available for the tracking of changes, consistency checks, dependency analysis, XML and Microsoft Excel data exchange, to name just a few.

1.6.3   BRFplus Rules Engine—Features

The BRFplus BRE provides an ABAP objects API for rules invocation:

▶ Specific rule entities can be accessed and processed with just a few lines of ABAP code.

▶ BRFplus provides several methods of rules invocation that vary in terms of performance and user comfort.

▶ Generated Web services and RFC-enabled function modules can be used for remote invocation.

▶ BRFplus incorporates a code generation framework for best performance and smallest footprint of rules processing. The framework is extensible by custom action and expression types.

▶ The code generation framework is able to generate on demand or dispose of generated ABAP classes without caller adoption or administration effort.

▶ A special code version can be generated that supports runtime traces. Tracing allows for verification, explanation, or justification of processed rules.

▶ BRFplus supports the concept of time-traveling: Rules can be processed for a specific timestamp so that the definitions that were valid at the specified point in time are applied.

1.6.4   BRFplus Rules Repository—Features

The rules repository of BRFplus has the capability to support a multitude of different usage and deployment scenarios:

► The rule artifacts can be stored client-dependent or client-independent as system, customizing, and master/application data.

► Local content is supported, as is transportable content. The latter is connected to the SAP Change and Transport System (CTS) so that client settings for automatic change recording apply.

► Data exchange via XML export and import is supported.

► The rule artifacts (objects) can be versioned to allow tracking of changes or time dependent rules processing.

► Permissions can be defined by means of SAP's standard authorization concept.

► Access levels can be defined to steer visibility and reuse of business rules artifacts.

► A sophisticated lifecycle concept allows for finely granular object management. Objects can be inactive, active, obsolete, marked for deletion, and eventually deleted.

► Automatic dependency analysis prohibits inconsistencies among the rule artifacts.

► A search infrastructure permits querying for objects with respect to almost all available object attributes.

1.6.5 SAP's Business Rules Strategy and Recommendations

In October 2007 SAP announced the acquisition of Yasu Technologies, with its flagship product Yasu QuickRules, a leading BRMS especially for the Java stack. The product was renamed SAP NetWeaver Business Rule Management (SAP NetWeaver BRM) and it has been integrated into the SAP NetWeaver Composition Environment (SAP NetWeaver CE). SAP NetWeaver BRM can thus be leveraged in conjunction with SAP NetWeaver Business Process Management (SAP NetWeaver BPM) to compose and integrate rules within the context of a modeled business process.

Today, with BRFplus and SAP NetWeaver BRM, SAP offers a pair of business rules management systems to embed business rules and decisioning power into business applications. Both provide optimal support for applications in terms of flexibility, performance, and total cost of ownership. The decision regarding which rules offering to use for a particular use case is often non-trivial and is based on the specific challenges to be solved. The choice may depend on a combination of the following factors:

► Technology stack (execution environment) of the application

► Technology stack in which application data resides

▸ Certain feature requirements such as Rete[6] algorithm, flow rules, or the ability to extend the BRMS

For best performance and rule editing experiences, a rule engine that integrates deeply into the execution stack of the business applications is generally recommended. For pure ABAP stack use cases, BRFplus shipped with the Business Suite is thus typically best suited, while SAP NetWeaver BRM fits usually best to pure Java use cases. For example, when a customer wants to leverage business rules in a Business Suite application or add flexibility to a Business Suite process, BRFplus would be the ideal choice. For customers creating composite applications and business processes using SAP NetWeaver CE, the SAP NetWeaver BRM would usually be more appropriate.

The decision as to which rules engine to use may, however, go beyond technology stack considerations; it may hinge on the requirements of a particular use case. The assignment of a use case to one of the four quadrants depicted in Figure 1.9 may serve as an indicator. On the horizontal axis, there are the BRMS offerings to be used—SAP NetWeaver BRM to the left and BRFplus to the right. On the vertical axis, there are the opposing ABAP and Java technology stacks. They typically correspond to usage scenarios of SAP Business Suite-related applications versus composite applications and modeled processes in SAP NetWeaver CE.

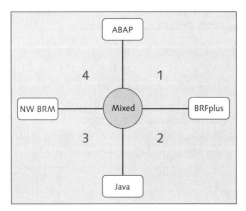

Figure 1.9 SAP BRMS Usage Scenarios

▸ Quadrant 1 characterizes use cases where the BRMS will solve business rules requirements for applications that extend the business suite functionality. Because the execution environment and the application data both reside on the

---

6 The Rete algorithm is a pattern-matching algorithm used by several business rules engines.

ABAP stack, BRFplus is the natural choice. It provides a deep integration and best performance.

▶ Quadrant 2 characterizes use cases where composite applications as well as modeled business processes in SAP NetWeaver BPM will access business rules of the business suite core. The rules should be designed with BRFplus and leveraged in SAP NetWeaver CE by calling them via Web services.

▶ Quadrant 3 characterizes use cases where composite applications and business processes modeled with SAP NetWeaver BPM will use the BRMS natively. Given the close integration, the SAP NetWeaver BRM should be used to solve decision making problems.

▶ Quadrant 4 characterizes use cases where applications for the suite require specific SAP NetWeaver BRM features: Rete algorithm capabilities, for example. The applications may also need to interact with other non-SAP systems in a heterogeneous landscape. In any case, access to the SAP NetWeaver BRM is required. The usage of the SAP NetWeaver BRM can, however, be made transparent by using BRFplus' BRMS connector expression type.

In addition to "BRFplus only" and "SAP NetWeaver BRM only" usage scenarios, there is an increasing demand for mixed scenarios in which "out-of-the-box" core business processes in the suite are enhanced or customized in composites using the SAP NetWeaver CE and business rules defined in BRFplus are used in SAP NetWeaver BRM and vice versa.

1.6.6 Outlook

BRFplus as well as SAP NetWeaver BRM continue to focus on best integration into the corresponding stack to serve ABAP and Java use cases in the best possible way. This goal requires further investments in the expressiveness and usability of the products, especially with respect to business experts. However, for use cases that are not strictly attributable to one technology stack, alignment activities as depicted in Figure 1.10 have been identified.

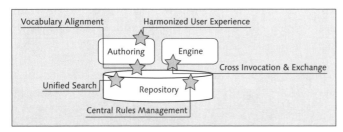

Figure 1.10 BRMS Alignment at SAP

▶ **Harmonized User Experience**
Business users prefer an easy to use, intuitive user interface to modify and maintain business rules. The goal is to provide a harmonized user experience across SAP NetWeaver BRM and BRFplus UIs, especially for frequently used artifacts such as decision tables.

▶ **Vocabulary Alignment**
It is important to have a common set of terms and definitions shared between SAP NetWeaver BRM and BRFplus to model business rules. The vocabulary can be specified by means of ABAP data dictionary objects (DDIC), SAP Global Data Types (GDTs), and native XSD schemas, allowing SAP NetWeaver BRM to benefit from the capabilities provided in BRFplus.

▶ **Unified Search**
The possibility to search and navigate to business rules that are spread across several systems and repositories is of foremost importance in complex and heterogeneous IT environments. Such a feature will lead to a higher degree of control and overview, and ultimately to better decisions. A unified search interface for BRFplus and SAP NetWeaver BRM with respect to business rule artifacts is thus planned.

▶ **Cross Invocation and Data Exchange**
Currently it is possible to invoke SAP NetWeaver BRM rules from BRFplus. The next natural step is to support the opposite direction as well, with an according invocation infrastructure. Further, an easy exchange of business rules artifacts such as decision tables or rule flows from SAP NetWeaver BRM to BRFplus and vice versa is planned.

▶ **Central Rules Management**
The provisioning of a central business rules management console could ease the alignment of SAP NetWeaver BRM and BRFplus. The console should permit managing the lifecycle of rule artifacts across both frameworks. Furthermore, it should include a centralized authorization management, facilitate the exchange of rules, and support monitoring of rule executions.

The five alignment themes outlined above will bring the two SAP BRMS offerings closer together. They are, however, still subject to change and will include feedback from SAP customers.

This chapter introduces the reader to BRFplus with help of an example. The rules workbench as well as the important artifacts and concepts are shown in context of a use case for price calculations.

2   BRFplus—a Brief Walk-Through

This chapter will provide you with a complete tour through all tools of the BRF-plus Workbench. In addition, we will introduce all objects used in the context of rule creation with BRFplus. The different topics will be dealt with in more detail in later chapters of this book.

2.1   BRFplus Workbench

The term *BRFplus Workbench* refers to the Web-enabled rule authoring and management tool that provides an environment with common paradigms for the maintenance, testing, and management of business rules content in BRFplus. The Workbench includes search and navigation capabilities to find specific BRFplus objects. It provides editors to create and change all the different types of BRFplus objects such as functions, data objects, and rulesets, as well as all kinds of expressions. Objects can be transported and deleted. Additional tools allow the simulation of rules, detection of unused objects, creation of Web Services, XML export and import, and many more capabilities.

2.1.1   Prerequisites

Appropriate authorizations are the main prerequisite to allow users to work with the BRFplus Workbench. `SAP_BC_FDT_ADMINISTRATOR` is the role for BRFplus administrators. It needs to be included in the user profile with transaction SU01.

The BRFplus Workbench is developed in Web Dynpro for ABAP and therefore requires an appropriate system setup to become executable. This setup includes correct administration of the Internet Communication Framework (ICF), which is an integrated component of the application server. The ICF allows for communication with the SAP system via Internet standard protocols such as HTTP, HTTPS, and so on. For HTTP(S) requests, suitable services can be registered and maintained with transaction SICF.

As depicted in Figure 2.1 the services are hierarchically organized. For the BRFplus Workbench, all nodes of the following service paths need to be enabled:

▶ /SAP/BC/WEBDYNPRO/SAP/FDT_WD_WORKBENCH

▶ /SAP/BC/WEBDYNPRO/SAP/FDT_WD_OBJECT_MANAGER

▶ /SAP/BC/WEBDYNPRO/SAP/FDT_WD_CATALOG_BROWSER

ICF Nodes

The tooltip on a `service/host` node provides information about the current state. The state can be changed individually for each node via a context menu by an administrator with the required authorization. In case of problems note 1109215 may be helpful.

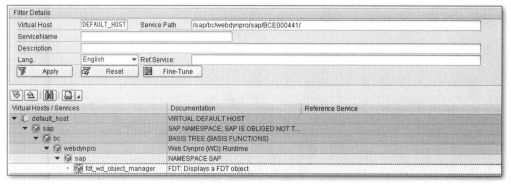

Figure 2.1 Internet Communication Framework—Web Dynpro Services

2.1.2 Starting the BRFplus Workbench

By default the BRFplus Workbench can be launched from an SAP system by entering the transaction code BRF+ or BRFPLUS. This will open a new browser window and invoke the Workbench by a URL. The URL can be used later to call the Workbench directly.

Starting the BRFplus Workbench in SAP NetWeaver 7.0 EHP1

Transactions BRF+ and BRFplus were introduced in SAP NetWeaver 7.0 Enhancement Package 2. The old transaction was FDT_WORKBENCH.

When you start the Workbench the first time, it will probably look like the screen shown in Figure 2.2. There is a menu bar at the top, a navigation panel on the left-hand side, the main display and editing area in the middle, and a status bar at the bottom.

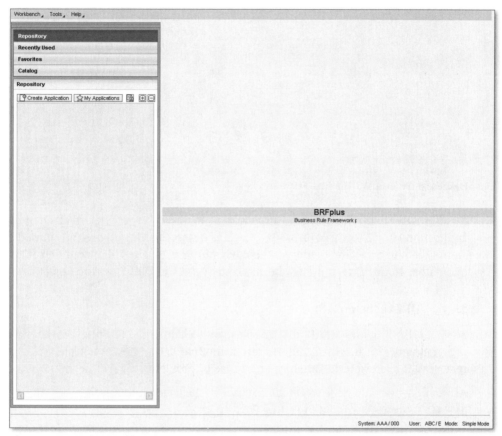

Figure 2.2 BRFplus Workbench

The Workbench allows you to provide the identifier of a specific BRFplus object with the URL-parameter ID in the form &ID=<Object ID>. If a valid identifier is provided, the object will instantly be displayed in the main area.

Technically, the Web Dynpro application FDT_WD_WORKBENCH will be started with the optionally given parameter ID. Users can therefore easily create individual favorites in the SAP GUI, selecting entry ADD OTHER OBJECTS from the context menu, choosing the type WEB DYNPRO APPLICATION, and entering data, as shown in Figure 2.3.

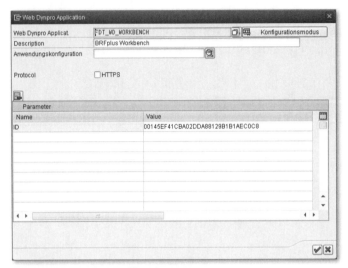

Figure 2.3 BRFplus Workbench—Favorites

An alternative to the Web Dynpro application FDT_WD_WORKBENCH is the Web Dynpro application FDT_WD_CATALOG_BROWSER. It will also start the Workbench but immediately switch to a specific catalog in the navigation panel. The URL-parameter ID is mandatory in this case and must be set to the valid UUID of a catalog object.

2.1.3 UI Execution API

BRFplus also provides an API that enables you to launch the BRFplus Workbench programmatically. Internally, the function module CALL_BROWSER is used, so you may read the relevant documentation in case of problems.

As the first step, you need to get an instance of the execution interface IF_FDT_WD_UI_EXECUTION as illustrated in Listing 2.1.

```
DATA: lo_ui_execution TYPE REF TO if_fdt_wd_ui_execution.
lo_ui_execution = cl_fdt_wd_factory=>if_fdt_wd_factory~get_instance(
  )->get_ui_execution( ).
```

Listing 2.1 Retrieval of the UI Execution Interface

To execute the Workbench, you may then do the following call:

```
lo_ui_execution->execute_workbench( ).
```

The ID of an existing object can optionally be provided in parameter IV_ID. Alternatively, you may call the catalog browser like this:

```
lo_ui_execution->execute_catalog_browser(iv_id = <catalog_id>).
```

2.1.4 Layout

To get a first impression on the layout of the BRFplus Workbench, you should look at Figure 2.4. It shows the display of a ruleset object in change mode. Although this figure shows the object display, you can recognize again the *menu bar* at the top, the *navigation panel* to the left, and the *status bar* at the bottom.

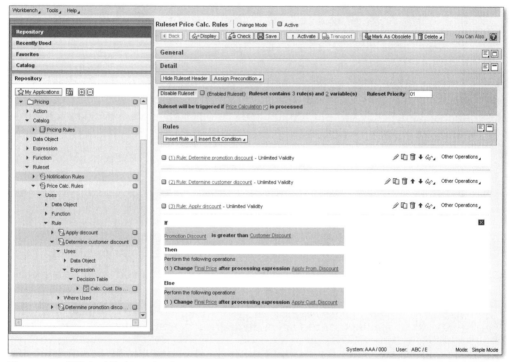

Figure 2.4 BRFplus Workbench—Layout

The menu bar, which is separately shown in Figure 2.5, provides three menus: one to access general functions of the Workbench, one to access several Tools, and one to access related Help.

Figure 2.5 BRFplus Workbench—Menu Bar

The *status bar* at the bottom of the Workbench shows information that is related to the current session. Figure 2.6 shows how the following information is summarized.

- SYSTEM: includes the system ID, client, and system time zone of the application server.
- USER: includes the user name, logon language, and user time zone.
- MODE: displays the current UI mode, by default either Simple Mode or Expert Mode.

System: ABC/000/UTC+01:00   User: ABCABABC/E/UTC+02:00   Mode: Expert Mode

Figure 2.6 BRFplus Workbench—Status Bar

The navigation panel is positioned on the left-hand side of the Workbench. As depicted in Figure 2.7, it can contain up to four different views. The visibility of the views depends on user settings and can be changed with WORKBENCH • PERSONALIZE in the VIEWS tab.

- *The Repository View* provides, in principle, access to all BRFplus objects in the repository.
- *The Recently Used View* provides access to objects that have recently been displayed or edited. This list can hold up to 20 objects.
- *The Favorites View* allows you to maintain and access a list of favorite objects. Favorites are intended to keep a permanent list with objects of interest.
- *The Catalog View* can display catalog objects that group and organize a specific subset of objects. Each user can setup a list of favorite catalogs, including a default catalog. The list can be maintained with menu entry WORKBENCH • PERSONALIZE... in the CATALOG tab of the user configuration dialog.

The objects shown in the navigation panel are not simple entries in a flat list. Rather, each object is the entry point to a hierarchy of sub-elements and usages. You can drill down through the object hierarchy by clicking on the triangle sign to the left of each object. The used or included objects are organized according to their type.

The object type is reflected by an icon on the left side of each object entry. Objects displayed in bold typeface are transportable. The icon on the right-hand side visualizes the object's status. Active objects have, for example, a green icon, inactive objects a grey one, and erroneous objects a red icon. A detailed overview can be obtained with menu entry HELP • LEGEND.

For each entry in the navigation panel, a rich context menu is provided. As illustrated in Figure 2.8, the menu includes, for example, entries for object creation, displaying, editing, copying, or accessing connected tools. The menu is dynamically composed based on the entry it is called on. The complexity of the menu depends also on the user's personalization.

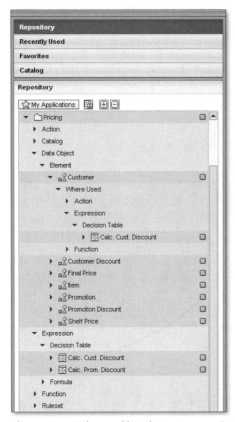

Figure 2.7 RFplus Workbench—Navigation Panel

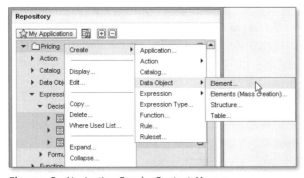

Figure 2.8 Navigation Panel—Context Menus

When you click on an object in the navigation panel or select the menu entry DISPLAY ... in its context menu, the object is shown in an editor on the right hand side.

An object can always be visualized in two modes in the main area of the Workbench. In display mode the object cannot be altered but it is therefore presented in a more readable way in which rather distracting UI elements for editing are hidden. Switching to change mode is possible only if the system settings allow you to do so and the object is not currently locked by another user.

Figure 2.9 BRFplus Workbench—Object Header

An *object header* as depicted in Figure 2.9 is always shown at the top of the object display. Here the type and name of the object are shown, followed by the current display mode and the object's status.

Below the header is the *object toolbar* illustrated in Figure 2.10. It mainly consists of a row of buttons. The BACK button on the left-hand side allows for navigation to a previously displayed object. The next button toggles between display and change mode. The rest of the buttons trigger different actions for the currently displayed object. Many of these actions can also be accessed via the context menus in the navigation panel. Some less often used options are contained in the YOU CAN ALSO menu on the right-hand side. There you also find a HELP button to invoke the *Help Center* for the BRFplus Workbench.

Figure 2.10 BRFplus Workbench—Object Toolbar

The rest of the screen is occupied by the actual *object editor*. It always consists of two parts: the *general section* and the *detail section*. The GENERAL section contains a set of attributes common to all objects in BRFplus, whereas the DETAIL section is specific to the current object type (see Figure 2.4 above).

2.1.5 Help

In the BRFplus Workbench several help functions are available to assist the user in his work. Each help function aims at a different aspect of the UI.

▶ The *Help Center* is the central place where a comprehensive UI documentation and some more features, such as a note editor, are available. You start the Help Center with a click on the HELP button in the object toolbar. Figure 2.11 gives you an idea of what the Help Center looks like.

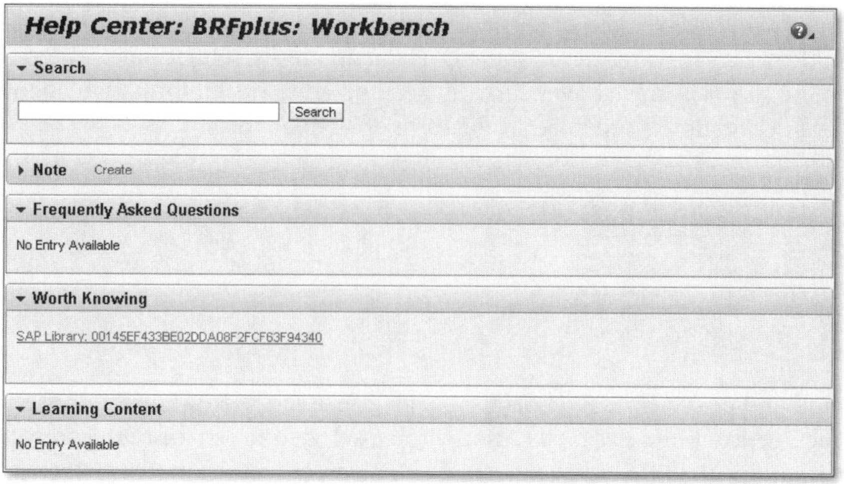

Figure 2.11 Help Center

In the WORTH KNOWING section there is a link to help in the SAP Library. This is the standard SAP documentation that is stored in the Knowledge Warehouse. The link is context sensitive. It will navigate to a help chapter that corresponds to the currently displayed object.

▶ Another type of help is *Quick Help*. It provides additional explanatory texts directly within the UI. Figure 2.12 shows an example of such a help text. Quick Help can be switched on by selecting the menu entry SHOW QUICK HELP in context menus that appear when you click on the right mouse button. If the mouse pointer hovers over an empty area of the screen, the context menu is limited to the entries shown in Figure 2.13.

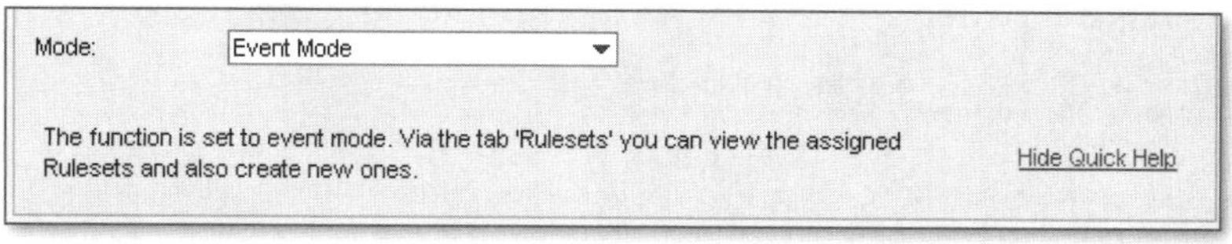

Figure 2.12 Quick Help

Figure 2.13 Switching on Quick Help

When *Quick Help* is switched on, some UI elements are also underlined in green. When the cursor is moved over such an element, additional information about the field in question is provided in the form of an extra tooltip.

Figure 2.14 Attribute Explanation

▶ Yet another type of help is *Field Help,* which is also accessible via context menus. The menu entry More FIELD HELP needs to be selected in this case. In contrast to Quick Help, Field Help depends on the UI element that the mouse pointer is currently pointing to.

Field Help may provide even more detailed information for a specific field on the screen. Figure 2.15 shows, for example, the help for the SOFTWARE COMPO-NENT field that is contained in the application object UI. With the link TECHNI-CAL HELP, technical information that is based on the Web Dynpro UI technology can be accessed.

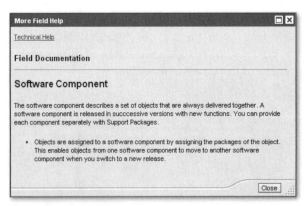

Figure 2.15 Field Help

2.1.6   Personalization

Several aspects of the BRFplus Workbench can be personalized by each user individually, according to his preferences and skills. The PERSONALIZATION mainly entails the hiding or showing of specific features. In this section we will list only the features that are connected to the personalization settings. Their detailed description follows in subsequent chapters.

As depicted in Figure 2.16, the user may first of all choose among different user modes in the WORKBENCH menu. A user mode can be regarded as one configuration of personalization settings. Each user mode provides some default settings that the user can adjust to his needs separately. So the user modes allow easy switching among different sets of personalization settings.

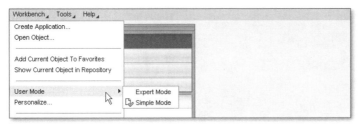

Figure 2.16   User Mode Selection

By default the SIMPLE MODE is used, which is intended for the standard business user. The EXPERT MODE addresses administrative users and provides appropriate pre-configured settings. The personalization settings for the currently selected user mode can be changed in a dialog that opens up when the menu entry WORKBENCH • PERSONALIZE … is selected. The dialog is shown in Figure 2.17.

At the bottom of the personalization dialog is the button RESTORE DEFAULT SETTINGS that resets all settings to the defaults of the currently active user mode. Clicking on the SAVE button will retain the current configuration in the database. However, to ensure that changed settings actually take effect, you should restart the BRFplus Workbench afterwards.

The various personalization settings are grouped into several tabs. On the GENERAL tab that is shown in Figure 2.17, the following aspects can be configured:

▶ NUMBER OF ENTRIES SHOWN IN A QUERY
Sets a default for the maximal number of result entries in search or respectively query dialogs.

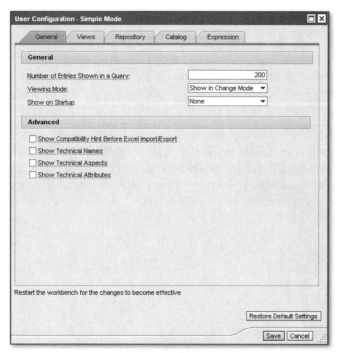

Figure 2.17 Personalization—General Settings

▶ VIEWING MODE
Allows choosing whether objects are opened in display or change mode by default.

▶ SHOW ON STARTUP
Offers the possibility of opening a specific application or the last displayed object when the Workbench is started.

ADVANCED general settings are the following:

▶ SHOW COMPATIBILITY HINT BEFORE EXCEL IMPORT/EXPORT
When data needs to be exchanged with Excel, for example in the simulation tool or in the decision table expression, the user can get information about the compatible versions.

▶ SHOW TECHNICAL NAMES
Objects are visualized by their technical names rather than by their short text descriptions.

▶ SHOW TECHNICAL ASPECTS
The TOOLS menu in the Workbench offers a bunch of additional entries for

administrative tasks. The *object toolbar* includes a separate TRANSPORT button to record objects directly onto a transport request.

▶ SHOW TECHNICAL ATTRIBUTES
Additional technical information is displayed in the UI. The function UI includes, for example, an additional tab that lists the ABAP classes created by the code generation. Or, in the UI of Search Tree and Decision Tree expressions, the internal identifiers of nodes can be displayed.

The VIEWS tab shown in Figure 2.18 allows you to choose the views that will be available in the navigation panel. At least one view must be selected. The DEFAULT VIEW setting determines the view that is preselected when the BRFplus Workbench is started.

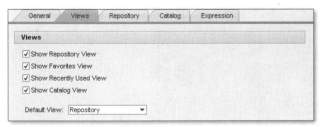

Figure 2.18   Personalization—Views

The list of objects displayed in the REPOSITORY VIEW can be filtered by settings in the REPOSITORY tab. For example, objects that are set to be obsolete or that are marked for deletion can be suppressed. Conversely, objects that have been deleted logically (but still persist physically in the database) are normally no longer shown. They can be made visible again.

As can be seen in Figure 2.19, the objects can also be filtered by their storage type. Master data objects might, for example, not be of interest to the user and can thereby be ignored.

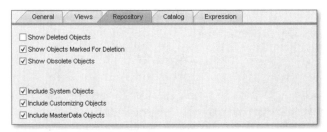

Figure 2.19   Personalization—Repository

On the CATALOG tab the user can maintain a list of favorite catalogs. Those catalogs are then easily selectable in the CATALOG VIEW with a SELECT CATALOG button choice. With the button MAKE DEFAULT one of the favorite catalogs can be set as the default catalog. It will be displayed in the CATALOG VIEW whenever the CATALOG VIEW would otherwise be empty.

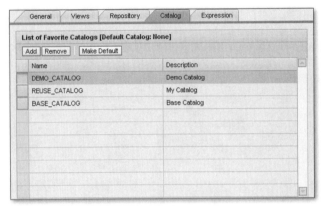

Figure 2.20   Personalization—Catalogs

Last but not least, there is an EXPRESSION tab that contains expression-type-specific settings. For Decision Table expressions the button for the TABLE SETTINGS can be hidden. This option may be useful if the user wants to edit only table content and not layout. The NUMBER OF ROWS TO BE SHOWN IN DECISION TABLE without scrolling can also be configured.

When a ruleset is opened in the object editor, the definitions of the contained rules can immediately be expanded. For long lists of rules this may become confusing. Therefore, it is possible to personalize a maximum NUMBER OF RULES EXPANDED IN RULESETS by default.

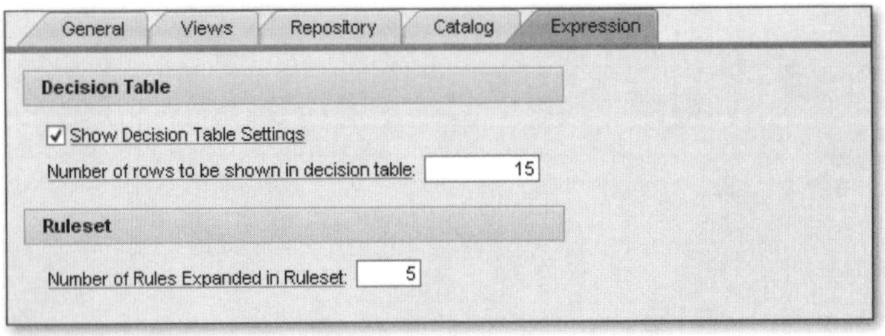

Figure 2.21   Personalization—Expressions

2.2   Workflow

The usage of BRFplus for scenarios involves several recurring steps as shown in Figure 2.22. The first step consists of creating an application. Then the function and its signature consisting of data objects are created. Usually most work is required in the modeling of the business logic that happens in rulesets, rules, expressions, and actions. Finally, all the objects need to be activated and may also be simulated. When everything works as expected, the call to the function can be implemented.

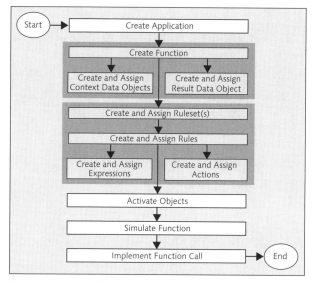

Figure 2.22   Workflow for BRFplus Scenarios

2.3   The Example

The example offered in this chapter shows business rules used in a pricing scenario. Purchase data is passed to a BRFplus function. Two rulesets are assigned to the function. The first ruleset contains rules to calculate a price based on the product and promotions. The second ruleset contains a rule to compose and send a notification email to a manager. This example is also used in a similar form in other chapters of the book.

The pricing scenario uses objects as shown in the following tables (Tables 2.1 to 2.7). The objects are discussed in more detail in the following sections of this chapter.

Application	
Name	**Text**
PRICING	Pricing

Table 2.1 Introduction Example—Application

Function	
Name	**Text**
PRICE_CALCULATION	Price Calculation

Table 2.2 Introduction Example—Function

Data Objects		
Name	**Text**	**Usage**
CUSTOMER	Customer	Context
ITEM	Item	Context
PROMOTION	Promotion	Context
SHELF_PRICE	Shelf Price	Context
FINAL_PRICE	Final Price	Result
CUSTOMER_DISCOUNT	Customer Discount	Ruleset Variable
PROMOTION_DISCOUNT	Promotion Discount	Ruleset Variable

Table 2.3 Introduction Example—Data Objects

Rulesets	
Name	**Text**
PRICE_CALCULATION_RULES	Price Calculation Rules
NOTIFICATION_RULES	Notification Rules

Table 2.4 Introduction Example—Rulesets

Rules	
Text	**Ruleset**
Determine promotion discount	PRICE_CALCULATION_RULES
Determine customer discount	PRICE_CALCULATION_RULES
Apply discount	PRICE_CALCULATION_RULES
Notify manager	NOTIFICATION_RULES

Table 2.5 Introduction Example—Rules

Expressions		
Name	**Text**	**Expression Type**
CALC_CUSTOMER_DISCOUNT	Calculate Customer Discount	Decision Table
DT_PROMOTION_DISCOUNT	Calculate Promotion Discount	Decision Table
APPLY_PROMOTION_DISCOUNT	Apply Promotion Discount	Formula
APPLY_CUSTOMER_DISCOUNT	Apply Customer Discount	Formula

Table 2.6 Introduction Example—Expressions

Actions		
Name	**Text**	**Action Type**
EMAIL_MANAGER	Email Manager	Email

Table 2.7 Introduction Example—Actions

Named and Unnamed Objects

For some object types, such as rules and expressions, a name is an optional attribute. When no name has been set, the object is shown with a description based on attributes of the object. For reuse of an object, a name is mandatory.

2.4   Application—Container for BRFplus Objects

Before we look at the BRFplus objects for implementing the example, we need to understand the purpose of the BRFplus *application*. A BRFplus application object is a container to organize and manage BRFplus objects. The application can be compared with a package in ABAP or with a project as used in several development environments such as Eclipse. But the application is more than that. Other objects, such as functions or rulesets, are created in the scope of an application. They inherit technical constraints, defaults, navigation options, etc. from the application.

▶ **Defaults and Constraints**
An application defines default behavior and constraints of BRFplus objects. The creation process of an application requires the selection of a storage type. The storage type defines whether an application is relevant for the change and transport system in the scope of system and client settings. Transport recording can be mandatory or optional or, in the case of local objects, it may also be unsupported.

There are also application properties that define defaults for the objects, such as a default for language dependency, for text and documentation, a message log object, or the versioning mode of the objects.

▶ **Navigation**
An application defines a root object in the repository navigation. When the Workbench is started for the first time, the repository is empty and it is necessary to use the menu bar to create a first application. Once there is an application, it is shown in the repository as a root object that can be expanded to see its content. Only with an application it is possible to create other objects.

▶ **Reuse**
The application attributes can contain information about the application component. The application component is used in combination with the *Access Level* to define visibility and reuse of objects for other applications.

▶ **Exits**
With the concept of application exits, BRFplus allows you to extend its common features in the scope of an application and its contained objects. For example, it is possible to restrict access to BRFplus objects with an additional authorization check of a finer granularity. The validity of data entered in an expression may need to be cross-checked against some external data sources. Or you may simply want to be notified in case a BRFplus object is saved so that some dependent adaptations or other post-processing can be started. An application exit is technically based on an ABAP class that implements the specific interface IF_FDT_APPLICATION_SETTINGS. The class name can be set as an attribute of an application.

▶ **API**
In some methods in the API, it is possible to provide an application ID to define the scope of an operation such as in the creation of new objects, search, or the packaged processing of objects. The application ID can be found in the expanded GENERAL section in the field APPLICATION ID.

▶ **Administration**
The application is the key entity used in some administration tools and reports.

2.5 Function—Interface Between Code and Rules

The function is the business rules service interface. It defines inputs and outputs and thus acts as the contract between caller and the business logic implemented within the rules. Functions also define the purpose of what is to be done in the business rules. Business rules are organized into rulesets. Multiple rulesets can be assigned to one function in the so-called *Event Mode* (see the PROPERTIES tab). The *Functional Mode* (also on the PROPERTIES tab) allows you to attach a top expression that implements very simple logic, e.g., in the form of a single decision table or a formula. Figure 2.23 illustrates how rules are invoked from ABAP code.

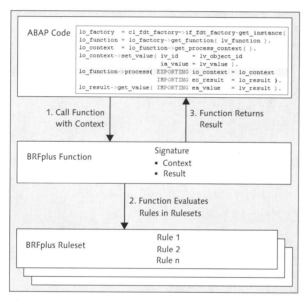

Figure 2.23 Rules Invocation with Functions

Functions define the signature consisting of context and result. Context and result are data carriers. The parameters consist of data objects that define a type and during runtime provide a variable as a data container. The data objects from the context and the result can be used by rules, expressions, and actions to implement the business logic.

Figure 2.24 shows the signature for the function PRICE_CALCULATION with text "Price Calculation." The function has four elementary inputs:

▶ CUSTOMER

▶ ITEM

▶ PROMOTION

▶ SHELF_PRICE

It returns the elementary result FINAL_PRICE.

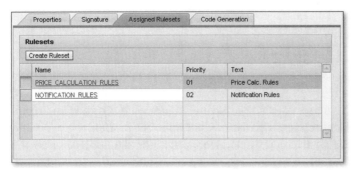

Figure 2.24 Function "Price Calculation"—Signature

The ASSIGNED RULESETS tab shows the rulesets that will be used to retrieve rules for evaluation when the function is processed. The rules are evaluated according to their priority. In this example, first rules from ruleset PRICE_CALCULATION_RULES (Price Calc. Rules) with priority one and then rules from ruleset NOTIFICATION_RULES (Notification Rules) with priority two will be evaluated.

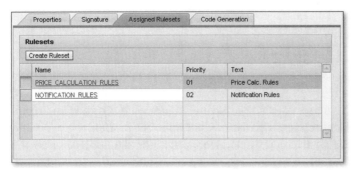

Figure 2.25 Function "Price Calculation"—Assigned Rulesets

BRFplus supports the generation of RFC enabled function modules and Web services for functions. It is also possible to simulate functions.

2.6 Data Object—Data Carriers

Data objects describe data types and at the same time serve as data carriers in the context or the result. Three general types of data objects exist, comparable to data types in the Data Dictionary. Table 2.8 compares these types in BRFplus and DDIC.

BRFplus Data Object Type	DDIC Data Type
Element	Data Element
Structure	Structure
Table	Table Type

Table 2.8 Data Object Types Versus DDIC Data Types

An elementary data object has a sub type called element type. The available sub types are shown in Table 2.9.

Element Type	Description	ABAP Type
Amount	Number with currency	IF_FDT_TYPES=>ELEMENT_AMOUNT
Boolean	Boolean value (true or false)	IF_FDT_TYPES=>ELEMENT_BOOLEAN
Number	Number with decimals	IF_FDT_TYPES=>ELEMENT_NUMBER
Quantity	Number with unit of measure	IF_FDT_TYPES=>ELEMENT_QUANTITY
Text	Character	IF_FDT_TYPES=>ELEMENT_TEXT
Timepoint	Date, time, timestamp	IF_FDT_TYPES=>ELEMENT_TIMEPOINT

Table 2.9 Elementary Data Object Types

Some of the elementary BRFplus types are mapped to a structured type in ABAP and the Data Dictionary:

▶ IF_FDT_TYPES=>ELEMENT_AMOUNT
   Consists of components NUMBER and CURRENCY

▶ IF_FDT_TYPES=>ELEMENT_QUANTITY
   Consists of components NUMBER and UNIT

▶ IF_FDT_TYPES=>ELEMENT_TIMEPOINT
   Consists of components DATE, TIME, TIMESTAMP, OFFSET_TIME, OFFSET_SIGN and TYPE

For elements, several more attributes are available, such as length and the number of decimals places. Some of the attributes depend on the element type. Figure 2.26 shows an example.

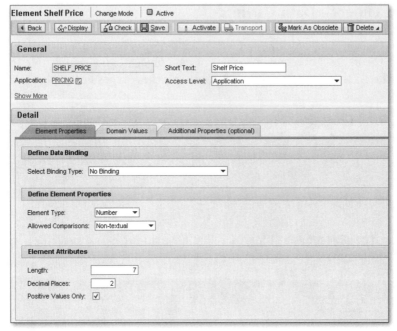

Figure 2.26 Data Object "Final Price"

Data objects of type structure can have several components of type element, structure, or table. Data objects of type table have exactly one line type, which is either an element or a structure. Data objects can be bound to the types of the Data Dictionary. This makes sure that all the attributes, including name, texts, technical type, and documentation, are derived from the supplied Data Dictionary type. Additionally, value help may be provided based on the Data Dictionary type.

The data objects used in the context of function PRICE_CALCULATION are listed in Table 2.10.

Name	Text	Element Type
CUSTOMER	Customer	Text
ITEM	Item	Text
PROMOTION	Promotion	Text
SHELF_PRICE	Shelf Price	Number

Table 2.10 Data Objects in the Context of Function "Price Calculation"

Data object FINAL_PRICE defines the result of the function. It is an element of type number.

2.7   Ruleset—Collection of Rules

Rulesets are collection of rules. Each ruleset can be assigned to exactly one function. Rulesets can have a priority, ranging from 01 (highest) to 99 (lowest). With the priority it is possible to influence the order of processing. A ruleset with a higher priority is processed completely before rulesets with lower priority are processed. Rulesets also can have preconditions. When a precondition is defined, it needs to be evaluated to true for processing of the rules in the ruleset; otherwise, the ruleset will be omitted from processing. The rules in a ruleset as well as the preconditions of the ruleset can use the data objects in context and result of the function the ruleset is assigned to.

Figure 2.27 shows the header of ruleset NOTIFICATION_RULES. This ruleset is defined with priority 02. Ruleset PRICE_CALCULATION_RULES is defined with priority 01. Both rulesets are assigned to function PRICE_CALCULATION. As a result, rules for the price calculation are processed before notification rules are processed. As mentioned above, rulesets can also have preconditions. If a precondition is not satisfied, rules from the ruleset are excluded from processing.

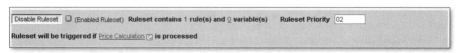

Figure 2.27   Ruleset "Notification Rules"—Header

There may be a need to store intermediate data or read additional data during the processing of the rules. In this case, the ruleset provides the possibility of defining variables and initializations. A variable is a data object that extends the context and can be used as any other data object in the context. The ruleset may optionally use expressions to initialize the variables with specific values.

Figure 2.28 shows the variables for customer and promotion discount defined for ruleset PRICE_CALCULATION_RULES. The rules in the ruleset determine the discounts before they are used for price calculation.

An initialization is an expression. Expressions have results that are defined by data objects. The result returned by the initialization expression updates the ruleset variable.

Figure 2.29 shows ruleset PRICE_CALCULATION_RULES with the rule "Apply discount" being expanded in the DETAIL SECTION.

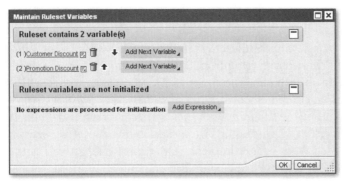

Figure 2.28 Ruleset "Validation Rules"—Variables

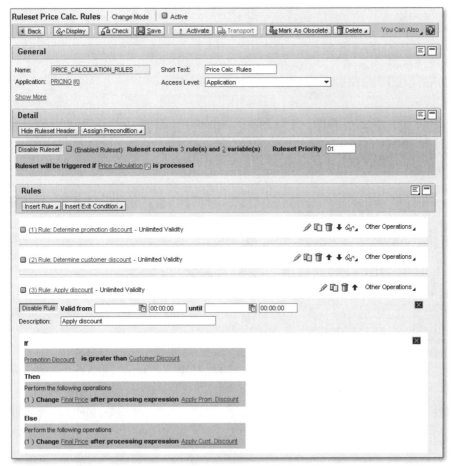

Figure 2.29 Ruleset "Price Calculation Rules"

It is possible to enable or disable each rule in the ruleset individually. Further, a description field is provided and each rule can be restricted to a validity interval. Using meaningful descriptions makes it easy to understand the business logic implemented in rulesets that contain many rules.

2.8   Rule—Central Entity

While rulesets organize which rules are evaluated, the rule itself is the central entity of BRFplus that builds the business logic. Rules have a simple structure:

```
IF
    condition
THEN
    operation(s)
ELSE
    operation(s)
```

First an optional condition is evaluated. Conditions can be developed in three different ways:

▸ Elementary data object from context with Boolean type

▸ Built-in Value Range comparisons (for simple conditions)

▸ Expression that returns a Boolean result (for complex conditions)

If the condition is left empty or the condition is evaluated to true, the THEN block is executed. If the condition is evaluated to false the ELSE block is executed. Both blocks provide the same capabilities:

▸ Assigning values to data objects in the context/result

▸ Processing expressions and updating context/result data objects from expression results

▸ Executing actions

▸ Processing other values

A block can include many operations that are executed sequentially. Therefore, it is possible to first execute an expression to calculate the value of a ruleset variable, and then to use it in another expression within in the same block of a rule.

Rules are self-contained objects. They can be maintained embedded into a ruleset or standalone. Figure 2.30 shows the unnamed rule "Apply discount" in the rule editor.

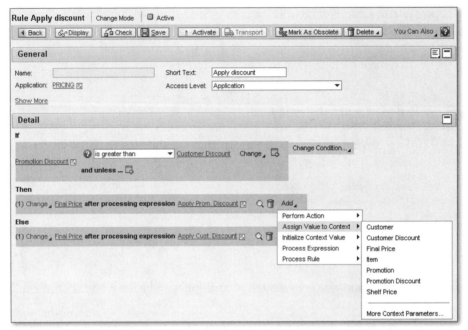

Figure 2.30 Rule "Apply Discount" in Rule Editor

In the pricing application, the rules are unnamed. A name is not required when a rule is used only in one place. In this case, a readable description based on the attributes of the object will be displayed. This is true not only for rules but also for any other expression or action type in BRFplus. The rules of the pricing application use expressions and actions. Figure 2.30 shows two formula expressions for the discount calculation being used in the THEN and the ELSE block in rule "Apply discount."

2.9   Expressions—Computational Units

The available expression types define the computational power of BRFplus. Each expression type is a self-contained computational unit with a well-defined logic. The data actually to be processed via an expression type is defined by expressions. Thus, an expression can be considered to be an instance of an expression type, behaving according to the expression type's logic.

In general an expression uses some input to calculate or derive some output, called a result. The input sources may be either context data objects or the results of nested expressions.

BRFplus comes with a set of common expression types and is regularly enhanced with new expression types. The expression types are part of the standard application FDT_SYSTEM (BRFplus system application).

Expression Type	Description
Boolean	Boolean arithmetic for any number of operands (all combinations with AND, OR, and NOT are possible)
BRMS Connector	Connects to an external Business Rule Management System (BRMS) like SAP NetWeaver BRM
Case	Arbitrary number of results, depending on input value; works like the ABAP CASE statement
Constant	Returns a constant value
DB Lookup	Retrieves values from the database or performs an existence check
Decision Table	Sequentially processes a table of conditions and results; returns either the first or all rows where the condition matches
Decision Tree	Traverses a binary tree with nodes carrying conditions and leaves carrying results
Dynamic Expression	Processes a dynamically specified expression
Formula	Allows the definition of complex formulas to be evaluated at runtime
Function Call	Calls another BRFplus function and thereby allows nesting of functions
Loop	Repeats a sequence of operations on an array of data
Procedure Call	Calls an ABAP procedure (method or function module)
Random Number	Returns a random value or indicates whether a specified probability was met
Search Tree	Traverses a non-binary tree with nodes carrying conditions and leaves carrying results
Step Sequence	Processes a number of single process steps
Table Operation	Operates on entire tables to carry out aggregations, existence checks, and line counts
Value Range	Checks whether a given value lies within a certain range
XSL Transformation	Performs an XSL transformation

Table 2.11 Expression Types in "BRFplus System Application"

All expression types provide their own user interface that allows properties to be set when maintaining expressions. BRFplus offers an open API so that there is virtually no limit to customer-specific extensions in frontend and backend with customer-specific expression types.

In many cases only a few of the expression types are actually used. This is also true for our Pricing scenario. There are decision table expressions and formula expressions.

Figure 2.31 shows the expression APPLY_PROMOTION_DISCOUNT in the formula editor in change mode. Formulas in general include context data objects, operands, and formula functions.

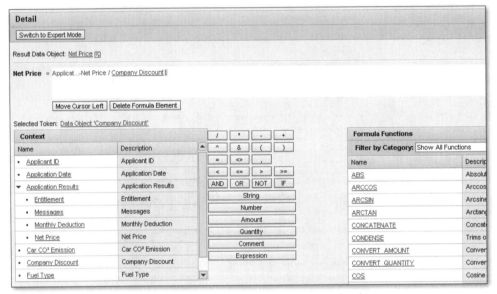

Figure 2.31 Expression "Apply Promotion Discount" in the Formula Editor

In the pricing application there are four expressions:

▶ CALC_CUSTOMER_DISCOUNT: an expression of type Decision Table to determine the customer discount

Detail		

Export To Excel | Table Settings

Table Contents

Customer	Item	Customer Discount
SAP	Ballpen	0.15
SAP	Pencil	0.12
		0

Figure 2.32 Expression "Calculate Customer Discount" in the Decision Table Editor

▶ `DT_PROMOTION_DISCOUNT`: an expression of type Decision Table to determine the promotion discount

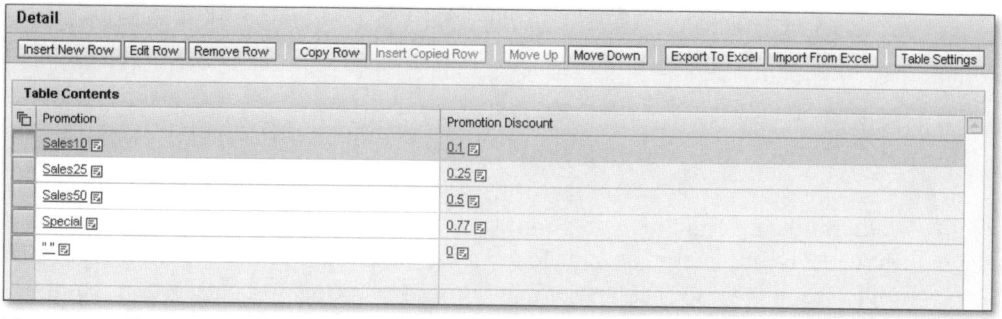

Detail

| Insert New Row | Edit Row | Remove Row | Copy Row | Insert Copied Row | Move Up | Move Down | Export To Excel | Import From Excel | Table Settings |

Table Contents

Promotion	Promotion Discount
Sales10 🖉	0.1 🖉
Sales25 🖉	0.25 🖉
Sales50 🖉	0.5 🖉
Special 🖉	0.77 🖉
"" 🖉	0 🖉

Figure 2.33 Expression "Calculate Promotion Discount" in the Decision Table Editor

▶ `APPLY_PROMOTION_DISCOUNT`: an expression of type Formula to perform the calculation:

Final Price = Shelf Price / (1+ Promotion Discount)

▶ `APPLY_CUSTOMER_DISCOUNT`: an expression of type Formula to perform the calculation:

Final Price = Shelf Price / (1+ Customer Discount)

2.10 Actions—Performing Tasks Outside of BRFplus

Action types define the interactive part of BRFplus. They can be regarded as a special kind of expression type. An instance of an action type is called an action. Actions do not have a result, except for the technical ID of the action performed. However, they can carry out activities that go beyond the borders of BRFplus. Similar to expressions, actions can use nested expressions and context data as input to accomplish their work.

Usually, action types are more application-dependent than expression types. Hence, only a few generic action types are shipped with BRFplus. The currently available standard action types are shown in Table 2.12. They are part of application `FDT_SYSTEM` (BRFplus System Application).

Action Type	Description
Procedure Call	Calls an ABAP procedure (method or function module)
Log Message	Writes a message into a message log
Send Email	Sends an email to a specified list of recipients
Start Workflow	Triggers the Business Workflow
Workflow Event	Raises a Business Workflow event

Table 2.12 Action Types in "BRFplus System Application"

Similar to the creation of expression types, new customer-specific action types can be created to implement specific logic to the customer use case. Actions types also provide their own user interface that allows properties to be set when maintaining actions.

In the pricing scenario a Send Email action is used in a rule of ruleset NOTIFICA-TION_RULES. The EDITOR VIEW of the action is shown in Figure 2.34.

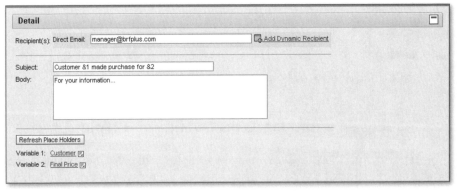

Figure 2.34 Expression "Email Manager" in the Send Email Editor

2.11 Catalog—Visualization and Navigation Help

A catalog simplifies the rules maintenance process for the business user by hiding the overall repository. Catalogs display only the relevant objects that are necessary for the maintenance of business rules in a given business scenario. They comprise structure nodes, object nodes, and catalog link nodes. Working with and organizing BRFplus objects into catalogs can be compared with working in Microsoft Explorer, which also allows you to create folders, organize files, and use shortcuts (links).

Figure 2.35 shows the Catalog PRICING_RULES (Pricing Rules) with an object being displayed to the right. The Navigation Panel shows only the CATALOG VIEW. In principle, there can be also other views such as the REPOSITORY VIEW. In combination with personalization options and authorizations, catalogs can be an effective way to simplify the User Interface and manage visibility of objects and features for different user groups.

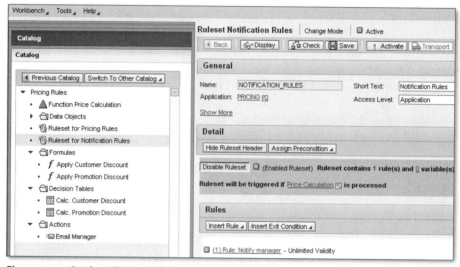

Figure 2.35 Catalog "Pricing Rules"

2.12   Simulating and Testing Rules

The business logic modeled in business rules can become very complex. In this case, it is helpful to use the simulation capabilities of BRFplus to test the rules against sample data. The simulation tool allows function testing with test data in two modes:

▶ SHOW ONLY RESULT

▶ SHOW ALSO RESULTS OF INTERMEDIATE STEPS

Especially the second mode with the intermediate steps can be useful for finding the source of a problem when the processing output does not meet the expectations.

The simulation tool can be opened in four ways:

▶ Menu bar: TOOLS • SIMULATION

▶ Repository View: FUNCTION CONTEXT menu • TOOLS • SIMULATION...

▶ Catalog View: FUNCTION CONTEXT menu • ACTIVITY • TOOLS • SIMULATION...

▶ Function Detail section: START SIMULATION button

The tool opens a dialog to define the inputs for the various data objects in the context of the function. It is also possible to upload data from a Microsoft Excel file (XLSX).

Figure 2.36 shows the screen of the simulation tool for the function PRICE_CAL-CULATION (Price Calculation). The data in the input fields is for the data objects in the context of the function. This data will be used for the simulation. At the bottom you can see the two simulation modes. SHOW ALSO RESULTS OF INTERMEDIATE STEPS is selected.

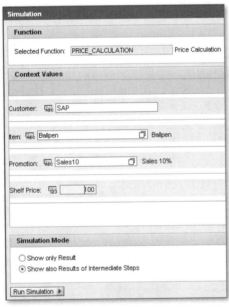

Figure 2.36 Simulation of Function "Price Calculation"—Data Entry

With the RUN SIMULATION button you start the simulation; afterwards, the result screen shown in Figure 2.37 is displayed. The screen is composed of two parts, Result and Process. At the top you can see the function result with the value provided by the business logic implemented in the rulesets.

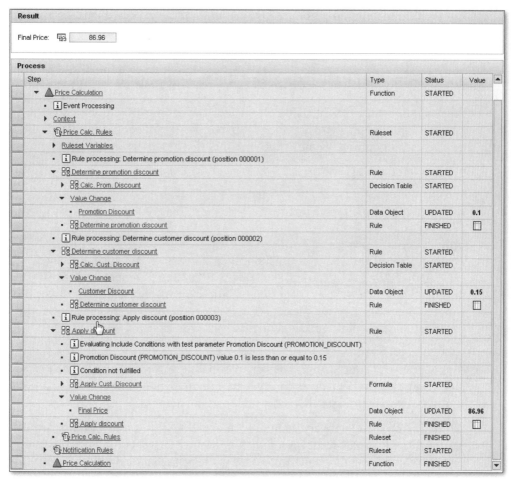

Figure 2.37 Simulation of Function "Price Calculation"—Result

In the PROCESS section you can see the simulation protocol in form of an execution tree. It is organized in a hierarchy so that users can expand and collapse complete rulesets, rules, and expressions for a better overview. The tree starts with a line of header information, including the time stamp of the simulation and the user. Next the function is listed. It is possible to click on the links to navigate to relevant objects, such as functions, expressions, or data objects. Below the function, the context is shown, including the values that have been supplied for the execution in column VALUE. The following entries are listed in chronological order. This means, for example, that the rule shown first in the simulation protocol has been executed first. With the simulation tool it is possible to trace the execution and understand exactly why those results are returned for the given set of inputs.

2.13 Function Processing and Rules Evaluation

When all the setup work has been completed, a call of the BRFplus function can be implemented. BRFplus provides four ways to process a function so that application developers can optimally embed BRFplus into their scenario:

- ▶ Instance method (`IF_FDT_FUNCTION->PROCESS`)
- ▶ Static method (`CL_FDT_FUNCTION_PROCESS=>PROCESS`)
- ▶ Function module (local or RFC)
- ▶ Web service

All four ways of processing a function internally result in calling a method in a generated ABAP class. A class is generated per function to reflect the logic defined in the objects such as rules, data objects, and expressions. The possibilities provided to process a function decouples the code to invoke the rules from the code generated for the rules. Consequently, rules can be changed but the calling code does not have to be.

A very powerful concept for code generation and re-generation has been implemented that not only involves code generation on demand but also automatically abolishes outdated classes that must not be used anymore.

Listing 2.2 shows exemplary code for the processing of the function "Price Calculation. The first part retrieves a function instance `LO_FUNCTION` from the factory `CL_FDT_FACTORY`. The function can be used to create the context object `LO_CONTEXT`. Then various values are set for the context data objects. The process call is based on the instance method `PROCESS` in interface `IF_FDT_FUNCTION`. At the end, the result object `LO_RESULT` is used to access the results of the rules evaluation.

```
* get function instance for function PRICE_CALCULATION
lo_function =
  cl_fdt_factory=>if_fdt_factory~get_instance(
    )->get_function(
iv_id = '00505683359D02DE97FAB4E171B5054E' ).

TRY.
*    provide context
    lo_context = lo_function->get_process_context( ).
    lo_context->set_value( iv_name  = 'CUSTOMER'
                           ia_value = lv_customer ).
```

```
    lo_context->set_value( iv_name  = 'ITEM'
                           ia_value = lv_item ).
    lo_context->set_value( iv_name  = 'PROMOTION'
                           ia_value = lv_promotion ).
    lo_context->set_value( iv_name  = 'SHELF_PRICE'
                           ia_value = lv_shelf_price ).
*   run rules
    lo_function->process( EXPORTING io_context = lo_context
                          IMPORTING eo_result  = lo_result ).
*   take results
    lo_result->get_value( IMPORTING ea_value = lv_result ).
  CATCH cx_fdt INTO lx_fdt.
*   todo: some error handling
ENDTRY.
```

Listing 2.2 Code Example to Process Function "Price Calculation"

2.14   **BRFplus Releases**

Developers and system administrators do not need to learn how to install and configure software to work with business rules. Instead, BRFplus is part of the SAP NetWeaver ABAP server and is available immediately. To use BRFplus you need a system with SAP NetWeaver 7.0 Enhancement Package 2 or higher. In the GUI you can see the SAP NetWeaver release of a system with menu option SYSTEM • STATUS… On popup SYSTEM: STATUS click on the icon SELECT DETAIL and popup SYSTEM: COMPONENT INFORMATION shows you all the installed software components of the system, including the release and support package information. Figure 2.38 shows the popup for a system that has only SAP NetWeaver installed.

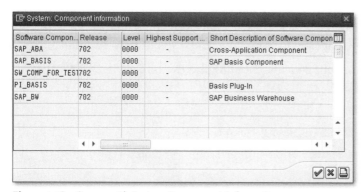

Figure 2.38 Popup with System Component Information

BRFplus is part of the software component SAP_BASIS, which is included in SAP NetWeaver. Release 702 is the technical name of SAP NetWeaver 7.0 Enhancement Package 2. If you see such a line in your system, you can start using BRFplus with the features described in this book. If you see a similar line but with values 701, 700 or even lower in the release column, your server is based on an older version and does not include BRFplus or includes it in an older version.

The first shipment of BRFplus took place with SAP NetWeaver 7.0 in 2006. The technical release name is SAP_BASIS 700. This shipment was not disclosed and the API was not released. The focus was on piloting the major concepts in some selected use cases. Large portions of BRFplus were not completed at that point in time. These include the code generation framework, user interface, and documentation. Based on the results from the pilot project, some concepts were reworked and the API was modified. Because of the incompatibility issues arising from these changes, we strongly discourage use of this version of BRFplus.

The second shipment of BRFplus took place with SAP NetWeaver 7.0 Enhancement Package 1 in 2008. The technical release name is SAP_BASIS 701. This version of BRFplus still has several limitations:

- Code generation not supported for all expression and action types
- Limited usability of several screens in the user interface
- Sufficient documentation not available
- Missing optimization of data management and database layout
- Several pitfalls in backend and UI when using DDIC binding
- Limited usage of table and structure components
- Ruleset and rules incomplete

Nevertheless, BRFplus gained a lot of attention and several projects at SAP started to adopt BRFplus, including projects in SAP Transportation Management, SAP Customer Relationship Management (SAP CRM), and SAP Business ByDesign.

As a rule of thumb, the following parts of BRFplus can be used in SAP NetWeaver 7.0 Enhancement Package 1:

- Application
- Function (not in combination with event mode)
- Data Objects (no code generation supported for structured types)
- Expressions
- Boolean
- Case

- Constant
- Decision Table
- Formula
- Value Range

It is possible to upgrade from SAP NetWeaver 7.0 Enhancement Package 1 to a higher version of BRFplus. The content created in SAP NetWeaver 7.0 Enhancement Package 1 will not be invalidated and the rules still can be executed. However, there are some changes that may make it necessary for you to make some changes in your code for a smooth upgrade. In SAP note 1305978 these changes are described in detail.

The third shipment of BRFplus comes with SAP NetWeaver 7.0 Enhancement Package 2. The technical release name is SAP_BASIS 702. Although not all features required by customers and SAP projects are included in the shipment, this release can be considered the first release without any restrictions. The feedback from the previous releases has been incorporated and known restrictions have been removed:

- All gaps in code generation closed
- Nearly all screens reworked to improve usability, navigation options improved, and configuration concept introduced
- Documentation completed
- Improved versioning features and version comparison
- Database layout improved and simplified
- Full support of DDIC binding including support of nested types and re-bind capabilities to reflect changes in BRFplus
- Very powerful and flexible concept with ruleset and rules
- New action and expression types
  - Loop expression
  - Send Email action
  - Start Workflow action
  - Table Operation expression
  - Workflow Event action
- Improved action and expression types
  - Boolean expression
  - Procedure Call expression and Procedure Call action

- ▸ DB Lookup expression
- ▸ Decision Table expression
- ▸ Decision Tree expression
- ▸ Rule expression
- ▸ Search Tree expression
- ▶ New services in backend and UI for the implementation of custom action and expression types
- ▶ Various tools for the management of the BRFplus content

BRFplus is already included in many projects at SAP as part of new development or renovation effort. With SAP NetWeaver 7.0 EHP2, BRFplus is ready for mass adoption and able to cope with complex scenarios.

"Learning by doing" is the motto of this chapter. It will guide the reader step by step through the definition of an example with help of the BRFplus Workbench or the BRFplus API.

3 Tutorials

This chapter describes how to build a pricing application similar to the one described in the previous chapter. The first part of this chapter focuses on the creation of an example in the BRFplus Workbench. The second part explains how the same example can be created with help of the API.

3.1 Creation of a Pricing Application with the BRFplus Workbench

The example application will consist of a function, seven data objects, a ruleset with one rule, two Decision Table expressions, and also two Formula expressions. An application, which is the starting point of rule definitions in BRFplus, is of course also required.

3.1.1 Application

After starting the Workbench, for example with transaction BRFplus, we will first create a new application. We therefore select the menu entry WORKBENCH • CREATE APPLICATION…, as depicted in Figure 3.1.

Figure 3.1 Create Application

An application creation dialog will open up. There we enter the NAME "PRICING" and the SHORT TEXT "Pricing" for the application. As STORAGE TYPE we choose "Customizing" and mark the CREATE LOCAL APPLICATION flag, as in Figure 3.2. We then click on the CREATE AND NAVIGATE TO OBJECT button.

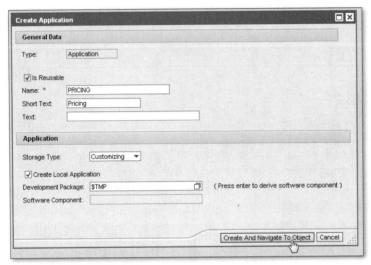

Figure 3.2 Application Setup

The application does not require any further changes, so we can now activate it with the applicable toolbar button, as illustrated by Figure 3.3.

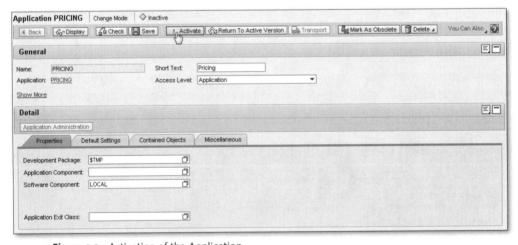

Figure 3.3 Activation of the Application

In the DETAIL section of the application UI, we select the CONTAINED OBJECTS tab. Of course no objects are listed yet. By default the object TYPE "Function" is preselected. As shown in Figure 3.4, we can thus immediately click on the button CREATE OBJECT to the right to create a new function. It is also possible to create objects with the context menu on the application in the repository tree.

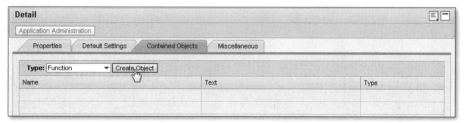

Figure 3.4   Creation of a New Function in the Application

3.1.2   Function

In the creation dialog for the function, we specify the NAME "PRICE_CALCULATION" and a suitable SHORT TEXT as in Figure 3.5.

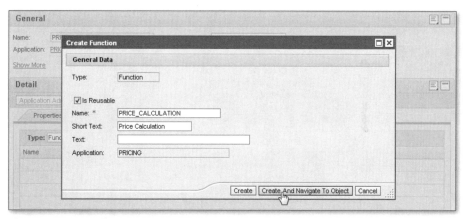

Figure 3.5   Setup of New Function

After clicking on the button CREATE AND NAVIGATE TO OBJECT, we can see several tab strips in the DETAIL section of the function UI. To allow the subscription of rulesets, the function has to run in Event Mode. Because this is the default setting, we do not need to change anything on the PROPERTIES tab. We continue with the SIGNATURE tab.

For the function input we need multiple, elementary CONTEXT parameters. We therefore select a button option accordingly, as shown in Figure 3.6.

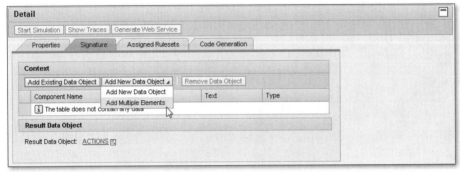

Figure 3.6 Adding Multiple Elements to the Function Context

In the dialog, we first define three new data elements of type "Text" with the names "CUSTOMER," "ITEM," and "PROMOTION". To keep the example simple, we add another data element "SHELF_PRICE" of type "Number." The SHORT TEXT entries can be taken over from Figure 3.7.

Type		Element Type		Reference	Name	Short Text	
Built-In Type	▼	Text	▼		CUSTOMER	Customer	
Built-In Type	▼	Text	▼		ITEM	Item	
Built-In Type	▼	Text	▼		PROMOTION	Promotion	
Built-In Type	▼	Number	▼		SHELF_PRICE	Shelf Price	
Built-In Type	▼	Text	▼				
Built-In Type	▼	Text	▼				
Built-In Type	▼	Text	▼				
Built-In Type	▼	Text	▼				
Built-In Type	▼	Text	▼				
Built-In Type	▼	Text	▼				

Create New Elements

Application: PRICING

Ok Cancel

Figure 3.7 Creation of Multiple Data Elements

Having confirmed the creation of elements, we will now first save the function together with the elements by clicking on this toolbar button.

We could use the defined context elements as they are, but we want to characterize them more precisely. As depicted in Figure 3.8 we thus simply click on the listed "CUSTOMER" element to navigate to its details.

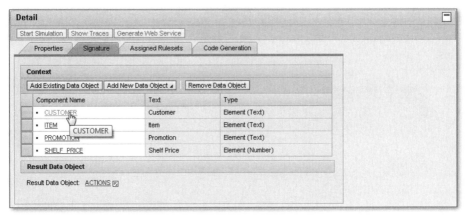

Figure 3.8 Navigation to Context Element

For the CUSTOMER element we only change the setting for the maximum LENGTH to 30 characters, as illustrated in Figure 3.9.

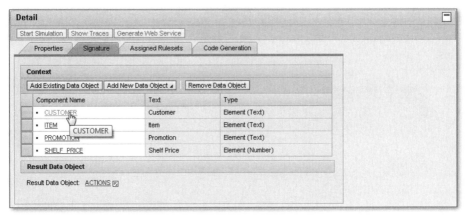

Figure 3.9 Changing Element Length

To navigate to the previous function screen, we can click on the BACK button in the toolbar.

Because we have not yet explicitly saved the changes to the element, a dialog box will appear that warns us against a possible loss of data. As Figure 3.10 illustrates we can simply confirm the dialog to save the changes now and continue navigating to the function.

A dialog box warning about loss of changes may also appear in the following steps without explicitly being mentioned. Changes should always be saved in such cases.

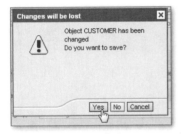

Figure 3.10 "Loss of Changes"—Dialog

Looking at the REPOSITORY VIEW on the left-hand side of the Workbench, we can see our created "Pricing" application at the top level. To find and edit any of the already created objects within, we can drill down to them following the object type hierarchy. Next, let us select the new "Item" element, just as shown in Figure 3.11.

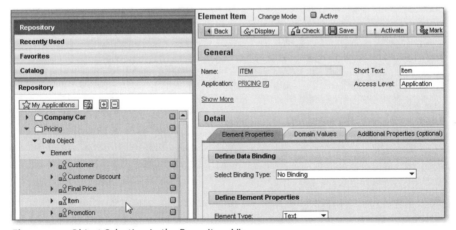

Figure 3.11 Object Selection in the Repository View

For the "Item" element, we first also specify a maximum Length of 30 on the Element Properties tab. To define a list of valid item identifiers, we switch to the Domain Values tab. To create a new domain value, we click on the button Create Value (see Figure 3.12).

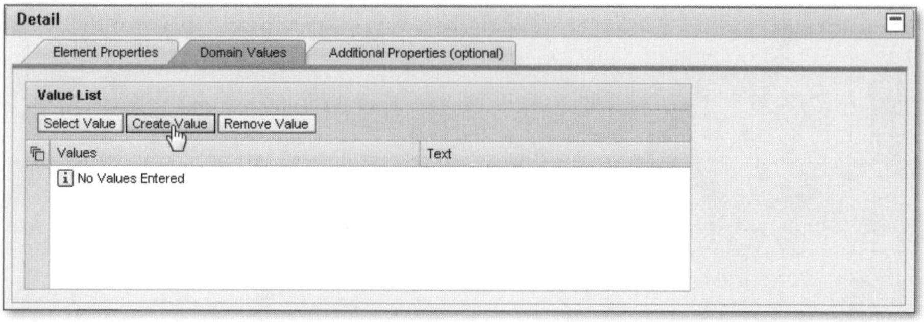

Figure 3.12 Creating Domain Values for Elements

A creation dialog for a new constant value will open up. For the short text description and the actual domain value we use the same entry "Pencil" in our example. This is, however, not required in general. To create the constant we click this time the Create button at the bottom of the dialog. Thus, the new constant is created, but without navigation to the newly created object.

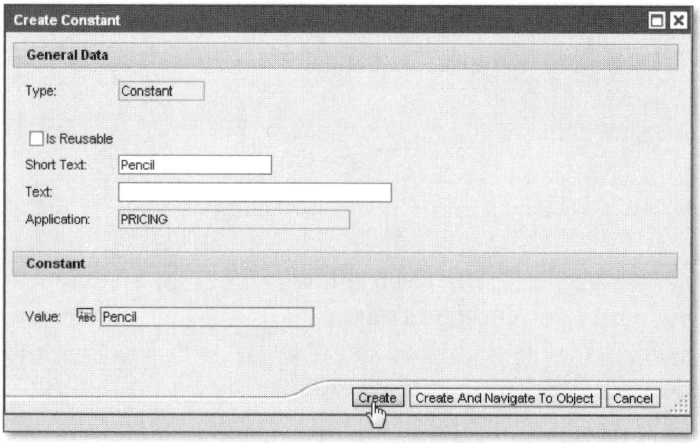

Figure 3.13 Creating a Constant as Domain Value

As explained earlier, we create two more domain values: "Ballpen" and "Pen." The results should look like those in Figure 3.14.

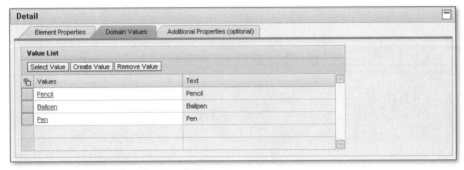

Figure 3.14 Domain Values for "Item" Element

We will next adapt the properties of the "Promotion" element. We restrict the maximum Length to 20, and enter the domain values "Sales10," "Sales25," "Sales50," "Special," and " " ("None") as demonstrated in Figure 3.15.

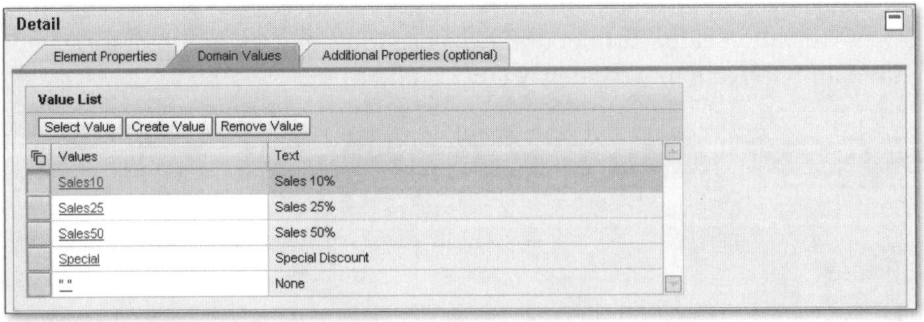

Figure 3.15 Domain Values for "Promotion" Element

Last but not least, we adapt the "Shelf Price" element, which has some additional properties due to its numeric type. On the ELEMENT PROPERTIES tab (see Figure 3.16) we set the maximum LENGTH to 7, the number of DECIMAL PLACES to 2, and mark the flag POSITIVE VALUES ONLY (see Figure 3.16).

To complete the definition of our function for "Price Calculation," we have to set its RESULT DATA OBJECT on the SIGNATURE tab to a suitable new type. Figure 3.17 shows the menu option CREATE... that can be used for this purpose.

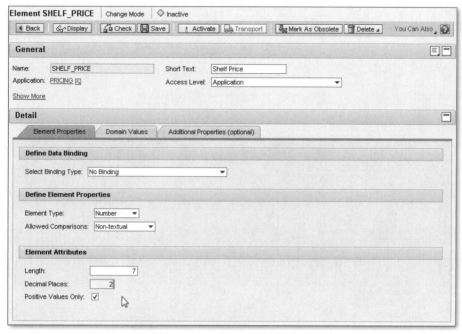

Figure 3.16 Properties of "Shelf Price" Element

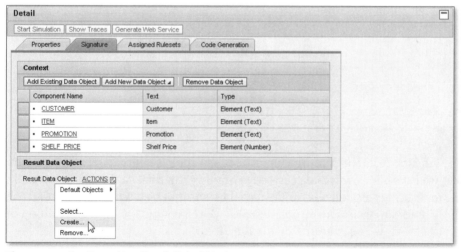

Figure 3.17 Creating a New Result Data Object

In the standard creation dialog for a data object (see Figure 3.18), we specify that the new result data object shall be of Type "Element" (default). We enter "FINAL_

PRICE" as Name and enter "Final Price" as Short Text. We can directly set the standard properties Length to 7, Decimal Places to 2, and allow Positive Values Only. By clicking on the Create button at the bottom of the dialog, we stay on the function UI in the background.

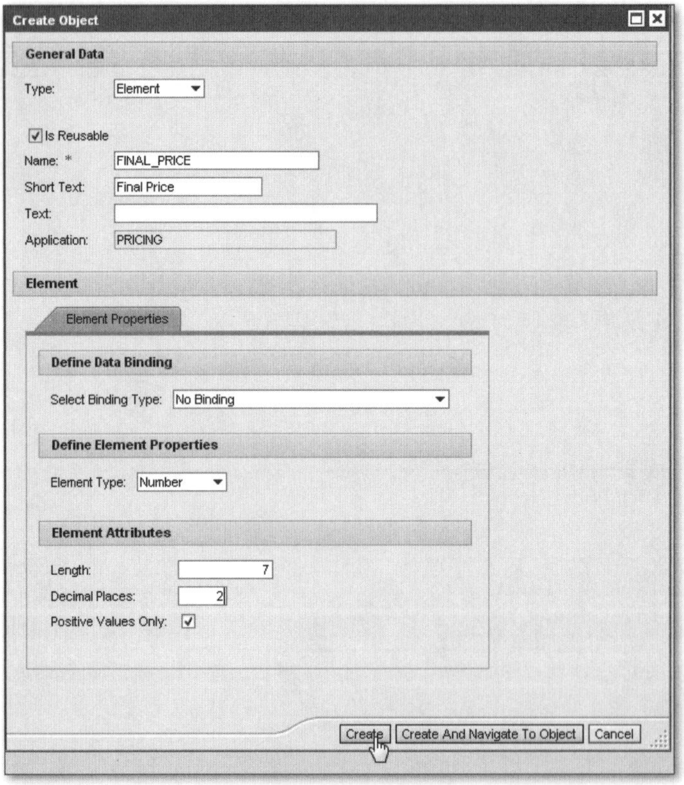

Figure 3.18   Creation of the Result Data Object

The function that represents the interface to our rules is now completed. To ensure that we have done everything correctly so far, we can click on the Check button in the toolbar. It is located next to the Save button, as depicted in Figure 3.16. If the check does not reveal any inconsistencies, we can continue with the definition of a ruleset that will be triggered by the function.

3.1.3   Ruleset

The easiest way to create such a ruleset is clicking on the button Create Ruleset on the tab Assigned Rulesets in the function editor. This is shown in Figure 3.19.

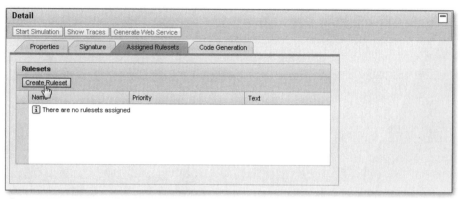

Figure 3.19   Creation of a Ruleset for the Function

The ruleset Name will be "PRICE_CALCULATION_RULES" and for the Short Text we enter the abbreviation "Price Calc. Rules." We thus require an additional longer Text "Price Calculation Rules," as depicted in Figure 3.20. Then we click on the button Create And Navigate To Object.

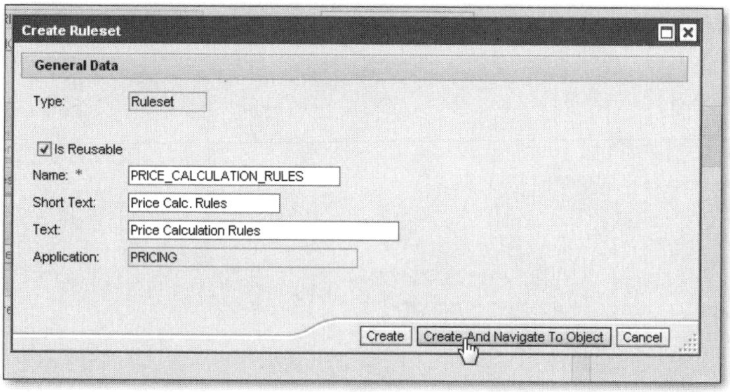

Figure 3.20   Creation of Ruleset

At the beginning of the Detail section, the properties of the ruleset header are gathered. We will require two temporary variables in the ruleset to store calculated customer and promotion discounts respectively. To analyze or create ruleset variables, we need only to click on the number shown in the header section in front of Ruleset Variables. Figure 3.21 points out the link. We might alternatively select a corresponding menu entry from the tray menu of the Detail section.

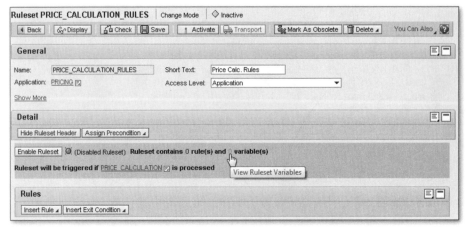

Figure 3.21 Access to Ruleset Variables

Because no ruleset variables are defined yet, we create a new one with the relevant menu entry (see Figure 3.22).

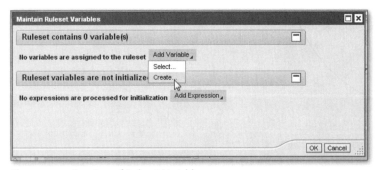

Figure 3.22 Creation of Ruleset Variable

Our first ruleset variable will be an element of type "Number." It gets the Name "CUSTOMER_DISCOUNT" and the Short Text "Customer Discount." The number will represent a percentage and shall thus have a Length of 3 digits with 2 Decimal Places and support Positive Values Only (see also Figure 3.23).

After clicking the Create button, we add just another ruleset variable "PROMO-TION_DISCOUNT" and text "Promotion Discount." It has the same technical settings as "Customer Discount." Again, we confirm the element creation with the Create button at the bottom of the dialog window. The ruleset variables definition should appear as in Figure 3.24.

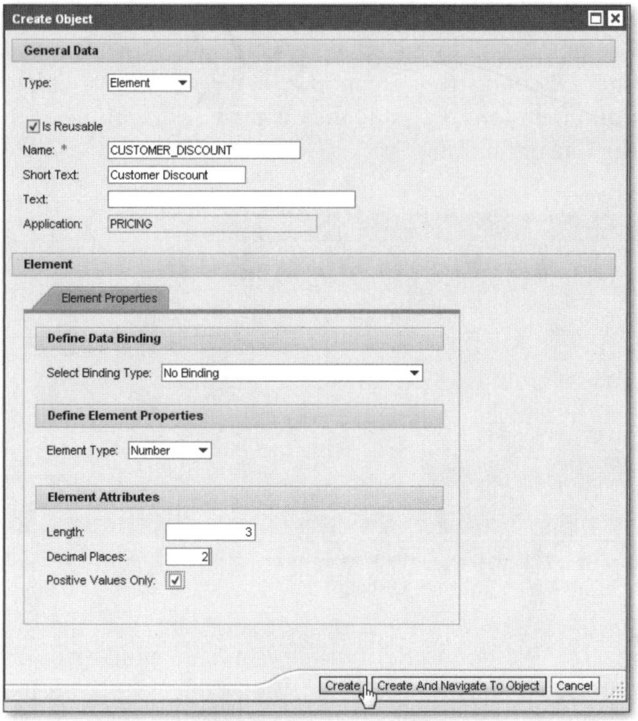

Figure 3.23 "Customer Discount" Element Definition

The variables will be initialized with respective discount values. We will use the logic of Decision Table expressions for this purpose. For the initialization we select CREATE as depicted in Figure 3.24.

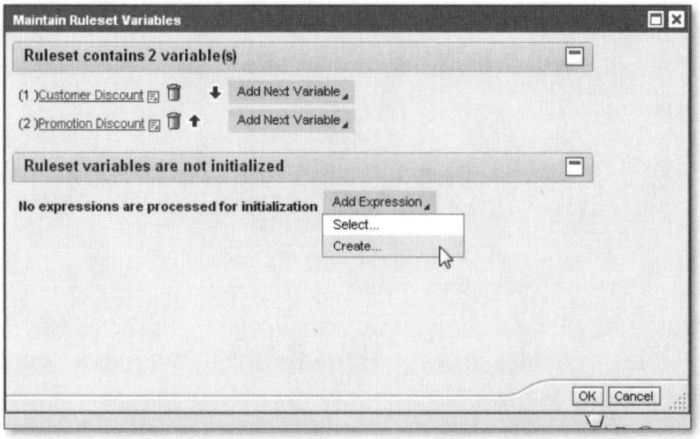

Figure 3.24 Creation of Initialization Expression

In the appearing object creation dialog, select TYPE "Decision Table" and enter the NAME "CALC_CUSTOMER_DISCOUNT," the SHORT TEXT "Calc. Cust. Discount" and the TEXT "Calculate Customer Discount" (see Figure 3.25). We want to complete the ruleset definition now and therefore postpone the detailed design of the decision table by clicking on the CREATE button.

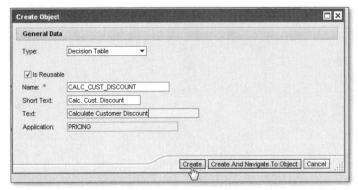

Figure 3.25 Creation of Decision Table for "Customer Discount"

For the second ruleset variable, "Promotion Discount," we add an additional initialization expression as before. We create another decision table, similar to the first one with NAME "CALC_PROMOTION_DISCOUNT," SHORT TEXT "Calc. Prom. Discount" and TEXT "Calculate Promotion Discount" (see Figure 3.26).

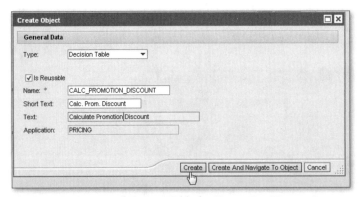

Figure 3.26 Creation of Decision Table for "Promotion Discount"

After definition of the ruleset variables and the initializations have been completed, the screen should look like Figure 3.27.

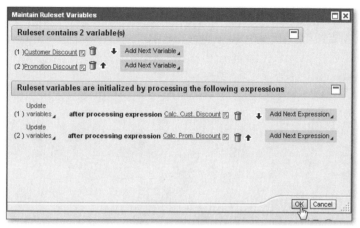

Figure 3.27 Ruleset Variables and Initializations

3.1.4 Rule

We now proceed to definition of a rule within the ruleset. By selecting the button choice INSERT RULE • CREATE, as depicted in Figure 3.28, we add a ruleset-specific rule. Reusable rule definitions could, for example, be created via the context menu in the Repository View.

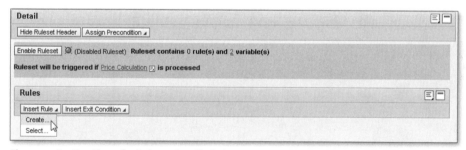

Figure 3.28 Creation of a Ruleset-Specific Rule

The rule will compare the promotion discount against the customer discount and the higher discount will be used to calculate the final item price. Therefore, we insert the description "Apply discount." For the comparison we select the menu entry USE VALUE RANGE FROM • PROMOTION DISCOUNT, next to the IF clause. This is shown in Figure 3.29. In case the element is not directly listed in the menu, we can select entry MORE CONTEXT PARAMETERS… to search for it. You may look ahead to Figure 3.31.

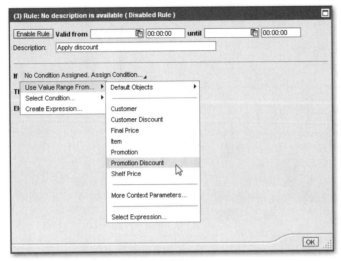

Figure 3.29 Choosing a Rule Condition

In the displayed condition area we select the comparison operator "is greater than" from the dropdown. By default the selected "Promotion Discount" element is compared to a value. In the CHANGE menu to the right, we can select another context parameter instead, as depicted in Figure 3.30.

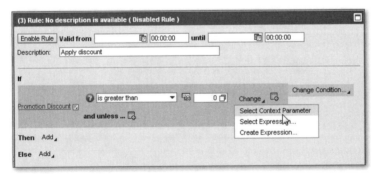

Figure 3.30 Selecting a Comparison Parameter

A context search dialog will open up. It enables searching for data objects that are part of the associated function context. We have to select the element "Customer Discount" as shown in Figure 3.31.

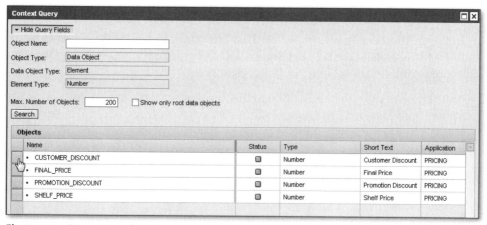

Figure 3.31 Context Search Dialog

The definition of the rule condition is completed now. For the action part we can define two respective lists of operations. The operations under the THEN clause are executed at runtime, if the condition is fulfilled. The operations of the ELSE clause are executed otherwise.

We will create single Formula expressions for each case. They will calculate the function result—the final price—according to the rule condition. First we add a new expression next to the THEN clause for this purpose. This is shown in Figure 3.32.

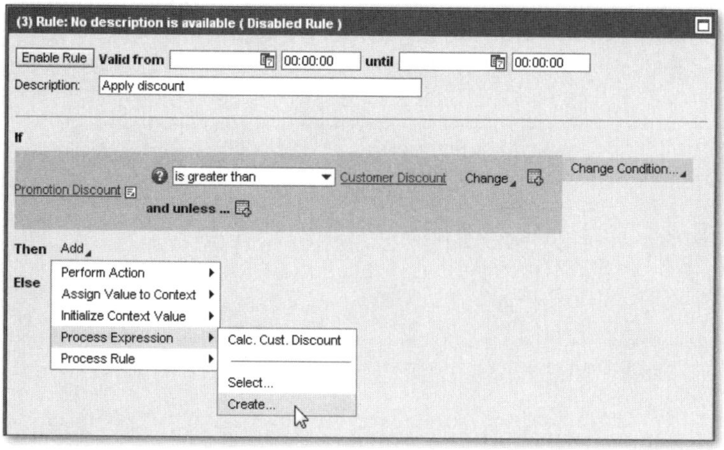

Figure 3.32 Adding a New Expression as Rule Operation

3.1.5 Formula Expressions

In the creation dialog we choose the TYPE "Formula" and enter the NAME "APPLY_PROMOTION_DISCOUNT," the SHORT TEXT "Apply Prom. Discount" and the TEXT "Apply Promotion Discount" as in Figure 3.33.

This time we navigate immediately to the new Formula expression by clicking the CREATE AND NAVIGATE TO OBJECT button. During this process we will have to save the changes that we have applied to the ruleset and the rule.

Figure 3.33 Creation of Formula Expression "Apply Promotion Discount"

The formula we want to define shall be *Final Price = Shelf Price / (1+ Promotion Discount)*. As RESULT DATA OBJECT we therefore have to select element "Final Price." In the menu that is pointed out in Figure 3.34, we choose the SELECT entry to trigger a search dialog for existing data objects. In the dialog we can search for and select element "Final Price."

Figure 3.34 Selection of Result Data Object for the Formula

Now it is time to define the actual formula string. We can add the "Shelf Price" context parameter to the formula simply by clicking on the corresponding entry in the CONTEXT box. This procedure is illustrated in Figure 3.35.

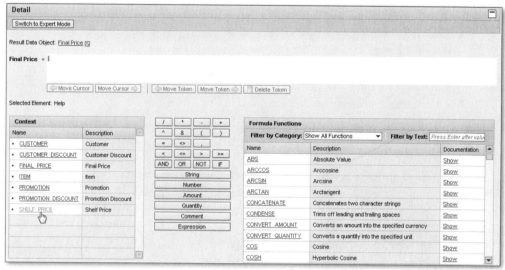

Figure 3.35 Adding Context Parameters to the Formula

The division operator / and the opening bracket (can be appended by clicking the corresponding buttons in the middle of the editor. To enter a number we click on the NUMBER button, as depicted in Figure 3.36. A small popup window will appear. There we enter the value 1 and press OK afterwards.

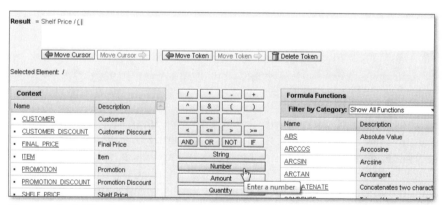

Figure 3.36 Adding Numbers to the Formula

Now we add a + operator, the context parameter "Promotion Discount," and a closing bracket) just as before. The final formula should appear as shown in Figure 3.37.

Figure 3.37 Formula "Apply Promotion Discount"

The rule definition is not completed yet. Thus we navigate back to our ruleset "Price Calc. Rules" and edit the rule as depicted in Figure 3.38.

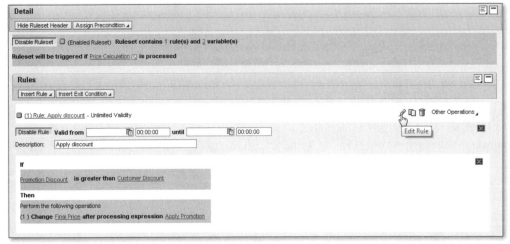

Figure 3.38 Editing a Rule in the Ruleset

For the ELSE branch of the rule we also add a new expression, just as we have done for the THEN branch (Figure 3.32). In the appearing creation dialog we again choose TYPE "Formula." Similar to our first Formula expression, we enter the NAME "APPLY_CUSTOMER_DISCOUNT," the SHORT TEXT "Apply Cust. Discount" and the TEXT "Apply Customer Discount," as depicted in Figure 3.39. We then navigate immediately to the new Formula expression by clicking on the button CREATE AND NAVIGATE TO OBJECT.

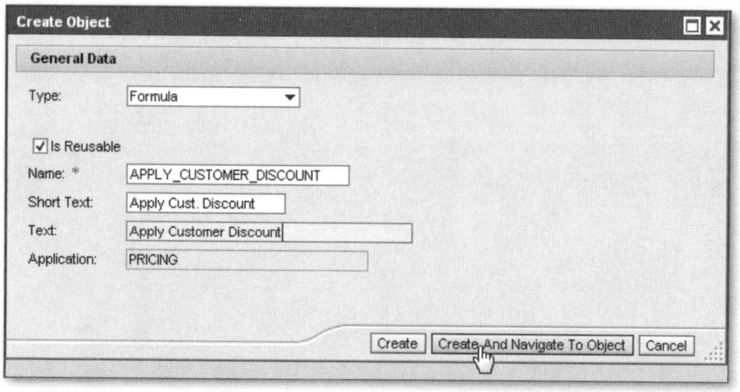

Figure 3.39 Creation of Formula Expression "Apply Customer Discount"

The formula we want to define shall be *Final Price = Shelf Price / (1+ Customer Discount)*. As RESULT DATA OBJECT we therefore again select element "Final Price." The formula string can be entered the same way as before, except that we have to use context parameter "Customer Discount" instead of "Promotion Discount" this time. The resulting Formula expression should look like Figure 3.40.

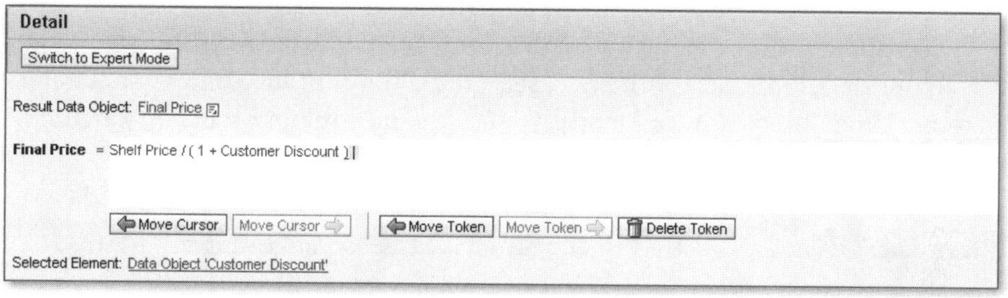

Figure 3.40 Formula "Apply Customer Discount"

3.1.6 Decision Tables

Still missing is the detailed design of the decision tables that we have created for the initialization of the ruleset variables. Therefore, we have to open expression "Calc. Cust. Discount" (CALCULATE_CUSTOMER_DISCOUNT) in the editor now. For this purpose we can select the expression in the REPOSITORY VIEW, for example.

In the editor we are immediately requested to specify the table settings that determine the layout of the decision table. As illustrated in Figure 3.41, we first select the RESULT DATA OBJECT. The already known search dialog for data objects will open up. Because the decision table will initialize our ruleset variable "Customer Discount," we need to select the element.

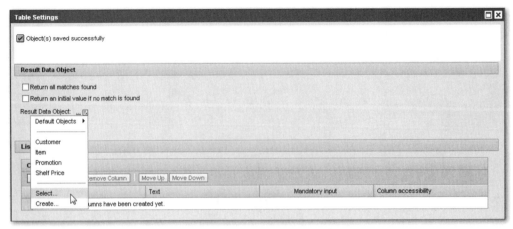

Figure 3.41 Selection of Result Data Object in Decision Tables

Having selected the result data object, the editor will immediately ask whether we want to automatically update the result columns of the decision table. This functionality offers a convenient way to get a correct table definition. We confirm the request.

For the computation of the customer discount, we will use two CONDITION COLUMNS in our decision table. Both are based on the input of the context parameters "Customer" and "Item." Consequently, we use the button option INSERT COLUMN • FROM CONTEXT DATA OBJECTS... as shown in Figure 3.42.

Figure 3.42 Inserting Condition Columns for Context Parameters

Once more, a search dialog will open up for the retrieval of context parameters. However, this time it is possible to indicate multiple entries at once, by holding down ⌈Ctrl⌋. The SELECT button at the bottom of the dialog window has to be pressed afterwards.

The complete decision table settings should appear as shown in Figure 3.43 and can be confirmed with OK.

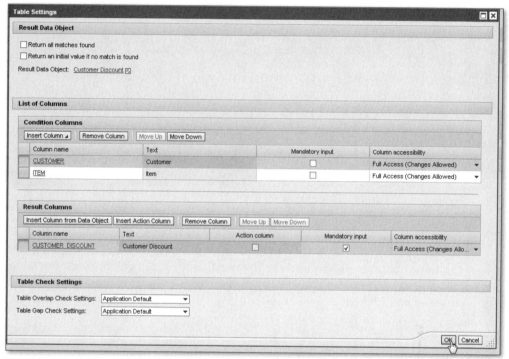

Figure 3.43 Decision Table Settings for "Customer Discount"

Now it is the time to enter some data into the decision table. We just click on the INSERT NEW ROW button in the toolbar of the DETAIL section, as shown in Figure 3.44. A new, empty line will be added to the table content.

Figure 3.44 Inserting Rows into a Decision Table

To enter values into the table cells, we only need to click on the links in the cells. An additional area will be expanded that allows entering simple conditions and values directly. As condition in the first cell of the "Customer" column, we enter a simple "is equal to" comparison for customer "SAP." This is illustrated in Figure 3.45. The new or changed cell value needs to be confirmed with OK.

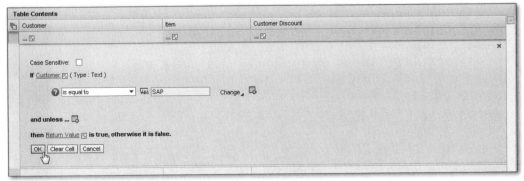

Figure 3.45 Conditions in Decision Tables

To create the table content that is summarized in Table 3.1, we need to add additional rows and enter corresponding cell values. The last row has no entries in the condition columns. The value 0 (no discount) in the result column will thus serve as a default. At runtime it is always chosen, in case the conditions of the above rows are not fulfilled.

Customer	Item	Customer Discount
SAP	Ballpen	0.15
SAP	Pencil	0.12
		0

Table 3.1 Decision Table Content for "Customer Discount"

The resulting decision table definition should look like Figure 3.46 and can be saved now.

We now have the knowledge to design the second Decision Table expression "Calc. Prom. Discount" in the editor. It will initialize the ruleset variable "Promotion Discount." Thus we need to select the appropriate element as RESULT DATA OBJECT of the expression. The result column of the decision table can once more be configured automatically via the editor.

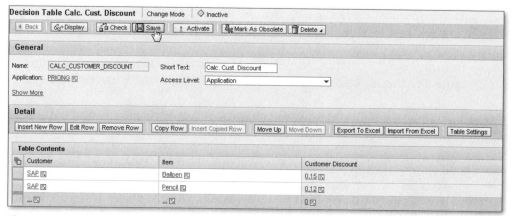

Figure 3.46 Decision Table Content for "Customer Discount"

We specify only one condition column for the table. It shall be based on the context parameter "Promotion." The final table settings should look like Figure 3.47.

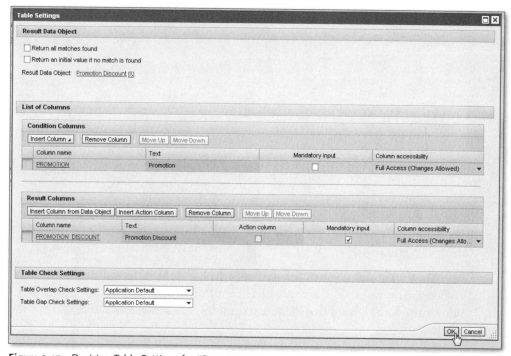

Figure 3.47 Decision Table Settings for "Promotion Discount"

Table 3.2 summarizes the data that we enter as decision table content. In the last table row we compare the "Promotion" context parameter to an initial value (space). This is in fact different from not specifying any condition at all. At runtime, an illegal "Promotion" value will not match any condition in our case and will cause a processing error. The final decision table should look like Figure 3.48.

Promotion	Promotion Discount
Sales10	0.10
Sales25	0.25
Sales50	0.50
Special	0.77
" "	0

Table 3.2 Decision Table Content for "Promotion Discount"

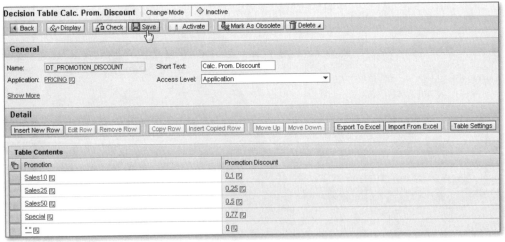

Figure 3.48 Decision Table Content for "Promotion Discount"

3.1.7 Activation

All objects that are required for our scenario have been created and set up now. To become processable, the only task left is primarily the activation of the objects. But we also must ensure that the ruleset and rule are actually enabled. This is what we do next.

The enabled status of rulesets and rules is indicated in the header sections. For the ruleset, a status icon can be found directly next to the ENABLE RULESET button, which is depicted in Figure 3.49. If necessary, we simply click on the button.

Figure 3.49 Enabling Rulesets

Each rule of the ruleset can individually be enabled and disabled, independent from the ruleset itself. A status icon is displayed at the upper left corner of each rule. If the rule is disabled, we need to access its complete header section. Figure 3.50 illustrates how the header section for the rule can be made visible.

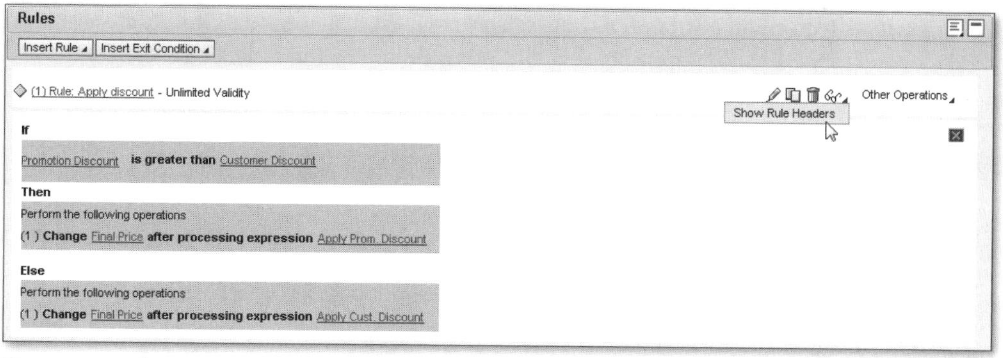

Figure 3.50 Showing Rule Headers

As for the ruleset, we can enable our rule simply by clicking on the ENABLE RULE button (see Figure 3.51). As an alternative, we could also edit the rule and enable it in the appearing rule editor.

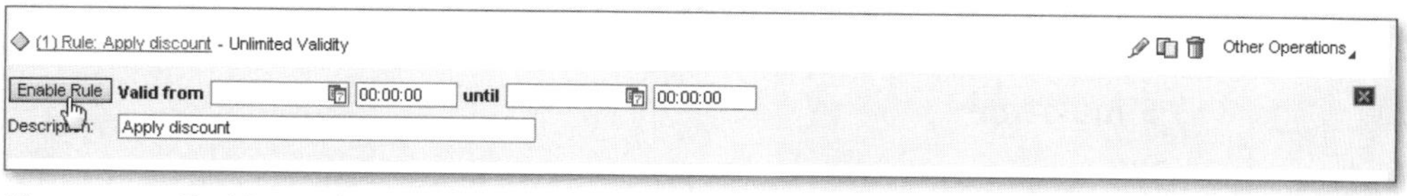

Figure 3.51 Enabling Rules

The activation of all our objects can be triggered through the activation of the ruleset only. This is because the ruleset references all other objects we have created, either directly or indirectly. When the ruleset is opened in the editor, we only need to click on the ACTIVATE button in the toolbar, which is depicted in Figure 3.52.

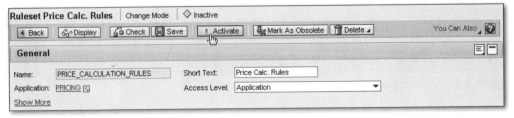

Figure 3.52 Activation of the Ruleset

After we click on the button, a confirmation dialog will appear. It asks whether we want to activate and whether the referenced objects shall be activated as well. With the confirmation of this dialog, we should be done. However, the activation is possible only if the involved objects are consistently defined. If not, any remaining errors will show up now. It is also possible to see the object state in the repository tree and activate the objects with the context menu.

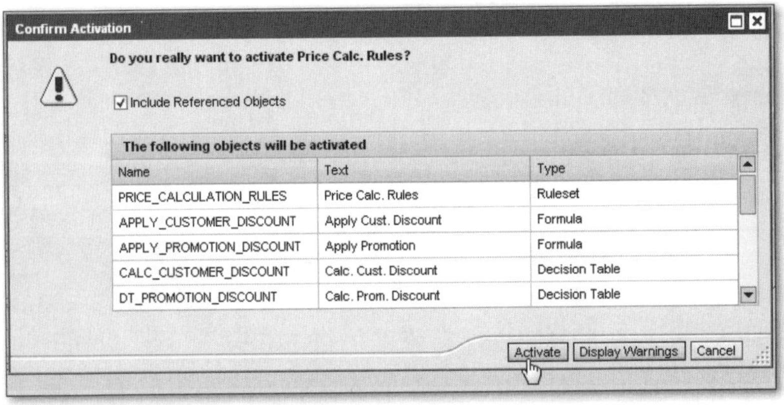

Figure 3.53 Confirmation Dialog for the Activation of Referenced Objects

3.1.8 Simulation

The activation has ensured that our objects are syntactically correct and can be processed. But it is not yet clear whether the defined logic actually works as expected. As the final step in our tutorial, we will run a simulation of the function.

We open our function "Price Calculation" in the editor and click on the START SIMULATION button in the toolbar of the DETAIL section, as shown in Figure 3.54. The simulation tool can also be started from the context menu in the repository tree.

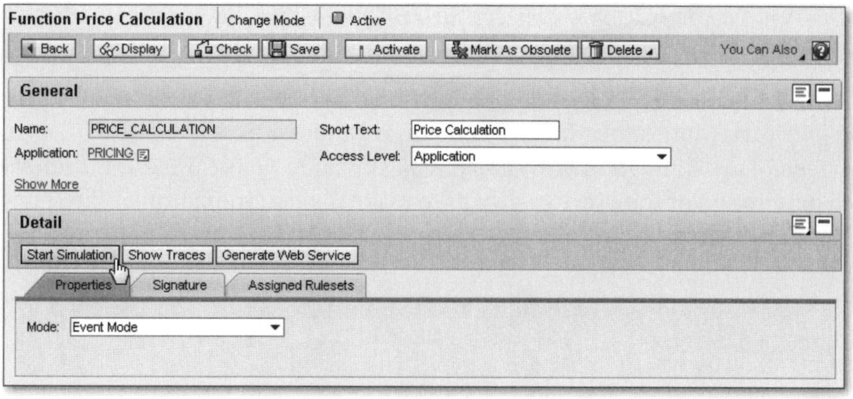

Figure 3.54 Starting the Function Simulation

The simulation tool of BRFplus will appear. For our function we can now directly enter test values for the four context parameters, for example:

▶ CUSTOMER: SAP

▶ ITEM: Ballpen

▶ PROMOTION: Sales10

▶ SHELF PRICE: 1.99

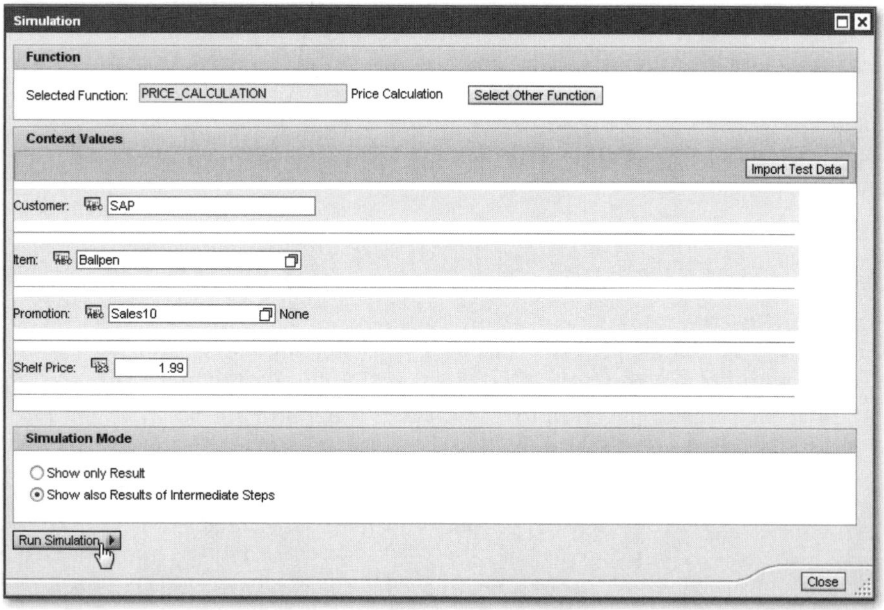

Figure 3.55 Simulation Setup

In Simulation Mode section we select the option Show also Results of Intermediate Steps. As depicted in Figure 3.55 we can start the simulation by clicking on the Run Simulation button.

For the given test values, our function should compute a final price of 1.73. The result screen of the simulation tool should look similar to Figure 3.56. It includes a detailed description of the processed steps to make the determination of the result value comprehensible.

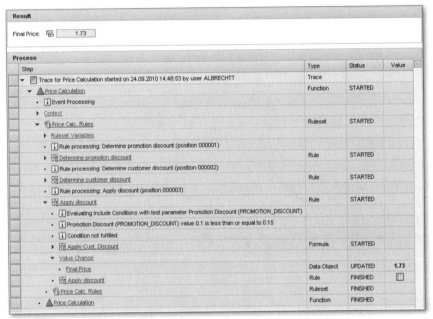

Figure 3.56 Simulation Result

3.2 Creation of a Pricing Application with the API

The previous sections showed the idea of the pricing application and how it can be created with help of the user interface, the BRFplus Workbench. This section shows how the same application can be created programmatically with the BRFplus API.

Package SFDT_DEMO_OBJECTS

Package SFDT_DEMO_OBJECTS is part of the BRFplus shipment. It contains many other example and tutorial programs. The programs are a good source to copy code and development patterns.

3.2.1 Application

The approach with the API is very similar to that of the UI. First, an application has to be created as a container for all other BRFplus artifacts. Listing 3.1 shows the code needed to create the application.

```
DATA: lo_factory          TYPE REF TO if_fdt_factory,
      lo_application      TYPE REF TO if_fdt_application,
      lt_message          TYPE if_fdt_types=>t_message,
      lv_boolean          TYPE abap_bool.

FIELD-SYMBOLS: <ls_message> TYPE if_fdt_types=>s_message.

lo_factory = cl_fdt_factory=>if_fdt_factory~get_instance( ).
lo_application = lo_factory->get_application( ).
lo_application->if_fdt_transaction~enqueue( ).
lo_application->set_development_package( '$TMP' ).
lo_application->if_fdt_admin_data~set_name( 'PRICING' ).
lo_application->if_fdt_admin_data~set_texts(
  iv_short_text = 'Pricing' ).
lo_application->if_fdt_transaction~activate(
          IMPORTING et_message           = lt_message
                    ev_activation_failed = lv_boolean ).
write_errors lt_message. "macro, which exits in case of error
lo_application->if_fdt_transaction~save( ).
lo_application->if_fdt_transaction~dequeue( ).
"Get an application specific factory instance
lo_factory = cl_fdt_factory=>if_fdt_factory~get_instance(
  iv_application_id = lo_application->mv_id ).
```

Listing 3.1 Creation of an Application

Any new object is created with help of the BRFplus factory. The object variables are always typed with an appropriate interface and not with classes. The classes that implement the interfaces are not published for usage and may change in an incompatible way in future releases. In the case of the application above, the interface is IF_FDT_APPLICATION.

All object interfaces embed the interfaces IF_FDT_TRANSACTION and IF_FDT_ADMIN_DATA. They allow performing common transactional actions and respectively changing common object properties.

Objects need to be locked when changes are saved. As for the application of our example, it is best done right after the creation with method ENQUEUE.

By default a created application has the storage type customizing. We thus only have to set local development package $TMP to ensure a local customizing application. We can omit an explicit call of method CREATE_LOCAL_APPLICATION in this way. After activating, saving and unlocking the application, a new, application-specific factory instance is created. This will make sure that all objects created with help of this factory are automatically assigned to the newly created application.

The handling of errors has been simplified in the sample code of this tutorial. The statement WRITE_ERRORS is actually a macro that writes an error message to the output screen and stops the processing of the program. Listing 3.2 shows the code for the macro.

```
DEFINE write_errors.
  IF &1 IS NOT INITIAL.
    LOOP AT &1 ASSIGNING <ls_message>.
      WRITE: <ls_message>-text.
    ENDLOOP.
    RETURN. ">>>
  ENDIF.
END-OF-DEFINITION.
```

Listing 3.2 Macro for Message Handling

In productive code it is not sufficient to take only error messages into account that are returned as method parameters. The code should also be embedded into an appropriate TRY-CATCH block, because many methods of the BRFplus API may throw exceptions. All exception classes of BRFplus inherit from class CX_FDT. They therefore share the common attribute MT_MESSAGE, which stores messages with detailed information about the problem that led to the exception.

3.2.2 Function

Similar to the UI tutorial, the next step is the creation of a function. Listing 3.3 shows how to do it.

```
DATA: lo_function    TYPE REF TO if_fdt_function,
      lts_context_id TYPE if_fdt_types=>ts_object_id,
      lv_result_id   TYPE if_fdt_types=>id.

lo_function ?= lo_factory->get_function( ).
lo_function->if_fdt_transaction~enqueue( ).
lo_function->if_fdt_admin_data~set_name( 'PRICE_CALCULATION' ).
lo_function->if_fdt_admin_data~set_texts(
  iv_short_text = 'Price Calculation' ).
```

```
lo_function->set_function_mode(
  if_fdt_function=>gc_mode_event ).

* code for context creation (lts_context_id) and result
* creation (lv_result_id) to be inserted here
lo_function->set_context_data_objects( lts_context_id ).
lo_function->set_result_data_object( lv_result_id ).

lo_function->if_fdt_transaction~activate(
  EXPORTING iv_deep                = abap_true
  IMPORTING et_message             = lt_message
            ev_activation_failed   = lv_boolean ).
write_errors lt_message. ">>> exit in case of error
lo_function->if_fdt_transaction~save(
  EXPORTING iv_deep = abap_true ).
lo_function->if_fdt_transaction~dequeue(
  EXPORTING iv_deep = abap_true ).
```

Listing 3.3 Creation of a Function

New compared to the application are the function-specific method calls such as SET_UNCTION_MODE. At the place of the comment (*code for...to be inserted here) the creation of the result and context data objects still has to be inserted. This part will be covered later. This substitution pattern is followed for the rest of this tutorial.

In the additional coding there is a slight difference in the way the function is activated, saved, and unlocked. Those operations are all done "deeply" by handing over parameter IV_DEEP. The methods will therefore include all referenced objects of the function, such as context and result data objects.

> **Types and Constants**
>
> Type and constant definitions are often included in the object-type-specific interface, for example, IF_FDT_FUNCTIONS. Common types are, however, included in the interface IF_FDT_TYPES and common constants can be found in the interface IF_FDT_CONSTANTS.

The creation of data objects for the function signature, which has been omitted from Listing 3.3, follows now. Listing 3.4 illustrates the creation of one data object for the context. The other context data objects have to be created in the same way.

```
DATA lo_element TYPE REF TO if_fdt_element.
lo_element ?= lo_factory->get_data_object(
    iv_data_object_type = if_fdt_constants=>gc_data_object_type_element ).
```

```
lo_element->if_fdt_transaction~enqueue( ).
lo_element->if_fdt_admin_data~set_name( 'CUSTOMER' ).
lo_element->if_fdt_admin_data~set_texts(
  iv_short_text = 'Customer' ).
lo_element->set_element_type(
  if_fdt_constants=>gc_element_type_text ).
lo_element->set_element_type_attributes( iv_length = 30 ).
INSERT lo_element->mv_id INTO TABLE lts_context_id.
```

Listing 3.4 Creation of a Context Data Object

For the creation of the other data objects, only a few changes are needed to pass different values. The values are listed in Table 3.3.

Name	Text	Element Type	Type Attributes
CUSTOMER	Customer	Text	length = 30
ITEM	Item	Text	length = 30
PROMOTION	Promotion	Text	length = 20
SHELF_PRICE	Shelf Price	Number	length = 7, decimals = 2, only positive = true

Table 3.3 API Tutorial—Context Data Objects

The creation of domain values for the elementary data objects is optional. To keep the tutorial simple, they have been left out. Information on this topic is available in Sections 5.2.2 and 5.5.2.

The function also requires a result data object. Creating a result data object is no different than creating the context data objects. Listing 3.5 shows how to do it.

```
lo_element ?= lo_factory->get_data_object(
    iv_data_object_type = if_fdt_constants=>gc_data_object_type_element ).
lo_element->if_fdt_transaction~enqueue( ).
lo_element->if_fdt_admin_data~set_name( 'FINAL_PRICE' ).
lo_element->if_fdt_admin_data~set_texts(
  iv_short_text = 'Final Price' ).
lo_element->set_element_type( if_fdt_constants=>gc_element_type_number ).
lo_element->set_element_type_attributes(
  iv_length        = 7
  iv_decimals      = 2
  iv_only_positive = abap_true ).
lv_result_id = lo_element->mv_id.
```

Listing 3.5 Creation of a Result Data Object

3.2.3 Ruleset

The next step is the creation of the ruleset. In this tutorial we use a second report for this purpose. The new report also includes the macro for error handling in Listing 3.2. The objects created so far are referred to by their technical ID, which is assumed to be known. In the Workbench the ID can be found in the GENERAL section of the editor. Listing 3.6 shows how to create the ruleset.

```
DATA: lo_ruleset      TYPE REF TO if_fdt_ruleset,
      lts_rule        TYPE if_fdt_ruleset=>ts_rule,
      lts_variable    TYPE if_fdt_ruleset=>ts_variable,
      lts_expression  TYPE if_fdt_ruleset=>ts_init_expr.

lo_factory = cl_fdt_factory=>if_fdt_factory~get_instance(
  iv_application_id = '00505683359D02EE98FC41ECA7650AA3' ).

lo_ruleset ?= lo_factory->get_ruleset( ).
lo_ruleset->if_fdt_transaction~enqueue( ).
lo_ruleset->set_ruleset_switch(
  iv_switch = if_fdt_ruleset=>gc_switch_on ).
lo_ruleset->if_fdt_admin_data~set_name(
  'PRICE_CALCULATION_RULES' ).
lo_ruleset->if_fdt_admin_data~set_texts(
  iv_short_text = 'Price Calc. Rules'
  iv_text       = 'Price Calculation Rules' ).
lo_ruleset->set_function_restriction(
  iv_function_id = '00505683359D02EE98FC41EE6215CAA4' ).

* code for ruleset variables (lts_variable) to be inserted here
lo_ruleset->set_ruleset_variables( lts_variable ).

* code for ruleset initializations (lts_expression) to be
* inserted here
lo_ruleset->set_ruleset_initializations( lts_expression ).

* code for rules (lts_rule) to be inserted here
lo_ruleset->set_rules( lts_rule ).

lo_ruleset->if_fdt_transaction~activate(
  EXPORTING iv_deep              = abap_true
  IMPORTING et_message           = lt_message
            ev_activation_failed = lv_boolean ).
write_errors lt_message. ">>> exit in case of error
lo_ruleset->if_fdt_transaction~save(
  EXPORTING iv_deep = abap_true ).
```

```
lo_ruleset->if_fdt_transaction~dequeue(
  EXPORTING iv_deep = abap_true ).
```

Listing 3.6 Creation of a Ruleset

As you can see, the function does not hold any reference to the ruleset but vice versa. The ruleset makes the execution of its rules dependent on the function with method IF_FDT_RULESET~SET_FUNCTION_RESTRICTION.

A common mistake is forgetting to enable the ruleset for processing by switching it on with method IF_FDT_RULESET~SET_RULESET_SWITCH.

Some Tips and Tricks when Working with the BRFplus API

▶ Intermediate calls of method IF_FDT_TRANSACTION~CHECK can help to identify problems with newly created objects early. Later those checks can be removed.

▶ In messages of type IF_FDT_TYPES=>S_MESSAGE there can be information about the source, where exactly the message was created.

Three important steps have been left out in Listing 3.6. They are replaced by comments, which indicate what has to be implemented at the specified places:

1. Definition of ruleset variables — LTS_VARIABLE

2. Definition of initialization expressions — LTS_EXPRESSION

3. Definition of a rule — LTS_RULE

3.2.4 Ruleset Variables

Ruleset variables extend the function context, but within the scope of the ruleset only. They are also based on data objects. Listing 3.7 shows how to create the two ruleset variables for our example. To conveniently pass them to the ruleset, they are stored in a table LTS_VARIABLE at the end.

```
DATA: lo_element      TYPE REF TO if_fdt_element,
      ls_variable     TYPE if_fdt_ruleset=>s_variable,
      lv_pro_discount TYPE if_fdt_types=>id,
      lv_cus_discount TYPE if_fdt_types=>id.

lo_element ?=
  lo_factory->get_data_object( iv_data_object_type =
    if_fdt_constants=>gc_data_object_type_element ).
lo_element->if_fdt_transaction~enqueue( ).
lo_element->if_fdt_admin_data~set_name( 'CUSTOMER_DISCOUNT' ).
lo_element->if_fdt_admin_data~set_texts(
```

```
      iv_short_text = 'Customer Discount' ).
lo_element->set_element_type(
   if_fdt_constants=>gc_element_type_number ).
lo_element->set_element_type_attributes(
   iv_length       = 3
   iv_decimals     = 2
   iv_only_positive = abap_true ).
ls_variable-position       = 1.
ls_variable-data_object_id = lo_element->mv_id.
INSERT ls_variable INTO TABLE lts_variable.
lv_cus_discount = lo_element->mv_id.

lo_element ?= lo_factory->get_data_object(
   iv_data_object_type = if_fdt_constants=>gc_data_object_type_element ).
lo_element->if_fdt_transaction~enqueue( ).
lo_element->if_fdt_admin_data~set_name( 'PROMOTION_DISCOUNT' ).
lo_element->if_fdt_admin_data~set_texts(
   iv_short_text = 'Promotion Discount' ).
lo_element->set_element_type( if_fdt_constants=>gc_element_type_number ).
lo_element->set_element_type_attributes(
   iv_length       = 3
   iv_decimals     = 2
   iv_only_positive = abap_true ).
ls_variable-position       = 2.
ls_variable-data_object_id = lo_element->mv_id.
INSERT ls_variable INTO TABLE lts_variable.
lv_pro_discount = lo_element->mv_id.
```

Listing 3.7 Creation of Ruleset Variables

The variables LV_CUS_DISCOUNT and LV_PRO_DISCOUNT store the technical IDs of the two ruleset variables. They are needed for the creation of decision tables, formulas, and the rule below.

3.2.5 Decision Tables as Initialization Expressions

Next the two Decision Table expressions that initialize the ruleset variables have to be created. The following listings show only the creation of decision table "Customer Discount," which is based on the data objects "Customer" and "Item." The second decision table DT_PROMOTION_DISCOUNT can be created similarly with only a few modifications.

Listing 3.8 contains only the basic steps to create a decision table in general. The detailed column definition and the table data are transferred into subsequent listings.

```
DATA: lo_decision_table TYPE REF TO if_fdt_decision_table,
      lts_column      TYPE if_fdt_decision_table=>ts_column,
      lts_table_data TYPE if_fdt_decision_table=>ts_table_data,
      ls_expression  TYPE if_fdt_ruleset=>s_init_expr.


lo_decision_table ?=
  lo_factory->get_expression( iv_expression_type_id =
    if_fdt_constants=>gc_exty_decision_table ).
lo_decision_table->if_fdt_transaction~enqueue( ).
lo_decision_table->if_fdt_admin_data~set_name(
  'CALC_CUSTOMER_DISCOUNT' ).
lo_decision_table->if_fdt_admin_data~set_texts(
    iv_short_text = 'Calc. Cust. Discount'
    iv_text      = 'Calculate Customer Discount' ).

* code for table definition (lts_column) to be inserted here
lo_decision_table->set_columns( lts_column ).
lo_decision_table->if_fdt_expression~set_result_data_object(
  lv_cus_discount ).   "customer discount

* code for table content (lts_table_data) to be inserted here
lo_decision_table->set_table_data( lts_table_data ).

ls_expression-position    = 1.
ls_expression-id          = lo_decision_table->mv_id.
ls_expression-change_mode =
  if_fdt_ruleset=>gc_change_mode_update.
INSERT ls_expression INTO TABLE lts_expression.
```

Listing 3.8 Ruleset Variable Initialization with Decision Tables

Listing 3.9 shows how the decision table columns are defined. The code has to be inserted at comment `* code for table definition ...` into Listing 3.8.

```
DATA: ls_column TYPE if_fdt_decision_table=>s_column.

ls_column-col_no    = 1.                    "customer
ls_column-object_id = '00505683359D02EE98FC41EEC610CAA5'.
ls_column-is_result = abap_false.
INSERT ls_column INTO TABLE lts_column.
ls_column-col_no    = 2.                    "item
ls_column-object_id = '00505683359D02EE98FC41EEF243CAA6'.
```

```
ls_column-is_result =  abap_false.
INSERT ls_column INTO TABLE lts_column.
ls_column-col_no    = 3.                    "customer discount
ls_column-object_id = lv_cus_discount.
ls_column-is_result =  abap_true.
INSERT ls_column INTO TABLE lts_column.
```

Listing 3.9 Decision Table Column Definition

Listing 3.10 shows the code for the creation of the decision table cells. It has to be inserted at the comment `* code for table content` ... into Listing 3.8.

```
DATA: ls_range       TYPE if_fdt_range=>s_range,
      ls_table_data  TYPE if_fdt_decision_table=>s_table_data.

FIELD-SYMBOLS <lv_number> TYPE if_fdt_types=>element_number.

ls_range-position = 1.
ls_range-sign     = if_fdt_range=>gc_sign_include.
ls_range-option   = if_fdt_range=>gc_option_equal.

ls_table_data-col_no = 1.                      "start of row 1
ls_table_data-row_no = 1.
GET REFERENCE OF 'SAP' INTO ls_range-r_low_value.
INSERT ls_range INTO TABLE ls_table_data-ts_range.
INSERT ls_table_data INTO TABLE lts_table_data.
CLEAR ls_table_data-ts_range.
ls_table_data-col_no = 2.
ls_table_data-row_no = 1.
GET REFERENCE OF 'Ballpen' INTO ls_range-r_low_value.
INSERT ls_range INTO TABLE ls_table_data-ts_range.
INSERT ls_table_data INTO TABLE lts_table_data.
CLEAR ls_table_data-ts_range.
ls_table_data-col_no = 3.
ls_table_data-row_no = 1.
CREATE DATA ls_table_data-r_value TYPE
  if_fdt_types=>element_number.
ASSIGN ls_table_data-r_value->* TO <lv_number>.
<lv_number> = '0.15'.
INSERT ls_table_data INTO TABLE lts_table_data.
CLEAR ls_table_data-r_value.

ls_table_data-col_no = 1.                      "start of row 2
ls_table_data-row_no = 2.
GET REFERENCE OF 'SAP' INTO ls_range-r_low_value.
```

```
INSERT ls_range INTO TABLE ls_table_data-ts_range.
INSERT ls_table_data INTO TABLE lts_table_data.
CLEAR ls_table_data-ts_range.
ls_table_data-col_no = 2.
ls_table_data-row_no = 2.
GET REFERENCE OF 'Pencil' INTO ls_range-r_low_value.
INSERT ls_range INTO TABLE ls_table_data-ts_range.
INSERT ls_table_data INTO TABLE lts_table_data.
CLEAR ls_table_data-ts_range.
ls_table_data-col_no = 3.
ls_table_data-row_no = 2.
CREATE DATA ls_table_data-r_value TYPE
   if_fdt_types=>element_number.
ASSIGN ls_table_data-r_value->* TO <lv_number>.
<lv_number> = '0.12'.
INSERT ls_table_data INTO TABLE lts_table_data.
CLEAR ls_table_data-r_value.

ls_table_data-col_no = 3.                    "start of row 3
ls_table_data-row_no = 3.
CREATE DATA ls_table_data-r_value TYPE
   if_fdt_types=>element_number.
ASSIGN ls_table_data-r_value->* TO <lv_number>.
<lv_number> = '0'.
INSERT ls_table_data INTO TABLE lts_table_data.
```

Listing 3.10 Decision Table Cell Data

Values for result columns are handed over in the reference variable LS_TABLE_DATA-R_VALUE. It is necessary to create new variables with the ABAP statement CREATE DATA each time. Otherwise all lines would point to the same data in the memory. This is a very common mistake.

3.2.6 Rule

In the ruleset sample code of Listing 3.6 there is the comment * code for rules... as a replacement for the actual rule creation coding. Listing 3.11 shows how the rule of our example application can be created. It is submitted with parameter LTS_RULE to the ruleset afterwards with method IF_FDT_RULESET~SET_RULES.

In this tutorial an unnamed rule is created, which is only valid within the scope of the ruleset it is assigned to. The rule can be identified by the text description setting within the ruleset.

```
DATA: lo_rule              TYPE REF TO if_fdt_rule,
      ls_rule              TYPE if_fdt_ruleset=>s_rule,
      ls_cond_range        TYPE if_fdt_range=>s_param_range,
      ls_rule_expr         TYPE if_fdt_rule=>s_expression,
      lt_rule_expr         TYPE if_fdt_rule=>t_expression,
      lv_formula_cus_disc  TYPE if_fdt_types=>id,
      lv_formula_pro_disc  TYPE if_fdt_types=>id.

lo_rule ?= lo_factory->get_expression(
  iv_expression_type_id = if_fdt_constants=>gc_exty_rule ).
lo_rule->if_fdt_transaction~enqueue( ).
lo_rule->if_fdt_admin_data~set_texts(
  iv_text = 'Apply Discount' ).

* promotion discount > cusomter discount
CLEAR ls_range.
ls_cond_range-parameter_id = lv_pro_discount.
ls_range-position          = 1.
ls_range-sign              = if_fdt_range=>gc_sign_include.
ls_range-option            = if_fdt_range=>gc_option_greater.
ls_range-low               = lv_cus_discount.
INSERT ls_range INTO TABLE ls_cond_range-ts_range.
lo_rule->set_condition_range( ls_cond_range ).

* define formulas, insert missing code later

ls_rule_expr-position    = 1.
ls_rule_expr-change_mode = if_fdt_rule=>gc_change_mode_update.
ls_rule_expr-expression  = lv_formula_pro_disc.
INSERT ls_rule_expr INTO TABLE lt_rule_expr.
lo_rule->set_true_action_extended(
  it_expression = lt_rule_expr ).

CLEAR lt_rule_expr.
ls_rule_expr-expression  = lv_formula_cus_disc.
INSERT ls_rule_expr INTO TABLE lt_rule_expr.
lo_rule->set_false_action_extended(
  it_expression = lt_rule_expr ).

ls_rule-position = 1.
ls_rule-rule_id  = lo_rule->mv_id.
ls_rule-switch   = if_fdt_ruleset=>gc_switch_on.
INSERT ls_rule INTO TABLE lts_rule.
```

Listing 3.11 Creation of a Rule

The rule uses the "Promotion Discount" data object as its test parameter and compares it to the "Customer Discount" data object. The comparison happens in form of a value range condition (method SET_CONDITION_RANGE). However, it would also be possible to set any expression or data object of Boolean type as a condition. In such a case method SET_CONDITION would be used.

Like the ruleset, also the rule needs to be explicitly enabled for processing. This is achieved with the component SWITCH in the rule table LTS_RULE.

Rule operations are referred to as actions in the API. To specify the rule actions there are two methods available in interface IF_FDT_RULE, SET_TRUE_ACTION_EXTENDED and SET_FALSE_ACTION_EXTENDED. They have exactly the same parameters.

Listing 3.11 shows how an expression can update the value of a context data object. In a similar way it would also be possible to set actions or define updates between context data objects. You can find more explanations of the rule capabilities in Section 5.4.

The creation of the Formula expressions had been omitted so far, to keep the focus on the rule. The next section shows how to create the Formula expressions. The variables LV_FORMULA_CUS_DISC and LV_FORMULA_PRO_DISC will store the respective IDs afterwards.

3.2.7 Formula Expressions

The creation of the Formula expressions is the last required step in this API tutorial. Listing 3.12 contains the missing piece of code that has to be inserted into Listing 3.11 instead of comment * define formulas....

```
DATA: lo_formula TYPE REF TO if_fdt_formula,
      lv_formula TYPE string.

lo_formula ?= lo_factory->get_expression(
  iv_expression_type_id = if_fdt_constants=>gc_exty_formula ).
lo_formula->if_fdt_transaction~enqueue( ).
lo_formula->if_fdt_admin_data~set_name(
  'APPLY_PROMOTION_DISCOUNT' ).
lo_formula->if_fdt_admin_data~set_texts(
    iv_short_text = 'Apply Prom. Discount'
    iv_text       = 'Apply Promotion Discount' ).
lo_formula->if_fdt_expression~set_result_data_object(
  '00505683359D02EE98FC41EF79D24AA9' ). "Final Price
* Final Price = Shelf Price / ( 1 + Promotion Discount )
lv_formula = '00505683359D02EE98FC41EF3591CAA8' &&
            ` / ( 1 + ` && lv_pro_discount && ` )`.
```

```
lo_formula->set_formula( lv_formula ).
lv_formula_pro_disc = lo_formula->mv_id.
```
Listing 3.12 Creation of a Formula Expression

Formulas can simply be defined as a text string, which is passed to method `IF_FDT_FORMULA->SET_FORMULA`. When (context) data objects are used as operands, they are represented by their technical ID in the formula string. In the listing the variable `LV_PRO_DISCOUNT` contains the ID of the "Promotion Discount" data object, while the ID of the "Shelf Price" data object is statically declared.

The second formula, which will calculate the customer discount, can be built in exactly the same way as the first one. Its technical ID has to be stored in variable `LV_FORMULA_CUS_DISC`. Only the formula string has to differ slightly. The "Customer Discount" data object has to be used instead of the "Promotion Discount" data object. Listing 3.13 shows how to do this.

```
* Final Price = Shelf Price / ( 1 + Customer Discount )
lv_formula = '00505683359D02EE98FC41EF3591CAA8' &&
             ` / ( 1 + ` && lv_cus_discount && ` )`.
```
Listing 3.13 Formula String

3.2.8 Embedding the Function into ABAP Code

The design time part is now complete. The last step in this tutorial is the creation of an ABAP program that will execute the created function. The code of that program is provided in Listing 3.14.

```
DATA: lo_function TYPE REF TO if_fdt_function,
      lo_context  TYPE REF TO if_fdt_context,
      lo_result   TYPE REF TO if_fdt_result,
      lx_fdt      TYPE REF TO cx_fdt,
      lv_string   TYPE string.

FIELD-SYMBOLS <ls_message> TYPE if_fdt_types=>s_message.

lo_function =
  cl_fdt_factory=>if_fdt_factory~get_instance(
)->get_function( iv_id = '00505683359D02EE98FC41EE6215CAA4' ).

TRY.
    lo_context = lo_function->get_process_context( ).
    lo_context->set_value( iv_name  = 'CUSTOMER'
                           ia_value = 'SAP' ).
    lo_context->set_value( iv_name  = 'ITEM'
```

```
                                ia_value = 'Pencil' ).
        lo_context->set_value( iv_name  = 'PROMOTION'
                                ia_value = ' ' ).
        lo_context->set_value( iv_name  = 'SHELF_PRICE'
                                ia_value = '10' ).
        lo_function->process( EXPORTING io_context = lo_context
                               IMPORTING eo_result  = lo_result ).
        lo_result->get_value( IMPORTING ea_value = lv_string ).
        WRITE lv_string .
      CATCH cx_fdt INTO lx_fdt.
        LOOP AT lx_fdt->mt_message ASSIGNING <ls_message>.
          WRITE / <ls_message>-text.
        ENDLOOP.
    ENDTRY.
```

Listing 3.14 Function Processing

The function is processed with help of the function object's PROCESS method. BRF-plus provides also a static PROCESS method in class CL_FDT_FUNCTION_PROSSESS for the same purpose. The static call is less elegant but optimized for better performance. More information about performance in BRFplus can be found in Section 7.1.

In BRFplus rules are assembled using objects of different types. This chapter provides information on how to handle and manage the objects in general. Besides transactional aspects that address the lifecycle and distribution of the objects, common object properties are described in detail. Also relevant for object management are two specific object types, the application and the catalog. They are presented in this chapter as well.

4   Object Management

For composing new rules in BRFplus, it is important to know how the BRFplus objects are defined, used, and linked to each other in general. Objects can be maintained either by using the BRFplus Workbench or via the BRFplus application programming interface (API). Both approaches address different types of users and use cases.

▶ The Workbench is a graphical user interface on top of the API. It can be used by administrators or business experts to define and adjust rules in a convenient way.

▶ Inherently the API is intended for programmers, for example to dynamically generate new rules on demand. The description of the API is encapsulated into separate sections at the end of each topic. You may therefore easily skip these parts.

In this chapter we will first look at the general handling and lifecycle of objects. The corresponding API section, Section 4.2, includes an introduction to the standard programming aspects of BRFplus, such as naming conventions, types, and constants. The properties and attributes that all objects have in common are presented afterwards in Section 4.3. This is followed by a section about the application object, which is a prerequisite for all other objects. The catalog object is introduced in Section 4.5. It is not relevant for the evaluation of rules, but allows the user to organize other objects in a convenient way.

4.1 Basic Object Handling

Before we go into details about the various object types and their properties, some ordinary actions within the BRFplus Workbench will be explained first. Let us begin with the creation of objects.

4.1.1 Object Creation

Using the BRFplus Workbench, new objects—except applications—are usually created either via a context menu in the navigation panel, or where needed within the DETAIL SECTION of objects.

The context menu in the navigation panel contains a CREATE entry, depending on the underlying item. It links to a sub menu offering the possible object types. As shown in Figure 4.1, for data objects, only the corresponding subtypes element, structure, and table can be created.

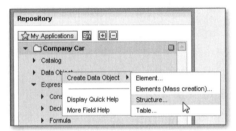

Figure 4.1 Object Creation in the Repository View

Within the DETAIL section of objects, referenced objects are typically represented by a link with an attached menu. Figure 4.2 shows such a menu within the function UI as an example. In the menu you can usually select existing objects or create new ones, whenever it makes sense. There may also, however, be ways other than links to represent associated objects.

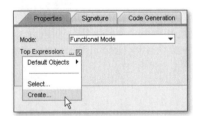

Figure 4.2 Object Creation via Link Menu

When you choose to create a new object, a popup like the one in Figure 4.3 will be shown, where you can enter some basic data. You then have two options to continue:

▶ By clicking on the CREATE button, you can create the new object but continue working on the currently displayed object. The detailed design of the new object can be postponed to a later point in time.

▶ By clicking on the CREATE AND NAVIGATE TO OBJECT button, you can leave the currently displayed object and switch immediately to the new object. After having specified the details for the new object, you can navigate to the previous object, using the BACK button on the left-hand side of the object toolbar.

It is a matter of taste which of the two design approaches—top-down or bottom-up—you use.

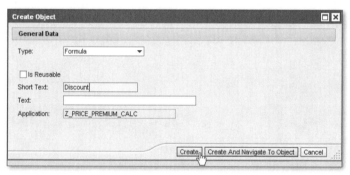

Figure 4.3 Object Creation Popup

4.1.2 Object Selection

Speaking of object selection, we address actually two different scenarios. One is simply the finding of an object you intend to display or edit. The other is the linking of one object to another.

In the first case you may already know the unique ID of an object. Then you can simply use the menu entry WORKBENCH • OPEN OBJECT … to show the object in the editor. Otherwise, the REPOSITORY view in the navigation panel gives you the opportunity to browse through the available content.

By default the objects created by the current system user are displayed. The objects are hierarchically ordered in a tree structure by their types, sub types, and so on. From an object item, you can drill down to all its used objects. Inversely, you can also drill from an object item to the objects that are using it. An object tree is depicted in Figure 4.4.

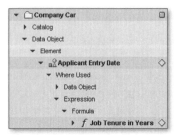

Figure 4.4 Object Tree in the Repository View

To locate the currently displayed object in the repository view, you can select menu entry WORKBENCH • SHOW CURRENT OBJECT IN REPOSITORY. You may alternatively select entry DISPLAY WHERE USED LIST in the YOU CAN ALSO menu of the object toolbar. In a popup, all referencing objects will be listed as links that you can navigate to.

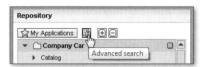

Figure 4.5 Search in the Repository View

The REPOSITORY view offers a button, shown in Figure 4.5, to search for any kind of BRFplus objects. The search dialog depicted in Figure 4.6 will open up. It allows you to enter search patterns for many different object attributes.

When you enter the wildcard characters * and +, they match any number of characters or respectively to a single unspecific character. If all input fields are left empty an unrestricted search that includes the complete repository content will be executed (not recommended). The NUMBER OF ENTRIES SHOWN field should, however, be set to a reasonable value and limit the result list. After the SEARCH button has been clicked on, the found objects will be listed directly in the REPOSITORY view. To switch back to your own objects, you can click on the MY APPLICATIONS button.

When you click on an object in the navigation panel, it is displayed in an editor in the main area of the Workbench. While editing an object you often need to link other objects to it. The linking is commonly done via a SELECT... menu entry or button. They will open an object search dialog that is also called a query dialog.

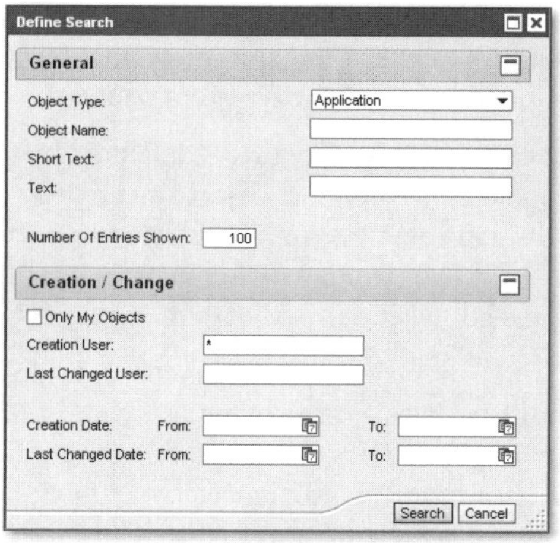

Figure 4.6 Repository Search Dialog

Figure 4.7 shows a screenshot of a query dialog. In the dialog you may first switch between CUSTOM OBJECTS and BRFPLUS DEFAULT OBJECTS. These are objects that BRFplus ships in the standard application FDT_SYSTEM. In the first case you may specify any application by providing its name. You can also enter search patterns using the wildcards + and * as placeholders for one or many arbitrary characters. Likewise, you may enter an OBJECT NAME that needs to be matched.

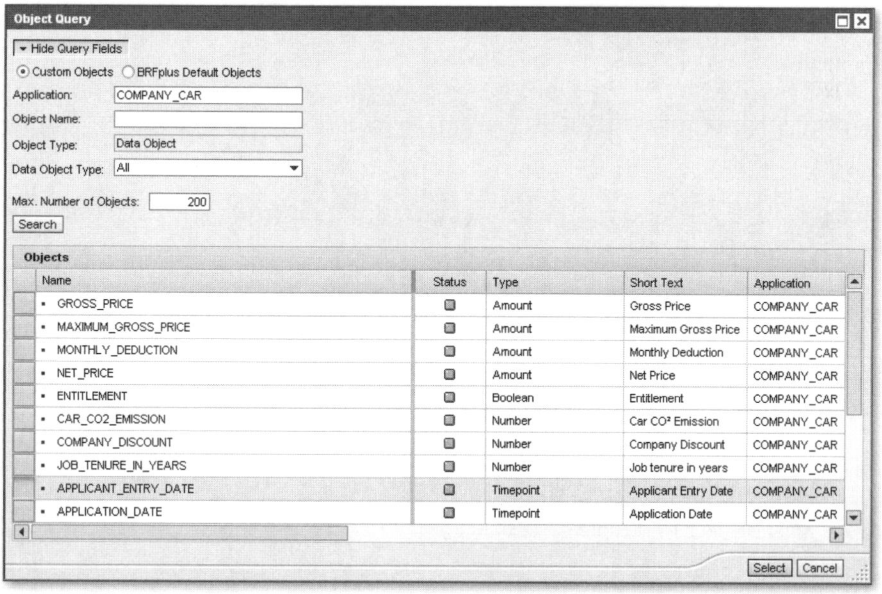

Figure 4.7 Query Dialog

The query is often context sensitive, so only objects of a specific type or expressions with a feasible result type can be selected. Thus you may restrict the object type and/or subtypes to be searched for only according to the current context.

You should also consider the MAX. NUMBER OF OBJECTS entry that is defaulted by a corresponding user profile setting. In case you do not find the object you are looking for, you might have to extend this value. In some cases it is possible to select multiple objects at once, holding down `Ctrl`. The popup will then have a SELECT button in the lower right corner to confirm the selection, as shown in Figure 4.7.

Sometimes only data objects that are contained in the context of a function or ruleset will be linked to the currently edited object. In this case you typically find the menu entry SELECT CONTEXT PARAMETER in the link menu. However, this option is feasible only if the current object is directly or indirectly referenced by a function or ruleset. It is thus recommended that you always create new objects within the realm of functions and rulesets.

Last but not least, the menus of links typically include shortcuts. They allow selecting a BRFplus DEFAULT OBJECT and/or recently used object directly. Such a menu is shown in Figure 4.8.

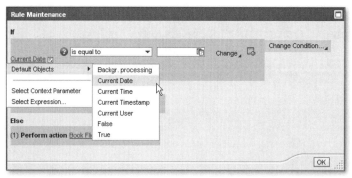

Figure 4.8 Object Linkage Menu

4.1.3 Object Maintenance

The object toolbar of the Workbench is depicted in Figure 4.9. With the buttons it contains, various actions can be performed on the currently displayed object.

Figure 4.9 Object Toolbar—Actions

Many actions can also be extended to include objects that are directly or indirectly referenced by the current object. Figure 4.10 shows, for example, the activation of multiple, connected objects at once. However, only objects that belong to the same BRFplus application are taken into account.

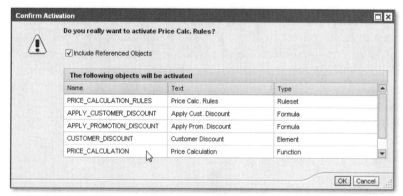

Figure 4.10 Actions Including Referenced Objects

Almost all actions require an internal locking of the current object to prevent other users from modifying it at the same time. Conversely, if the object is already locked by another user or in another system client, most actions will not be possible.

Whether an object is changeable depends on the object's storage type and according system and client settings. These settings may, for example, forbid changes entirely or they may require recording the changes onto a transport request. Section 4.4 contains more information about the storage types.

To perform an action, the user eventually needs to have the appropriate authorization. An administrator can assign a matching role or authorization profile to the user with Transaction SU01.

Authorization Settings

Technically the authorization check for BRFplus objects is based on the authorization object FDT_OBJECT. It defines the fields FDT_APPL, FDT_OBJTYP and FDT_ACT so that the standard checks depend on the BRFplus application the object is assigned to, the object's type, and the action to be performed. The available actions are listed in Table 4.3. Additional, custom defined authorization checks can be realized with an application exit. This is explained in detail in Section 7.3.1.

All the above mentioned preconditions must be fulfilled to edit an object. The preconditions are checked when the object editor is switched into change mode with the EDIT button in the object toolbar. (The button will transform into a DISPLAY button to switch back into display mode.)

With the CHECK button, you can check the object for consistency. This is mostly relevant when the object has been edited and may contain invalid settings. Used objects will, however, always be checked as well. The check result consists of a list of messages that are displayed in a separate area below the toolbar. For each message, the issuing object is represented by a link at the beginning. This link allows you to directly navigate to the object. The DETAILS link at the end of each message will show rather technical information about the message's origin. For some messages a more detailed description is available. In such cases an additional DISPLAY LONGTEXT link will be visible to show the description.

Figure 4.11 Check Result Messages

The SAVE button in the object toolbar is active only when the object is shown in edit mode. Clicking on the SAVE button will have an effect only if the current object has actually been changed. In case automatic change recording is turned on in the system, a dialog may appear the first time, requesting a valid transport request. Later, saving will automatically record onto the same transport request. Object changes are always retained as an inactive object version at first. On the one hand, the inactive version of the object does not need to be consistent and thus allows intermediate changes also to be preserved. On the other hand, an inactive object version is never considered during rules processing.

Non-local BRFplus objects can in general be transferred into other systems by means of the standard transport mechanism. Only the last active version of an object is transportable. The application's storage type influences the type of transport request that can be used for recording. Customizing objects, for example, require a customizing request for the current client, whereas system objects are recorded onto Workbench requests. Because no object can exist without its application, the corresponding application object is always recorded onto the same transport request as well. The package assigned to an application may allow only certain target system settings for the transport request. If a specific transport request or task cannot be chosen for recording, it may not be of the required type. Transport requests can be maintained and released with Transaction SE09.

Release of Transport

BRFplus allows transporting of only active and consistent objects. When you try to release a transport request, all recorded BRFplus objects are automatically checked in this respect. In case inactive or inconsistent object versions are detected, the release of the transport request is cancelled and error messages are issued. The objects to which the messages refer have to be activated or corrected. Objects that are locked, for example because they are still opened in the Workbench in edit mode, also cannot be released.

Usually only changed objects are recorded onto a transport request or task. When the checkbox SHOW TECHNICAL ASPECTS has been marked in the user personalization, an additional TRANSPORT button, depicted in Figure 4.12, becomes available in the object toolbar. It allows you to record an object directly onto a transport request, no matter if the object has been changed or not. Tasks of transport requests are not supported in this case.

Figure 4.12 Object Toolbar—Transport Button

Only active versions of an object are taken into account in the processing of rules. To transform a currently inactive version of the opened object into an active version, the ACTIVATE button in the object toolbar needs to be clicked on. The object will be checked for consistency and if no errors are found it will be saved as an active version to the database. Checking and saving consequently do not need to be performed separately. In case an active version of the object exists already, it is also possible to discard the inactive version by clicking on the RETURN TO ACTIVE VERSION button. All changes in the inactive version will thereby be lost.

The typical lifecycle of a BRFplus object is illustrated in Figure 4.13. Once created, the object is ready to be used by other objects. If changes are required the status can switch an arbitrary number of times between inactive and active.

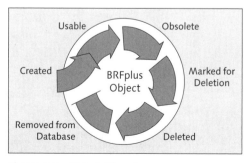

Figure 4.13 Object Lifecycle

The next lifecycle phase is often reached when the object will not be used any more by other objects because there is, for example, a better replacement available. The object shall, however, not be deleted but remain for existing usages. In such a case, the object status can be set to obsolete with the button MARK AS OBSOLETE in the toolbar. Obsolete objects can neither be changed nor newly linked by other objects. The obsolete status can be revoked at any time.

Deletion of an object may be prevented by the existing references from other objects. Either the referencing objects must be deleted first, or the linkage among the objects must be broken. As a third option, BRFplus provides an intermediate object status: Objects can be marked for deletion only. In this state an object is at first treated the same way as an obsolete object. The status can also still be revoked. An administrator can periodically try to delete objects that are marked for deletion with the application administration tool. See Section 6.5 for more details. As soon as the object is no longer in use, it will then be deleted.

Objects that are not referenced by any version of another object in the system can immediately be deleted via the DELETE button in the object toolbar. Clicking on the button will in fact set a deletion status for the object first. The object is still saved in the database, but BRFplus treats such objects as non-existent. With the setting SHOW DELETED OBJECTS in the user personalization, such objects can still be made visible. For emergency reasons it is temporarily possible for administrators to undelete such objects. They will ultimately be removed from the database either manually by an administrator or automatically after a retention time of 180 days.

4.2   Basic Object API

The BRFplus API is written in object-oriented ABAP and mainly exposed via interfaces. They make the individual functionality accessible but hide the technical implementation. Before we go into further programming details, let us first look at some general naming conventions.

4.2.1   Naming Conventions

For interfaces and classes, BRFplus uses the following conventions:

▶ Interfaces start with prefix IF_FDT_...

▶ Classes start with prefix CL_FDT_...

▶ Exception classes start with prefix CX_FDT_...

The abbreviation FDT stems from the formerly used internal name for BRFplus, which was "Formula & Derivation Tool."

Within these objects the following naming conventions apply for attributes:

▶ Constant definitions start with prefix GC_...
▶ Static attribute definitions start with prefix GV_...
▶ Member attribute definitions start with prefix MV_...

Parameter names within class and interface methods (or also function modules) have a prefix that consists of two to three characters. The first character defines the parameter's usage type:

▶ I for importing parameters
▶ E for exporting parameters
▶ C for changing parameters
▶ R for returning parameters

The second character of the prefix describes the parameter's data type:

▶ V for simple variable types
▶ S for structure types
▶ T for table types
▶ R for reference types
▶ O for object types
▶ A for generic/unspecific data types like ANY or DATA

For table types an additional third character may further refine the type of the parameter:

▶ H for hashed table types
▶ S for sorted table types

Here are some examples: IA_VALUE describes an importing parameter with generic data type, RO_FUNCTION refers to a returning object parameter, and ETS_TEXT eventually corresponds to an exporting parameter of a sorted table type.

Most object type-specific methods deal with setting or getting some property values. These methods are usually respectively named SET_<PROPERTY> and GET_<PROPERTY>. Importing parameters of the setter-methods are then typically mirrored by analogously named exporting parameters in the getter-methods. For simple properties, the getter-methods may provide single values in the form of a returning parameter.

If you understand the signature of the setter-methods, the usage of the getter-methods is usually straightforward. When there is no deviation from the described schema, the getter-methods are thus not explicitly described.

4.2.2 Interface Hierarchy

The object-oriented approach of the API perfectly fits the object based BRFplus model. Each BRFplus object type or sub type is represented by an according ABAP interface. The behavior of the object type is modeled with a class that implements the interface.

Each BRFplus object definition contains individual settings according to its type. In ABAP the analogy to a BRFplus object is thus a class instance that implements the corresponding type's interface. The instance can hold the individual settings the processing logic is based on.

The interfaces reflecting the BRFplus types are hierarchically structured to bundle common aspects. This hierarchy is shown in Figure 4.14. The fundamental interfaces are IF_FDT_TRANSACTION and IF_FDT_ADMIN_DATA, which all objects share (and can be cast to). The implementation of these two interfaces is contained in the non-public base class CL_FDT_MAINTENANCE.

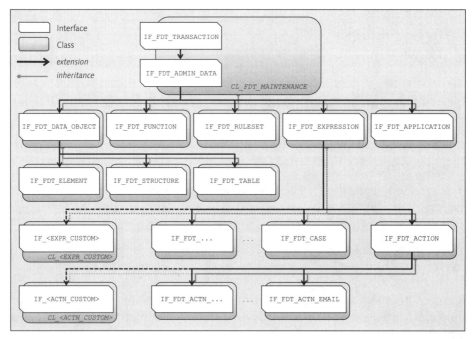

Figure 4.14 Object Hierarchy

On the next level there are interfaces for the different main object types. The list in Figure 4.14 is actually not complete because the interfaces for catalogs or expression types are missing. These types are, however, somewhat special because they are not relevant to processing. Additional object types may of course evolve in the future.

For data object and expression types there are further sub-interfaces. Action types are actually a special kind of expression types, so they are represented by yet another sub-interface of the expression interface.

For all sub-interfaces of IF_FDT_ADMIN_DATA there exists a corresponding class that provides the implementation for the interface. Apart from the prefix CL_ instead of IF_ these classes share the same name. Class CL_FDT_EXPRESSION implements, for example, the common functionality for expression types, which is defined by interface IF_FDT_EXPRESSION. The inheritance of the classes is similar to the extension of the interfaces.

Customers who develop their own expression or action types may stick to this convention as well. IF_FDT_EXPRESSION and IF_FDT_ACTION are the interfaces, they will have to be extended similarly.

In addition to the interfaces representing the various BRFplus object types, the API comprises many more interfaces that deal with processing of rules, querying objects, data exchange, and other functional aspects. The following, central interfaces are commonly used.

4.2.3 Types, Constants, and Messages

ABAP types that are widely used within the BRFplus API are centrally defined within the interface IF_FDT_TYPES. For example, there are definitions for the available element types like ELEMENT_NUMBER, ELEMENT_AMOUNT and so on.

Some types are specific to an object's type and therefore directly declared within the respective interface. For example, the data type for an application component is used only for application objects. It is thus declared as type APPLICATION_COMPO-NENT in interface IF_FDT_APPLICATION.

As for the type definitions, common constants are likewise centrally declared in interface IF_FDT_CONSTANTS. For example, there are constants for the standard object-, expression- and data object types available, which follow the name pattern GC_OBJECT_TYPE_*, GC_EXTY_* and GC_DATA_OBJECT_TYPE_* respectively. Object type specific constants are again directly declared within the respective interface.

Messages issued by the BRFplus API are of the structure type IF_FDT_TYPES=>S_MESSAGE. In addition to ABAP's standard message variables SY-MSG*, the structure contains the following useful fields:

- TEXT: the resulting message text, ready to use.
- ID: usually refers to the issuing object.
- OBJECT_TYPE: contains the type of the issuing object.
- RELATED_ID: may refer to another object that is related to the cause of the message.
- SOURCE: contains information about where the message was issued.

Messages are for example contained in exceptions raised by the BRFplus API: All exception classes inherit from the root class CX_FDT and thus have a table type member attribute MT_MESSAGE. There the related messages are stored.

4.2.4 The Factory Class: Central Point of Access

BRFplus follows the common approach for defining a standard entry point to its API by providing a factory class. The class has the obvious name CL_FDT_FACTORY and exposes its functionality via the implemented interface IF_FDT_FACTORY. Commonly, the first line of coding with respect to BRFplus retrieves a singleton instance of the factory interface via the static method GET_INSTANCE:

```
DATA: lo_factory TYPE REF TO if_fdt_factory.
lo_factory = cl_fdt_factory=>get_instance( ).
```

Listing 4.1 Factory Retrieval

By convention, the methods of the BRFplus API provide only the IDs of objects rather than references to object instances. In case an object instance is actually required, it can be retrieved only via the factory class.

Besides the access to an instance of itself, the factory interface provides the methods listed in Table 4.1 to access the various BRFplus object types.

The methods return an instance of the respective interface type and allow you to either create new objects or retrieve existing[1] object definitions. Their signatures look very similar. For the creation, you may need only to pass the desired sub type in case of expression or data object types. A new object instance will be

---

1 Objects may exist only in memory or they may already have been saved to the database. They are automatically loaded by the factory, if required.

returned with an automatically generated universal identifier in the member variable IF_FDT_ADMIN_DATA~MV_ID.

Method Name	Description
GET_INSTANCE	Gets a factory singleton instance.
GET_APPLICATION	Gets or creates an application type object.
GET_CATALOG	Gets or creates a catalog type object.
GET_DATA_OBJECT	Gets or creates a data object type object.
GET_EXPRESSION	Gets or creates an expression or action type object.
GET_EXPRESSION_TYPE	Gets or creates an expression type object.
GET_FILTER	Not supported in release 7.02. Do not use!
GET_FUNCTION	Gets or creates a function type object.
GET_ISSUER	This method is deprecated. Do not use!
GET_RULESET	Gets or creates a ruleset object.

Table 4.1 Interface IF_FDT_FACTORY—Access to BRFplus Object Instances

To retrieve an existing object, its identifier of type IF_FDT_TYPES=>ID has to be passed via parameter IV_ID. If the parameter is passed, an object with the provided identifier must exist and be of the correct type. Otherwise, a CX_FDT_INPUT exception will be thrown.

Through the factory interface you may access further entities besides BRFplus object types. The corresponding methods are not listed in Table 4.1 but are described in the relevant chapters.

Public Interfaces

The factory class shall also ensure that only public interfaces are used. The instances provided by the factory class may implement further, BRFplus internal interfaces that must not be used. There are, however, also some public interfaces that exist standalone. In doubt, you should check package interface FDT of package SFDT. All objects that are included in this package interface can be used without restrictions. Objects that are exposed only by the package interface FDT_EXTENDED are usually not required and should be considered only in exceptional cases, such as the implementation of a new action or expression type.

4.2.5 Transactional Behavior

Whenever you change, save, or delete a BRFplus object, you also change its transactional state. Using the BRFplus Workbench, some transactional operations like authorization checks or locking are done automatically. All related kinds of operations are available through interface IF_FDT_TRANSACTION. As already mentioned in

Section 4.2.2., this interface is included with all BRFplus object related interfaces. The methods of interface IF_FDT_TRANSACTION are summarized in Table 4.2.

Method Name	Description
AUTHORITY_CHECK	Checks whether the user is allowed to perform a specific action on the object.
GET_CHANGEABILITY	Checks whether the object is changeable and optionally returns transport relevant information.
ENQUEUE	Locks the object.
CHECK	Checks object consistency.
ACTIVATE	Activates the object.
DISCARD_CHANGES	Discards unsaved changes.
COPY	Creates a copy of the object.
MARK_OBSOLETE	Marks the object as obsolete.
DELETE	Deletes or marks the object for deletion.
SAVE	Saves the object.
DEQUEUE	Unlocks the object.
TRANSPORT	Writes the object onto a task/request for transport.

Table 4.2 Methods in Interface IF_FDT_TRANSACTION

All methods except method GET_CHANGEABILITY can be called in a deep mode by setting parameter IV_DEEP to ABAP_TRUE: The transactional operation is then performed not only on the object itself but also on all referenced objects within the same application. The application defines an implicit boundary for deep operations.

Before you perform any kind of activity on a BRFplus object, you might first want to check whether the current user has the required authorization. Method AUTHORITY_CHECK can be used for that purpose: It will return a Boolean value for the requested activity, passed in parameter IV_ACTIVITY. The parameter can have the values listed in Table 4.3, which are defined in interface IF_FDT_CONSTANTS. The further parameter IS_SUB_ACTIVITY is currently not evaluated by BRFplus itself. It is only potentially forwarded to a custom defined application exit. Currently the only defined sub activity is GC_SUB_ACTIVITY_COPY. It is intended for the copying of an object in combination with activity GC_ACTIVITY_CREATE.

Value	Description
GC_ACTIVITY_DISPLAY	Displays the object.
GC_ACTIVITY_CHANGE	Changes the object.
GC_ACTIVITY_CREATE	Creates the object.
GC_ACTIVITY_ACTIVATE	Activates the object.
GC_ACTIVITY_DELETE	Deletes the object.

Table 4.3 Authorization—Activities

Method AUTHORITY_CHECK does not have a parameter dedicated to messages. However, in case an authorization is not granted, the message variables in the global ABAP structure SYST are set accordingly.

Explicit Call
Method AUTHORITY_CHECK needs to be explicitly called before an activity is performed. The method is not automatically evaluated!

If you try to change an object, you might want to know beforehand whether (apart from authorization restrictions) the system and client settings allow changes on the object in general. The application determines the changeability of an object. The system settings apply to the storage type and package assignment of the object's application. For transportable objects the existence of a usable transport request or task may cause an additional precondition for changeability. Method GET_CHANGE-ABILITY provides the relevant information as summarized in Table 4.4.

Parameters	Description
EV_CHANGEABLE	ABAP_TRUE, if the object is changeable in general.
EV_CHANGE_RECORDING	ABAP_TRUE, if the object needs to be recorded on a transport request or task upon saving.
EV_RECORDED	ABAP_TRUE, if the object is already recorded on a transport request or task.
ET_TRANSPORT_REQUEST	May provide a list of suitable transport requests for change recording.
ET_MESSAGE	May provide related system messages, especially in case the object is not changeable.

Table 4.4 Parameters of Method IF_FDT_TRANSACTION~GET_CHANGEABILITY

The provided information can be especially useful when you try to save a transportable object. A transport request or task must be provided only under the following circumstances:

1. The object is changeable in general.

2. Changes on the object need to be recorded onto a transport request or task, according to the system and client settings.

3. The object is not yet recorded onto a transport request or task.

If the transactional state of an object is changed and persisted (saved) to the database, the object has to be locked first. The locking prevents persistent changes from being performed by other user sessions on the same object at the same time. Locking implies the following aspects:

▶ Only one system process can lock an object at a time.

▶ Objects that are not locked cannot be saved.

▶ Upon locking, all unsaved, previous changes of the object are lost.

Also: new objects need to be locked before they are altered. Otherwise, all changes will be lost and the objects cannot be saved. Locking is therefore best be done directly after the creation via the factory class. However, if you only want to temporarily test changes on objects, you should *not* lock them to ensure that the changes *cannot* be saved.

Locking is performed with a call to method ENQUEUE.[2] The optional parameter IV_ENQUEUE_MODE allows a more finely granular way of locking (e.g., read/write locks) but is seldom required. The method returns a parameter RV_ENQUEUE_FAILED. It is set to ABAP_TRUE in case the object is already locked externally and the enqueue fails. If the object can successfully be locked, the returning parameter is set to ABAP_FALSE.

After supposedly having locked an object, altering any of its properties may result in inconsistent settings. Calling method CHECK will return a list of messages for any critical or ambiguous settings. If the message list contains an error message, the object is not consistent and can therefore not be activated for processing.

The same checking is implicitly done when you try to activate an object calling method ACTIVATE. There may even be additional checks performed due to relations with or dependencies on other objects. If the activation fails for any rea-

---

2   The object is actually enqueued into a locking list; thus, enqueue is a common term for locking at SAP.

son, parameter EV_ACTIVATION_FAILED is set to ABAP_TRUE. Related messages are then contained in table parameter ET_MESSAGE. The currently active version of the object is provided in parameter EV_ACTIVE_VERSION. The value depends upon the success of the activation and on the versioning setting of the object (see also Section 4.3.3).

If checking or activation was not successful, you might want to explicitly restore the object to its last saved version. Method DISCARD_CHANGES can be used for that purpose. Alternatively, unlocking a locked object or locking an unlocked object has the same effect. The only difference with the explicit discarding is that you can set an optional parameter IV_CLEAR_DB_BUFFERS to ABAP_TRUE. It will enforce a reload from the database. However, this is required only if you expect that the object might have been changed externally.

Objects that are not to be used any more by other objects can first simply be marked to be obsolete, using method MAKE_OBSOLETE. Obsolete objects can neither be changed nor be newly linked to by other objects any longer. It is possible to revoke the obsolete status using the same method by setting the optional parameter IV_REVERSE_MAKE_OBSOLETE to ABAP_TRUE.

If you intend to delete an object, you have two choices using method DELETE:

▸ You can mark only the object for deletion by setting the optional parameter IV_MARK_FOR_DELETE to ABAP_TRUE. This is the recommended way because it retains the possibility of revoking the status and yields the actual deletion to an administrator. Parameter IV_REVERSE_MARK_FOR_DELETE needs to be set in this case.

▸ You can directly delete the object. As a precondition the object must not be used any more in any way or version by other (not deleted) objects. From the API perspective, a deleted object no longer exists. However, it persists on the database with such a status for a retention time of 180 days. In emergency cases an administrator might be able to undelete the object.

The current status of an object with respect to deletion is considered to be an attribute of the object. It can be retrieved using method IF_FDT_ADMIN_DATA~GET_CHANGE_INFO.

The COPY method allows you to create a copy of the current object with the same settings, except the object's ID and version history. The new object can even be created within a different application, passing the optional parameter IV_APPLICATION_ID.

If an object is deeply copied, exactly one copy is created for each referenced object of the same application. The references among the created objects are accordingly adapted. All created new objects are automatically locked and may thus immediately be saved afterwards.

After having changed, activated, copied, or deleted an object, you need to invoke the SAVE method to make the changes become persistent. As already mentioned, the object needs to be locked as a prerequisite. If automatic change recording is switched on for the current system or client, a transport request might be required in addition. It can be passed via parameter IV_TRANSPORT_REQUEST the first time the object is saved. If the object cannot be saved for any reason, an exception of type CX_FDT will be raised. Inactive object versions can be saved, even though they have an inconsistent state.

Locked objects that have finally been successfully saved should be unlocked afterwards to avoid blocking of other processes that need to lock the same object. A call to method DEQUEUE will remove the object from the internal locking list. Unsaved changes on the object will thereby be lost.

Non-local system and customizing objects can explicitly be recorded onto a transport request. They do not have to be changed for that purpose. The current system and client settings must, however, allow transport in general. The method TRANSPORT requires only a valid transport request in parameter IV_TRANSPORT REQUEST.

Because an object needs to be locked during recording, it is automatically enqueued and dequeued when necessary. A CX_FDT exception is raised in the case that an object cannot be recorded onto the provided request for any reason.

As a synopsis Listing 4.2 shows the typical steps involved in creating and saving new objects via the API. It only leaves out authorization and changeability checks for simplification.

```
DATA: lo_factory  TYPE REF TO if_fdt_factory,
      lo_constant TYPE REF TO if_fdt_constant,
      lo_function TYPE REF TO if_fdt_function,
      lt_message  TYPE if_fdt_types=>t_message,
      lx_fdt      TYPE REF TO cx_fdt.
FIELD-SYMBOLS <ls_message> TYPE if_fdt_types=>s_message.
TRY.
  "Get a factory instance
  lo_factory = cl_fdt_factory=>if_fdt_factory~get_instance(
    if_fdt_constants=>gc_application_tmp ).
  "Create and setup a function
  lo_function ?= lo_factory->get_function( ).
  lo_function->if_fdt_transaction~enqueue( ).
  lo_function->if_fdt_admin_data~set_name( 'HELLO_WORLD').
  "Create and setup a constant expression
```

```
lo_constant ?= lo_factory->get_expression(
  iv_expression_type_id = if_fdt_constants=>gc_exty_constant ).
lo_constant->if_fdt_transaction~enqueue( ).
lo_constant->set_constant_value( 'Hello World' ).
"Link the constant expression to the function
lo_function->set_expression( lo_constant->mv_id ).
"Activate and save everything
lo_function->if_fdt_transaction~activate(
  EXPORTING iv_deep            = abap_true
  IMPORTING et_message         = lt_message ).
lo_function->if_fdt_transaction~save( iv_deep = abap_true ).
lo_function->if_fdt_transaction~dequeue( iv_deep = abap_true ).
CATCH cx_fdt into lx_fdt.
  APPEND LINES OF lx_fdt->mt_message TO lt_message
ENDTRY.
"Output
LOOP AT lt_message ASSIGNING <ls_message>.
  WRITE / <ls_message>-text.
ENDLOOP.
```

Listing 4.2 Object Creation with the API

First an instance of the factory class is retrieved for the local standard application TMP, which is always available and intended for temporary objects only. A function object is then created, enqueued, and provided with a name. Next a Constant expression object is created, enqueued, and equipped with the return value "Hello World." For the function the constant is set via its ID as the expression to be processed. The function object thus references the Constant expression object from that point in time on.

The following deep activation of the function ensures that all required objects are activated as well. The Constant expression is thereby included. The function is then also deeply saved and dequeued, whether the activation was successful or not. Again, the Constant expression is included.

The coding is framed by a TRY-CATCH block, which handles all exceptions that might occur. Eventually all messages that may result either from the activation or from an exception are output on the screen.

Now that we have cast some light on the creation and change of BRFplus objects in general, the following sections deal with the individual object settings. The common object settings are described first.

4.3   Common Object Settings

All BRFplus objects have a certain set of general properties and attributes in common. The term "attribute" refers to non-changeable properties. Their values are automatically generated or derived from the system status. Some properties might be defaulted from the associated application object, but are changeable in general.

In the BRFplus Workbench the general properties are displayed in the GENERAL section of the screen. By default a reduced view that contains only a selection of the most important properties is displayed (see Figure 4.15).

Figure 4.15   General Section—Reduced View

Clicking on the link SHOW MORE will expose an extended view that contains the full set of general properties, organized into individual tabs. Let us begin with the non-changeable general attributes.

Figure 4.16   General Section—Extended View

4.3.1   Attributes

Attribute values are automatically generated or derived from the system status. As shown in Figure 4.16, you can see the following attributes on the first tab in the GENERAL section:

- ID
A generated, universally unique identifier for the object. With menu entry WORKBENCH • OPEN OBJECT ... you can for example display a certain object after entering its ID.

- OBJECT TYPE
Once created, the type of an object cannot be changed.

- APPLICATION ID
Each object is associated with an application object, that has its own unique ID. From the application the object inherits further technical settings, like the storage type, package assignment, etc.

- CREATED BY
The name of the user that has created the object

- CREATION DATE
The date the object was created

- CREATION TIME
The time when the object was created

- CHANGED BY
The name of the user that last changed the object

- CHANGE DATE
The date the object was last changed

- CHANGE TIME
The time the object was last changed

At the bottom of the GENERAL tab the storage type of the object is described. In addition it is indicated whether the versioning setting for the object is switched on or off.

Under the ADDITIONAL INFORMATION tab, some additional, less frequently required attributes are displayed:

- IMPORTED BY TRANSPORT
The transport request by which the latest version of the object has been imported into the system. If the field is empty, the object has not been transported.

- SOURCE SYSTEM ID
The system where the object has originally been created in. For objects delivered by SAP to customers, this attribute is set to "SAP."

- SOURCE SYSTEM CLIENT
The client where the object was originally been created.

On the GENERAL TAB some changeable properties are displayed as well. They are explained in subsequent sections, starting with Section 4.3.2.

Attributes API

The most basic object attributes are directly available also as attributes of interface IF_FDT_ADMIN_DATA. They are listed in Table 4.5.

Attribute	Description
MV_ID	The universal identifier of the object.
MV_OBJECT_TYPE	The (main) object type.
MV_LOCAL_OBJECT	A flag indicating whether it is a local object.
MV_SYSTEM_OBJECT	A flag indicating whether it is a system object.
MV_CUSTOMIZING_OBJECT	A flag indicating whether it is a customizing object.
MV_MASTERDATA_OBJECT	A flag indicating whether it is a master data object.

Table 4.5 Basic Attributes in Interface IF_FDT_ADMIN_DATA

The flags for the system-, customizing- and master data- storage types are mutually exclusive, so only one of them is set to ABAP_TRUE. All sub-interfaces usually define an alias as a shortcut to directly access these attributes, e.g., MV_ID rather than IF_FDT_ADMIN_DATA~MV_ID.

The ID of an object's application can be retrieved or set via the methods GET_APPLICATION and SET_APPLICATION respectively. When you set the application for an object, you also define its storage type and other default settings.

For the creation of new objects, it is recommended that you obtain a factory instance for the intended target application:

```
lo_factory = cl_fdt_factory=>if_fdt_factory~get_instance(
    iv_application_id = <ID of the application> ).
```

For objects that are created by such a factory, the application is automatically preset. Otherwise, you need to do this explicitly with method SET_APPLICATION. The application should be set only once, directly after the creation of an object.

Application Setting

The nature of the application setting is that of a final attribute. It is strongly recommended that you do not change the application for an object at a later point in time, due to possible usage and access inconsistencies afterwards. For objects that have already been saved, there is also the restriction that they cannot be assigned to applications of a different storage type. Based on experience, the better approach is to copy rather than move an object to another application. The latter option is, however, not strictly forbidden via the API.

The following, basic information about the current object version can be retrieved with method `GET_CHANGE_INFO` of interface `IF_FDT_ADMIN_DATA`:

Exporting Parameter	Description
EV_CREATION_USER	Name of the user that has created the object
EV_CREATION_TIMESTAMP	Timestamp when the object was created
EV_CHANGE_USER	Name of the user that last changed the object
EV_CHANGE_TIMESTAMP	Timestamp when the object was last changed
EV_TRANSPORTED	A flag indicating whether the current version has been transported
EV_WTT_TIMESTAMP	Timestamp when the object was written to a transport request or task
EV_OBSOLETE	A flag indicating whether the object is set to be obsolete
EV_MARKED_FOR_DELETE	A flag indicating whether the object is marked for deletion
EV_DELETED	A flag indicating whether the object is logically deleted

Table 4.6 Attributes Provided by Method IF_FDT_ADMIN_DATA~GET_CHANGE_INFO

Additional information about the current version and possible multiple versions of the object are available through method `GET_VERSIONS`. Details are described in Section 4.3.3.

4.3.2 Names

Names have a special meaning in the creation of an object. Giving the object a name implicitly means that the object can be reused by other objects and has a lifecycle of its own. Otherwise, the object can be linked only from within the using object it was created in. Unnamed objects share the lifecycle of their using objects. They are, for example, deleted when their using object is deleted. An unnamed object can be changed into a named object, but the other way around is not possible. Some objects, like applications, functions or data objects, are inherently reusable. You always have to specify a name for them.

Names may consist only of the characters 0-9, A-Y, _, and /. The first character of a name needs to be a letter of the alphabet or a slash. Furthermore, the special name `TABLE_LINE` is reserved and not allowed. It is recommended not to use a name starting with FTD because of internal usage.

The slash / is intended for the inclusion of a SAP-namespace and can only be used with the pattern `/<namespace>/*`. Also, customers and partners can reserve such namespaces.

In general names do not have to be unique, but using different names makes it easier to distinguish objects, especially if they are of the same type. There are two exceptions:

▶ Application names must be unique. For customers it is recommended to use either reserved SAP-namespaces (setup with Transaction SE03) or the standard customer namespaces Y* and Z*.

▶ Function names have to be unique within their application.

In the Workbench there is a standard object creation popup where you can enter the most basic data. The first setting is the name for the object. When created within another object, the name field can be optional to allow the creation of unnamed objects. In addition to the name you should, however, always define a descriptive short text, since it is used to represents the object within the Workbench.

An object can be renamed using the tray menu of the GENERAL section (see Figure 4.17). Renaming of actively used applications, functions, or data objects is often critical. The objects may already be addressed by their names outside BRFplus, for example, when calling a BRFplus function.

Figure 4.17   Rename Object

Names API

The API for setting or getting an object name consists mainly of the two methods SET_NAME and GET_NAME of interface IF_FDT_ADMIN_DATA. They are basically self-explanatory. If you try to set an invalid name that contains illegal characters, namespaces, or clashes with existing names, an exception of type CX_FDT_INPUT is raised. For convenience, the common mistake of using whitespaces or dashes (-) within a name is automatically corrected by replacing them with an underscore _.

If you need to dynamically create a unique name, static method GET_UNIQUE_NAME in class CL_FDT_SERVICES may serve that purpose. It allows you to optionally provide a prefix of up to five characters with parameter IV_PREFIX, and returns a name that is based on a generated, unique identifier.

4.3.3 Versioning

For all BRFplus objects, versioning can individually be switched on or off. Versioning allows you to track changes and to run older versions of an object at a given time point. It makes the processing of an object implicitly time dependent. Explicit time dependency can be modeled within rulesets and rules definitions. For details see Section 5.3.

In general BRFplus objects can always have two versions—an active and an inactive version. Whenever an object is created or changed, this is done on the inactive version (which is thus also called the "working version"). The inactive version is automatically generated if it does not currently exist. It can be seen as a playground for adjusting the object to the intended, final state. The inactive version can be saved, even if it contains faulty settings. It can, however, never be processed. This is only possible for active versions (also called "runtime versions"). Thus, to make changes become effective, the (error-free) inactive version needs to be activated. Here the versioning setting comes into play.

If versioning is switched off—which is the default—the inactive version becomes an active version that will replace a possibly existent, previous active version. So typically only one active version of the object exists, which can be processed at runtime.

If versioning is switched on, the BRFplus object can have multiple active versions: Upon activation the inactive version becomes a new active version, without influencing any previous active versions. Each active version has its own creation timestamp, which is technically set when the activated object is saved. The timestamp induces an interval of validity. It extends either until the creation timestamp of the next active version, or to "infinity" in case of the latest active version. For the processing of a versioned object, this has the following time dependency effect:

▶ If the versioned object is processed for no specific point in time (which means "current time"), the latest active version will always be evaluated.

▶ If the processing takes place for a specifically passed timestamp, BRFplus will determine and evaluate the active version whose interval of validity overlaps with the given timestamp. As for non-versioned objects, an error occurs if no active version exists for the processing timestamp.

The following table shows an example how different actions might affect a versioned object.

Action	Version	State	Change Timestamp
Object is created and saved	1	Inactive	01/01/2010 08:01:00 AM
Object is activated and saved	1	Active	01/01/2010 01:05:45 PM
Object is changed and directly activated and saved	2	Active	02/02/2010 05:34:05 PM
Object is changed and saved but not activated	3	Inactive	03/03/2010 11:59:59 AM

Table 4.7 Versioned Object Example

If the object in the example were evaluated at runtime on 01/02/2010, the active version 1 would be used. Any processing after 02/02/2010 05:34:05 PM would use active version 2 of the object.

The versioning setting of an object is defaulted by the application it is assigned to (see Section 4.4.2). It can, however, individually be changed any time. Switching a versioned object back to non-versioned mode will not delete any existing active versions. Instead, only the latest active version will be overwritten by any newly activated changes from that point in time on.

To get rid of older versions that are no longer used by other objects, it is possible to truncate active versions from an object. More details on this topic are described in Section 6.5.

In the BRFplus Workbench the current versioning setting is displayed in the first tab of the GENERAL section. Like the object name, the property can be changed via an entry in the tray menu (see Figure 4.17). If you change the versioning setting for an object, you will be asked whether versioning for all referenced objects should be set accordingly too. This option is highly recommended because it is more fail-proof to have the same versioning setting also for referenced objects. Think, for example, of a versioned object that references an object without versioning. If the latter were changed, it might have an impact on all versions of the using object. To support a common versioning setting, the application has a default setting. It is automatically applied upon the creation of new objects (see also Section 4.4.2).

The VERSIONS tab in the GENERAL section offers an overview of all versions of a versioned object. For each version, you may drill down to the used objects. For each object and version, you see the name, creation user, and creation timestamp. Clicking on the timestamp link shows the object definition for the corresponding version. Furthermore, for each object and version, the changes made with respect to the previous version can be displayed. For convenience, the changes are separated into processing and non-processing relevant changes, e.g., change of texts only. You simply need to click on the corresponding icon to see the change details. On top of the table display, you find the link DISPLAY OBJECT HISTORY, which gives a summary of all changes made in a specific time interval.

You can also display and thereby compare two versions of an object next to each other: Simply select two version entries and click on the COMPARE button. Eventually it is possible to use an existing version as a template for a new version by clicking on the COPY VERSION button on a selected version entry.

Versioning affects almost all properties of an object: For each version the properties may have a different setting. Only for the text and documentation properties is this by default not the case.

Versioning API

The versioning setting of a BRFplus object is technically a Boolean flag that can be changed with method SET_VERSIONING of interface IF_FDT_ADMIN_DATA. The method of retrieving the versioning setting is GET_VERSIONS. It also provides additional information, listed in Table 4.8.

Exporting Parameter	Description
ETS_VERSION	Information for all object versions, sorted by the version number.
EV_LAST_DB_VERSION	Version number of the last saved version.
EV_LAST_DB_VERSION_STATE	State (active/inactive) of the last saved version.
EV_VERSIONING	Versioning setting flag, indicating whether versioning is currently switched on or off for the object.

Table 4.8 Parameters of Method IF_FDT_ADMIN_DATA~GET_VERSIONS

The table parameter ETS_VERSION contains an entry for each version of the object. Its table structure IF_FDT_ADMIN_DATA=>S_VERSION consists of the fields in Table 4.9.

For two consecutive versions there may be gaps in the numbering. Therefore, to retrieve information about the latest version, you should select the last entry of the table by index rather than by version number.

If an object is transported, only its last active version is taken into account and imported into the target system. Thus, the version number in the original system may differ from the version number in the target system, created by the transport. To be able to identify which version in the original system corresponds to a version imported by transport, the fields TRTIMESTAMP, TRVERSION, TRSYSID, TRCLIENT and OVERS_ID leave a footprint of the original version. They are not changed after the transport. Field OVERS_ID is set directly upon creation of a new version in the original system. The other fields of the footprint are determined when the object version is activated and thus changed last time.

Field	Description
VERSION	Version number.
USER	Name of the user that created the version.
TIMESTAMP	Timestamp when the version was created.
STATE	State (active/inactive) of the version. Only the last version may be inactive.
VERSIONING	Versioning setting.
CUSTOMER_CHANGE	A flag indicating whether the version has been created or changed within a customer system.
TRREQUEST	Transport request, in case the version has been imported by a transport.
TRTIMESTAMP	Timestamp the version has been last changed (and activated) in the original system, in case it has been imported via transport.
TRVERSION	Version number in the original system, in case it has been imported via transport.
TRSYSID	System where the version was originally created, in case it has been imported via transport.
TRCLIENT	Client in which the version was originally created, in case it has been imported via transport.
OVERS_ID	A universal ID for version in the original system.

Table 4.9 Fields of Structure IF_FDT_ADMIN_DATA=>S_VERSION

A general aspect of the BRFplus API is that all GET_<PROPERTY> methods commonly have an importing parameter IV_TIMESTAMP. Using the parameter allows you to retrieve the value for the version that was active at the specified point in time. If you want to retrieve the value of the last active version, you simply need to pass a current timestamp, usually retrieved with the ABAP statement GET TIME STAMP FIELD.

If you pass a timestamp in IV_TIMESTAMP before the creation timestamp of the object's first active version, a CX_FDT_INPUT exception will be raised. An error occurs, of course, also if no active version exists.

If you do not pass the parameter, the value for the latest version—be it active or inactive—will be passed.

4.3.4 Texts and Documentation

As already mentioned, all BRFplus objects can (and should) have a specific short text that represents the object in the UI. The length of the short text is restricted to 20 characters. A longer descriptive text having a length of up to 80 characters can be specified in addition. For more sophisticated objects and especially for objects that are intended for reuse, there is the possibility of defining or referencing a documentation of any length.

In the BRFplus Workbench, the short text can be entered directly upon creation of an object. It can also be entered any time in the reduced view of the GENERAL section. Some advanced options and the text and documentation properties are accessible only via the extended view. Let us have a look at the TEXTS tab depicted in Figure 4.18.

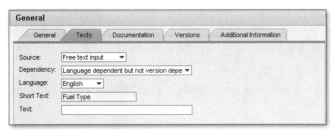

Figure 4.18 Object Texts

Texts can be retrieved from three different sources. By default texts are directly entered as "Free text input" and saved together with the BRFplus object. For this text source it is possible to specify a text dependency setting, which is defaulted from the assigned application. The setting is actually a mixture of two dependencies that can individually be switched on or off:

▶ **Language dependency**
Texts may be stored on language-dependent database tables. The creator of an object typically enters the texts in the current logon-language only. Translation usually takes place by information developers with special tools afterwards. However, using the LANGUAGE dropdown makes it possible to display or change the texts for all available system languages also in the Workbench.

▶ **Version dependency**
This kind of dependency is only available if versioning is switched on for the object. In contrast to other properties, texts are stored version-independent by default. Since the meaning or purpose of a BRFplus object does usually not

change, it would normally be pointless to store the same texts multiple times for each object version. This would be even more true if texts were stored language-dependent. However, if the need arises, it is possible to adjust and store different texts for each object version.

Loss of Data

You should be aware that changing the text source or the text dependency at a later point in time may result in loss of data. If you switch, for example, the dependency setting from "language dependent" to "language independent," the translations will no longer be available.

Instead of newly specifying texts for each BRFplus object, it is also possible to reuse texts that have already been entered within an existing program. The text source needs to be set to "Text Symbols" in this case. Then you simply need to enter the program name and the three-digit text symbol key to be referenced. The corresponding text will be retrieved and displayed in the selected language. (You might need to press Enter to update the text display.) If the referenced text symbol has no more than 20 characters, it is used as short text description and otherwise as (long) text only.

Text symbols are always retrieved language-dependent and version-independent. The Language dropdown in the UI is only used for displaying purposes in this case.

Text Symbol Sources

You can find text symbols in any kind of ABAP program. Here are two examples:

▶ Start Transaction SE38 in the SAP GUI, enter a valid program name and click on the Display button. Then choose menu entry Goto • Text Elements • Text Symbols to display the available text symbols.

▶ Alternatively, an ABAP class is inherently also a "program." Start Transaction SE24 in the SAP GUI, enter a valid class name, and click on the Display button. Then choose menu entry Goto • Text Elements to display the available text symbols.

Exit Class

The most flexible way to retrieve texts from any kind of repository is the usage of an "exit class" as text source. Texts can thereby be retrieved programmatically. This option is available only if the user personalization setting Display Technical Aspects is enabled. You find this setting under menu Workbench • Personalize…, tab General, section Advanced.

Technically, an ABAP class that implements interface `IF_FDT_TEXT_DOCU_EXIT` needs to be specified (and created beforehand). Whether texts are then retrieved language-, version- or even time-dependent is completely in the hands of the programmer of the exit class.

Documentation

The settings for documentation are similar to text settings. You can access them on the separate tab DOCUMENTATION. As for texts, documentation can by default be defined via "free text input." This type of documentation source allows the entry of a simple, unformatted string of any length. Again it is possible to specify a dependency on language and version, as described for the texts above.

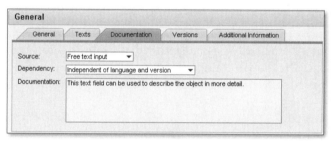

Figure 4.19 Object Documentation

Another type of source may be a *SAPscript*, a standard format at SAP that allows the definition of rich-text-like documents. SAPscripts are typically used to document data dictionary types, programs, methods, etc. As for text symbols, existing SAPscripts can be reused for BRFplus objects.

SAPscripts are always retrieved language-dependent and version-independent. The LANGUAGE field in the UI is intended for displaying purposes only. To reference a SAPscript, you need to provide its ID (type) and OBJECT (name).

SAPscript Sources

SAPscripts can be edited with Transaction SE61. In transactions like SE80 and SE38 you find the documentation for an existing program, function module, or data type normally via menu entry GOTO • DOCUMENTATION. On the top of the documentation display, you find the ID and object value, for example `RE` and `ZFDT_DOCUMENTATION` as in Figure 4.20.

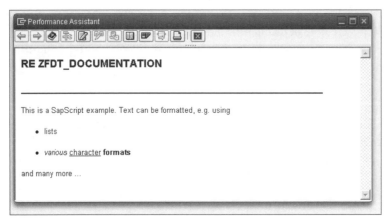

Figure 4.20 SAPscript Documentation

Last but not least, you may use an exit class to retrieve a documentation text programmatically. This approach allows, again, only unformatted texts. The same exit class you might have defined for texts can be reused also for documentation retrieval.

Text and Documentation API

The definition of text settings can be accomplished using method SET_TEXTS in interface IF_FDT_ADMIN_DATA.

The actual texts can be set either for the currently used system language SY-LANGU only, or for all available system languages at once. In the first case, you need to use the plain parameters IV_TEXT and IV_SHORT_TEXT. In the second, case you need to use the table parameters ITS_TEXT and ITS_SHORT_TEXT respectively, which have a sorted language key in common. Setting the texts for multiple languages will replace all existing entries. So if you want to change the text for one specific language only, you should first get the existing table of texts, modify the relevant entry, and set back the complete table.

In parallel you can apply a different text dependency setting with parameter IV_TEXT_DEP_TYPE. It can have the following four values, defined in interface IF_FDT_ADMIN_DATA:

▶ GC_TEXT_DEP_NO: No dependencies

▶ GC_TEXT_DEP_LANGU: Language dependency

▶ GC_TEXT_DEP_VERSION: Version dependency

▶ GC_TEXT_DEP_LANGU_VERSION: Language and version dependency

If you want the texts to be retrieved from a text symbol, you need to specify parameter IS_TEXT_SYMBOL. The structure is of type IF_FDT_TYPES=>S_TEXT_SYMBOL and consists of two fields for the program name and the text symbol key.

If you want the texts to be derived programmatically from an exit class, you may set the class name with parameter IV_EXIT_CLASS.

The parameters for texts, text symbol, and exit class are mutually exclusive. Per call, only one of the parameters must be passed or an exception occurs. The passed parameter will automatically clear the settings for the respective other two parameters.

Changing documentation settings can be done analogously to text settings with the method SET_DOCUMENTATION. You may use parameter IV_DOCUMENTATION to set a documentation text for the current system language or the table parameter ITS_DOCUMENTATION for all system languages. The dependency setting can be provided with parameter IV_DOCUMENTATION_DEP_TYPE.

If you want the documentation to be retrieved from a SAPscript, you need to specify parameter IS_SAPSCRIPT_OBJECT. The structure is of type IF_FDT_TYPES=>S_SAPSCRIPT_OBJECT and consists of two fields for the type-ID and object name.

If you want the documentation to be derived programmatically from an exit-class, you may set the class name with parameter IV_EXIT_CLASS.

Again, the parameters for texts, SAPscript, and exit class are mutually exclusive. They must not be used simultaneously and will automatically clear the settings for the respective other two parameters.

4.3.5 Access Level

Named objects can be referenced and thereby reused by other objects. However, if a reused object needs to be changed, this may affect and require modification of all using objects. Also, a used object cannot be deleted unless all using objects are deleted as well or the usages have been removed. With the access level setting, BRFplus allows you to restrict the usage of an object to objects of a specific domain only. The domains are defined by different access levels. They depend mainly on application components.

Application components represent areas of responsibility. One application component can be assigned per BRFplus application. Application components are hierarchically structured. The hierarchy levels are separated by a - (dash) delimiter in their names. For example, for standard BRFplus content, the application component is BC-SRV-BR. It consequently comprises a three-level hierarchy.

The following access levels are available for BRFplus objects.

▶ **Same Application**
This is the default setting. The object is accessible only for objects of the same application.

▶ **Same Application Component**
The object is accessible only for objects of the same application component.

▶ **Same Superior Application Component**
The object is accessible only for objects that share the same superior application component. The superior component for BC-SRV-BR is BC-SRV.

▶ **Same Top Application Component**
The object is accessible only for objects that share the same top application component. The top component for BC-SRV-BR is BR.

▶ **Global**
The object is accessible for all objects without restrictions.

As a rule of thumb, an object should always have as little accessibility as possible but as much accessibility as needed. By default the most restrictive access level is used. For objects that may already be productively used, the access level should never be reduced because dependent objects could become inconsistent through such a change.

The accessibility of an object is not only explicitly determined by the access level setting: it implicitly also depends on the object's storage type. See Section 4.4.1 for more details.

Access Level API

The API to set or change the access level simply consists of the methods SET_ACCESS_LEVEL and GET_ACCESS_LEVEL in interface IF_FDT_ADMIN_DATA. The following constants defined in interface IF_FDT_CONSTANTS reflect the different access levels:

▶ GC_ACCESS_LEVEL_APPLICATION: Same application

▶ GC_ACCESS_LEVEL_APPL_COMPONENT: Same application component

▶ GC_ACCESS_LEVEL_SUPERIOR: Same superior application component

▶ GC_ACCESS_LEVEL_COMPONENT: Same top application component

▶ GC_ACCESS_LEVEL_GLOBAL: Global

Constant value GC_ACCESS_LEVEL_SAP is obsolete and must no longer be used.

4.4 Applications

An application is considered to define a logical unit for the creation of BRFplus artifacts. It can be compared to a development project in common programming environments: all objects required for a set of related rules are intended to be "collected" into one application.

In BRFplus, the application is an own object type. It acts as a container in which objects of other types are created. For the created objects, their application is essential. If an object is written to a transport request, its application is therefore also added to the same request.

Some basic application settings such as storage type are imposed on the created objects and cannot be changed later on. Some other settings serve as default for new objects only.

4.4.1 Application Creation

If you have not yet created any application, the REPOSITORY section of the BRFplus Workbench will show no entries but offer a button to create a new application, as depicted in Figure 4.21. It is always possible to create a new application object via the menu entry WORKBENCH • CREATE APPLICATION ... otherwise.

Figure 4.21 Creation of a First Application

For applications you are required to specify a name that is unique. Customers should also use a namespace prefix, either an explicit one or one of the standard customer namespaces Y* and Z*. See also Section 4.3.2.

In addition to the GENERAL DATA field, the creation popup for the application (see Figure 4.22) will request some further required settings. It starts with the STORAGE TYPE that is propagated to all objects of the application. The storage type does not only determine the way the application and its contained objects are saved on the database. It also implies which system settings influence the changeability and transportability of the objects. The relevant system settings are typically maintained by administrators with Transaction SCC4.

The following storage types are supported by BRFplus:

- ▶ *System* objects are stored client-independent and can be transported with Workbench requests. They can reference only other system objects, but can be referenced themselves by objects of all storage types. System objects are typically of constant nature and might be defined for reuse purposes. They can best be compared to program code. Customers are not allowed to change delivered system objects.

  As an example, BRFplus provides the standard system application FDT_SYSTEM. It contains some default data objects and expressions that can be reused by all other applications.

- ▶ *Customizing objects* are stored client-dependent and can be transported with Customizing requests. They can reference system or other customizing objects, but can be referenced by customizing objects and by master data objects. Customizing objects are typically intended to define some default behavior that can be adapted by customers later on.

- ▶ *Master Data* objects are stored client-dependent as well and not intended to be distributed. They are also local objects that cannot be transported to other systems. Master data objects can reference objects of all storage types, but can be referenced only by other master data objects.

If the flag CREATE LOCAL APPLICATION is set, the application and its objects are restricted to local system usage only. Except for master data they are typically created for test purposes. For local applications, only local packages can be used. Their objects cannot be transported to other systems and also cannot be accessed by non-local objects because they would not be available in the target systems of transported objects.

BRFplus offers a special local application *TMP*, that is always available and created automatically. As the name indicates, it is intended to create objects for temporary use cases only. Objects of the *TMP* application are automatically deleted after 30 days.

One more setting is the DEVELOPMENT PACKAGE that the application and its objects are assigned to. It defines the technical domain that all kinds of development objects and data in general are created for. Local applications can be assigned only to a local package, starting with a $ character. By default, the $TMP package is used for local applications.

For system objects the development package is a mandatory field. It influences the changeability of the objects in a dedicated system. If you use a package with a namespace prefix (/<namespace>/), the application name must start with this prefix as well.

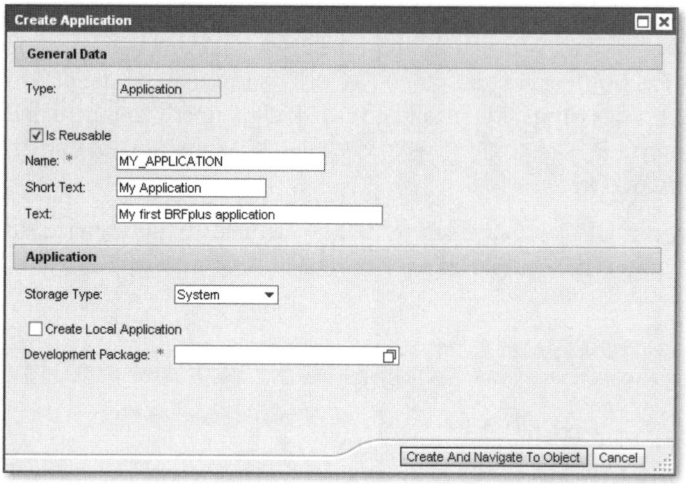

Figure 4.22 Application Creation Popup

Having defined all basic properties for the new application, you may actually create it and navigate to the full object display. Because objects of the application can be activated only when the application itself has been activated, it is recommended that you adapt further application settings and activate the application directly afterwards.

4.4.2 Application Properties

The DETAIL section for the application object contains several tab strips.

The PROPERTY tab contains the settings that are relevant for the application object itself. In addition to the development package, you can see and change here the SOFTWARE COMPONENT and the APPLICATION COMPONENT. The former is kind of a top-level assignment for packages, whereas the latter can be used, for example, to address problems to the responsible development team. From non-local development packages, the two settings are automatically inherited.

Customizing at SAP

Non-local customizing applications that are created at SAP must have unique names. The explicit assignment of a software component is required if no development package is provided.

Eventually there is the possibility of defining an APPLICATION EXIT CLASS. This offers an easy way to programmatically enhance specific capabilities of BRFplus on the level of an application. It is, for example, possible to restrict access to BRF-plus objects with a custom authorization check mechanism of a finer granularity. The validity of data entered in an expression might be cross-checked against some external data sources. Or, upon saving an object, a notification may be needed to trigger some additional processing. Technically an ABAP class needs to be created that implements the interface IF_FDT_APPLICATION_SETTINGS. More information on application exits is provided in Section 7.3.1.

On the DEFAULT SETTINGS tab, you can define default values for newly created objects. The tab is illustrated in Figure 4.23.

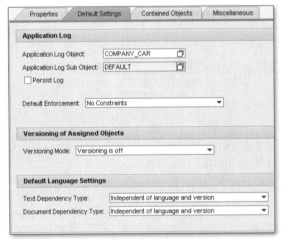

Figure 4.23 Application—Default Settings

The APPLICATION LOG is relevant only for specific object types that actually do log information, such as *Message Log* actions. A log instance is always assigned to a LOG OBJECT and LOG SUB OBJECT. They impose a hierarchical categorization and can be maintained in the system with Transaction SLG0.

Logs can be persisted to the database or be kept only in memory for temporary use cases. You may set the flag PERSIST LOG accordingly.

The usage of the default application log objects can be restricted in the following way:

▸ **No Constraints / Optional**
The settings serve as defaults only. They are displayed and can be changed in using objects

▸ **Mandatory**
The settings are displayed but cannot be changed in using objects.

▸ **Mandatory and Hidden**
The settings must be used implicitly. In the using objects they are completely hidden from the user and consequently cannot be changed.

The VERSIONING OF ASSIGNED OBJECTS can be switched on by default for processing relevant object types. Processing relevant object types are all object types that can influence the outcome of a BRFplus function call. A catalog is, for example, not processing relevant, whereas functions, rulesets and rules, expressions, actions, and data objects are processing relevant.

Underneath DEFAULT LANGUAGE SETTINGS you may alter the default dependency settings for texts and documentation, which have already been mentioned in Section 4.3.4.

On the tab CONTAINED OBJECTS, you can see the list of objects that belong to the application. When you inspect an application, you probably first want to know which of the functions that it contains can be processed. Therefore, by default function objects are displayed. With the TYPE drop down above the table display, you may choose any other object type or even all object types. If feasible, you may then also select a corresponding sub type as well.

By clicking on the CREATE OBJECT button, you can create a new object of the selected type within the application. Alternatively, you may right-click on an application entry in the REPOSITORY view of the navigation panel and select the CREATE entry in the context menu. Thirdly, you can by convention create new objects directly where needed within the DETAIL SECTION of using objects.

On the MISCELLANEOUS tab, you find additional, more special application settings. Currently you may activate option RESTART RULESETS ENABLED here. It allows a deferred processing of rules, for example, for performance reasons. More details are provided in Section 5.3.3.

4.4.3 Application API

The application object type is technically defined with interface `IF_FDT_APPLICATION`. Let us first of all look at how to create a new BRFplus application.

As for other object types, you first need to retrieve a new, initial application instance via the corresponding factory method IF_FDT_FACTORY~GET_APPLICATION. As usual, it then needs to be locked, if you want to save it. The creation process may now require further steps. By calling one of the following three, parameter-free methods, you define the storage type for the application:

▶ CREATE_CUSTOMIZING_APPLICATION

▶ CREATE_SYSTEM_APPLICATION

▶ CREATE_MASTERDATA_APPLICATION

By default a customizing application is created. If you want to create a local application, you have to call method CREATE_LOCAL_APPLICATION. Except for master data applications, the reversal into a non-local application is also possible, by passing parameter IV_REVERT_LOCAL with value ABAP_TRUE.

Change of Storage Type Settings
All of the CREATE... methods can only be called as long as the application is neither saved nor referenced by any other (probably new) object; otherwise, an exception occurs. As mentioned in Section 4.3.1, these settings become non-changeable attributes.

Depending on the storage type, you need to provide additional settings, or the application cannot be saved. For non-local system applications, the development package is for example a mandatory setting. The paradigm that normally allows you to save also inconsistent object states is not valid in this case.

Properties

With method SET_DEVELOPMENT_PACKAGE you can assign an appropriate development package to the application. If you pass an invalid package name you will cause a CX_FDT_INPUT exception. For local applications only package names that start with a $ are allowed. By default the default $TMP package is used.

If a development package is defined, the corresponding software and application components are automatically derived. Otherwise, you may optionally want to set them using methods SET_SOFTWARE_COMPONENT and SET_APPLICATION_COMPONENT in respect. As for the development package, only a valid software component can be set without causing an exception. Software component LOCAL is allowed for local objects only.

Default Settings

The following methods deal with default settings for new objects of the application. First, the default versioning setting can be adjusted with method SET_VER-SIONING_MODE. The passed parameter IV_VERSIONING_MODE can have two values, defined in interface IF_FDT_APPLICATION:

▶ GC_VERSMODE_DEFAULT_OFF: No versioning by default.

▶ GC_VERSMODE_DEFAULT_PR: Versioning is switched on for processing relevant object types.

The inverse method GET_VERSIONING_MODE provides not only the current setting in exporting parameter EV_VERSIONING_MODE, but also on request the two table parameters ET_VERSIONED_DEFAULT and ET_NOT_VERSIONED_DEFAULT. They contain an explicit list of all object types that will or will not be affected by the default versioning setting.

Default dependency settings for texts and documentation can be set quite straightforwardly with method SET_LANGUAGE_SETTINGS. It has accordingly two parameters, IV_TEXT_DEP_TYPE_DEFAULT and IV_DOCU_DEP_TYPE_DEFAULT, that can be set to the values GC_TEXT_DEP_... of interface IF_FDT_TYPES, which have already been mentioned in Section 4.3.4.

Finally the default log settings can be applied with method SET_LOG_SETTINGS. It has the parameters listed in Table 4.10.

Parameter	Description
IV_LOG_OBJECT	Logs object name, as maintained in transaction SLG0.
IV_LOG_SUBOBJECT	Logs sub object name, as maintained in transaction SLG0.
IV_PERSIST_LOG	A flag indicating whether the log shall be persisted onto the database.
IV_LOG_CONSTRAINT	Usage constraints for the default log.

Table 4.10 Parameters of Method IF_FDT_APPLICATION~SET_LOG_SETTINGS

The parameter IV_LOG_CONSTRAINT can have the following values, defined in interface IF_FDT_APPLICATION:

▶ GC_LOG_CONSTRAINT_NONE: No default log is set.

▶ GC_LOG_CONSTRAINT_OPTIONAL: Default log is optional.

▶ GC_LOG_CONSTRAINT_MANDATORY: Default log cannot be changed.

▶ GC_LOG_CONSTRAINT_HIDDEN: Default log is hidden and not changeable.

Advanced Settings

For advanced use cases, two further application properties can be set:

- An application exit class can be applied with method SET_SETTING_CLASS to extend the capabilities of BRFplus. The class needs to implement interface IF_ FDT_APPLICATION_SETTINGS. If the passed class name is not valid, a CX_FDT_INPUT exception is raised. Details on application exits are explained in Section 7.3.1.
- Rulesets can be made restartable to defer the processing. This special functionality can be activated on the application level with the Boolean parameter IV_ RULESET_RESTART of method SET_RESTART_SETTINGS. The inverse method is named GET_RESTART_OPTIONS.

At the end of this chapter it is finally worth mentioning that the application object can be cast to interface IF_FDT_APPLICATION_OBJECTS. The interface exposes methods to perform actions that involve all objects of the application.

4.5 Catalogs

All BRFplus objects are stored in a general repository that can be browsed mainly on application and object type level. A catalog defines an explicit, structured view for a collection of BRFplus objects. Its main purpose is to organize specific objects for and by business users, independent from the storage in the repository. In contrast to the object types described so far, a catalog object is not processing relevant. It can only be used to make the access to BRFplus objects more convenient in the user interface.

The basic structure of a catalog is usually set up by an administrator in the DETAIL section of the BRFplus Workbench, as shown in Figure 4.24. Business users typically use and extend the existing catalog later on in the CATALOG VIEW as an alternative to the REPOSITORY VIEW on the left-hand side of the BRFplus Workbench. The CATALOG VIEW is shown in Figure 4.25.

Similar to a file directory, a catalog consists of a tree-like folder structure that can store references to BRFplus objects and other catalogs. Basically the catalog is a tree with three different types of nodes:

- Folder nodes nest all node types including sub folder nodes. They define the main structure of the catalog.
- Object nodes reference a BRFplus object of the repository. The displayed name and text of the node can differ from the name and text of the referenced object.
- Catalog nodes can reference nodes of other catalogs. Entire catalogs or specific parts of catalogs can thereby easily be reused.

An initial catalog consists of a root folder node that shares the name of the catalog itself. In the UI, new nodes can easily be added using the context menu for existing nodes. Nodes can also be moved up and down, cut and pasted, or eventually deleted. Each node can have a rather technical name and/or a descriptive text that is translatable.

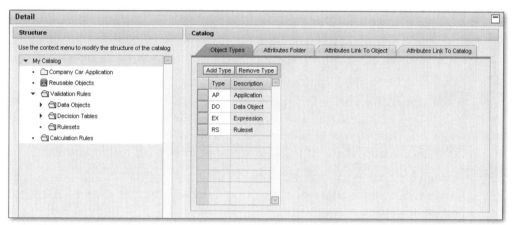

Figure 4.24 Catalog Editor

In the editor for catalogs, the properties for a node can be edited by selecting a node in the Structure area. For the root node an administrative user can set up special settings that are valid for the entire catalog. As Figure 4.24 illustrates, they are distributed across several tab strips:

▶ OBJECT TYPES

The catalog can be restricted to allow object nodes to reference only a specific set of object types. Business users may, for example, not need to create applications and functions themselves. Unnecessary complexity can therefore be hidden with this setting.

▶ ATTRIBUTES

For each node type a set of up to six attributes can optionally be defined. Business users may then set according values for the attributes on each respective node. The attribute type is described by an element of type text, number or Boolean. There is no standard use case for the node attributes, but they might, for instance, be used to define responsibilities, comments, technical references, status information, etc.

Once the catalog has been set up in the editor, it should be activated to ensure that it is defined error-free. To display the catalog in the CATALOG VIEW on the left-hand side of the Workbench, there are three different approaches:

▶ In the CATALOG VIEW you can click on the button SELECT CATALOG or respectively SWITCH TO OTHER CATALOG at the top of the view. A popup opens where you can search for a specific catalog in the repository.

▶ If the desired catalog is listed in one of the other views of the navigation panel, you can select a context menu entry DISPLAY IN CATALOG VIEW ....

▶ In the user personalization (menu entry WORKBENCH • PERSONALIZE...) you can define a list of favorite catalogs. One of these catalogs is marked as default and will be shown in the CATALOG VIEW whenever it would normally be empty. One can easily switch to other favorite catalogs using the SWITCH TO OTHER CATALOG button choice.

When you click on an object entry in the CATALOG VIEW, the respective object is displayed in the main area of the Workbench. Selecting a reference to catalog folder will switch to the respective catalog within the CATALOG VIEW. The button PREVIOUS CATALOG on top of the view will appear, to allow back-navigation.

Extending or editing a catalog directly in the CATALOG VIEW is also possible, as Figure 4.25 demonstrates. All changes performed within the CATALOG VIEW are immediately saved and activated.

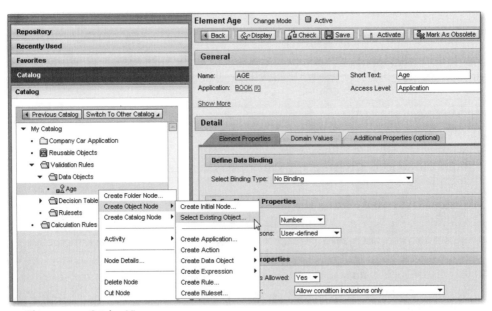

Figure 4.25 Catalog View

Catalog API

Catalogs are programmatically represented by interface IF_FDT_CATALOG that comprises the methods shown in Table 4.11.

Method	Description
SET_CATALOG_PROPERTIES	Defines object type restrictions and attributes for the catalog.
CREATE_NODE	Creates a new node in the catalog tree structure.
SET_NODE_PROPERTIES	Sets properties for a specific node of the catalog tree.
MOVE_NODE	Moves a node to another position within the catalog tree structure.
DELETE_NODE	Deletes a node from the tree structure.
GET_CHILDREN	Provides the sequence of child nodes for a parent folder node.
GET_CATALOG_STRUCTURE	Provides a list of information for all nodes of the catalog.
GET_WHERE_USED	Finds out which other catalogs reference the current catalog.
GET_NODE_ID	Provides the identifier of the first catalog node that references a given object.

Table 4.11 Methods of Interface IF_FDT_CATALOG

The overall catalog properties can be set with method SET_CATALOG_PROPERTIES. First of all, a list of allowed object types may be set. If no such list or an empty list is specified, all object types are allowed. Catalog entries that refer to not allowed objects will lead to check errors. Attributes for the various node types can optionally be specified via according lists of elementary data objects.

The catalog structure consists technically of a tree structure with nodes of three different types. The types are reflected by the following constant definitions:

▶ GC_NODE_TYPE_STRUCTURE: For folder nodes that define the structure of the tree.

▶ GC_NODE_TYPE_LEAF: For nodes that reference an object from the repository.

▶ GC_NODE_TYPE_LINK: For catalog nodes that reference the folder of another catalog.

Each node automatically incorporates an internal ID by which it can be referenced. Only the root node that represents the complete catalog has no such ID. New nodes can be created with method CREATE_NODE, which provides the node ID in exporting parameter EV_NODE. To specify a specific position in the tree structure, the ID of either a parent node and/or or a preceding sibling node needs to be passed. If no ID is passed, the new node is created as the first node under the root node.

The properties for a node can be set or changed with method SET_NODE_PROPERTIES. For object nodes, the referenced object can be passed in parameter IV_OBJECT_ID. For catalog nodes, the referenced catalog and node can be specified with parameter IS_LINK of type S_LINK. The field NODE_UUID of that structure is not used any more and can be ignored.

Nodes can be moved to another position within the tree structure, or they can be deleted with the corresponding methods MOVE_NODE and DELETE_NODE. To browse through the catalog's tree structure, the methods GET_CHILDREN and GET_CATALOG_ STRUCTURE can be used. The former provides only the sequence of sub/child nodes for a specific folder node, whereas the latter provides a sorted list of all nodes, together with respective position information.

Finally, there is a separate method GET_WHERE_USED available in addition to the equally named standard method of interface IF_FDT_ADMIN_DATA. This is required because catalogs reference each other only lazily. A catalog can for example be deleted, even though it is still referenced by another catalog. The standard GET_ WHERE_USED method of interface IF_FDT_ADMIN_DATA works only for strong references and will therefore not yield any results.

This chapter provides a description of all the different object types and sub types that BRFplus provides for the assembly of rules. The focus for the definition and usage of the objects lies in the UI provided by the BRFplus Workbench. But the most important aspects of the respective programming API are also included.

5 Objects

Application and catalog objects have already been introduced in Sections 4.4 and 4.5. They are the foundation for deploying and managing the vast majority of all the other object types that BRFplus has to offer for the definition of rules. This chapter shall illuminate the purpose, definition, and usage of the different object types. Especially when it comes to expressions, there may exist multiple approaches to define a rule in a more or less elegant way. Thus it is recommended that you get at least a rough overview of all the object types.

The description of the different object types in this chapter follows the recommended way of defining business rules with BRFplus. It starts with the fundamental function and data objects, continues with rulesets and rules, and eventually addresses the huge variety of standard expression and actions types. As in the previous chapter, for each object type the description of the respective API is condensed into a separate section that may be skipped for later reading.

5.1 Functions

The glue between application code and BRFplus rules is the function object. It is the starting point for triggering the processing of BRFplus rules. Within their application, the function objects must have a unique name.

To ensure fast rule processing, BRFplus generates and executes program code in the form of an ABAP class, the first time a function is executed.

Function objects incorporate a so-called *context*, a set of *data objects* to pass data. It can roughly be compared to the list of importing or changing parameters of a function module. Data objects are the equivalent of a variable in programming languages, combined with a specific type. An additional, single *result data object* allows for returning the outcome of the rule processing.

If you want to define new rules for your application, you typically start with the definition of a function object. Here, you first need to think about the required mode of operation.

5.1.1 Mode of Operation

Three different modes of operation exist and need to be considered when designing new rules

▶ **Functional Mode**
A single, top-level expression can be processed and its result will be returned in the result data object. Even though the nesting of expressions into each other allows for some quite sophisticated logic, this mode is especially suitable for rather simple use cases. If you intend to use condition-based and sequential processing of multiple expressions, you should use the event mode.

▶ **Event Mode**
The actual rule logic is not directly determined by the function. Rather, the logic is contained in one or several rulesets that can subscribe to the function. When the function is processed, all subscribed rulesets are executed. Thus the function becomes extensible. The order of the ruleset execution can depend on a priority setting in the ruleset. Each ruleset can incorporate rules that may change the state of the context or trigger the execution of external activities.

By default, the result data object becomes a table that collects the IDs of all executed actions. But any other data object can also be set as a result. Within rule definitions, the result can be used just like any other data object of the function context. Rulesets can also have an additional, temporary context that allows more flexibility in the rule design. In short, the event mode is the preferred way to unleash the full potential of BRFplus rules design.

▶ **Functional and Event Mode**
The third mode is actually a mixture of the other two modes. First a top-level expression is evaluated to prefill the result data object. Then a list of subscribed rulesets is optionally processed. The mode exists largely for historic reasons. With the current release, the same logic can be designed with rules in the event mode meanwhile.

In the BRFplus Workbench, the function settings are distributed across several tabs. The MODE is set on the first tab, the PROPERTIES tab which is shown in Figure 5.1. If the mode requires a top-level expression, it can be specified directly beneath as Top Expression. For the pure functional mode, the result data object needs to be defined on the Signature tab because there is no default available.

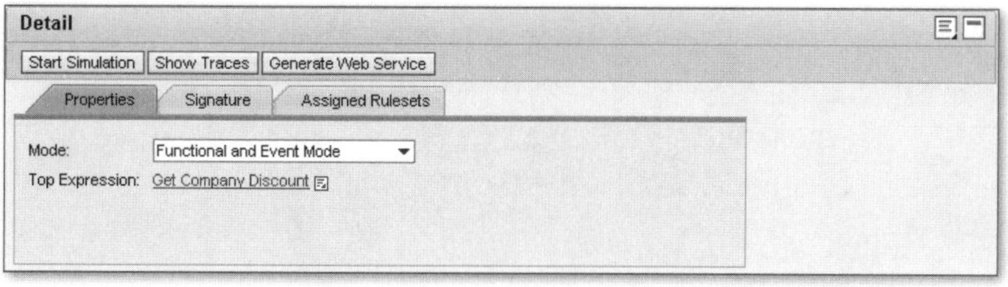

Figure 5.1 Function Properties

If the mode allows the subscription of rulesets, an additional tab, Assigned Rulesets, is displayed. Here you will see the list of all subscribed rulesets together with their priority setting. Rulesets of priority 0 (zero) may be executed in an arbitrary order. Priority 1 is the highest priority. Clicking on the button Create Ruleset will create a new ruleset object that automatically subscribes to the function.

> **Tip**
>
> Before you continue with the detailed design of the connected top expression or ruleset, it is recommended that you define the function's signature first. Data objects defined in the signature can then easily be accessed as context parameters in the UI.

5.1.2 Signature

The signature of a BRFplus function consists of the *context* and a *result data object*. The data objects in the context serve as a list of primarily optional parameters. Parameters that are not passed get an initial value. The context is mainly intended to pass required data the rule logic is based on. But it is also possible to read values from the context, after the function processing has been completed. Especially in the event mode, rules may be used to alter the values in the context.

In the BRFplus Workbench, you can assign existing data objects to the context on the Signature tab with the button Add Existing Data Objects (see Figure 5.2). For simple cases, you may reuse the standard data objects of application FDT_SYSTEM. The button Add New Data Object offers two options to create and assign new data objects to the context. There is the "classical" way of creating a single new data object of any type. Multiple elementary data objects can be created at once in a rapid way, using option Add Multiple Elements. For details see Section 5.2.2.

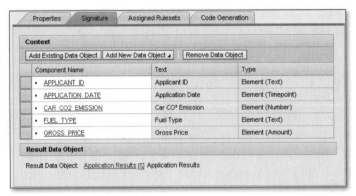

Figure 5.2 Function Signature

The result data object will basically contain the rule evaluation result. Using a structure or table type data object allows you to pass back multiple values at once.

When the function is set to event mode, the standard data object actions of application `FDT_SYSTEM` is set by default. This is a table that will collect the IDs of all action objects that are actually processed. You may, however, replace the actions data object or include it in a custom-defined, structured result data object.

A data object must be used only one time in the signature of the function. For example, it is not possible to use the same data object in the context and also as the result data object. When using structures and tables, you must also take care that the data objects they reference as components are only used once. In general, it is recommended that different structures and tables should not share the same data objects.

The usage of a table in the function signature will implicitly also make the table's structure and/or elements accessible within the connected rule definitions. Expressions can easily retrieve or change data of a single table line by using the Table Operation expression, which is described in detail in Section 5.5.17.

5.1.3 Simulation, Web Services, Code Generation, and Tracing

The execution of BRFplus functions is usually triggered from within application code. To be executable, an active version of the function and its referenced objects must exist.

In the BRFplus Workbench, a simulation tool exists that allows you to analyze the processing and outcome of an active function with test values. The tool can be

invoked either for a currently displayed function with the button Start Simulation, or for any function via the menu entry Tools • Simulation.

If the Display Technical Aspects setting is activated in the user's personalization,
an additional tool is available to generate a Web service for a BRFplus function. In
this way the BRFplus function can easily be consumed from external systems as
well. Similar to the simulation tool, the Web Service generation tool is available
for the currently displayed function via a button Generate Web Service, or for
any function via the menu entry Tools • Web Service Generation. To complete
the picture of the BRFplus function, we will now take a quick glance at some more
technical aspects.

When a function is processed, BRFplus will try to execute generated ABAP code
to boost the speed of evaluation. The code is automatically generated when the
function is executed the very first time. It has to be regenerated when a used object
of the function was changed. As a fallback, there always exists a slower interpretation mode. You can switch to this mode, if, for example, an object type does not
support code generation.

The code generated for a function is encapsulated into ABAP classes. If one or several used objects have multiple versions, also multiple classes may be required to
cover different time intervals.

If you have switched on the Display of Technical Attributes setting in the user
personalization, you can see all generated classes of a function on the tab Code
Generation. It lists the class names and the time intervals of validity. A flag indicates whether the generated code supports lean tracing.

Tracing is actually available in two different flavors: the *technical trace* and the *lean
trace*. The technical trace shows the full details of what happens during function
processing. It works only in interpretation mode and is mainly used for debugging
purposes, for example, by the simulation tool. When the simulation tool is used,
no ABAP class will therefore be generated.

The lean trace addresses the need to keep a record of all executions of a function,
also for mass processing. It is integrated into the code generation and will store
only a subset of the data to keep a high performance. More details about this topic
are provided in Section 7.2.

5.1.4 Function API

The function object type is technically reflected by interface `IF_FDT_FUNCTION`. It
provides the methods listed in Table 5.1.

Method	Description
SET_FUNCTION_MODE	Sets the mode of operation.
SET_EXPRESSION	Sets a top expression for the functional mode.
SET_CONTEXT_DATA_OBJECTS	Defines the function context.
SET_RESULT_DATA_OBJECT	Defines the function result.
PROCESS	Processes the function.
SET_CONTEXT_CLASS	Obsolete
SET_FILTER	Obsolete
SET_TRACE_MODE	Obsolete

Table 5.1 Methods of Interface IF_FDT_FUNCTION

For a new function you usually first set the mode of operation with method SET_FUNCTION_MODE. It has a single parameter, which accepts one of the following values that are defined in the function interface:

- GC_MODE_FUNCTIONAL: for the functional mode
- GC_MODE_EVENT: for the event mode
- GC_MODE_FUNCTIONAL_AND_EVENT: for functional and event mode

For the functional mode, a top expression has to be specified with method SET_EXPRESSION. The subscription of rulesets for the event mode is not maintained in the function, but in the individual rulesets.

The function context can be specified or changed by passing a list of data object IDs with method SET_CONTEXT_DATA_OBJECTS. The result data object can be set independently, passing a data object ID in method SET_RESULT_DATA_OBJECT.

In the current release of BRFplus, there is a filter setting for functions under evaluation. However, you actually should not use the related methods SET_FILTER and GET_FILTER. The methods SET_TRACE_MODE and SET_CONTEXT_CLASS are obsolete as well and must not be used any more.

Function Processing API

What mainly differentiates the API of the function from the API of all other object types is its method IF_FDT_FUNCTION~PROCESS—or, in other words, the possibility of triggering the execution of BRFplus rules. The method signature allows to initiate the processing in different ways. Table 5.2 summarizes its parameters.

Parameter	Description
IO_CONTEXT	A runtime context instance of type IF_FDT_CONTEXT.
ITS_ID_VALUE	An alternative to parameter IO_CONTEXT. One can use this list to assign values to the context parameters.
IV_TIMESTAMP	Allows function processing for a previous point in time (time travelling).
IV_TRACE_MODE	Activates tracing during function processing in the specified mode.
EO_RESULT	Provides a handle to the actual function result after the processing is completed.
EO_TRACE	A trace instance to read out the traced information.

Table 5.2 Parameters of Method IF_FDT_FUNCTION~PROCESS

The runtime context for the function can be provided by a separate object in parameter IO_CONTEXT, which has to implement interface IF_FDT_CONTEXT. The interface allows a wide range of context manipulation. It defines the methods that are listed in Table 5.3.

Method	Description
GET_INSTANCE	Returns a new instance of the context interface implementation for a specific timestamp.
COPY	Returns a copy of this context instance.
SET_VALUE	Sets a value for a specific data object in the context. The data object may be referred to by its ID or name. Attribute MV_TIMESTAMP_VALUE_CHANGE is updated.
REMOVE_VALUE	Removes the value for a specific data object in the context. The data object may be referred to by its ID or name. Attribute MV_TIMESTAMP_VALUE_CHANGE is updated.
GET_VALUE	Gets the currently set value for a specific data object in the context. The data object may be referred to by its ID or name.
HAS_VALUE	Checks if a value has been set for a specific data object in the context. The data object may be referred to by its ID or name.
INSERT_DATA_OBJECT	Adds a data object to the context
REMOVE_DATA_OBJECT	Removes a specific data object from the context
GET_DATA_OBJECTS	Returns a list of all context data objects

Table 5.3 Methods of Interface IF_FDT_CONTEXT

With method GET_PROCESS_CONTEXT a default instance with a preset list of context data objects can be retrieved. The context instance is mainly used to set context values for the function processing. But it also allows you to retrieve possibly changed context values afterwards.

To begin, the context interface defines the following two read-only attributes:

▶ MV_TIMESTAMP contains the processing timestamp the context instance is created for

▶ MV_TIMESTAMP_VALUE_CHANGE contains the timestamp when a context value has last been changed.

Passing a context instance via parameter IO_CONTEXT to method PROCESS is one option for setting context values. A faster approach with respect to performance is using table parameter ITS_ID_VALUE instead. The creation of an explicit context object instance is then not required. The structure type IF_FDT_TYPES=>S_ID_VALUE of the parameter defines the mapping of a context data object ID to a value by data reference. On the one hand, it is therefore required to know the IDs of the involved data objects; on the other hand, name changes to the data objects do not matter.

Processing of the function can be triggered for a specific timestamp, which becomes relevant when versioned objects are part of the underlying rule definition. The timestamp needs either to be passed upon creation of the context instance in method GET_PROCESS_CONTEXT, or directly in the PROCESS method via parameter IV_TIMESTAMP. If no timestamp is passed, the latest active version of the processed BRFplus objects will be used.

If you want to trace the function processing, you need to request a trace object with parameter EO_TRACE. Tracing can be requested in different modes by using parameter IV_TRACE_MODE. The following constant values of interface IF_FDT_CON- STANTS are supported:

▶ GC_TRACE_MODE_TECHNICAL
Activates the technical trace which enforces processing in interpretation mode.

▶ GC_TRACE_MODE_LEAN
Activates the lean trace, if possible.

▶ GC_TRACE_MODE_LEAN_REQUIRED
Enforces the lean trace. If lean tracing is blocked, for example because code generation is not possible, an exception occurs.

If parameter IV_TRACE_MODE is not passed, the technical trace is used by default. Details on tracing and how to use the provided trace object are given in Section 7.2.

The result of the function processing can be accessed via paramater EO_RESULT of type IF_FDT_RESULT. Like the context interface, the result interface contains the two read-only attributes MV_TIMESTAMP and MV_TIMESTAMP_VALUE_CHANGE. Most important is method GET_VALUE, which provides the value of the result data object. When nested data objects like structures and tables are used, it is possible to retrieve only specific values by passing the name or ID of the corresponding data object in parameter IV_ID or respectively IV_NAME. The value can be requested either by direct value assignment with the exporting parameter EA_VALUE, or by data reference using parameter ER_VALUE. To ensure that the passed variables are of compatible types, you may dynamically create them using methods of the data object interface. See Section 5.2.1 for details. In Table 5.4 you find a complete overview of the methods defined in interface IF_FDT_RESULT.

Method	Description
GET_VALUE	Retrieves the value of the result data object or a part of it.
GET_DATA_OBJECT	Returns an instance of the result data object.
SET_VALUE	Sets the value for the result data object or a part of it.
SET_DATA_OBJECT	Sets the result data object.
COPY	Returns a copy of the this result object instance.

Table 5.4 Methods of Interface IF_FDT_RESULT

The execution of a function may fail with an exception. It is therefore recommended that you encapsulate the method call into a TRY – CATCH – ENDTRY block. Besides exceptions of type CX_FDT_INPUT or CX_FDT_SYSTEM, which typically occur due to a false method call or some general system problem, a CX_FDT_PROCESSING exception may occur. Processing errors can therewith be handled in a separate way.

As a synopsis let us look at a typical piece of code to call a BRFplus function.

```
DATA: lo_function      TYPE REF TO if_fdt_function,
      lo_context       TYPE REF TO if_fdt_context,
      lo_result        TYPE REF TO if_fdt_result,
      lv_result_string TYPE string,
      lx_fdt           TYPE REF TO cx_fdt.
FIELD-SYMBOLS: <ls_message> TYPE if_fdt_types=>s_message.
CONSTANTS: lc_fct_id TYPE if_fdt_types=>id
VALUE '00145EF41CBA02DDA8819E3B1652013A'.
TRY.
  lo_function = cl_fdt_factory=>get_instance( )->get_function(
iv_id = lc_fct_id ).
  lo_context = lo_function->get_process_context( ).
```

```
    lo_context->set_value( iv_name = 'INPUT'
                           ia_value = 'Hello World' ).
    lo_function->process( EXPORTING io_context = lo_context
                          IMPORTING eo_result = lo_result ).
    lo_result->get_value( IMPORTING ea_value =
                          lv_result_string ).
  CATCH cx_fdt_processing.
   lv_result_string = 'PROCESSING ERROR!'.
  CATCH cx_fdt INTO lx_fdt.
   LOOP AT lx_fdt->mt_message ASSIGNING <ls_message>.
     WRITE: / <ls_message>-text.
   ENDLOOP.
ENDTRY.
WRITE:/ 'The result is : ' , lv_result_string.
```

Listing 5.1 Function Call Example

First the function object with a specific ID is retrieved. A context object for the function is created afterwards, and the value "Hello World" is set for context parameter INPUT. Next the function is processed and the result value of type string is retrieved. In case a processing error should occur, the result string is set to "PROCESSING ERROR!" If any other exception occurs, the error messages are output. Finally, the determined result string is simply output.

To support function processing with even higher performance, the BRFplus API includes the extra class CL_FDT_FUNCTION_PROCESS. It allows you to trigger function processing statically, without the need to instantiate a function object.

Static Function Processing API

Processing a function with method IF_FDT_FUNCTION~PROCESS is quite intuitive. But it requires the creation of multiple BRFplus object instances with according database selections. These are rather costly actions in terms of the speed of execution. For use cases that are performance critical and/or call many functions, BRFplus offers an additional approach. Class CL_FDT_FUNCTION_PROCESS contains a static PROCESS method that can be used as an alternative to its counterpart in interface IF_FDT_FUNCTION. At first glance its signature looks quite similar, but it has the following deviations:

▶ IV_FUNCTION_ID
  ID of the function to be processed. No function object instance is required.

▶ CT_NAME_VALUE
  A table of name/value pairs. It depicts another option for setting and retrieving context parameter values.

▶ EA_RESULT

It replaces the parameter EO_RESULT of type IF_FDT_RESULT. The result value is directly stored into the passed variable so no intermediate result object is required.

All other parameters that are described in Section 5.1.4 exist as well and have the same meaning.

The table parameter CT_NAME_VALUE constitutes a further option for setting the values for context parameters. Its structure type ABAP_PARMBIND maps a context parameter name to a value by data reference. Because CT_NAME_VALUE is a changing parameter, it also contains the latest context values after the processing.

The use of a static method without any function, context, or result objects can noticeably improve the execution speed. The ultimate optimization measure with respect to performance is, however, not obvious. Context data that is passed to the function usually needs to be converted into a BRFplus internal format. The data conversion requires an instantiation of the corresponding context data objects, and in turn several accesses to the database. The data conversion can be avoided by providing the context values in the BRFplus internal format. For elementary context data objects, you may simply use variables that are of the corresponding type in interface IF_FDT_TYPES:

▶ ELEMENT_TEXT

▶ ELEMENT_NUMBER

▶ ELEMENT_BOOLEAN

▶ ELEMENT_AMOUNT

▶ ELEMENT_QUANTITY

▶ ELEMENT_TIMEPOINT

For structure and table types, you can either define a matching type yourself, or dynamically get a suitable data reference with the static method GET_DATA_OBJECT_REFERENCE of class CL_FDT_FUNCTION_PROCESS.

An optimized way to invoke function processing could look like the following simple example. It assumes that the function uses a structure NUMBER_DESCRIPTION in its context. The structure has the two components NUMBER of type number and DESCRIPTION of type text.

```
DATA: lt_name_value TYPE abap_parambind_tab,
      ls_name_value LIKE LINE OF lt_name_value,
      lv_result_string TYPE string.
CONSTANTS lc_fct_id TYPE if_fdt_types=>id VALUE
```

```
'00145EF41CBA02DDA8819E3D1652013A'.
FIELD-SYMBOLS <la_data> TYPE ANY DATA.
TRY.
  ls_name_value-name = 'NUMBER_DESCRIPTION'.
  cl_fdt_function_process=>get_data_object_reference(
    EXPORTING iv_function_id = lc_fdt_id
              iv_data_object = ls_name_value-name
    IMPORTING er_data = ls_name_value-value ).
  ASSIGN COMPONENT 'NUMBER' OF STRUCTURE ls_name_value-value->*
                                         TO <la_data>.
  <la_data> = '3.14159'. "Set the number value
  ASSIGN COMPONENT 'DESCRIPTION'
   OF STRUCTURE ls_name_value-value->* TO <la_data>.
  <la_data> = 'PI'. "Set the text value
  APPEND ls_name_value to lt_name_value.
  cl_fdt_function_process=>process(
    EXPORTING iv_function_id = lc_fdt_id
    CHANGING  ct_name_value = lt_name_value
    IMPORTING ea_result = lv_result_string ).
  WRITE: / 'The result is : ' , lv_result_string.
CATCH cx_fdt.
  WRITE / 'Error'.
ENDTRY.
```

Listing 5.2 High-Performance Function Call Example

5.2   Data Objects

Data objects are the carriers of values in BRFplus. They combine the aspects of a variable and a data type definition. Data objects incorporate a type with individual characteristics. They may additionally impose usage restrictions, for example, for allowed comparisons. At runtime the data object represents a single parameter or variable instance.

Three different sorts of data objects exist in BRFplus: elements, structures, and tables. They have in common that they can be bound to existing data type definitions in the *Data Dictionary* (DDIC). When you bind a data object, it is by default named like the underlying type definition. Because names do not need to be unique in BRFplus, you may create multiple data objects with the same name, potentially the same binding, but different IDs. For equally named data objects, it is recommended that you define different short text descriptions.

In the case that a data object is bound, all settings that can possibly be derived from the existing type definition are automatically set and become unchangeable.

This partly affects also the text and documentation properties. The dependency types are automatically set to be language- but not version-dependent. By default the bound data object has no own texts set. Instead the texts are dynamically retrieved from the corresponding definition in the data dictionary. It is, however, still possible to change the texts and thereby overwrite the usage of the data dictionary definitions.

Even though the binding is a common feature for all data object types, it has different, type-specific consequences. For example, the binding for a table type implies the creation of a bound structure type. Binding for a structure type requires the creation of appropriately bound data objects that constitute the components of the structure. Because tables and structures may be deeply nested, a binding can result in the creation of an arbitrary number of required data objects.

The context of a function should contain only data objects that are actually required for the rules processing. It is thus recommended that you use binding against complex data structures only, if all contained elements are actually needed.

If a bound DDIC-type has been changed, the binding can be refreshed. For elementary types, this refreshing will update all derived settings. For structures or tables, it may also result in the creation of new data objects for added components.

> **Caution**
>
> If you refresh the DDIC-binding for a structure that has been extended, new data objects are created only for the added components. But when you first remove the DDIC-binding and then bind against the same structure again, new data objects will be created for *all* components of the structure! Rules may already reference the former data objects and thus become invalid.

At runtime, values are assigned to the used data objects according to their type. A value transfer among data objects is possible only if the value is convertible. For data objects of type element, any value can be converted into a text string, for example, but a text must consist only of numeric digits to be convertible into a number.

As a precondition of being convertible, the involved data objects need to match structurally. If the source data object is a table or structure, the target data object needs to provide an equally named and matching counterpart for each structure component. In addition, a table can be converted only into a flat structure or element at runtime if it has exactly one line of entry.

For very simple use cases you will not need to create any data object yourself. For each element type the following default data objects in Table 5.5 of standard application FDT_SYSTEM are available for reuse.

Data Object	Description
TEXT	Text type without restrictions
NUMBER	Number type without restrictions
BOOLEAN	Boolean type without restrictions
AMOUNT	Amount type without restrictions
QUANTITY	Quantity type without restrictions
TIMEPOINT	Timepoint type without restrictions
TIMESTAMP	Timepoint of type Universal Time Coordinated (UTC) timestamp, including date and time
DATE_TIME	Timepoint of type date and time (local)
DATE	Timpoint of type date
TIME	Timepoint of type time
USER_NAME	Text type, bound to DDIC type SYUNAME
BACKGROUND	Boolean type, bound to DDIC type SYBATCH
ACTION	Text type, intended to store IDs of actions

Table 5.5 Default Data Objects

5.2.1 Data Objects API

The common parts of data objects are reflected by interface IF_FDT_DATA_OBJECT. The defined methods are supported by all data object types, but mostly implemented in a special way for each type.

The type of a data object is available in attribute MV_DATA_OBJECT_TYPE. Alternatively, method GET_DATA_OBJECT_TYPE can be used for that purpose. The three possible constant values are defined in interface IF_FDT_CONSTANTS:

- GC_DATA_OBJECT_TYPE_ELEMENT: for elements
- GC_DATA_OBJECT_TYPE_STRUCTURE: for structures
- GC_DATA_OBJECT_TYPE_TABLE: for tables

Method IS_DEEP returns a Boolean value that indicates whether the data object deeply nests other data objects. Deep nesting is in fact only possible for structure or table types. It means that an involved (table) structure embeds another structure or table, which may again be deeply nested.

Binding

With method SET_DDIC_BINDING the data object can be bound to a specific data dictionary type. You simply have to pass the desired type name. To refresh the binding, you can simply call the method with the currently set type name again. If you want to remove an existing DDIC-binding, you have to pass an empty type name. Settings that have been derived from the DDIC-binding will, however, not be cleared.

> **Binding for Global Data Types**
>
> Similar to DDIC-binding, method SET_GDT_BINDING can be used to bind a data object against a global data type in *SAP Business ByDesign* systems. The method accepts a path definition in parameter IV_PROXY_BINDING_PATH that points to the attribute of a business object's *node*. The attribute's global data type will be used for the binding.[1] The format of the proxy path is <bo_name>.~BO_NODE_NAME.<bo_node>[.<bo_node>]*.~ATTRIBUTE.<attr_name>[.<attr_name>]*.
>
> <bo_name> is the proxy name of the business object, <bo_node> is a contained node, and <attr_name> a node attribute.

Since only one type of binding is possible at a time, calling a binding method will invalidate any previously set, different binding. The current type of binding can be retrieved with method GET_BINDING_TYPE. It will return one of the following constant values:

▶ IF_FDT_DATA_OBJECT=>GC_BINDING_TYPE_NONE: no binding

▶ IF_FDT_DATA_OBJECT=>GC_BINDING_TYPE_DDIC: binding against a data dictionary type

▶ IF_FDT_DATA_OBJECT=>GC_BINDING_TYPE_GDT: binding against a global data type

▶ IF_FDT_ELEMENT=>GC_BINDING_TYPE_REF_ELEMENT: binding against another BRF-plus element; this is possible only for elementary data objects.

Unlike other properties, the setting of a binding property may result in the creation of an arbitrary number of required data objects for structures and tables. The IDs of the created data objects are listed in the exporting table parameter ETS_OBJECT_ID.

---

1 The alternative binding parameter IV_ESR_BINDING_PATH has become obsolete. The related utility-method CREATE_ESR_BINDING_PATH is therefore also of no importance any more.

> **Precaution**
>
> Structures and tables should be activated and saved only in deep mode to prevent inconsistencies. Required components may otherwise be missing or may not reflect the latest state of the origin type.

Derivation

Method SET_DDIC_BINDING implicitly reuses method DERIVE_DATA_OBJECT, that allows to derive settings from *any* ABAP data type. The data type can either be explicitly passed by the type's name in parameter IV_TYPENAME or dynamically be determined from a variable passed through parameter IA_DATA. With the Boolean parameter IV_INCL_TEXTS the adaption of text settings can be included or excluded. Method DERIVE_DATA_OBJECT will also create additionally required data objects for structure or table types. The corresponding object IDs are available in parameter ETS_OBJECT_ID. In contrast to method SET_DDIC_BINDING, the passed ABAP type is not stored and all settings remain changeable.

Data Creation

The data object itself does not store any runtime values. Rather, this is the task of the runtime context and result. But the data object allows you to dynamically create a reference to an appropriate variable. Method CREATE_DATA_REFERENCE provides the variable via a suitable reference in parameter ER_DATA. Information about the created data field can be retrieved in parallel, using parameter EO_DATADESCR. It provides a matching instance of the *ABAP Runtime Type Services*.

Data Conversion

Method IS_CONVERTIBLE_TO allows you to check whether data of one data object can in principle be transferred to another data object that is specified in parameter IO_TARGET_DATA_OBJECT. The method can return three different values:

▶ GC_CONVERSION_POSSIBLE
Data can always be transferred.

▶ GC_CONVERSION_DATA_DEPENDENT
Data can be transferred only if it fits the type and characteristics of the target data object. A text can, for example, be transferred into a number, if it consists only of numeric digits.

▶ GC_CONVERSION_IMPOSSIBLE
Data cannot be transferred to the target data object.

The actual conversion of a value from one data object to another can be achieved with method CONVERT_TO. It requires the parameters listed in Table 5.6.

Parameter	Description
IV_TIMESTAMP	Timestamp to determine the active version for the involved data objects
IA_SOURCE_DATA	Value that is compatible with the source data object
IO_TARGET_DATA_OBJECT	The target data object that determines the output format
CA_TARGET_DATA	The target value that is adapted

Table 5.6 Parameters of Method IF_FDT_DATA_OBJECT~CONVERT_TO

If the target data object is of type table, the source data will be inserted into the provided target table data. For structures, only the common components that occur in the source and target data object are filled. In case the conversion is not possible, a CX_FDT_CONVERSION exception is raised.

5.2.2 Elements

Elements—or rather data objects of type element—define simple value entities of a specific type. The element definition consists of a basic data type such as a number or text, together with some optional properties. A list of valid domain values can be provided too.

Creation

For the creation of elements, the BRFplus Workbench offers two different approaches—the standard approach for a single element and also a mass creation tool. The object creation popup for elements shown in Figure 5.3 includes an area with the most important properties.

In the DEFINE DATA BINDING section, you may directly bind the element against a DDIC type and thereby derive all basic settings. Through binding even the name is defaulted, if you have not yet entered one. Without binding you need to specify or rather change the ELEMENT TYPE (the default is "Text"). Some corresponding ELEMENT ATTRIBUTES can also be set. To adjust further, more special properties, you need to navigate to the element object.

Another way to swiftly create multiple elements at once is the mass creation popup. In the REPOSITORY VIEW you may access it within the context menu of an APPLICATION, DATA OBJECT or ELEMENT node by selecting menu entry CREATE DATA OBJECT • ELEMENTS (MASS CREATION).

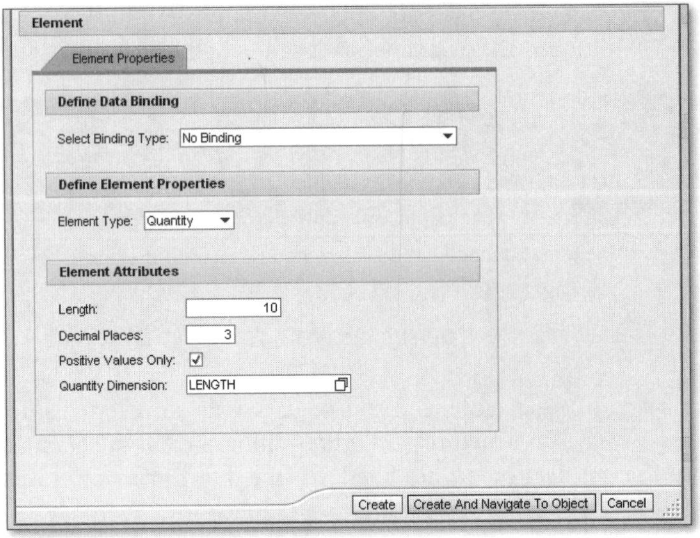

Figure 5.3 Element Creation Popup

In the popup you can enter a list of up to ten new elements to be created. For each line you simply need to specify the ELEMENT TYPE, NAME, and a SHORT TEXT. It is also possible to define a binding against a DDIC-type or other BRFplus element by choosing the corresponding option in the TYPE column. The element type will then automatically be derived from the reference type or element, which you enter into column REFERENCE. Figure 5.4 shows how the popup is used.

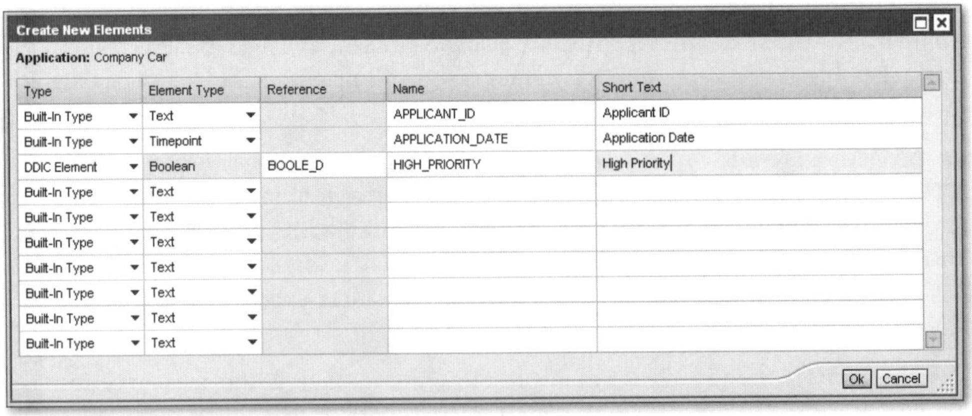

Figure 5.4 Element Mass Creation Popup

Creating the intended elements in this way allows you to immediately continue with the rules definition, and to adjust the element details at a later point in time. We will now have a closer look at the details.

Element Types and Attributes

Each element supports only a specific type of values. The following element types are available:

▶ **Text**
Text strings can be used for any kind of character-like data. Texts stored by BRF-plus are limited to a length of 255 characters. At runtime there is no such limitation. Strings retrieved from external sources or string concatenations during processing may have any length.

▶ **Number**
This element type can be used for any numeric data. With SAP NetWeaver 7.02 BRFplus uses the new base type `Decfloat34`. It allows you to handle a wide range of numbers regarding length and precision. Numbers stored by BRFplus are, however, limited to a maximum length of 31 digits and a precision of 10 decimals.

▶ **Boolean**
A Boolean element supports only two values, representing a logical "True" or "False." It is mainly used to store the result of a condition evaluation. BRFplus takes over the ABAP convention to store Boolean values as a character of length 1, which may have the value "X" for "True" and " " (space) for "False."

▶ **Amount**
This type is intended for monetary amounts. In BRFplus an amount always consists of two values: a number and a currency value. At design time, the decimals of the number value must not exceed the currency's decimals setting, that has been customized in table TCURX for the current client. At runtime you should take care to pass amount values in the right format. Outside BRFplus, amounts of ABAP type `CURR` are sometimes shifted to be stored with 2 decimals on the database, independent of the used currency. They might need to be shifted back to the actual decimals, by using an appropriate conversion routine.

▶ **Quantity**
This type can be used for unit-dependent quantity values. Analogous to amounts, a quantity always consists of two values in BRFplus: a number and a unit value. A quantity element can be restricted to allow only units of a specific dimension, such as "length," "mass," etc. For units BRFplus uses the standard data type `UNIT`. Consequently, the valid units are customized for each client in

table T006, field MSEHI. Because data type `UNIT` uses a conversion routine, the external representation MSEH3 of table T006A is displayed the UI and automatically transformed into the corresponding MSEHI value.

▶ **Timepoint**
This type can be used for time- and date-related values. The timepoint element supports several timepoint types. Depending on the type, a time and/or date value can be entered. The type may also impose different semantic meaning. For example, a timestamp may refer to local time or to universal time coordinated (UTC).

> **Client Dependency**
>
> Units and currencies are customizing data and thus are stored client-dependent. In case you define amount or quantity values within system objects that are stored client-independent, they might not be valid in every client. Also elements of type quantity that are defined on system level and imply a dimension restriction might not be usable everywhere.

Depending on the element type, the following attributes can be maintained to restrict the allowed values.

▶ **Length**
Defines the allowed, total number of characters within a text string or digits within a numeric value. Length 0 has the meaning of "no restriction." It corresponds, however, to the maximal supported length.

▶ **Decimals**
Defines the allowed decimal digits within a numeric value.

▶ **Only Positive**
A flag that indicates that only positive numeric values are allowed.

▶ **Dimension**
Restricts the usage of units within a quantity. To be convertible, the units of two quantities usually must be of the same dimension, such as "length," "mass," and so on. Setting a dimension can reduce the risk of creating rules with incompatible quantity data.

▶ **Timepoint Type**
Restricts a timepoint element to a specific timepoint type. The available timepoint types are: *time*, *date*, *timestamp* and *UTC timestamp*.

Table 5.7 summarizes the element types together with their technical type and the applicable attributes.

Type	Length (max.)	Decimals (max.)	Only Positive	Dimension	BRFplus Type in IF_FDT_TYPES	ABAP Base Types
Text	255	–	–	–	ELEMENT_TEXT	SSTRING
Number	31	10	x	–	ELEMENT_NUMBER	DF34_RAW
Boolean	–	–	–	–	ELEMENT_BOOLEAN	CHAR1
Amount	31	–	x	–	ELEMENT_AMOUNT	DF34_RAW, CHAR5
Quantity	31	10	x	x	ELEMENT_QUANTITY	DF34_RAW, CHAR3
Timepoint	–	–	–	–	ELEMENT_TIMEPOINT	DATS,TIMS, TIMESTAMP

Table 5.7 Element Types and Attributes

Binding

If you bind an element against a DDIC type, all element attributes that can be derived are automatically set and become unchangeable. The used DDIC type must however match to the element type. The following Table 5.8 shows the compatibility matrix.

ABAP Type Kind	BRFplus Element Type	Max Length	Max Number of Decimals	Only Positive Values	Timepoint Type
Char	Text	1–255	n/a	n/a	n/a
String	Text	255	n/a	n/a	n/a
Numc	Text	1–255	n/a	n/a	n/a
Int1	Number	1–3	0	Yes	n/a
Int2	Number	5	0	No	n/a
Int, Int4	Number	10	0	No	n/a
Packed	Number	1–31	0–10	No	n/a
Float	Number	16	0–10	No	n/a
Decfloat16	Number	16	0–10	No	n/a
Decfloat34	Number	31	0–10	No	n/a
CURR (DDIC)	Amount	1–31	n/a	No	n/a

Table 5.8 Element Types Compatibility Matrix

ABAP Type Kind	BRFplus Element Type	Max Length	Max Number of Decimals	Only Positive Values	Timepoint Type
QUAN (DDIC)	Quantity	1–31	0-10	No	n/a
Date	Timepoint	n/a	n/a	n/a	Date
Time	Timepoint	n/a	n/a	n/a	Time
Timestamp	Timepoint	n/a	n/a	n/a	UTC Timestamp

Table 5.8 Element Types Compatibility Matrix (Cont.)

Text elements cover any string or character-like type, including numeric characters. Hexadecimal types of length 16 that may represent a 32 characters UUID are exceptionally supported too.

All kind of numeric types are supported by the number element type.

Boolean types must be characters of length 1 and have exactly the two domain values: "X" and " " (space).

Amounts and quantities may only be bound against their special DDIC type counterparts. When used within a function signature, you should not forget also to pass a currency or a unit value, which are always part of the BRFplus representation. In general it is recommended that you use DDIC structures that contain both a value field and a reference field for the currency or unit.

Eventually date and time types can be mapped to a timepoint element of the corresponding type. For timestamp types the mapping is ambiguous because they are actually packed number types. Currently a packed number type is recognized as a timestamp when it fulfills the following constraints, which are still subject to change:

▶ The type must use domain TZNTSTMPS or its name must include the key word "timestamp"

▶ The used decimal number must be of length 15 and with no decimals.

Elements can be bound not only to DDIC-types, like all data objects. They additionally support binding against another BRFplus element of the same element type. In this case all attributes of the bound element type become directly valid also for the referencing element. This feature is useful if, for example, you need two element instances of exactly the same type within a function or ruleset context.

Comparisons

Within business rules, the values of context parameters or expression results are often compared against each other or against fixed value ranges. This allows you to discriminate between different processing paths or to trigger some conditional action. BRFplus therefore supports a wide range of comparison operations and operators.

The operations can semantically be categorized into three groups: ordinal comparisons such as "is greater than," string comparisons such as "matches pattern," and implicit comparisons, such as "is initial."

Table 5.9 lists all comparison operations available in BRFplus. The ID is the technical representation of the operator. It corresponds to its ABAP counterpart when feasible.

Category	ID	Description	Comment
Ordinal comparisons	EQ	Is equal to	
	NE	Is not equal to	
	LT	Is less than	
	LE	Is less than or equal to	
	GT	Is greater than	
	GE	is greater than or equal to	
	BT	Is between	The values defining the upper and lower limit of the comparison interval are included.
	NB	Is not between	The logical inverse to "Is between"
String comparisons	CA	Contains any	The sequence of characters does not matter
	NA	Does not contain any	The sequence of characters does not matter
	CO	Contains only	The sequence of characters does not matter
	CN	Does not contain only	The sequence of characters does not matter
	CS	Contains string	The sequence of characters must be identical in the test and comparison parameter
	NS	Does not contain string	Logical inverse of "Contains string"

Table 5.9 Comparison Operations

Category	ID	Description	Comment
	CP	Matches pattern	The following wildcards are supported: + – matches exactly one character * – matches any number of characters Example: "Hello" matches "He*o" but not "He+o". Hero matches "He*o" and "He+o" as well.
	NP	Does not match pattern	Logical inverse of "Matches Pattern"
Implicit comparisons	I1	Is initial	An initial string is empty or contains only whitespace. An initial number is zero. An initial Boolean parameter equals "false." Initial amounts and quantities are zero and have no currency or unit. An initial time point has either no time point type or the respective fields are initial. Initial time and date fields are empty or consist only of zeros.
	I2	Is not initial	Logical inverse of "Is initial"

Table 5.9 Comparison Operations (Cont.)

For ordinal comparisons of texts, case-sensitivity is not taken into account. For example, *a is less than B* is evaluated as true, although a has a higher ASCII code value than B.

For string comparisons, leading and trailing whitespace is removed from the test parameter; but whitespace inside of a string is retained. Pattern matching comparisons are always performed case-insensitive. Otherwise, case-sensitivity can only be explicitly be set in range or Case expressions. See also Sections 5.5.3 and 5.5.6 for details.

All operations involve an incoming test parameter and—except for implicit comparisons—a comparison parameter. Whether a particular operator can be used or not depends on the operator category and the type of the parameters involved. Implicit comparisons are always possible because no comparison parameter is required.

If the test and comparison parameters are of the same type, all ordinal comparisons are applicable in general. The only exceptions are Boolean parameters that support only the two comparisons "Equal to" and "Not equal to." If the test and comparison parameters are of different types, ordinal comparisons can be performed only among texts and numbers. If possible, the text parameter is converted into a number and the parameters are compared numerically. Otherwise, the numeric parameter is converted to text and an alphanumeric comparison is performed.

String comparisons are possible for all but Boolean test parameters if the comparison parameter is either of type text or number. All non-textual parameters are translated into text in these cases.

> **Normalization**
>
> The way an operator actually works on the involved parameter types may require some internal conversion into a normalized format first. For alphanumeric comparisons, text parameters are internally converted into a byte sequence, according to the ABAP command CONVERT TEXT. On the one hand, this kind of normalization avoids inconsistencies when characters belong to different codepages; on the other hand, the behavior may sometimes differ from the expected outcome.
>
> Parameters of type amount or quantity may have different currencies or units. In case the values are not zero, a conversion into one of the involved currencies or units is implicitly executed. The values are then numerically compared.
>
> Date and time fields are compared numerically to each other. Currently only parameters of the same timepoint type can be compared.

Allowed Comparisons

In addition to technical restrictions, it is possible to further limit the allowed comparisons. In the Workbench, you may change the setting for ALLOWED COMPARISONS within the ELEMENT PROPERTIES tab (see Figure 5.5):

▸ **No Restrictions**
This is the default. All supported comparison operations are allowed.

▸ **Equals**
It is only allowed to use operator "Is equal to" against a single value.

▸ **Single Value**
It is allowed to use the operators "Is equal to" or "Is not equal to" against a single value.

▸ **Value List**
It is allowed to use the operators "Is equal to" or "Is not equal to" against one or multiple values.

▸ **Non-textual**
It is allowed to use all but string comparisons against one or multiple values.

▸ **User-defined**
An explicit list of allowed operators can be specified.

When "user-defined" comparisons are chosen, some additional settings are available in the emerging section Uem-Defined Properties, as depicted in Figure 5.5.

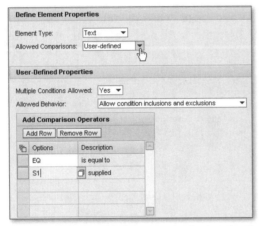

Figure 5.5 User-Defined Comparison Settings for Elements

With Multiple Conditions Allowed you may specify whether the comparison consists only of a single condition, or whether multiple conditions are allowed that will be semantically concatenated with a logical OR.

With the Allowed Behavior setting, the comparisons can be restricted to consist of:

▶ **Condition Inclusions**
Conditions that need to be fulfilled.

▶ **Condition Exclusions**
Conditions that must not be fulfilled.

If both types are allowed, there is no restriction in this respect.

Eventually it is possible to define an explicit list of comparison operators that shall be available when the data object is used for a comparison definition.

Checking an expression or action object that defines a comparison that is not allowed by the used element results in an error message by default. The severity of such a violation may, however, be altered on the tab Additional Properties. With the field Comparison Check Messages you may specify whether an error message, warning message or no message at all will be raised in such a case.

Domain Values

An elementary data object may be intended to support only values within a specific domain. These values are listed on the tab Domain Values.

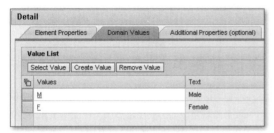

Figure 5.6 Element Domain Values

In case the element is bound against some reference type, the domain values are automatically derived from that type. In the case of DDIC-binding to a type that is using a DDIC domain, the allowed list of values is retrieved from the domain's Value Range (see Transaction SE11). BRFplus currently supports only Single Value or Value Table definitions in DDIC domains. Intervals of values are ignored.

If the elementary data object is not bound, it is possible to use a list of constant definitions as domain values. Constants are the most primitive type of expression objects. It is possible to reuse named constant objects with the button Select Value. New constants can be created by clicking on the button Create Value. You should consider creating unnamed constants if the constant values are only required for the element.

By default only a warning message will be displayed if a value is defined within some action or expression that is not contained in the list of domain values in the underlying element. To enforce valid values, you can increase the severity of such messages to type error on the tab Additional Properties in the field Existence Check Messages.

Element API

For each element type, BRFplus uses a corresponding ABAP type that is defined in interface IF_FDT_TYPES. The underlying base types impose the technical limitations for element values. All element attributes, such as length or decimals, are within the range of the base type. The types and ABAP base types are listed together in Table 5.10.

Type	BRFplus Type	ABAP Base Types
Text	ELEMENT_TEXT	SSTRING
Number	ELEMENT_NUMBER	DF34_RAW
Boolean	ELEMENT_BOOLEAN	CHAR1
Amount	ELEMENT_AMOUNT	DF34_RAW,CHAR5
Quantity	ELEMENT_QUANTITY	DF34_RAW,CHAR3
Timepoint	ELEMENT_TIMEPOINT	DATS,TIMS,TIMESTAMP

Table 5.10 ABAP Types for Element Types

The characteristics of elements mentioned above are reflected programmatically by interface IF_FDT_ELEMENT. The provided methods are summarized in Table 5.11.

Method	Description
SET_ELEMENT_TYPE	Sets the element type.
SET_REFERENCED_ELEMENT	Binds the element to another element.
SET_ELEMENT_TYPE_ATTRIBUTES	Specifies additional characteristics, according to the element type.
SET_ALLOWED_COMPARISONS	Defines which comparisons are allowed in connection with the element.
SET_VALUE_LIST	Sets a list of domain values, if the object is not bound.
SET_MSG_SEVERITY	Adjusts the severity of messages for some checks.

Table 5.11 Methods of Interface IF_FDT_ELEMENT

Most important is the specification of the element type with method SET_ELE-MENT_TYPE, if it has not already been derived through DDIC-binding. Binding to another BRFplus element can be achieved with method SET_REFERENCED_ELEMENT, which simply requires a valid element ID. To revoke an existing element binding, an initial ID needs to be passed.

Element type specific attributes can be set with the corresponding importing parameters in method SET_ELEMENT_TYPE_ATTRIBUTES. If attributes are passed that are not supported by the element type, a CX_FDT_INPUT exception is raised. A dimension can, for example, be set only for elements of type quantity, and a timepoint type only for elements of type timepoint.

Allowed timepoint types are available as constants in interface IF_FDT_CONSTANTS:

- GC_TP_DATE: local date
- GC_TP_TIME: local time

- ▸ `GC_TP_DATETIME`: local timestamp
- ▸ `GC_TP_TIMESTAMP_UTC`: UTC timestamp
- ▸ `GC_TP_DATETIME_OFFSET_UTC`: UTC timestamp with offset (only available in *SAP Business ByDesign* systems)

For the length and decimals attributes, the maximal allowed values are available as constants directly in interface `IF_FDT_ELEMENT`:

- ▸ `GC_MAXIMUM_TEXT_LENGHT`: maximal number of characters for textual values
- ▸ `GC_MAXIMUM_NUMBER_LENGTH`: maximal number of digits for numeric values
- ▸ `GC_MAXIMUM_NUMBER_OF_DECIMALS`: maximal number of decimals for numeric values

To refine the allowed comparisons for an element, method `SET_ALLOWED_COMPARISONS` provides the following parameters:

- ▸ `IV_ALLOWED_COMPARISONS`
  Defines the type of comparison restrictions. Possible values are defined as constants `GC_COMPARISONS_*`. The passed type also limits the allowed values for the other parameters. Only if the type is set to `GC_COMPARISONS_USER_DEFINED` is any combination of restrictions allowed.
- ▸ `IV_MULTIPLE`
  Allows or forbids the definition of multiple conditions within a comparison.
- ▸ `ITS_SIGN`
  Lists the allowed condition types. The table may contain any combination of the two constant values `GC_SIGN_INCLUDE` for including conditions and `GC_SIGN_EXCLUDE` for excluding conditions.
- ▸ `ITS_OPTION`
  Lists the comparison operations that are allowed. Possible values are defined as constants `GC_OPTION_*`.

If the element is not bound, a list of valid domain values can be specified with method `SET_VALUE_LIST`. The values need to be created as Constant expression objects beforehand. Their IDs can then be passed in the table parameter `ITS_CONSTANT_ID`.

Eventually it is possible to specify the type of messages that are issued, when objects that define inconsistent values or comparisons for the element are checked for consistency. Method SET_MSG_SEVERITY has two parameters that support the following options, defined in interface IF_FDT_CONSTANTS:

- ► GC_MSG_SEVERITY_ERROR: always issue an error message
- ► GC_MSG_SEVERITY_WARNING: always issue a warning message
- ► GC_MSG_SEVERITY_NONE: issue no message at all
- ► GC_MSG_SEVERITY_UNDEFINED: default behavior which can be a mixture of all the above for different messages

5.2.3 Structures

A structure in BRFplus is simply an ordered collection of data objects. This implies that the components of a structure are self-contained data objects with their own UUID, which can also be used independently. Access to the component of a structure simply means access to the corresponding data object.

Because data objects are inherently reusable, they may in principle also be part of several structures at once. You should, however, consider that two structures using the same data object cannot be used in a function context together.

Structures can contain not only elements but also other structures and tables, which then leads to a deeply nested data object. However, a recursive nesting where structure A includes structure B that again includes structure A is not allowed.

The names of the data objects used within a structure are important with respect to data conversion. Moving data from one structure to another is only possible if each component in the source structure has an equally named, compatible counterpart in the target structure. When data objects with the same name are created for such use cases, it is recommended that you give them at least different short text descriptions to make them easily distinguishable.

Creation

A newly created structure object initially has no components. In the BRFplus Workbench, you may assemble the structure either by adding already existing data objects or by creating new ones. The corresponding buttons are depicted in Figure 5.7.

Another way to create the structure components is using binding to a DDIC structure. If the components cannot directly be altered any more, they can only be refreshed after the DDIC structure has been modified.

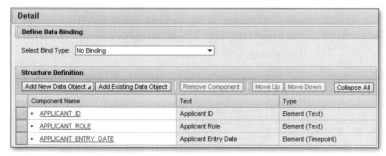

Figure 5.7 Structure Definition

Binding

When you bind a structure object to a DDIC structure, a data object is automatically generated for each structure component and is bound to the corresponding DDIC type as well. Fields of type CURR for monetary amounts and QUAN for quantities are treated specially. In DDIC structures these fields need to reference a currency field of type CUKY or unit field of type UNIT respectively. Three cases are distinguished by means of amounts:

1. Both fields, the amount field and the currency field, are contained within the bound DDIC structure. In the BRFplus structure they will be merged into a single element of type amount, which inherently consists of a corresponding number and currency field. At runtime BRFplus will recognize the correlation when values are exchanged using the DDIC structure type, for example, to and from the function context.

2. Multiple amount fields reference the same currency field within the bound DDIC structure. For each amount field, a corresponding element of type amount will be created in the bound BRFplus structure. The currency field is omitted and not explicitly available any more. Instead, each amount can theoretically have its own currency. At runtime BRFplus will recognize the one-to-many correlation for the currency field. Exporting data via the DDIC structure to BRFplus, the currency value will be distributed to all the amount fields in the BRFplus structure. Importing values from the BRFplus structure into the DDIC structure is, however, possible only if either all amounts share the same currency or if the amounts with a deviating currency are zero. Rules should therefore take care to set or alter currencies consistently. Figure 5.8 illustrates the different scenarios.

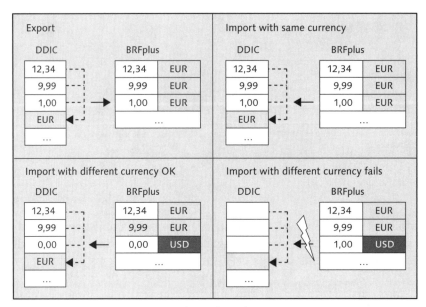

Figure 5.8 DDIC-Structure Data Exchange for Reference Types

3. The amount field references a currency field that is not contained in the bound DDIC structure but is part of an external (table) structure. In this case, an element of type amount that includes a currency field will be created for the BRFplus structure. At runtime it does not make sense to exchange data using the DDIC structure because the currency is not included. When the BRFplus structure is imported into the DDIC-structure, the currencies will be omitted. This scenario may be subject to change.

Structure API

Apart from the common data object API, interface IF_FDT_STRUCTURE allows you to set the components of the structure with method SET_ELEMENTS. The name of the method stems from SAP NetWeaver 7.0, enhancement package 1, when structures supported only elementary types.

The single table parameter ITS_ELEMENT has the line type S_ELEMENT. It consists of the position field the table is ordered by, and three component fields to separately store either an element-, structure- or table-ID. The extra fields to be used for structures or tables ensures backwards compatibility with the previous release.

5.2.4 Table

The table data object can be used to hold multiple lines of data at runtime. The line type can be defined either by an elementary or a structure data object type. By default, table data can be accessed only as a whole. To extract or manipulate single table lines and cells, you need to use expressions like the Table Operation expression, the Loop expression or also the Formula expression, described in Sections 5.5.11, 5.5.13, and 5.5.17.

When a table is added to the function signature, the data object defining the line type automatically becomes accessible as context, too. This feature makes the retrieval of table line data within rule definitions more convenient because no duplicate of the table line data object is required in addition.

Creation and Binding

The table data object has only a single property: the line type. In the BRFplus Workbench you can simply select or create an element or structure data object for that purpose. As for structures, the alternative approach is to use DDIC-binding, which will automatically create all required data objects for the line type.

In the case of a structure line type, the structure components are shown, but only editable within the structure data object itself.

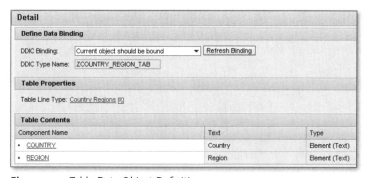

Figure 5.9 Table Data Object Definition

Table API

The API for table data objects is even more simple than that for structures. Interface `IF_FDT_TABLE` defines the single method `SET_STRUCTURE` to pass the ID of a structure or element, which shall be used as the table line type.

5.3 Rulesets

In BRFplus a ruleset object has three main tasks:

▶ It encapsulates a set of rules, but also defines under which conditions the rules shall be processed.

▶ It connects the contained rules to a specific function object, which becomes the main trigger for the rules processing.

▶ It enhances the function context with variables. Variables are additional, temporary data objects that can be accessed as context parameters within the nested rules and expressions.

At design time, the relationship between rulesets and functions is unidirectional. One or multiple rulesets can subscribe to a single function, but functions do not directly reference any ruleset. Functions need to be set up in event mode to allow rulesets to subscribe to them (see also Section 5.1.1). Changing a function object may have impact on many connected ruleset and rule definitions, whereas changing a ruleset object does not affect the referenced function object.

At runtime a function in event mode will trigger the processing of all subscribed rulesets. If multiple rulesets are involved, the order of processing can be influenced by a priority setting of the rulesets. With the default priority setting (zero), the subscribed rulesets may, however, be processed in arbitrary order. The event concept allows an easy and flexible way to enhance pre-delivered BRFplus functions. Even system functions can be extended with additional rules of storage type customizing or application data. More information on this topic is provided in Chapter 8.

5.3.1 Ruleset Header

The concepts and properties that are of importance before any rule is actually processed form the *header* of a ruleset.

A ruleset can be enabled or disabled as a whole. If the ruleset is not enabled, it will be completely skipped by the triggering function at runtime. But even if the ruleset is enabled, it can define an additional precondition besides the triggering function. If the precondition is not fulfilled, all contained rules will be skipped as well. Such a condition may, for example, be based on the passed context values or depend on the system status.

By default, rules of a ruleset can use the data objects that are defined in the assigned function signature. However, those data objects are mainly intended for external data exchange. Having multiple rules within a ruleset often requires additional data objects to store and exchange intermediate results. Rulesets therefore allow the declaration of additional data objects as *variables*. Variables can be used just like context parameters within the rules.

> **Context Parameters**
>
> Within rule, expression, or action definitions, there is no differentiation between function context or result data objects and ruleset variables. They are all referred to as context parameters.

Variables are of a temporary nature at runtime, so values can neither be read nor set from outside. Before any rule is executed, the ruleset can set an initial value for each variable by using an adequate expression. In the simplest case this can be just some constant value.

If you expect or know that multiple rulesets are assigned to the same function, you can set a priority for each of them. With the priority setting a certain processing order can be enforced. Rulesets with a high priority then usually have more impact on the outcome of the function than rulesets with a lower priority.

By default no priority—or actually priority number 0—is set. It means that the ruleset may arbitrarily be processed before or after any other rulesets. If you set a priority, the according number ban ranges from 1 to 99. Priority number 1 is actually the highest priority! This is recommended for rulesets that shall intentionally be executed before any other ruleset. Rulesets with a lower priority number are evaluated before rulesets with a higher priority number. Rulesets with the same priority are executed in an arbitrary order.

In the BRFplus Workbench the ruleset header is shown in the area between the DETAIL toolbar and the RULES section. Figure 5.10 shows the initial display of the ruleset. With button HIDE RULESET HEADER you can hide the header part.

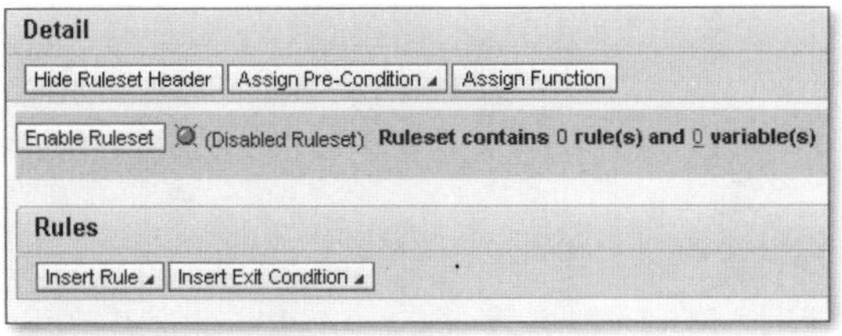

Figure 5.10   Initial Ruleset

Clicking on button ASSIGN FUNCTION, you may first select the function that will trigger the execution of the ruleset. When the ruleset is created from within a function, that function is automatically assigned to the ruleset by default. See also Section 5.1.1.

With button ASSIGN PRECONDITION you may add an additional condition that needs to be fulfilled to execute the ruleset. The condition can be defined in two ways:

► A simple condition that is based on a (context) value comparison can directly be entered.

► For other, more complex conditions, a separate expression with a Boolean result needs to be used.

Ruleset variables can be defined by clicking on the link displaying the number of variables. Or you select the menu entry MAINTAIN RULESET VARIABLES, which is contained under the menu icon on the right-hand side of the DETAIL tray. There you also find entries for other actions related to the ruleset header.

The variables are maintained in a popup window. The first section contains a list of the used data objects. Here you may simply add or remove entries. The lower section contains a list of expressions to initialize the variables. Per variable, only one expression with a corresponding result data object is allowed. For variables of type table, you can add expressions that deliver only a line of table data, using the table's structure as result data object. The table line will then simply be inserted into the table.

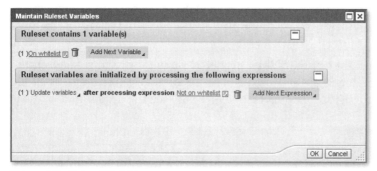

Figure 5.11 Ruleset Variables

If you want to set a specific ruleset priority that differs from the default, you need to choose menu entry ASSIGN RULESET Priority under the tray menu icon. An input field will then become available in the ruleset header area.

At the end of a ruleset definition, you must not forget to enable the ruleset as a whole by clicking on the button ENABLE RULESET in the header section. The header may then look like Figure 5.12.

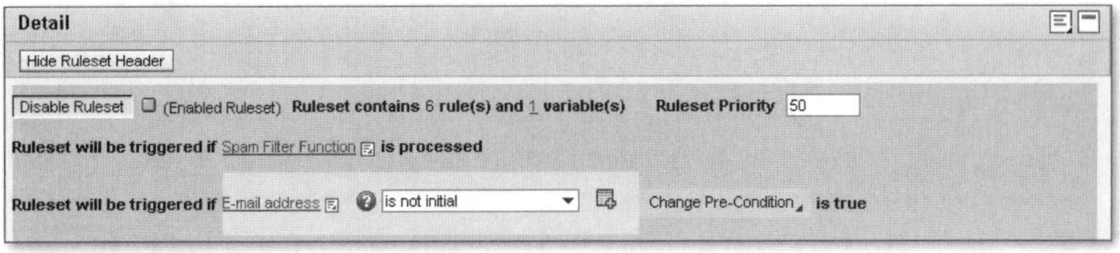

Detail

Hide Ruleset Header

Disable Ruleset ☐ (Enabled Ruleset) **Ruleset contains 6 rule(s) and 1 variable(s)** **Ruleset Priority** 50

Ruleset will be triggered if Spam Filter Function 🖻 **is processed**

Ruleset will be triggered if E-mail address 🖻 ❷ is not initial ▾ 🗔 Change Pre-Condition ◢ **is true**

Figure 5.12 Ruleset Header

5.3.2 Rules in the Ruleset

Without any rules a ruleset is, of course, still incomplete. In the RULES section of the ruleset user interface, you define an ordered list of rules and exit conditions. They will be executed top-down, one after another. Exit conditions can be regarded as special rules that allow to skip any subsequent rules and thereby end the ruleset processing.

☐ 🐜 (2) Rule: Check e-mail whitelist - Validity: 01.01.2010 - Unlimited (Time in UTC time zone)   ✏ 🗍 🗑 ⬆ ⬇ Other Operations ◢

Figure 5.13 Rule Toolbar in Rulesets

For each rule, a toolbar as shown in Figure 5.13 will be displayed. On the left-hand side it contains a short summary of the header information. From left to right the toolbar has the following content:

1. A status icon indicating whether the rule is enabled or not.

2. An optional icon may indicate that a precondition is specified for the rule.

3. A link with the position and description of the rule. Clicking this link will show or hide rule details below the toolbar. Each such detail section can be closed again with an according icon on the right-hand side. Further options to show or hide the details of all rules are available in the menu of the RULES tray.

4. The validity of the rule with respect to time

5. For rules that are not reusable, an icon to edit the rule is shown next.

6. There are icons to copy, delete, or move the rule within the list.

7. The complete rule header can be made visible and editable with the glasses icon.

8. Eventually the OTHER OPERATIONS menu includes entries that allow you to directly insert or replace rules and exit conditions at a specific position.

With the button INSERT RULE at the beginning of the RULES section you have two options to add rules to the top of the list:

1. You can select an existing, independently defined rule to be reused. For such rules you need to ensure that the data objects used by them are contained in the function context or as ruleset variables in respect. Referenced rules are displayed as links that allow navigating to the corresponding object.

2. You can create a new unnamed rule, which is only valid and changeable in the scope of the ruleset. Such rule definitions are edited inside a popup window, and a preview is directly shown in the ruleset list. To edit these rules once you have defined them, you have to click on the corresponding icon in the rule toolbar.

With the button INSERT EXIT CONDITION you can add an exit condition at the top of the list. You can either define a value range comparison for a context parameter or expression result. Or you reference any separate expression that provides a Boolean result.

Rule Header

For each rule, the ruleset stores additional settings that are relevant for the rules processing. Similar to the ruleset header, they are referred to as the *rule header*. The representation of the header in the Workbench is shown in Figure 5.14.

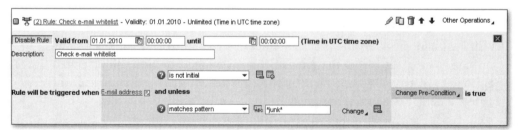

Figure 5.14   Rule Header in Rulesets

The rule header consists of the following settings:

▶ **Status**

Each rule can individually be enabled and disabled within the ruleset.

▶ **Description**

A textual description to easily identify the rule and its meaning.

▶ **Interval of validity**

Within the ruleset a rule can be made explicitly time dependent through the definition of an interval of validity. If processing of the assigned function is triggered outside such a validity period, the rule will be skipped.

▶ **Precondition**

It is even possible to define a precondition that must be fulfilled in order to actually process the rule. Such a precondition can be useful to define a more sophisticated period of validity or to prevent unnecessary execution of performance critical rules.

You can enable or disable the rule with a button at the beginning of the section. You can also enter the interval of validity and a description text. To set an optional precondition you need, however, to use the OTHER OPERATIONS menu in the rule toolbar and select entry ASSIGN PRECONDITION.

Example

Before going into details about rules in Section 5.4, let us have a look at an example. Figure 5.15 shows a ruleset that implements a very basic email filter.

Figure 5.15   Ruleset Example

The function and the ruleset shall provide a classification, whether an email is spam, not spam, or of unknown/ambiguous type. The sender's email address and the email text are available for analysis as function context.

The first rule of the ruleset will unconditionally classify the mail to be of unknown type by default. The second rule checks whether the sender of the email is on a "white" list of trusted mail addresses. If this is the case, the classification is set to "no spam," and the processing is ended by the subsequent exit condition.

The rule in the fourth step will check the opposite: whether the sender is on a "black" list of untrustworthy addresses. If this is the case, the classification is set to "spam" and again an exit condition will end the processing in the next step.

Last but not least, the email text will be analyzed and the classification is either set to "spam" or left as "unknown."

Assuming that the email whitelist or blacklist in this example might become inconsistent and require maintenance, it would be easy to deactivate the according rules temporarily.

5.3.3 Deferred Ruleset Processing

Exit conditions are typically intended to stop the ruleset processing when a valid result could be determined and no further rules are required for processing. However, there may also be use cases where the evaluation of subsequent rules is not possible due to some temporary constraints, e.g., missing data. When the constraints do not exist any longer, the rules processing could continue. In another scenario, the evaluation of some rules might be not time critical but performance critical and should then rather be executed by a batch process. In both cases, it is desirable to keep the current state of the rule processing and to be able to continue with it at a later point in time. This is exactly what deferred ruleset processing makes possible.

If deferred ruleset processing is enabled, an exit condition of a ruleset can not only quit the processing, but it can also be set up to remember the current processing state, including the values of all context data objects. This information can even be stored to the database and be used later on to restart the ruleset again. Two distinct points of entry for a restarted ruleset are possible:

▶ The ruleset is restarted *before* the exit condition. The exit condition is evaluated again and the processing of the ruleset may possibly be deferred yet another time at the same position.

▶ The ruleset is restarted *after* the exit condition. Processing of the ruleset simply continues with the next following rule or exit condition in this case.

Because deferred ruleset processing requires special calls to the BRFplus API, it needs to be enabled on the application level. Consequently, this feature is available only for all or no rulesets within an application. In the BRFplus Workbench, the corresponding setting can be changed on the MISCELLANEOUS tab of the application UI. See also Section 3.4.2.

Figure 5.16 Deferred Ruleset Processing

When deferred processing has been enabled, the following additional options for exit conditions become available in the ruleset UI, as illustrated in Figure 5.16:

▶ DO NOT INTERRUPT RULESET AT THIS EXIT: This is the standard exit condition behavior.

▶ INTERRUPT RULESET AT THIS EXIT: The ruleset can be restarted after the exit condition.

▶ RE-START RULESET BEFORE THIS EXIT: The ruleset can be restarted before the exit condition.

5.3.4 Ruleset API

A ruleset is represented by interface IF_FDT_RULESET. Table 5.12 summarizes the methods that deal with properties of the ruleset header.

Method	Description
SET_FUNCTION_RESTRICTION	Assigns the triggering function to the ruleset. Simply a valid function ID needs to be passed.
SET_RULESET_SWITCH	The ruleset can be switched on and off (or rather be enabled or disabled) with the passed Boolean value.
SET_RULESET_VARIABLES	An ordered list of data object IDs can be set that extends the context with temporary variables.
SET_RULESET_INITIALIZATIONS	A list of expressions that will be evaluated prior to the rules. The result data objects of the expressions must be variables of the ruleset.

Table 5.12 Ruleset Header API

Method	Description
SET_RULESET_PRIORITY	Sets a specific priority for the ruleset. Allowed values are 0 (no priority) and 1 (highest) to 99 (lowest).
SET_RULESET_CONDITION	Assigns an optional precondition to the ruleset. One may either pass the ID of a Boolean element or of an expression with Boolean result in parameter IV_CONDITION_ID. Alternatively, a value range comparison can be set using parameter IS_CONDITION_RANGE. More details on such a range definition are provided in Section 5.5.3.

Table 5.12 Ruleset Header API (Cont.)

The list of rules and exit conditions are set with method SET_RULES. The desired rules must have been created as separate rule objects beforehand. The table parameter ITS_RULE is of the structure type S_RULE, which consists of the fields shown in Table 5.13:

Field	Description
POSITION	Defines the position of the entry in a rule list in ascending order.
SWITCH	Indicates whether the rule shall be enabled or disabled in general.
VALID_FROM	Represents an optional timestamp that limits the validity of the rule. The rule will be evaluated only if the processing timestamp is after this timestamp.
VALID_TO	Represents an optional timestamp that limits the validity of the rule. The rule will be evaluated only if the processing timestamp is before this timestamp.
CONDITION_ID	Contains the ID of an expression or elementary context parameter with Boolean (result) type, which serves either as a rule precondition or as an exit condition.
CONDITION_RANGE	Can be used instead of the CONDITION_ID and depicts a value range comparison, that serves then as precondition or exit condition. More details on such a range definition are given in Section 5.5.3.
EXIT_RULESET	Indicates whether this rule entry represents an exit condition. When set to "true," no rule will actually be processed but the ruleset is exited in case the condition is fulfilled.
RULE_ID	Contains the ID of the rule object to be processed. The field is (only) required, in case EXIT_RULESET is "false."

Table 5.13 Structure IF_FDT_RULESET=>S_RULE

Field	Description
RESTART_OPTION	Indicates for exit-condition entries whether the ruleset can be restarted. Three values available as constants are possible: GC_NO_RESTART: **For standard exit conditions.** GC_RESTART_BEFORE_EXIT: **The ruleset can be restarted just before the exit condition.** GC_RESTART_AFTER_EXIT: **The ruleset can be restarted directly after the exit condition.**
FUNCTION_ID	This field must not be used any longer and is only relevant for legacy usages.

Table 5.13 Structure IF_FDT_RULESET=>S_RULE (Cont.)

For convenience there are also the two methods ADD_RULE and DELETE_RULE available. They will not exchange the whole list of rules but rather modify it by adding or deleting some entries.

5.4 Rules

Even though rules are technically similar to expressions, they are treated as an object type in BRFplus. This is mainly because rules allow some special kind of operations and can thus be used only within rulesets and some specific expressions like the LOOP expression.

A rule basically implements an IF <condition> THEN <do operations> ELSE <do operations> logic. So a rule definition consists of three parts: the condition and possibly two lists of operations. The first list of operations is processed if the condition evaluates to true (or if no condition is specified at all). The other list of operations is optional and will be processed if the condition evaluates to false.

The operations comprise either the processing of nested rules and actions or the change of context values. In detail the following operations are possible:

▶ Reset a context data object to its type-specific, initial value.

▶ Set a value for a context data object.

▶ Exchange values among context data objects.

▶ Process an expression to determine a new value for a context data object.

▶ Process a nested rule.

▶ Execute an action to perform some other (external) changes.

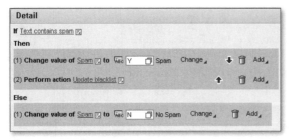

Figure 5.17   Rule Example

Figure 5.17 shows the screenshot of a rule example in the Workbench. In the UI you may first define the rule condition next to the If statement. In the context menu you have the following options:

▶ USE VALUE RANGE FROM
Allows you to directly enter a value range comparison for a context parameter.

▶ SELECT CONDITION
Allows you to select an existing expression result data object or context data object of Boolean type.

▶ CREATE EXPRESSION
Allows you to create a new expression that must have a Boolean result value.

In case you have already set a condition, you can also choose the following two options:

▶ ADD MORE CONDITIONS
Directly embeds a Boolean expression and thereby allows you to concatenate additional conditions logically. Details are available in Section 5.5.5.

▶ REMOVE CONDITION
Allows you to remove an existing condition. No condition corresponds to a condition that is always true.

The operations to be performed if the condition evaluates to true or false can be defined under the THEN and the ELSE statement the same way. Next to each defined operation, you will find clickable icons to change the order of the operations or to remove an existing operation. With the ADD menu on the right-hand side, you can append or insert additional operations:

▶ INITIALIZE CONTEXT VALUE
Reset the value of a context data object.

- ASSIGN VALUE TO CONTEXT
  To set either a value for a context data object or to take over the value from another data object. For the latter case, you need to replace the value with the intended data object using the CHANGE menu.

- PROCESS EXPRESSION
  Select or create an expression to be processed. The expression will set a new value for its result data object.

- PERFORM ACTION
  Select or create an action to be performed.

- PROCESS RULE
  Select or create a rule to be processed.

The first two types of operations are self-contained within the rule and only allow some basic data manipulations. For the other two types. additional expression or action objects are required. They unleash the full potential of rules in BRFplus.

Rule API

The API for rule objects, exposed by interface IF_FDT_RULE, has been enhanced greatly compared to the previous release. Some methods, which still exist for legacy usages, required a complete redesign of the signature. Therefore, new methods that enhance or replace the previous ones are now available. Table 5.14 provides an overview of the interface methods.

Method	Description
SET_CONDITION	Sets the rule condition using an expression or data object with Boolean result.
SET_CONDITION_RANGE	Sets the rule condition using a value range comparison (see also Section 5.5.3). A condition with method SET_CONDITION must not have been set yet, and vice versa.
SET_TRUE_ACTION_EXTENDED	Sets the operations to be executed when the rule condition evaluates to true. Multiple lists of actions, expressions, nested rules, data object, and value assignments can be passed. This method is a replacement for SET_TRUE_ACTION.
SET_FALSE_ACTION_EXTENDED	Sets the operations to be executed when the rule condition evaluates to false. This method supports the same parameters as method SET_TRUE_ACTION_EXTENDED and is a replacement for SET_FALSE_ACTION.

Table 5.14 Methods of Interface IF_FDT_RULE

213

Method	Description
CLEAR	Clears parts of the rule definition. For each property that can be defined by a SET method, there is a Boolean importing parameter to indicate whether the property shall be cleared.
SET_TRUE_ACTION	Sets an action object to be processed when the rule condition evaluates to true. It is recommended to use method SET_TRUE_ACTION_EXTENDED instead.
SET_FALSE_ACTION	Sets an action object to be processed when the rule condition evaluates to false. It is recommended to use method SET_FALSE_ACTION_EXTENDED instead.
COPY	Convenient method for copying a rule object non-deeply (deprecated). The method exists only for legacy reasons and implicitly performs if_fdt_transaction~copy(iv_deep = abap_false).

Table 5.14 Methods of Interface IF_FDT_RULE (Cont.)

The methods ending with *EXTENDED to set or get a list of rule operations use the same table parameter types. The used table types are:

▶ T_ACTION
A list of action objects to process.

▶ T_RULE
A list of nested rule objects to process.

▶ T_EXPRESSION
A list of expressions to process.

▶ T_DATA_OBJECT_ASSIGNMENT
A list of source and target data objects. The value of the source data object will be applied to the target data object.

▶ T_VALUE_ASSIGNMENT
A list of context data objects and values. At runtime the value will be applied to the data object at. An additional initialization flag can alternatively indicate that the context parameter shall be cleared.

All table types include the field POSITION. It defines the position for the operation within the concatenated list of *all* operations with all types.

The last three types include an additional field CHANGE_MODE. This field serves to modify the way values are applied to the context. The following constant values are applicable:

▶ GC_CHANGE_MODE_UDPATE

This is the default. A new value is set for the data object in the context and replaces any previous value.

▶ GC_CHANGE_MODE_INSERT

This option can be used for table or table structure types. The provided value is inserted into the corresponding context table.

▶ GC_CHANGE_MODE_NONE

This option must only be used in combination with actions or expressions. The according result is ignored and no context value is changed. The option is mainly intended for actions that can only return their ID as result. Some expression types like the Procedure Call expression may, however, also implicitly change context data, independent of the result data object.

5.5   Expressions

Expressions—together with the derived actions—form the building blocks of rules. They are available in a multitude of types that define the computational power of BRFplus. Each expression type is a self-contained unit with a well-defined logic. Table 5.15 lists all expression types available with the standard BRFplus shipment. Other SAP applications may provide additional, specialized expression and action types.

Expression Type	Description
Boolean	Implements Boolean arithmetic for any number of operands. All combinations with logical AND, OR and NOT are possible.
BRMS Connector	Connects to an external Business Rule Management System (BRMS) like the SAP NetWeaver BRM.
Case	Maps input values to a defined set of output values or actions
Constant	Simply returns a static, constant value.
DB Lookup	Analyzes or selects data from the database.
Decision Table	Sequentially processes a table of conditions and results. It returns either the first row or all rows where the conditions match.
Decision Tree	Traverses a binary tree, which consists of inner nodes carrying conditions and leaf nodes carrying the results.
Dynamic	Processes any other expression that can dynamically be determined by its ID.
Formula	Allows the calculation of formulas using a wide range of mathematical and logical functions and operators.

Table 5.15 Standard Expression Types

Expression Type	Description
Function Call	Calls another BRFplus function and returns its result.
Loop	Repeats a sequence of rules.
Procedure Call	Calls either the static method of an ABAP class or a function module to determine a result value. It also allows you to update multiple context parameters at once.
Random	Either returns a random value or indicates whether a specified probability was met.
Search Tree	Traverses a non-binary tree in various modes. The tree consists of nodes that may carry conditions and results as well.
Table Operation	Supports a wide range of operations on table type data.
XSL Transformation	Performs an XSL transformation to determine a result.

Table 5.15 Standard Expression Types (Cont.)

In general, expression types calculate or derive a result value, which usually depends on some input data. Besides fixed values, the input may be provided by context parameters, nested expressions, or external data.

Context Parameter Selection

Data objects that are used in the function signature or as ruleset variables are referred to as "context parameters" in the user interface. Using data objects as input for expressions usually makes sense only if the data objects are actually context parameters. Otherwise, no value can be supplied at runtime and the processing will fail. In the expression UIs, it is thus often possible to select context parameters only via a context search dialog.

If an expression is referenced by a single function or ruleset, the context search dialog will take the relevant context parameters into account. If an expression is, however, referenced by multiple functions or rulesets, the context search dialog will show only data objects that are included in the intersection of all according contexts. Only those data objects ensure that the expression can be processed by all the functions and rulesets.

If an expression is eventually not yet referenced by a function or ruleset, no context parameters are available. The context search dialog will issue a warning message in this case and take all data objects of the current application into account. The user must ensure that the chosen data object becomes a context parameter in all functions and rulesets that reference the expression later on.

An expression can be considered to be an instance of an expression type. On the one hand, it behaves according to the expression type's logic. On the other hand, it defines the data and input to be actually used. For example, the Constant expression type provides the simple logic to return some fixed value. But each Constant expression (instance) defines the value that will actually be returned. Describing an expression therefore automatically implies describing the expression's type.

All expressions have one property in common—the result data object. It primarily defines the result type of the expression. When used as context parameter, the result data object can also implicate the storage of the result value at runtime. The expression can then, for example, be used to initialize or update a ruleset variable.

Expressions can directly be assigned to functions in functional mode as top expression. When the function is processed, the expression—together with its nested expressions—will be evaluated and the result is returned. When embedded into rulesets or rules, expressions are typically evaluated only under certain conditions. Expressions with Boolean result type may, however, also be used to define such conditions.

5.5.1 Expression API

All expression types define an ABAP OO interface that extends the common interface IF_FDT_EXPRESSION and adds the expression type specific parts (see also Section 3.2.2). Technically, actions and rules are only specialized subtypes of expressions. Therefore, the interface defines the two Boolean attributes MV_ACTION and MV_RULE that indicate whether an expression actually implements an action or rule type (see Table 5.16).

The individual expression or action type is reflected by an ID in the attribute MV_EXPRESSION_TYPE_ID. BRFplus uses a separate object type "expression type" to store metadata information for an expression type. The expression type ID is therefore actually the ID of a corresponding expression type object. This concept allows customers and partners to create their own expression types for specialized of more sophisticated use cases. For all standard expression types that are available in BRFplus, the IDs are available as constants of interface IF_FDT_CONSTANTS. They share the common name pattern GC_EXTY_*.

Attribute	Description
MV_EXPRESSION_TYPE_ID	Universal ID of the underlying expression type.
MV_RULE	Indicates if the expression is actually a rule.
MV_ACTION	Indicates if the expression is actually an action.

Table 5.16 Attributes of Interface IF_FDT_EXPRESSION

New expression objects can be created with the factory method IF_FDT_FACTORY~GET_EXPRESSION. In parameter IV_EXPRESSION_TYPE_ID the ID of the desired expression type has to be passed in this case.

To retrieve an existing expression, you can use the same method but need to pass its object ID in parameter IV_ID. The returned instance can be cast to the interface of the corresponding expression type.

Expressions have only one property in common—the result data object. Consequently, interface IF_FDT_EXPRESSION provides only the setter-method SET_RESULT_DATA_OBJECT, which simply accepts the ID of the data object to be used. However, depending on the expression's type, only specific data object types or even element types may be allowed.

Expressions can typically nest other expressions as input. The setting of nested expressions for specific purposes is expression type-specific and can only be done via the corresponding sub-interfaces. But each expression type implements method GET_USED_EXPRESSIONS and thereby provides a list of all nested expressions. A timestamp can optionally be passed to get nested expressions of older versions.

If an expression is already used by functions or rulesets, the accessible context data objects can be retrieved with method GET_CONTEXT_DATA_OBJECTS. The method provides a list of data objects that are either used as context or as variable in all those functions or respectively rulesets. The list can further be filtered to include only context data objects that are actually used by the expression itself.

The expression interface declares several more methods that impose the common way expressions are processed. These methods are of interest when you want to define your own expression types. Table 5.17 therefore briefly summarizes all methods of interface IF_FDT_EXPRESSION.

Method	Description
SET_RESULT_DATA_OBJECT	Sets the data object to be used as result.
GET_USED_EXPRESSIONS	Returns a list of all used expressions, optionally for a specific timestamp.
GET_CONTEXT_DATA_OBJECTS	Returns a list of data objects that are included in the intersecting context of all functions and rulesets, which are using the expression.
SET_CONTEXT_DATA_OBJECTS	Obsolete
GET_EXPRESSION_TYPE	Returns the underlying expression type ID.
PROCESS	Triggers processing of the expression in interpretation mode.
IS_GENERATING	Indicates whether the expression type supports code generation.
GENERATE_PROCESS	Generates source code for processing

Table 5.17 Methods of Interface IF_FDT_EXPRESSION

The following sections describe the various expression types that are available with the standard shipment of BRFplus. The basic Constant and Value Range expression types are explained first. The other types follow in alphabetical order.

5.5.2 Constant Expressions

The *Constant* expression type is the most basic, standard expression type. It simply returns a fixed value. The type of the value is specified by the result data object, which must actually be an element. Structures and tables are not supported.

A typical constant would, for example, be the mathematical value Pi (π = 3,14159...). It must be defined only once and can be reused by other expressions for comparisons and calculations. The result data object of a Constant expression must typically define only its element type. Therefore, the standard data objects of type element in application FDT_SYSTEM can mostly be used for that purpose.

Creation

When you create a Constant expression in the *BRFplus Workbench*, you can enter the Constant type and value directly in the creation dialog. An example dialog is shown in Figure 5.18.

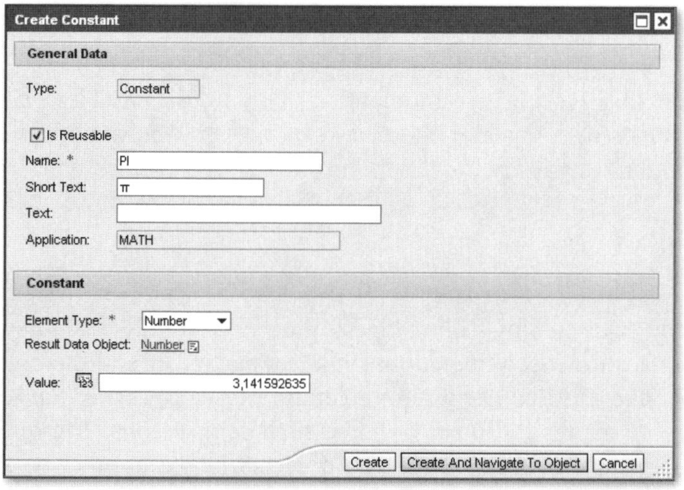

Figure 5.18 Constant Expression Creation

If you simply choose an ELEMENT TYPE, the corresponding standard data object of application FDT_SYSTEM will automatically be used as RESULT DATA OBJECT. But you can also select any other data object, which may then impose restrictions on the allowed values and/or comparisons.

In case the underlying element uses a list of domain values, value help (also called `F4` help) is available for the input field. Pressing `Enter` on such an input field checks the entered data against the domain value list. If a descriptive text is available for a domain value, it is shown next to the input field. Currency and unit fields of amount and quantity values respectively are always bound to a domain. The domain is defined through standard customizing in the client.

> **Search Helps**
>
> The result data object of the Constant expression may be bound to a DDIC type with an assigned search help definition. The search help will then automatically be attached to the corresponding input field in the BRFplus UI. However, only elementary search helps are supported. Search helps that defined on the level of a DDIC structure are ignored.

Constant Expression API

The Constant expression API defined by interface IF_FDT_CONSTANT contains only method SET_CONSTANT_VALUE to set the constant value. The passed data must be compatible with the result data object of the Constant expression. If no result data object has been set, the method will automatically derive a matching element type from the data and set the corresponding standard element of application FDT_SYS-TEM as result data object.

To pass data in a compatible way, it is recommended that you use variables that are of the corresponding ELEMENT*-type of interface IF_FDT_TYPES. You should also keep in mind, that amount, quantity, or timepoint data is of structure type in BRFplus.

5.5.3 Value Range Expressions

Conditions are typically expressed by value range comparisons in BRFplus. They perform one or multiple comparison operations on a test parameter and thereby check whether the parameter value lies within a certain range. The *Value Range expression type* is the very expression type to define such comparisons. The test parameter of the Value Range expression is a data object, which can either be a context parameter or an expression result. The result data object must always be of Boolean type.

In Section 5.2.2 all the comparison operations that BRFplus supports are listed. For tables and structures, it is possible only to check whether they are initial (empty).

The range comparison may have of two lists of comparison operations, one for including and one for excluding conditions. The conditions in each list are implicitly concatenated by a logical OR. When processed, at least one of the including conditions needs to be fulfilled and none of the excluding conditions may be fulfilled in order for the whole range comparison evaluates to true.

Figure 5.19 shows an example of a Value Range expression with multiple conditions. It uses the standard text element of application FDT_SYSTEM as test parameter. Including (If ...) and excluding (and unless...) conditions are defined as well.

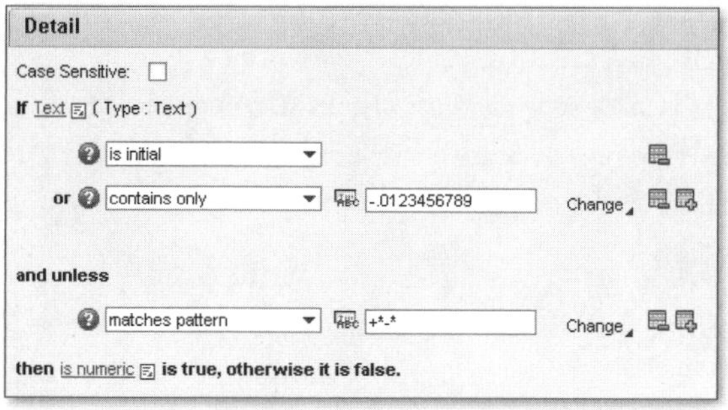

Figure 5.19   Value Range Expression Example

Each condition consists of a comparison operator together with the required comparison parameters. Some comparisons such as in between require two comparison parameters to define an interval. Comparisons like equals require only a single comparison parameter, and implicit comparisons like is initial require even no comparison parameter at all. A comparison parameter is often just a static value. It is, however, also possible to use dynamic comparison parameters in the form of context parameters and nested expressions.

The element used as test parameter may allow only certain kinds of comparisons. On the one hand, the element's type may impose implicit restrictions on the supported operators. On the other hand, the element definition can explicitly declare comparison constraints (see also Section 5.2.2):

▶ It can limit the list of available comparison operators.

▶ It can allow including or excluding conditions only.

▶ It can permit the definition of a single comparison only.

For test parameters of type text, the Value Range expression allows you to specify an additional restriction itself. It can specify whether comparison operations like equals are performed case sensitive or not.

In general, the Value Range expression is limited to a single test parameter, which is suitable for most use cases. To define conditions for multiple test parameters, you can use the Boolean expressions described in Section 5.5.5.

Value Range Expression API

The interface IF_FDT_RANGE for Value Range expressions offers the methods listed in Table 5.18.

Method	Description
SET_TEST_PARAMETER	Sets the data object or expression to be used as test parameter.
SET_RANGE	Defines the value range as a list of comparison operations.
SET_CASE_SENSITIVITY	Switches case sensitivity for comparison operations on or off. This flag is only relevant for test parameters of type text.
SET_CONVERSION	Obsolete
COMPARE_TO_RANGE	Required only for special use cases. The method compares the range to another Value Range expression using the same test parameter.

Table 5.18   Methods of Interface IF_FDT_RANGE

First, the ID for the test parameter should be defined with method SET_TEST_PARAMETER because the validity of the comparisons depends on it.

The actual range comparisons can be set up through a list of respective condition declarations with method SET_RANGE. Technically an ordered table of structure type S_RANGE is passed, which comprises the fields shown in Table 5.19.

Range Field	Description
POSITION	Defines the order of the entries that might influence processing speed.
SIGN	Specifies whether the entry represents an including or excluding condition. Allowed are the corresponding constant values GC_SIGN_INCLUDE and GC_SIGN_EXCLUDE.
OPTION	Contains the comparison operation to be performed. Allowed values are available as constants GC_OPTION_*. All available operations are listed in Table 5.9.
LOW R_LOW_VALUE	Represents the default comparison parameter. For intervals it defines the lower boundary. Either a referenced object or a direct value can be set.
HIGH R_HIGH_VALUE	Represents an optional second comparison parameter for the upper boundary of intervals. Either a referenced object or a direct value can be set.

Table 5.19   Fields of Value Range Conditions

Technically the Value Range expression supports all comparison operators that are available in ABAP. The fields SIGN, OPTION, LOW, and HIGH are semantically equivalent to the fields of ABAP range types. For the latter two fields, the paradigm for constant values is applicable. Constant values can directly be passed be means of data references with the respective fields R_LOW_VALUE and R_HIGH_VALUE.

Comparisons of the example shown in Figure 5.19 would result in the condition list shown in Table 5.20 below.

POSITION	SIGN	OPTION	LOW	R_LOW_VALUE	HIGH	R_HIGH_VALUE
1	I	I1				
2	I	CO		->{-.0123456789}		
3	E	CP		->{+*-*}		

Table 5.20 Condition List for the Example in Figure 5.19

5.5.4 Direct Values and Value Ranges

Constant values and value range comparisons are widely used in BRFplus. They are typically not reused but defined specifically for a single expression only. If all values and value ranges were defined as distinct expressions, the database would be flooded with thousands or millions of individual objects. This would negatively impact performance, memory consumption, and required database space as well.

To prevent such a scenario, almost all expression types allow integrating values and value range comparisons directly. Such definitions behave like unnamed Constant or respectively Value Range expressions, but their data is stored together with the other data of the using expression. In the Workbench, the integrated values and comparisons can directly be entered where needed. They are thus also referred to as "direct" values and value ranges in the following.

Figure 5.20 shows a Boolean expression with multiple value range comparisons. In each line a separate, direct value range is displayed. The comparisons are based on different context parameters with different element types. Thus, you can also see how different types of values are represented in the UI.

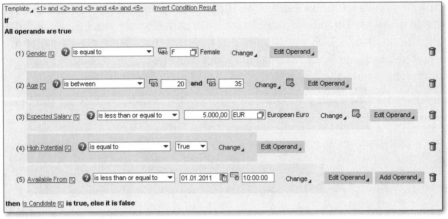

Figure 5.20 Direct Value Range Example

Direct Value and Value Range API

If an expression type can integrate direct values and value ranges, this is reflected in the signatures of its interface methods. The methods have typically equivalent but mutually exclusive parameters to set or get values and value ranges. Alternatively, the methods may use structured parameters that have equivalent but mutually excusive fields.

▶ One field or parameter is typically of type IF_FDT_TYPES=>ID and refers to the ID of a referenced object. The referenced object *might* be an explicit Constant or Value Range expression. It can, however, also be any other adequate expression or context data object.

▶ The other fields or parameters allow you to pass a value or value range directly:

  ▶ For values, the type REF TO DATA is used so that any data can be passed by reference. A data reference <dref> can be retrieved from an existing variable <dobj> with the ABAP statement GET REFERENCE OF <dobj> INTO <dref>.

  ▶ For value ranges, the type IF_FDT_RANGE=>TS_RANGE or a similar type is used. The value range data can thus be assembled or retrieved just like for a Value Range expression.

Method SET_OPERANDS of interface IF_FDT_BOOLEAN serves as a good example. It uses up to four parameter pairs like IV_FIRST_OPERAND_ID and IV_FIRST_OPERAND_RANGE to set the operands of a Boolean expression. An operand can consequently either be an object that provides a Boolean value, or it can be a direct value range comparison.

Referenced objects can usually be mixed with direct values or value ranges. When you retrieve a property of an expression or action, you might therefore have to consider multiple parameters or structure fields. This is especially the case when a property consists of a list of entries.

The content of a Decision Table expression is, for example, defined by a list of table cell entries. A cell entry is reflected by a structure with the following fields: COL_NO, ROW_NO, EXPRESSION_ID, R_VALUE and TS_RANGE. While the first two fields are required to define the cell position, only one of the other three fields has to be set to define the cell content. The cell content can consequently be determined *either* by a referenced object *or* by a direct value *or* by a direct value range. All three fields must be checked to find out which one is actually used.

5.5.5 Boolean Expressions

The *Boolean expression* type can be used to logically concatenate multiple Boolean values or conditions in respect. Consequently, the result of the expression is also of Boolean type.

The expression uses a template string that defines the structure of a logical expression. The string can consist of the following items, which must be used in a syntactically correct order:

▶ <#> — Placeholders for operands. For # any number from 1 to 99 can be used in ascending order.

▶ AND, OR, NOT — Boolean operators

▶ (,) — Brackets to determine the order of evaluation.

The expression provides some predefined, basic templates such as <1> and <2> or (<1> or <2>) and <3>. The operands can be any Boolean element or expression of Boolean result type. Value range comparisons can directly be embedded as operands.

Definition

When you define a Boolean expression in the BRFplus Workbench you should first select a template from the corresponding TEMPLATE link menu. You can choose among the predefined templates or select the entry CHOOSE YOUR OWN TEMPLATE. In the latter case, the popup window shown in Figure 5.21 will be opened, where you can freely enter any template string. With the CHECK button you can check whether the template string is syntactically correct.

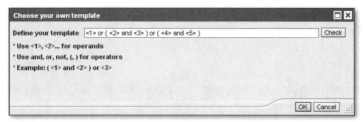

Figure 5.21 Boolean Expression Template

The logical formula defined by the template will be reflected in the UI. Figure 5.22 illustrates an example definition for the template of Figure 5.21. You can edit the chosen template any time by clicking on the proper link.

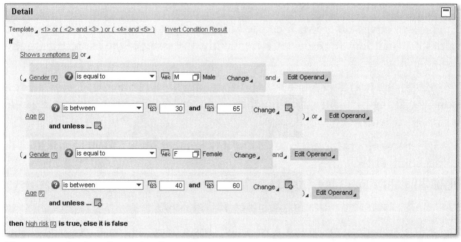

Figure 5.22 Boolean Expression Example

Each operand of the template can be edited within a separate line. You can use Boolean elements, expressions with Boolean result, or you can directly enter value range comparisons. Menu EDIT OPERAND at the right-hand side of each line allows you to change the operand any time later.

Sometimes it is easier to express a condition in the negative. With the link INVERT CONDITION RESULT the whole condition can be enclosed by a NOT operator to invert the expression result.

In case you have entered a free-style template, the logical formula is displayed in an extended mode. You can then directly modify the formula by adding or remove conditions and brackets via additional menu entries.

Boolean Expression API

Interface IF_FDT_BOOLEAN represents the Boolean expression type. The methods of the interface are summarized in Table 5.21.

Method	Description
SET_OPERATION	Specifies the Boolean operation.
SET_OPERANDS	Specifies the operands for predefined operations.
SET_USER_DEFINED_BOOLEAN	Sets an arbitrary, user-defined Boolean operation with according operands.

Table 5.21 Methods of Interface IF_FDT_BOOLEAN

To define a Boolean expression you first need to specify the mode of operation with method SET_OPERATION. (In the UI this mode is set by choosing one of the predefined templates.) Parameter IV_OPERATION can take one of the constant values, which are listed in Table 5.22. Parameter IV_INVERT can be used to encapsulate the chosen operation with a logical NOT.

Operation	Template	Group
GC_OPERATION_A_AND_B	<1> and <2>	Static
GC_OPERATION_A_OR_B	<1> or <2>	
GC_OPERATION_A_AND_B_AND_C	<1> and <2> and <3>	
GC_OPERATION_A_OR_B_OR_C	<1> or <2> or <3>	
GC_OPERATION_A_AND_B_OR_C	(<1> and <2>) or <3>	
GC_OPERATION_A_OR_B_AND_C	(<1> or <2>) and <3>	
GC_OPERATION_ALL_AND	<1> and <2> and ... and <#>	Dynamic
GC_OPERATION_ALL_OR	<2> or <2> or ... or <#>	
GC_OPERATION_USER_DEFINED	Any template	User-defined

Table 5.22 Boolean Expression Operations

The modes of operation can be assigned into three different categories: static, dynamic, and user-defined.

Static operations use a fixed template with a fixed set of operands. The operands can be set with method SET_OPERANDS using the corresponding parameters:

▶ IV_[FIRST|SECOND|THIRD]_OPERAND_ID for data objects or expressions.

▶ IS_[FIRST|SECOND|THIRD]_OPERAND_RANGE for direct value range definitions.

The parameters IV_[FIRST|SECOND|THIRD]_INVERT allow to invert the value of operands by a logical NOT.

Dynamic operations use a template with fixed operators but allow an arbitrary number of up to 99 operands. The operands can be set with method SET_OPERANDS using parameter ITS_ANDOR_OPERAND. It is a table of type S_ANDOR_OPERAND with the fields:

▶ POSITION
The position number of the operand within the template.

▶ ID
A Boolean element or expressions to be used as operand.

▶ S_RANGE
A direct value range definition to be alternatively used as operand.

▶ INVERT
A flag to use the inverse value of the operand via an implied logical NOT operation.

User defined operations allow templates with an arbitrary combination of operators and operands. The complete logical formula can be set with method SET_USER_DEFINED_BOOLEAN. Its importing table parameter IT_USER_DEFINED_TOKEN has the following structure:

▶ TOKEN
Represents a Boolean operator or an opening or closing parenthesis. The allowed values are defined as constants GC_TOKEN_*. If the field is left empty, the table entry represents an operand by one of the other two fields.

▶ OPERAND_ID
Defines a Boolean element or expression to be used as operand.

▶ S_RANGE
Defines a value range comparison to be used as operand.

The method automatically analyzes whether the table entries represent a syntactically correct Boolean expression. The exporting parameter EV_SYNTAX_ERROR is set accordingly.

For legacy reasons, the parameter IV_USER_DEFINED_BOOLEAN is also still supported. The Boolean expression can thereby be defined as a string of concatenated tokens and object UUIDs. However, value range comparisons cannot be used in this format. The string will internally be parsed and translated into the table format.

5.5.6 BRMS Connector Expression

A BRMS connector expression allows you to call rules that are hosted by an external rules engine. This may be required, for example, if data or actions outside the ABAP stack need to be considered. The expression also facilitates using features of other BRMS products that BRFplus is not (yet) capable of. When used as the top expression of a function, the BRMS connector expression can be used as a simple wrapper of an external rule.

The connection to the external BRMS is accomplished with the help of a remote-enabled function module. BRFplus provides two function modules for that purpose. One (`FDT_NW_BRMS_CONNECTOR_EXECUTE`) is specifically designed for connecting to the SAP NetWeaver BRM. The other (`FDT_EXT_BRMS_CONNECTOR_EXECUTE`) can be used for other third-party BRMSs. It provides a generic connection to a Java engine by means of the SAP Java Connector (JCo). However, as a prerequisite, a remote function call (RFC) destination with connection type TCP/IP needs to be set up with Transaction SM59.

For data exchange, a common business vocabulary is required that can be understood by both BRFplus and the external rule engine. For that purpose, an appropriate XML Schema Document (XSD) can be generated. It is based on a list of context parameters that serve as input for the called rule and on a result data object for the output of the called rule. The result data object is usually identical to the result data object of the expression. BRMS-specific connection parameters that are required to access the intended rule(s) can be set up with a generic list of name/value pairs.

At runtime, the BRMS connector expression communicates with the external rules engine, using the connection parameters. An XML document that is formatted according to the XSD will be conveyed to the connected BRMS. It contains actual values for the context parameters and a formal placeholder for the result. The external rules engine reads the context information, evaluates the relevant rules, and populates the XML document with the result data. The XML document is then sent back to BRFplus and the BRMS Connector expression maps its content to the expression's result data object.

The setup of a BRMS connector expression in the workbench is illustrated in Figure 5.23. With the CONNECTION TYPE setting you can define whether you want to connect to an SAP NetWeaver BRM or to a different external rules engine. The FUNCTION MODULE is automatically determined, but you have to specify an existing RFC DESTINATION that can be used for the connection.

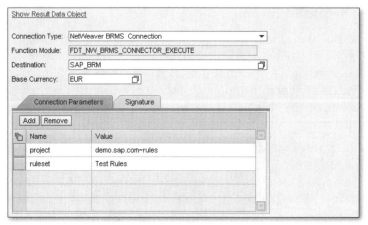

Figure 5.23 BRMS Connector Expression

The field BASE CURRENCY is optional. It may be used if parameters of type amount are passed to the external BRMS. In case a base currency is specified, the amounts will be converted to that common currency before they are transferred.

On the CONNECTION PARAMETERS tab, a list of BRMS-specific name/value pairs can be defined. They must provide the information that is required to establish the connection to the remote BRMS and to address the desired rule(s). For the SAP NetWeaver BRM, a "project" and a "ruleset" have to be specified. On the SIGNATURE tab shown in Figure 5.24, you can map the CONTEXT and RESULT of the external rule to data objects and expressions of BRFplus.

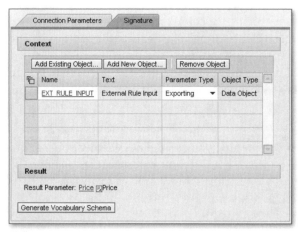

Figure 5.24 BRMS Connector Expression — Signature

The list of parameters in the CONTEXT area usually serves as input for the called rules only. The default PARAMETER TYPE "Exporting" marks the parameter as read-only, so that their content will not be altered. Therefore, context data objects as well as expressions can be used as parameters in this case. The PARAMETER TYPE "Changing" is allowed for data objects only. The remotely called rule may change the content of such parameters, in addition to the provided result.

The RESULT PARAMETER must be a data object that can store the result of the called rule(s). It is usually identical to the result data object of the BRMS Connector expression. However, it is possible that the called rules provide a structured result while the expression returns, for example, only a specific element of the structure.

When the signature is complete, you can click the GENERATE VOCABULARY SCHEMA button. An XML Schema document will be generated, which serves as the foundation for the data exchange with the remote BRMS.

BRMS Connector Expression API

Interface `IF_FDT_BRMS_CONNECTOR` defines the programmatic access to a BRMS Connector expression. Its methods are summarized in Table 5.23.

Method	Description
SET_PROPERTIES	Sets all properties that are required to establish a connection to the remote BRMS.
SET_IMPORTING_PARAMETER	Sets a data object that will import the result of the remote rules.
SET_EXPORTING_PARAMETERS	Sets a list of data objects and expressions that will populate the context for the remote rules.
SET_CHANGING_PARAMETERS	Sets a list of data objects that will populate the context for the remote rules. Changed context values will be transferred back to the data objects.
GET_VOCABULARY_SCHEMA	Generates an XML Schema document for the currently set importing, exporting, and changing parameters.

Table 5.23 Methods of Interface IF_FDT_BRMS_CONNECTOR

With method SET_PROPERTIES, you define the basic information that is required to connect to the remote BRMS. The parameters of this method are listed in Table 5.24. For parameter IV_CONNECTION_TYPE_ID the following two values are supported:

- ► N

 for connections to an SAP NetWeaver BRM

- ► E

 for connections to an external BRMS, which is not an SAP NetWeaver BRM

In parameter `IS_CONNECTION_SETTING`, an RFC-enabled function module can be specified. By default, the function module `FDT_EXT_BRMS_CONNECTOR_EXECUTE` will be used. For connections to SAP NetWeaver BRM, function module `FDT_NW_BRMS_CONNECTOR_EXECUTE` should be specified. It is also possible to use a custom function module as long as it adheres to a specific signature, which is described in the following section.

Parameter	Description
IV_CONNECTION_TYPE_ID	Defines the connection type, currently either 'N' or 'E'
IS_CONNECTION_SETTING	Points to the function module and destination used for the remote function call
IV_CONNECTION_CURRENCY	Sets a base currency for parameters of type amount
ITS_CALL_PARAMETER	Contains BRMS-specific connection parameters
ITS_CALL_PARAMETER_PROPERTIES	Obsolete

Table 5.24 Parameters of Method IF_FDT_BRMS_CONNECTOR~SET_PROPERTIES

With method `SET_IMPORTING_PARAMETER` a data object that must conform to the expected result type can be specified. The same data object is also set as result data object for the expression if the result data object is not yet defined. Method `SET_EXPORTING_PARAMETERS` accepts a list of data objects and expressions that provide the context for the called rules. Method `SET_CHANGING_PARAMETERS` allows you to specify an additional list of data objects only. They also provide context for the called rules. Their content will, however, be updated with possibly changed values after the remote rules have been processed.

BRMS Connections

The function modules that are used to connect to an external BRMS must have a certain signature. The signature consists of the parameters that are summarized in Table 5.25, and the exceptions that are listed in Table 5.26.

Parameter	Type	Data Type
ITS_CALL_PARAMETER	Importing	FDTT_BRMS_CALL_PARAM
IV_INPUT_XML	Importing	XSTRING
IV_DATE_TIME_ISO	Importing	/ISD/DATE_ISO
EV_OUTPUT_XML	Exporting	XSTRING

Table 5.25 BRMS Connection—Function Module Signature

When the function module is called, the importing parameter ITS_CALL_PARAM-ETER will hold a list of BRMS-specific connection properties, parameter IV_DATE_TIME_ISO will contain the rule processing timestamp, and parameter IV_INPUT_XML transfers context data in the form of an XML document. In the exporting parameter EV_OUTPUT_XML, the receiver of the remote function call has to provide an updated XML document that includes the result value.

Exception	Description
SYSTEM_FAILURE	Indicates a general system failure
COMMUNICATION_FAILURE	Indicates a network or other RFC-related failure
INVALID_INPUT	Indicates that invalid parameters were passed to the BRMS
CONFIGURATION_ERROR	Indicates an inconsistent configuration of the BRMS
PROCESSING_ERROR	Indicates an error during rule processing

Table 5.26 BRMS Connection—Function Module Exceptions

Connections to an external BRMS in the Java stack typically leverage the SAP Java Connector (JCo). In such scenarios, a small wrapper program has to be implemented on the Java side. On an SAP NetWeaver Java Application Server an Enterprise Java Bean (EJB) can be used for that purpose. To react to incoming JCo calls from BRF-plus, the EJB must only provide a remote method processFunction(JCo.Function), and the JNDI[2] name of the session bean must correspond to the name of the used function module, which is by default FDT_EXT_BRMS_CONNECTOR_EXECUTE.

The implementation of the wrapper program must basically accomplish three tasks:

▸ Context data has to be extracted from the provided XML document.

▸ The rules engine of the BRMS must be called with the provided connection parameters.

---

2 JNDI is an abbreviation for the Java Naming and Directory Interface.

▶ The XML document must be updated with values that are returned or changed by the processed rules.

Listing 5.3 provides a small example of how an EJB could extract importing data from the JCo call. Further programming code would have to be specific to the used BRMS and is therefore not provided here.

```
private void extractJCoParameters(Function function) {
  ParameterList importParameters =
    function.getImportParameterList();
  //BRMS-specific properties
  Table brmsProps = importParameters.getTable("ITS_CALL_PARAM");
  if (brmsProps == null) {
    throw new J2EEAbapException("INVALID_INPUT", "BRMS Props");
  }
  for (int i = 0; i < brmsProps.getNumRows(); i++) {
    String propName = brmsProps.getString("NAME");
    String propValue = brmsProps.getString("VALUE");
  }
  //XML document
  try {
    Document xmlDoc = getDocumentBuilder.parse(
      new InputSource( new ByteArrayInputStream(
        importParameters.getByteArray("IV_INPUT_XML"))));
    // Parse XML document and call BRMS here…
  } catch (SAXException e) { } // handle exception
  } catch (IOException e) { } // handle exception
```

Listing 5.3 Extracting BRMS Connection Data from JCo

5.5.7 Case Expressions

Case expressions basically define a simple mapping for input values to output values. They take an elementary input parameter, which is also called a *case parameter* or *when parameter*, and compare it to a list of *test parameters*. If the value of the test parameter is equal to the value of the case parameter, an according *return parameter* defines the outcome of the expression.

The special test parameter "others" allows to define a result parameter that is evaluated if no other test parameter matches the case parameter. In Figure 5.25 you see an example of a Case expression definition in the UI.

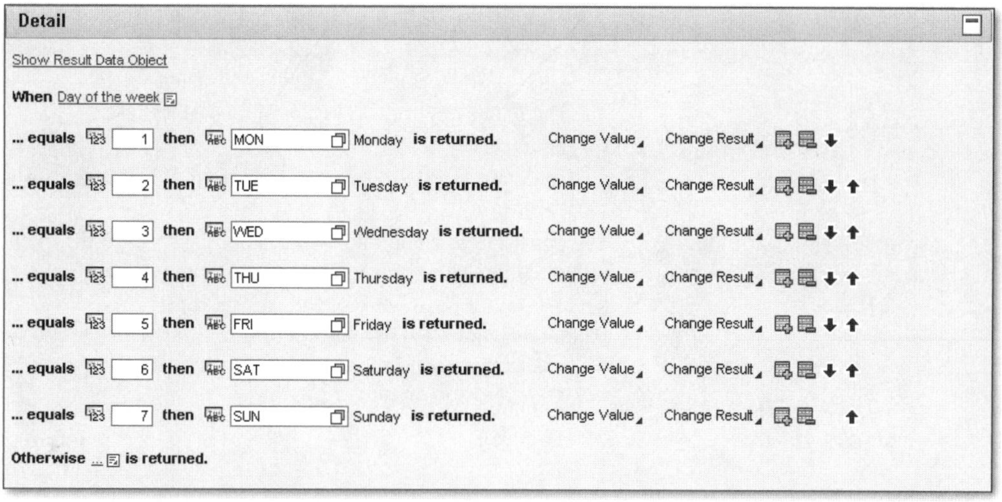

Figure 5.25 Case Expression Example

Next to the WHEN clause, you select the case parameter. Underneath you can add any number of test and corresponding return parameters. In the example only direct values are used. For the OTHERWISE case, deliberately no return parameter has been set. At runtime this will lead to a processing error if no explicitly defined test parameter matches.

In general, all parameters of the expression can be nested BRFplus objects. The case parameter is typically a context data object, the test parameters are often fixed values, and the result parameters usually consist either also of fixed values or of nested expressions.

By default the Case expression is used to return some value as result. In the Workbench the field RESULT TYPE is set to "Return Value" in this case and you can specify a RESULT DATA OBJECT for the expression. By changing the RESULT TYPE to "Perform Action," the result, and with it the return parameters, are, however, switched to actions. In this mode, the expression consequently defines a mapping of input values to actions instead of output values.

Case Expression API

The interface IF_FDT_CASE represents the Case expression type. The methods listed in Table 5.27 can be used to set the various properties.

Method	Description
SET_CASE_PROPERTY	Switches between value and action result type.
SET_CASE_PARAMETER	Sets the data object or expression to be used as case parameter.
SET_CASE_SENSITIVITY	Switches case sensitivity for the comparison of text type case parameters on or off.
SET_WHEN_TABLE	Sets the list of test and return parameter pairs. For both, either a direct value or a referenced object can be set.
SET_OTHER_VALUE SET_OTHER_PARAMETER	Sets the return parameter for the implied "others" test parameter. One method allows setting a direct value, while the other can be used to set the ID of a compatible data object, expression or action.

Table 5.27 Methods of Interface IF_FDT_CASE

5.5.8 DB Lookup Expressions

DB Lookup expressions allow for reading or checking data of a specific database table. The rows to be taken into account can be restricted by conditions.

The expression can be used in three different modes:

▶ **Data Retrieval**
By default the expression is used to retrieve actual data from a database table. Either a single line or multiple lines of data can be read. Accordingly, the result data object of the expression may need to be of table type or not. It is possible to read data only from selected columns and to map them to the fields of a data structure.

▶ **Aggregation**
Multiple values of one table column can be aggregated into a single value with the following functions: Minimum, Maximum, Average, Sum, Count. Mainly for the latter three functions, it can be specified whether only distinct values are taken into account or whether all values—no matter if they occur several times—are aggregated.

▶ **Existence Check**
In this mode the expression only checks whether there exists at least one table line that fulfills all defined conditions. Consequently, the result data object needs to be of elementary Boolean type.

Selection conditions can be defined for all three modes. A single condition consists of a value range comparison for a specific table column. If multiple conditions are defined for the same table column, at least one of them needs to be fulfilled. At runtime the conditions are evaluated for each table row and only matching rows are selected for the result.

For the definition of conditions, there are currently some restrictions, which may be subject to change:

▶ Conditions cannot be defined for columns of type amount (DDIC type CURR) or quantity (DDIC type QUAN).

▶ Conditions can compare the table data to direct values, context parameters, or nested expression results but not to other table data.

▶ The following comparison operations from Table 5.9 and their negative counterparts are not available for the DB Lookup expression:

  ▶ Contains only

  ▶ Contains any

  ▶ Contains String

Authorization

Access to database table information may be security relevant. Therefore, an additional authorization check is performed before a DB Lookup expression can be maintained for a specific table. The user requires an appropriate setting for authorization object S_TABU_DIS that is usually maintained by system administrators with Transaction SU21.

In the BRFplus Workbench the SELECTION MODE is the first property to be set. The UI for the definition of the data selection changes as explained below. When the mode is changed at a later point in time, dependent settings may be lost.

Data Retrieval Mode

Figure 5.26 illustrates the UI for the data retrieval mode. At the beginning of the selection definition, you can choose whether possibly multiple rows (ALL ENTRIES) or only a single row (SINGLE ENTRY) should be read from the database table. For single entries the first selected row will be used at runtime.

Next, the database table has to be entered into the FROM input field and ⌑Enter⌑ needs to be pressed to retrieve the columns of the table. Now conditions can be added and maintained below for the available columns. Conditions for different columns are logically concatenated with an AND operator, conditions for the same column are aggregated with an OR operator. The comparison value can directly be entered, next to the comparison operator. It can also be exchanged with a data object or expression result using the CHANGE menu.

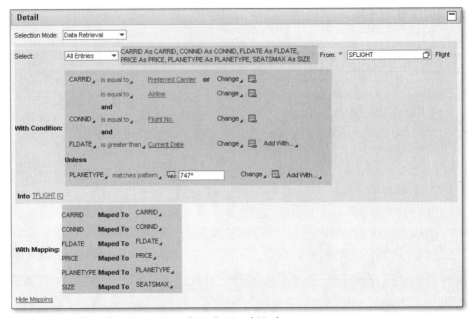

Figure 5.26 DB Lookup Expression—Data Retrieval Mode

The result data object of the DB Lookup expression constitutes also the target for the data selection. It is specified below the conditions, next to the INTO clause. For the selection of multiple rows, a table type data object is required. A new result data object that fits the structure of the database table can easily be generated by using the menu entry CREATE RESULT FROM TABLE. Simply, a name for the table and/ or the structure to be created needs to be specified within a popup window.

The result data object implicitly restricts the columns of the database table, which can be used for data retrieval. By default the columns of the database table are automatically mapped by name to the components of the result data object. Typically, the columns match the corresponding structure elements. If you want to assign the data of a column to a differently named element or you want to skip a column at all, the mapping can be adjusted. The link SHOW MAPPING needs to be clicked for that purpose.

Aggregation Mode

In aggregation mode, the expression delivers only a single value that is calculated from selected values of one specific column. In the UI the first setting is the aggregation function, followed by the aggregation mode. The mode determines whether all selected rows or only distinct rows that differ from each other are taken into account. Before you can select the column the aggregation shall be performed on, you need to specify the database table on the right-hand side and press ⎡Enter⎤. Also, conditions can be entered afterwards, just as in the data retrieval mode.

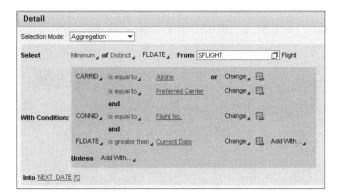

Figure 5.27   DB Lookup Expression—Aggregation Mode

For the result data object of the expression, you need to use an element that is compatible with the type of the chosen table column.

Existence Check Mode

The existence check is the simplest mode of the DB Lookup expression. You only specify the database table and the conditions that need to be fulfilled, just as for the other two modes.

For the result data object a Boolean element needs to be specified. It will be set to "true" at runtime if at least one table row matches the defined conditions.

DB Lookup Expression API

The API for the DB Lookup expression type consists of interface IF_FDT_DB_LOOKUP. Table 5.28 summarizes the methods of the interface.

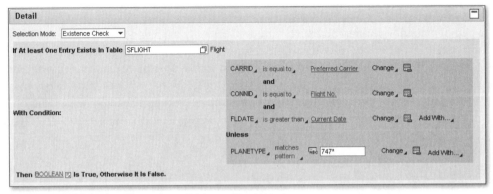

Figure 5.28 DB Lookup Expression—Existence Check Mode

Method	Description
SET_MODE	Sets the runtime mode for the expression.
SET_TABLE_NAME	Sets the name of the database table to be used.
SET_FIELD_CONDITIONS	Defines an optional list of conditions to select only specific rows from the database table.
SET_SINGLE	Indicates whether multiple or only a single line of data is selected in data retrieval mode. Accordingly, the result data object of the needs to be of table type or not.
SET_MAPPING	Defines a mapping of columns to the element(s) of the result data object.
SET_AGGREGATION	Sets aggregation mode specific options such as the function and column name.

Table 5.28 Methods of Interface IF_FDT_DB_LOOKUP

The name of the database table to be used can be set with method SET_TABLE_NAME. Of course, only valid table names are allowed.

The result data object of the expression determines what kind of value(s) are retrieved from the database table. It must be set according to designated selection mode that can be specified with method SET_MODE. Allowed parameter values for the method are defined as constants with the name pattern GC_MODE_*. According to the mode additional settings can be specified:

▶ GC_MODE_SELECT

This is the default mode for data retrieval. With method SET_SINGLE it can be specified whether a single or possibly multiple result lines should be selected. If the names of table columns do not match elements of the result data object, an individual mapping can be specified with method SET_MAPPING. For each column that shall be included in the result, an entry of structure type `S_FIELD_MAP-PING` needs to be provided. It assigns the column name to the ID of a corresponding element, which must be part of the result data object.

▶ `GC_MODE_AGGREGATION`
This is the aggregation mode. With method `SET_AGGREGATION` the function and the table column to be aggregated can be specified. The available aggregation functions are reflected by the constants `GC_AGGREGATION_FUNCTION_*`. Furthermore, it can be decided whether all or only distinct values will be selected for the aggregation.

▶ `GC_MODE_EXISTENCE_CHECK`
This is the existence check mode. Apart from optional conditions, no further special settings are required.

To select only specific rows from the database table, a list of conditions in the form of value range comparisons can be set with method `SET_FIELD_CONDITIONS`. The used table parameter is of structure type `S_FIELD_CONDITION`. It includes the same fields as structure `S_RANGE` of interface `IF_FDT_RANGE` (see also Table 5.19). The structure contains, however, an additional field `FIELDNAME`, which specifies the table column that is used for the comparison. For the `OPTION` field that defines the comparison operator, only the constant values `GC_OPTION_*` defined in interface `IF_FDT_DB_LOOKUP` are valid.

When a BRFplus function is called that uses a DB Lookup expression, security relevant data might be retrieved. Therefore, an additional authorization check can be enforced for the function processing by using method `AUTHORITY_CHECK_FOR_PRO-CESSING` of class `CL_FDT_FUNCTION_PROCESSING`. For DB Lookup expressions, authorization object `S_TABU_DIS` is checked.

5.5.9 Decision Table Expressions

A *Decision Table expression* is a very powerful concept for decision making. It sequentially processes rows of a table that consists of condition and result columns. For each row, the conditions are tested first. Empty table cells without a condition evaluate to true. If all conditions in a row are fulfilled, the corresponding result cells are evaluated. This may also include the execution of actions.

The Decision Table expression can work in two different modes, the default single match mode and the multiple match mode. They influence the result type and what impact the order of the decision table rows will have.

Detail								
Insert New Row	Edit Row	Remove Row	Copy Row	Insert Copied Row	Move Up	Move Down	Export To Excel	Import From Excel	Table Settings

Table Contents

Net Price	Car CO² Emission	Fuel Type	Company Discount	
[0 EUR..15,000 EUR]	<=170	Diesel	1.35	
[0 EUR..15,000 EUR]	<=170	Gas	1.3	
[0 EUR..15,000 EUR]	[171..200]	Diesel	1.3	
[0 EUR..15,000 EUR]	[171..200]	Gas	1.25	
>15,000 EUR	<=170	Diesel	1.32	
>15,000 EUR	<=170	Gas	1.28	
>15,000 EUR	[171..200]	Diesel	1.28	
>15,000 EUR	[171..200]	Gas	1.23	
...	<=220	...	1.05	
...	...	...	0	

Figure 5.29 Decision Table Expression—Example

Single Match Mode

In the single match mode, the processing stops at the first matching row and only a single result line can be returned. In case none of the decision table rows match, a processing error occurs by default. This behavior can be changed so that an initial result value will be provided instead.

Due to the processing order from top to bottom, the conditions in the upper rows of the table should be more specific than conditions in the lower rows. To prevent gaps among the decision table conditions, it is recommended that you define the last table row without any conditions at all. Such a row will serve as a default in case no other row matches. In general, the arrangement of the conditions is a semantic decision that has to be made by the editor of the expression.

At design time, the Decision Table can perform an overlap check that compares the conditions of a table row with all conditions of the upper rows. The aim is to detect and avoid rows that would never be reached because their conditions are a subset of more general conditions in the rows above. You can configure whether the check is active at all and whether a positive check results in a negligible warning or in an error that cannot be ignored.

Another type of available check is the gap check. It tries to detect conditions that are not yet covered by the decision table definition. The aim is to avoid empty results or even runtime errors in case none of the decision table rows match. Again, you can configure whether this check is active and whether a positive check results in an error or in a warning only.

Multiple Match Mode

In the multiple match mode, all table rows are always processed. The results of matching rows are collected into a table type overall result. The order of the result lines depends on the order of the corresponding rows in the decision table. If none of the decision table rows match, the result table remains empty.

Condition Columns

The condition column definitions are based on test parameters that are usually made up of context parameters of type element. Nested expressions can also be used to calculate a common input value for all conditions of the column. The content of the columns, the actual conditions, typically consist of value range comparisons. However, expressions returning a Boolean result can be used too.

Two column settings are relevant at design time for the column content. The first setting makes input into the column's table cells mandatory. This means that empty condition cells that always evaluate to true are not allowed any more for this column.

The second setting deals with the accessibility of the column content and is mostly relevant after a first, complete version of the decision table has been defined. Besides the default full access that allows changes on the column data, the column can be marked to become read only or even completely hidden. A use case for a hidden column might be that the column content shall be changed only programmatically, for example, by an application exit.

Result Columns

The result column definitions are based on data objects, which are usually of element type. The data objects impose the type of the decision table content, which typically consists of direct values or nested expression results.

Result columns are closely related to the decision table's result data object. A change in either of them usually has impact on the other one. Typically, the result columns are directly derived from the result data object. If the object is of element type, the table has one corresponding result column. If the result data object is a structure, the table includes a set of result columns, one for each structure component.

Table type result data objects can be used in two ways:

▶ The result columns are defined according to the table structure of the result data object. This mainly makes sense if the decision table is setup in multiple match mode and may thus return multiple result lines. In single match mode, only a single result line is inserted into the result table.

▶ The decision table has a single result column, which is of the same table type as the result data object. Each decision table row needs to provide a table result in this case. In multiple match mode, the results of multiple tables are appended. A possible scenario could be the nesting of decision tables. Each nested decision table would calculate the result for one row of the top-level decision table. All nested tables would be set up in multiple match mode and they would all deliver results of the same table type.

In addition to the standard result columns, the decision table allows you to add a single action result column. Each table row may thereby include an action that shall be triggered in case the conditions match at runtime. In general, the action column has no influence on the decision table result. Only if there is no other result column defined is the result automatically an actions table that contains the IDs of the executed actions.

Result columns also have a setting so that input into the corresponding table cells becomes mandatory. This means that empty table cells, which automatically evaluate to an initial value, are no longer allowed for this column. It is, however, still possible to *explicitly* set an initial result value. If this is not desired, you may implement custom checks with an application exit (see Section 7.3.1).

As for condition columns, the accessibility of result columns can also be restricted so that they become read-only or hidden.

Table Settings

Each decision table instance comprises general table settings like the table structure as well as the table content. In the BRFplus Workbench, the table settings are edited in a popup window that is automatically opened when you create a new instance. Later on, you can open the popup any time with a TABLE SETTINGS button in the table toolbar. See Figure 5.30.

The first table setting in the UI, RETURN ALL MATCHES FOUND, switches on the multiple match mode. Processing errors may be prevented by activating the option RETURN AN INITIAL VALUE IF NO MATCH IS FOUND.

When you select or change the RESULT DATA OBJECT of the expression, you will be asked whether the result columns should be adapted accordingly, which is usually a good idea. In case the result data object is of table type, an additional option SEGREGATE THE RESULT DATA OBJECT INTO ITS CONSTITUENT ELEMENTS is shown. The decision table will accordingly either have a single result column of table type or multiple result columns, one for each table structure element.

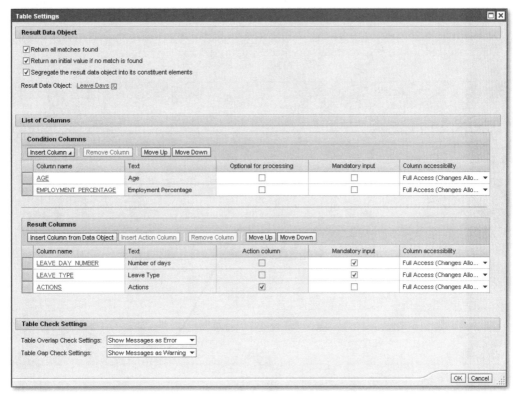

Figure 5.30 Decision Table Expression—Settings

In the LIST OF COLUMNS section you can set up the table structure. Condition and result columns are defined and configured separately. In the RESULT COLUMNS table you can include a special action column with the button INSERT ACTION COLUMN. In case multiple result columns—except the action column—do not match an existing data structure, a new structure object is automatically generated and used as result data object of the expression.

Eventually you can configure the overlap check and gap check settings at the bottom of the screen. By default the checks are active and show warnings if they detect a potential problem.

Table Contents

The main screen of the decision table UI is depicted in Figure 5.31. Here you can enter the actual content, once you have specified the general table settings. The condition columns of the decision table are aggregated on the left-hand side, while the result columns are highlighted on the right-hand side. Table rows can be inserted, removed, copied, and moved up and down.

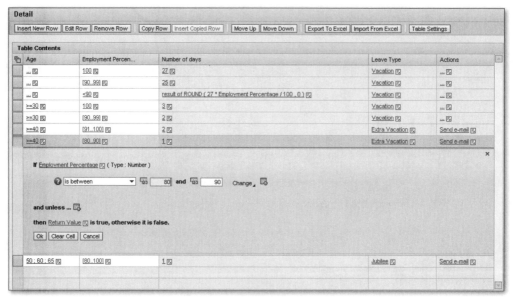

Figure 5.31 Decision Table Expression — Contents

Condition columns typically contain value range comparisons for the column's test parameter. Such conditions can directly be entered after clicking on the link of empty cells ("...") or by choosing the attached menu entry DIRECT VALUE INPUT. Figure 5.31 shows a typical example. More sophisticated conditions can be implemented using expressions that return a Boolean result.

Result column cells typically contain arbitrary values, which can be entered directly. Also any expression with a compatible result type can be used to determine or calculate a result value. For action result columns, it is of course only possible to reference an action object for processing.

Excel Support

If the decision table content consists only of directly entered range comparisons and values, it can easily be exported into a Microsoft Excel file. You simply need to click on the button EXPORT TO EXCEL in the table toolbar and specify the name and location for the Excel file. Conversely, the content can also be imported from an existing Excel file, which is especially useful for larger quantities of data.

Typically, you first export an empty decision table to create a valid template in Excel. Then you fill in the table data and import the Excel file back into BRFplus. Last but not least, you need to save the changes in the decision table.

Microsoft Excel integration in BRFplus currently supports the .xslx format of the version 2007. If you are using a lower version, like Excel 2003, you need to install the compatibility pack that is available for free from Microsoft.

Decision Table API

Table 5.29 gives an overview of all methods of interface IF_FDT_DECISION_TABLE.

Method	Description
SET_TABLE_PROPERTY	Allows for switching multiple match mode on or off with parameter IV_MULTIPLE_MATCH. Parameter IV_ALLOW_NO_MATCH activates default initial result.
SET_COLUMNS	Defines the table structure as a list of condition and result columns.
SET_TABLE_DATA	Defines the table content as a list of value to table cell assignments.
SET_MSG_SEVERITY	Adapts the severity of overlap checks and gap checks. The checks can thereby be completely disabled.

Table 5.29 Methods of Interface IF_FDT_DECISION_TABLE

Technically, the definition of a decision table consists mainly of two lists: One list contains the table column definitions, while the other contains the table content. However, if you want to create a decision table in multiple match mode, you should first switch to that mode with method SET_TABLE_PROPERTY. The expression then requires a table type result data object.

The columns of the decision table can be defined with method SET_COLUMNS, which uses a table parameter with structure type S_COLUMN. It consists of the fields described in Table 5.30 for condition and result columns as well.

Field	Description
COL_NO	Defines the internal number/position of the column, which must start with 1, 2, 3, onwards.
IS_RESULT	Specifies whether the column is a condition column (false) or result column (true). A decision table must include at least one condition and one result column.
OBJECT_ID	Is the data object or expression that either defines the condition test parameter or the result type. The same object must not be used twice within condition or result column definitions.
INPUT_REQUIRED	Indicates that table cells for the column must not be empty.
IS_OPTIONAL	Obsolete
IS_ACTION	Indicates that the entry represents an action result column. Field IS_RESULT needs to be true, OBJECT_ID must be set to the standard actions table with the constant ID GC_DOBJ_ACTION_TABLE defined in interface IF_FDT_ACTION. Also, only one action column is allowed in a decision table.
UI_MODE	Defines the accessibility of a column in the UI. Allowed values are defined in interface IF_FDT_CONSTANTS: ▶ GC_UI_MODE_CHANGEABLE ▶ GC_UI_MODE_DISPLAY_ONLY ▶ GC_UI_MODE_HIDDEN

Table 5.30 Fields of Structure IF_FDT_DECISION_TABLE~S_COLUMN

If you have not explicitly specified a result data object for the expression yet, it will be set automatically by method SET_COLUMNS, according to the result column definitions. If a generic structure is required to reflect the result columns, it will be generated too.

After the table columns are defined, the content can be set as a list of value assignments to individual table cells. The complete content needs to be passed to method SET_TABLE_DATA using a table with structure type S_TABLE_DATA. It consists of the fields described in Table 5.31.

Field	Description
COL_NO	Defines the column number for the table data.
ROW_NO	Defines the row number for the table data.

Table 5.31 Fields of Structure IF_FDT_DECISION_TABLE~S_TABLE_DATA

Field	Description
EXPRESSION_ID	References the expression that will calculate the table cell content. Context parameters are also valid in this release. The expression or context parameter must provide a Boolean value for condition columns and for result columns a compatible type.
R_VALUE	Sets a direct constant value for result columns, instead of EXPRESSION_ID.
TS_RANGE	Sets a direct value range comparison for condition columns, instead of EXPRESSION_ID.

Table 5.31 Fields of Structure IF_FDT_DECISION_TABLE~S_TABLE_DATA (Cont.)

Finally, you can adapt the severity of overlap checks and gap-checks with method SET_MSG_SEVERITY.

5.5.10 Decision Tree Expressions

Decision Tree expressions traverse a binary tree of conditions to inquire a result. They are thus especially useful because the rules can be formulated as a sequence of questions that can be answered with "Yes" and "No" only. The result type of such an expression can either be a value or an action that is executed.

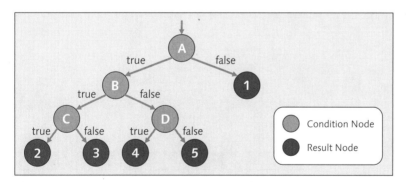

Figure 5.32 Decision Tree Structure

In Figure 5.32 the structure of a decision tree starts at the top node (also called root node) with an assigned condition A. It branches into two sub nodes that will either be processed when the condition is true or when it is false. The sub nodes may again represent a condition B or determine the expression's result 1. While nodes with a condition (A to D) always branch to two further sub nodes, nodes with an assigned result (1 to 5) represent the "leaves" of the tree where the processing stops.

In the BRFplus Workbench, the decision tree can be set up by means of a context menu that appears when clicking with the right mouse button on a node entry. To each node, either a condition or a result can be assigned. If a condition is assigned, two new sub nodes are automatically generated. Figure 5.33 shows an example.

The conditions may consist of Boolean elements or expressions with Boolean result. Value range comparisons can directly be entered. Results must be compatible with the result data object of the expression. Result values can also be entered by direct value input.

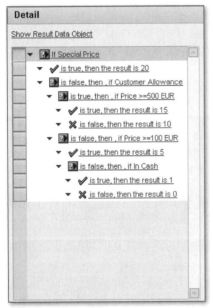

Figure 5.33 Decision Tree Expression

Technical Attributes

If the display of technical attributes has been switched on in the user personalization, an additional context menu entry NODE PROPERTIES is available in the context menu of the nodes. It provides information, such as an internally used node identifier and a sequence number, which is primarily relevant from the API perspective.

Decision Tree API

The Decision Tree expression type is represented by interface IF_FDT_DECISION_TREE. Its methods are summarized in Table 5.32.

Method	Description
SET_TREE_PROPERTY	Switches the action return type on or off.
GET_ROOT_NODE	Returns the internal ID for the root node.
SET_NODE_PROPERTY	Configures a node to represent either a condition or a result. Conditions and results can be defined by means of a referenced object, a range comparison, or value definition.
GET_CHILDREN	Provides the internal IDs of child nodes for a condition node.
GET_TREE_STRUCTURE	Provides the tree structure by listing all branches of the tree.

Table 5.32 Methods of Interface IF_FDT_DECISION_TREE

With method SET_TREE_PROPERTY of interface IF_FDT_DECISION_TREE the result type of a Decision Tree expression can be switched to ACTIONS. The result data object automatically becomes the standard actions table of application FDT_SYSTEM in this case.

The tree structure can be built up step by step. A new Decision Tree expression implicitly has a root node with an internal node ID. This node ID can be retrieved with method GET_ROOT_NODE.

With method SET_NODE_PROPERTY and the node ID, the node can be configured to become either a condition node or a result node. If it is configured as a condition node using parameter IV_CONDITION or IS_RANGE, two new child nodes are internally generated. The node IDs of the child nodes can be retrieved with method GET_CHILDREN. The child nodes may be configured again with method SET_NODE_PROPERTY. The same procedure can be repeated, unless both child nodes are configured as result nodes, using parameter IV_RESULT or respectively IR_RESULT.

The whole structure of the generated tree can be retrieved with method GET_TREE_STRUCTURE. It returns a list of node assignments that correspond to the branches of the tree. Each entry of type S_TREE_STRUCTURE contains a parent node and a child node ID, and is either assigned to the parent's "true" or "false" result.

5.5.11 Dynamic Expressions

Expressions are usually nested into other expressions in a static way: expression *A* checks, for example, whether expression *B* returns some specific result value so that expression *C* will be evaluated. Therefore, expressions *B* and *C* are statically linked to expression *A*. At runtime, all expressions share the same context.

Dynamic expressions, in contrast, take the ID of any expression as input and execute it in a separate context. It is not defined before runtime which expression will actually be called. The ID of the expression to execute can even be passed from the outside via a function context parameter, as exemplified in Figure 5.34. It is thus crucial to ensure that the expression ID is valid and points to a compatible expression:

▸ The result type of the called expression must be compatible with the result data object of the dynamic expression.

▸ The called expression must not require data objects outside the current runtime context of the dynamic expression.

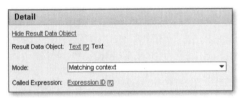

Figure 5.34 Dynamic Expression

Executing the called expression in a separate context prohibits changes on the original context. Only the result of the called expression is taken over. The separate context can be determined in two modes:

▸ **Standard Mode**
By default the entire original context is copied. Only if the ID for the called expression is defined by a context parameter is this parameter removed from the context copy.

▸ **Matching Mode**
Only those context parameters of the original context that intersect and thus match with the context of the called expression are copied. (For recapitulation: the context of the called expression is determined by all functions and rulesets using the expression.) The mode ensures that the called expression is running only within its own context.

Drawbacks

The use of the dynamic expression involves some significant drawbacks:

▸ At design time it is not possible to check whether valid expression IDs will be used at runtime. The probability of processing errors is essentially increased.

▶ Code generation is not possible for the dynamic expression. At runtime the called expression and all subsequent objects can be evaluated only in the rather slow interpretation mode.

▶ Lean tracing is not possible for the dynamic expression and all subsequently processed objects.

Therefore the dynamic expression is recommended only for special use cases and should be avoided when possible.

Dynamic Expression API

The relevant interface `IF_FDT_DYNAMIC_EXPRESSION` deals only with two properties, which are listed in Table 5.33.

Method	Description
SET_PARAMETER	Sets the parameter that determines the ID of the expression to call. The parameter can be a context data object or a nested expression.
SET_MODE	Sets the mode in which the context for the called expression is created. Two possible constant values are allowed: ▶ GC_MODE_COMPLETE_CONTEXT ▶ GC_MODE_MATCHING_CONTEXT

Table 5.33 Methods of Interface IF_FDT_DYNAMIC_EXPRESSION

5.5.12 Formula Expressions

The *Formula expression* type allows you to perform a wide range of calculations. All kind of mathematical operations and functions on numbers, Boolean values, text strings, amounts, quantities, table data, and more are available. Context parameters, expressions, and direct values can be used as operands within the definition of a formula.

In the BRFplus Workbench, the formula can be entered in a standard and an expert mode. In the standard mode, the formula can be edited only at a single position, marked by an orange cursor. The cursor is always positioned next to the currently selected formula element, which gets underlined. The cursor can be moved left or right with corresponding buttons, or it can be directly set by clicking on one of the formula elements depicted in Figure 5.35.

At the position of the cursor, you can insert new formula elements. In the middle of the screen, you find a button panel from which you can select basic mathematical and logical operations. They are used in infix notation in the form *<operand> <operator> <operand>*. Table 5.34 gives an overview of the available infix operators.

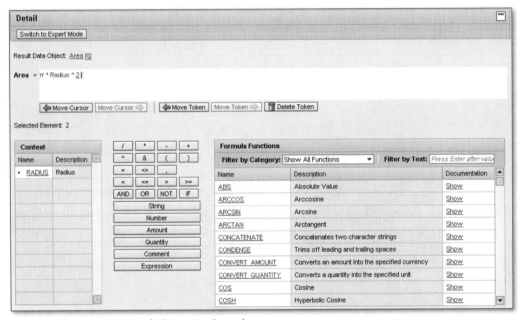

Figure 5.35 Formula Expression Example

Result Type	Operator	Description
Numeric	+	Addition
	-	Subtraction
	*	Multiplication
	/	Division
	DIV	Quotient without fraction
	MOD	Modulo, remainder of division
	^	Raise to a power
Any	&	Concatenate

Table 5.34 Formula Infix Operators

Result Type	Operator	Description
Boolean	=	Equals
	<>	Not equals
	>	Is greater than
	>=	Is greater than or equal
	<	Is less than
	<=	Is less than or equal
	AND	Logical and
	OR	Logical or
	NOT	Logical not

Table 5.34 Formula Infix Operators (Cont.)

As operands, different types of values can be entered directly or you can use data objects and expressions. On the left-hand side, you find a CONTEXT panel where you can directly select context data objects as operands. The panel remains empty as long as the Formula expression is not referenced by a function or ruleset. Operands can also be inserted at the position of the cursor using the context menu, which appears when you click on the right mouse button.

On the right-hand side of the screen, you find a vast list of formula functions that can be used. The list can be filtered by function categories and text patterns. For each formula function, a documentation is available that explains functionality and syntax. The currently available list of functions is summarized in Appendix A.

If you want to use the expert mode for editing the formula, you have to click on the button SWITCH TO EXPERT MODE at the top of the DETAIL area. The formula is then represented in a textual way. Expressions and data objects used as operands are defined by means of their UUIDs. Text strings need to be encapsulated by apostrophes. Amount and quantity values such as 100$EUR or 12.5&M include a $ or & character to delimit the currency or the unit from the number value.

Figure 5.36 Formula Expression—Expert Mode

Independent of the way the formula is defined, it needs to be syntactically correct. For example, opening and closing brackets must be used consistently, and the type of operands must fit to the connected operation.

Formula Expression API

The Formula expression has basically one property: the formula. The corresponding ABAP interface IF_FDT_FORMULA includes, however, several getter-methods to retrieve additional information, as described in Table 5.35.

Method	Description
SET_FORMULA	Defines the formula, either as a list of formula tokens or as a string representation.
GET_FUNCTIONALS	Provides a list of supported formula functions. With *application exits* the list can be adapted (see also Section 7.3.1).
GET_FUNCTIONAL_CATEGORIES	Provides a list of categories the formulas can be assigned to. With *application exits* the list can be adapted (see also Section 7.3.1).
GET_OPERATORS	Provides a list of supported operators. Operators like "plus," "minus," etc. can be regarded as a kind of special base functions that syntactically impose infix notation.
GET_ERROR_TOKEN	When the formula is syntactically incorrect, the first invalid token can be retrieved after a call to method IF_FDT_TRANSACTION~CHECK.

Table 5.35 Methods of Interface IF_FDT_FORMULA

The formula can be set in two different formats, which correspond to the standard and expert mode in the UI. With table parameter IT_TOKEN of method SET_FORMULA, the internal standard format is used. The formula is split into a list of tokens of structure type S_TOKEN, which consists of the following fields:

▶ TOKEN_TYPE
The type of the token. Supported token types are defined as constants with the name pattern GC_TOKEN*.

▶ TOKEN
The token itself. The syntax of the token is imposed by the token type. See also Table 5.36.

▶ ADD_INFO

Some token types require an additional field. For example, amount and quantity values store the currency or respectively the unit in this field.

Table 5.36 gives an overview of the most relevant token types.

Token Type	Description	Format (examples)	
GC_TOKEN_TYPE_BRACKET	Brackets	( )	
GC_TOKEN_TYPE_COMMA	Comma separator for functions with multiple operands	,	
GC_TOKEN_TYPE_CONST_AMOUNT	Direct values of different types	123.45	EUR
GC_TOKEN_TYPE_CONST_QUANTITY		1000	KG
GC_TOKEN_TYPE_CONST_NUM		123.4567	
GC_TOKEN_TYPE_CONST_STRING		'Text'	
GC_TOKEN_TYPE_DATA_OBJECT	Data object used as operand	UUID	
GC_TOKEN_TYPE_EXPRESSION	Expression used as operand	UUID	
GC_TOKEN_TYPE_FUNCTIONAL	Name of a formula function	SQRT EXP CONDENSE	
GC_TOKEN_TYPE_INFIX_OP	Name of a formula operator	+ - * / MOD	
GC_TOKEN_TYPE_COMMENT	Comment texts that	"Comment"	

Table 5.36 Formula Token Types

With parameter IV_FORMULA of method SET_FORMULA, the formula can be passed as a string of concatenated tokens. The method will internally parse the string and transform it into the internal token table format.

Formula Builder

Internally the Formula expression type uses the formula builder component of package S_FORMULA_BUILDER. In this package you can find some demo reports SFBE_EXAMPLE* to find out how the formula builder works in general.

5.5.13 Function Call Expressions

Function Call Expressions can call a separate BRFplus function and return the respective function result afterwards. With this type of expression, it is thus possible to reuse existing BRFplus functions. It also allows for the splitting of complex rules into a set of sub-rules with less complexity that can be maintained individually. For example, a tax calculation function could call country-specific sub-functions.

The execution of the called target function takes place in a detached context without access to the context of the calling expression. To pass data to the target function, its context can be mapped to data objects in the context of the Function Call expression. The mapping can also include data transformations using expressions. After the target function has been executed, its result automatically becomes the result of the calling Function Call expression.

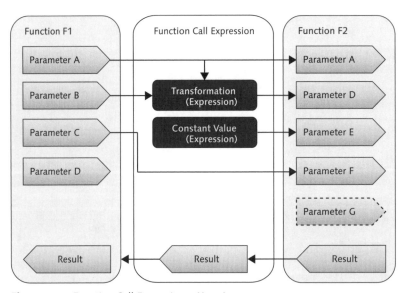

Figure 5.37 Function Call Expression—Mapping

Figure 5.37 outlines the context mapping in an abstract way: Within function F1 a Function Call expression is used to evaluate function F2. The first parameter A of function F2 is also contained in the context of F1 and can therefore be directly mapped. The value for parameter D of function F2 is derived from the context parameters A and B of function F1 by means of a nested expression. For parameter E of function F2 a static value is assigned. Parameter C of function F1 is again directly assigned to parameter F of function F2 and must therefore be of compatible type. Eventually parameter G of function F2 is not set at all. The result of the called function becomes the result of the Function Call expression and may thus affect the context or result of function F1 as well.

As Figure 5.38 illustrates, the definition of a Function Call expression in the BRFplus Workbench does not require many settings. First the TARGET FUNCTION to call needs to be selected or created. The context data objects of the target function are listed in the right column of the MAPPING table afterwards. For each target context data object, a source context data object or expression can be specified in the left column of the table.

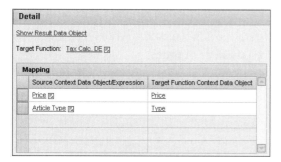

Figure 5.38 Function Call Expression

Function Call Expression API

The API for the Function Call expression type is reflected by interface IF_FDT_FUNCTION_CALL. It defines only the two methods described in Table 5.37.

Method	Description
SET_FUNCTION	Sets the ID of the target function to call.
SET_MAPPING	Defines a mapping for the context parameters of the target function.

Table 5.37 Methods of Interface IF_FDT_FUNCTION_CALL

With method SET_FUNCTION the ID of the target function to call is set. Method SET_MAPPING determines the context parameter mapping. Each context data object of the target function that is not optional must be listed in the table parameter ITS_MAPPING, together with a corresponding source data object or expression.

5.5.14 Loop Expressions

With *Loop expressions* a sequence of operations can be repeatedly executed. An operation is primarily the execution of a rule. Because rules can in turn (even unconditionally) execute any expressions and actions, this is no limitation.

Four different loop modes are available:

▸ FOR EACH ENTRY IN <TABLE>
Evaluates a sequence of rules for all or only selected rows of given table data. The selection of specific rows is optional and based on conditions for the row data. The structure object of the used table acts as a cursor to the individual row data. All rules and nested expressions within the loop can access the structure and structure elements as additional context. The rules can thereby read or change the table data for the selected rows, one after another.

▸ REPEAT <NUMBER> TIMES
Repeats the sequence of rules a fixed number of times.

▸ DO UNTIL <CONDITION>
Repeats the sequence of rules until a specific condition is fulfilled. The sequence of rules is evaluated at least one time. The rules must ensure that the condition becomes true after a finite number of repetitions.

▸ WHILE <CONDITION> DO
Repeats the sequence of rules as long as a specific condition is fulfilled. The rules may not be executed at all. The rules must ensure that the condition becomes false after a finite number of repetitions.

Figure 5.39 shows an example of a Loop expression that iterates over selected rows of a FLIGHTS table. The loop operations consist of a single rule. It triggers two different actions based on the value of a PRICE field in the table data.

As a special kind of operation, it is possible to define conditions that will skip all subsequent operations in the sequence. They can be used either to exit the loop processing completely or to continue with the next loop cycle under specific circumstances.

The Loop expression is typically used within rulesets to manipulate context data and/or execute actions. The standard actions table is used as result data object in this case. The expression can, however, also be used in the classical way to provide a value for a specific result data object, which is not already part of the context. In the UI, a RESULT TYPE option can be switched accordingly from PERFORM ACTION to RETURN VALUE.

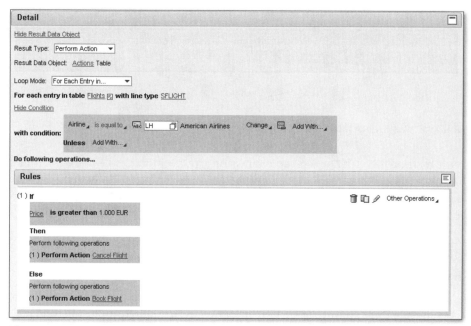

Figure 5.39 Loop Expression

In the BRFplus Workbench, you usually first choose the desired LOOP MODE. For the modes DO UNTIL and WHILE, you can then specify a condition in the form of a Boolean context element or expression result. For the REPEAT mode you simply enter the required number of repetitions. Last but not least, the FOR EACH ENTRY mode requires a table data object and optionally a list of table row conditions. As for DB Lookup expressions (see Section 5.5.7) or Table Operation expressions (see Section 5.5.17), the conditions consist of value range comparisons for specific table columns. In addition, it is possible to check whether the whole table line is initial or not.

In the section RULES the list of operations that shall be evaluated can be defined. Using the menu OTHER OPERATIONS you can add entries for rules and for conditions to exit or continue the loop execution. Existing, named rules can be reused or new rules can directly be defined in the scope of the Loop expression. Each rule or condition entry can be removed, copied, edited, or moved up and down when feasible.

Loop Expression API

For the Loop expression type, interface IF_FDT_LOOP is defined. It comprises the methods described in Table 5.38.

261

Method	Description
SET_LOOP_MODE	Specifies the loop mode via constant values GC_LOOP_MODE_*.
SET_LOOP_PROPERTIES	Sets properties according to the loop mode.
SET_RULES	Specifies the sequence of rules and exit conditions that shall be repeatedly evaluated within the loop.

Table 5.38 Methods of Interface IF_FDT_LOOP

With method SET_LOOP_MODE, the expression can be initialized for the intended runtime mode. Previously made settings for a different mode will thereby be cleared. The possible modes are reflected by constants with the name pattern GC_LOOP_MODE_*.

Method SET_LOOP_PROPERTIES accepts different parameters to configure the expression according to the chosen mode:

▶ Mode GC_LOOP_MODE_FOR_EACH
Parameter IV_FOR_EACH_TABLE assigns the table data object to use for the loop. In addition, conditions for the selection of specific table rows can be specified with parameter ITS_FOR_EACH_WHERE_CONDITION. Its structure type S_FOR_EACH_WHERE_CONDITION represents a value range comparison and deviates from type S_RANGE of interface IF_FDT_RANGE only by the field COMPONENT. This field refers to the table column or the corresponding element that is used as test parameter. For the field OPTION only values defined by the constants GC_OPTION_* in interface IF_FDT_LOOP are supported.

▶ Mode GC_LOOP_MODE_REPEAT_TIMES
Parameter IV_NUMBER_OF_REPEATS defines the fixed number of repetitions.

▶ Modes GC_LOOP_MODE_REPEAT_UNTIL and GC_LOOP_MODE_REPEAT_WHILE
Parameter IV_LOOP_CONDITION can be used to assign a Boolean element or an expression with Boolean result as loop condition. Alternatively, parameter IS_LOOP_COND_RANGE allows integrating a range comparison as loop condition directly.

The sequence of operations and exit conditions can be set with method SET_RULES. The used structure S_RULE contains the fields described in Table 5.39. Except for field POSITION only one of the other fields in the structure must be exclusively set.

Field	Description
POSITION	Specifies the position in the sequence of operations.
RULE_ID	Refers to a rule object to be evaluated.
EXIT_CONDITION_ID	Refers to a Boolean element or expression that serves as condition to exit the loop.
EXIT_COND_RANGE	Specifies a value range comparison that serves as condition to exit the loop.
CONTINUE_CONDITION_ID	Refers to a Boolean element or expression that serves as condition to continue the loop with the next cycle.
CONTINUE_COND_RANGE	Specifies a value range comparison that serves as condition to continue the loop with the next cycle.

Table 5.39 Fields of Structure IF_FDT_LOOP=>S_RULE

5.5.15 Procedure Call Expressions

The *Procedure Call* expression type is intended mainly for experienced users with ABAP programming skills. It allows the user to execute ABAP code to determine a result and/or to change the values of context data objects. The capabilities of BRF-plus can thereby be extended with arbitrary functionality in a convenient way.

The ABAP code to be executed can be accessed by calling either a public, static class method or a function module. Both are referred to as "procedure."

> **Downwards Compatibility**
>
> In former releases, the Procedure Call expression type was referred to as static method call. It allowed only calling a specific static method PROCESS with a predefined signature. The class had to implement the interface IF_FDT_STATIC_METHOD_TEMPLATE for that purpose. This kind of static method call has become obsolete, but it is still supported for downwards compatibility.

The Procedure Call expressions allow for mapping of importing, exporting, changing, or returning parameters of the called procedure. Table parameters of function modules are supported too. The parameters can be mapped either to context parameters or to the result data object of the expression. Importing parameters may also be supplied by nested expressions. All other kinds of parameters will update the mapped context or result data object. Context values can thus be changed independent of the specified result data object of the expression.

Concerning parameter types, there are some restrictions that need to be considered when using a Procedure Call expression. The following types cannot be mapped and are thus allowed only for optional parameters:

- ▶ Reference types (REF TO).
- ▶ Deeply nested table or structure types.
- ▶ Generic types like ANY or DATA. Only the types NUMERIC, CLIKE, CSEQUENCE, INDEX TABLE and ANY TABLE can be mapped. Type ANY can only be used for importing parameters.
- ▶ Type RAW. Type RAW16 is however supported.

To access dedicated runtime information, some special importing parameters can be defined in the signature of the called procedure. The parameter names and types must be exactly the ones listed in Table 5.40.

Parameter Name	Parameter Type	Description
IV_EXPRESSION_ID	IF_FDT_TYPES=>ID	ID of the calling expression
IV_TIMESTAMP	IF_FDT_TYPES=>TIMESTAMP	Timestamp of the rule evaluation
IO_TRACE	REF TO IF_FDT_TRACE	Currently used trace instance, if any

Table 5.40 Procedure Call Expression—Special Parameters

Exceptions that are declared in the signature of a procedure can be handled in two ways. By default they will cause a processing error at runtime. But it is also possible to list individual exceptions that will be ignored. If such an exception occurs at runtime, no context data will be altered and the rule processing continues.

Changes and Transport

For a new, transportable Procedure Call expression you must take care that the used class or function module exists also in all target systems. Especially if the relevant ABAP object has been newly developed as well, it is recommended that you record both the expression and the ABAP object onto the same transport request.

If the signature of the used function or method is changed afterwards in an incompatible way, the expression needs to be adapted. Again, if the expression is transportable, both changes should be recorded onto the same transport request.

The definition of a Procedure Call expression in the BRFplus Workbench is illustrated in Figure 5.40. The first field CALL TYPE specifies whether the expression shall execute a static method or a function module. Accordingly, either the function name or the name of the class and the method can be entered below. If the static method is defined by an interface that the class implements, the interface name also needs to be provided. [Enter] must be pressed afterwards to verify the entered values and to retrieve the signature of the method or function module.

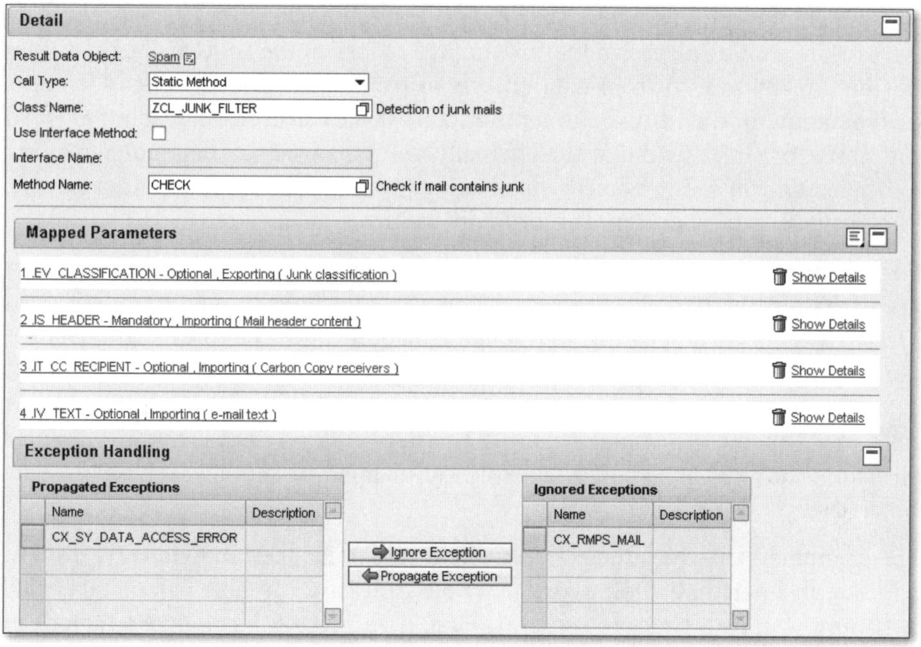

Figure 5.40 Procedure Call Expression

Those parameters of the function or method signature that shall be supplied or retrieved can be added to the section MAPPED PARAMETERS. Parameters that are not optional must always be mapped. An expanded mapping definition is illustrated by Figure 5.41.

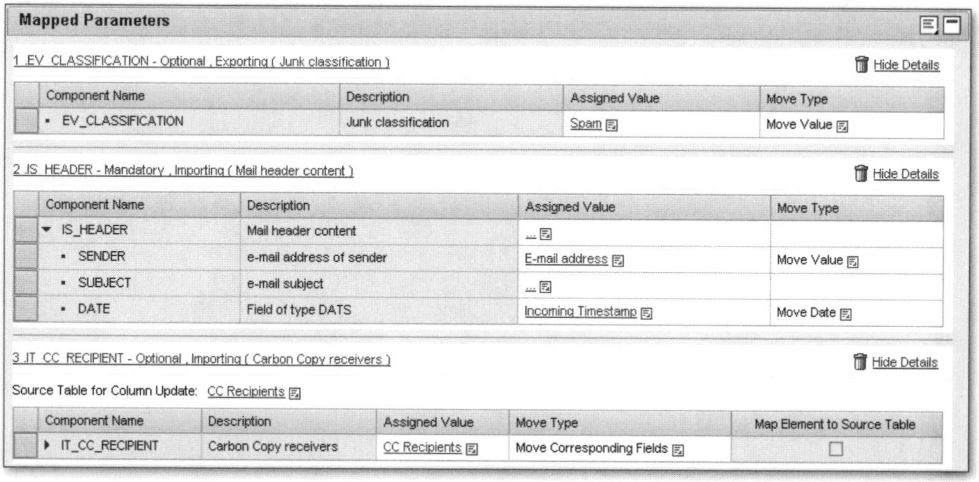

Figure 5.41 Procedure Call Expression — Parameter Mapping

A parameter is typically mapped to a data object of matching type. The way values are exchanged is displayed in the column MOVE TYPE in the UI. Usually, the values can be directly moved from data objects to parameters or vice versa. Elements of type amount, quantity, or timepoint consist, however, of multiple fields, so the source or target field that shall actually be exchanged can be ambiguous. For example, it might be intended to update only the date field of a timepoint element. The MOVE TYPE can be altered accordingly in such a case.

For structures and tables, only the fields that have an equally named counterpart are exchanged by default. The MOVE TYPE is then called MOVE CORRESPONDING FIELDS. It is, however, possible to refine the mapping, for example in case the field names do not match. You might also intend to exchange only some selected fields or to supply individual fields from another data source. If, for example, all but one field of a structured parameter should be supplied by a corresponding BRFplus structure, the extra field could be explicitly mapped to another elementary data object or expression.

For parameters of type structure, each field can be mapped individually, even in addition to a default mapping for the whole structure. For table parameters, such a mapping can be a bit more complex. First, each field of the table parameter can be mapped to an element. The element may or may not be part of a corresponding table structure. In the first case the option MAP ELEMENT TO SOURCE TABLE needs to be marked so that the complete table column data will be moved and not only a single element value. The relevant SOURCE TABLE FOR COLUMN UPDATE needs to be specified the first time the option is marked. Figure 5.42 shows such a case where only a single column shall be filled. If there is already a default mapping defined for the whole table, it must refer to the same BRFplus table. Table fields that are not mapped to a source table can be supplied with a common value for each row. This can be a single, fixed value but also the value provided by a context element or nested expression.

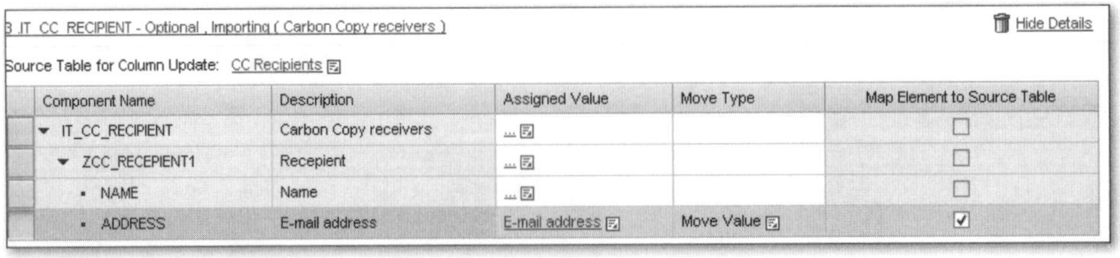

Component Name	Description	Assigned Value	Move Type	Map Element to Source Table
▼ IT_CC_RECIPIENT	Carbon Copy receivers	... 🗎		☐
▼ ZCC_RECEPIENT1	Recepient	... 🗎		☐
• NAME	Name	... 🗎		☐
• ADDRESS	E-mail address	E-mail address 🗎	Move Value 🗎	☑

IT_CC_RECIPIENT - Optional , Importing (Carbon Copy receivers) Hide Details
Source Table for Column Update: CC Recipients 🗎

Figure 5.42 Procedure Call Expression—Advanced Table Mapping

Procedure Call Expression API

Because the Procedure Call expression type is an update of the former static method call expression type, the interface IF_FDT_STATIC_METHOD is still used. The complete list of its methods is shown in Table 5.41.

Method	Description
SET_CALL_TYPE	Sets the type of procedure that shall be called.
SET_FUNCTION_MODULE	Defines the function module that shall be called.
SET_CLASS	Defines the class containing the static method that shall be called.
SET_METHOD	Defines the static method that shall be called.
SET_MAPPING	Specifies how individual parameters or parameter fields will be mapped.
SET_EXCEPTION_HANDLING	Specifies a list of exceptions that shall be ignored.
SET_SUB_EXPRESSIONS	Obsolete
CLEAR	Clears all settings to redefine the expression from scratch.

Table 5.41 Methods of Interface IF_FDT_STATIC_METHOD

With method SET_CALL_TYPE it can be specified whether the expression should call a function module or a static class method. According to the type, additional settings can be made. The allowed call types are available as constants with the name pattern GC_CALL_TYPE_*:

▶ GC_CALL_TYPE_FUNCTION
A function module shall be called. The function module name can be set with method SET_FUNCTION_MODULE.

▶ GC_CALL_TYPE_STATIC_METHOD
A public, static class method shall be called. The class name can be set with method SET_CLASS. The method name and optionally the name of the interface defining the method can be supplied with method SET_METHOD.

▶ GC_CALL_TYPE_TEMPLATE_IF
With this obsolete call type, the static method PROCESS of interface IF_FDT_STATIC_METHOD_TEMPLATE is called for a specific class. The class implementing the interface needs to be set with method SET_CLASS.

For all but the obsolete call types, a parameter mapping can be defined with method SET_MAPPING. The mapping consists of a table of structure type S_MAPPING. Each entry can map either a parameter as whole or only individual fields of structure parameters or table parameters. Structure `S_MAPPING` comprises the fields shown in Table 5.42.

Field	Description
POSITION	Determines a sequence for the mapping entries.
PARAMETER	Contains the name of the function or method parameter.
PARAM_COMP_PATH	If the entry shall map only a single field of a structure or table parameter, the path to the according component must be defined here. For structure parameters, this is simply the field name. For table parameters the path must be provided in the format `<table structure name>-<field name>`.
ID	Refers to the data object the parameter shall be mapped to. Field `R_VALUE` must not be used in this case.
ID_COMP_PATH	Obsolete, must not be used.
TOP_ID	Refers to the table data object, if the entry shall map only a single field of a table parameter. In this case, the field `ID` must refer to the corresponding element of the table structure.
R_VALUE	Refers to the value that shall be mapped to importing parameters. Field ID must be empty in this case.
MOVE_TYPE	The move type determines the way data is exchanged. The following constant values are possible. ▶ `GC_MOVE_TYPE_VALUE` — for direct value assignment. It is the default for elementary parameters or parameter fields. ▶ `GC_MOVE_TYPE_MOVE_CORR` — assigns only values of matching fields for structure parameters and table parameters. ▶ `GC_MOVE_TYPE_SUPPL` — assigns the currency or unit field of amount or quantity elements. ▶ `GC_MOVE_TYPE_DATE` — assigns the date field of timepoint elements. ▶ `GC_MOVE_TYPE_TIME` — assigns the time field of timepoint elements. ▶ `GC_MOVE_TYPE_TMSTMP` — assigns the timestamp field of timepoint elements.

Table 5.42 Fields of Structure IF_FDT_STATIC_METHOD=>S_MAPPING

Eventually the called procedure may raise some defined exceptions. In such a case, a list of exceptions that shall be ignored can additionally be provided with method `SET_EXCEPTION_HANDLING`.

5.5.16 Random Number Expressions

As expected, a *Random Number expression* dynamically creates a random number at runtime. BRFplus uses the standard ABAP random number generator with a new seed value every time. This ensures that the sequence of generated numbers is different each time the expression is processed.

The expression can be used basically for two purposes and hence in two different modes:

▶ The expression can return a random number between a defined minimum and maximum value. The precision of the random number is adaptable by means of the number of decimals.

▶ The expression can return a Boolean value, which becomes "true" with a defined probability between 0 and 1.

The MODE is the first property to be set for the Random Number expression in the UI. Depending on the chosen mode, the standard Number or Boolean element of application FDT_SYSTEM is set as result data object by default. Furthermore, the corresponding random number constraints MINIMUM, MAXIMUM, DECIMALS or respectively the PROBABILITY become editable.

By default, the constraints values are defined statically as constants. They may, however, also be determined dynamically using referenced data objects or expressions. In the UI you can use button SWITCH TO REFERENCING MODE to change the type of input.

Figure 5.43 shows an example simulating the outcome of dicing.

Figure 5.43 Random Number Expression—Dice Example

Another example shows the usage of the probability mode (see Figure 5.44). Here the random expression references a Formula expression to calculate a probability between 0 and 1.

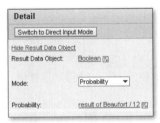

Figure 5.44 Random Number Expression—Probability Example

Random Expression API

The API for the random expression in interface IF_FDT_RANDOM has no method for explicitly setting the mode of operation. Instead, the mode is derived by the expression's result data object. If it is of type number, the expression will return a random number value. If it is of type Boolean, the expression will run in probability mode.

If no result data object is set, the mode is derived from the set properties. The methods of setting the properties are listed in Table 5.43. Only if a probability value is set will the expression run in probability mode.

Method	Description
SET_BORDERS	Defines the minimum and maximum value for the generated random number.
SET_DECIMALS	Sets the precision of the generated random number. By default the random numbers have no (zero) decimals.
SET_PROBABILITY	Defines the probability of returning a Boolean "true" value in probability mode.
GET_MODE	Returns the current runtime mode which is derived from the set properties.

Table 5.43 Methods of Interface IF_FDT_RANDOM

The mode of operation can be requested with method GET_MODE. It will return either of the two constant values GC_MODE_RANDOM_NUMBER or GC_MODE_PROBABILITY.

All but the decimals property can either be defined by means of a direct value or in the form of a referenced object's ID.

5.5.17 Search Tree Expressions

Search Tree expressions traverse a tree structure of nodes and branches to determine a result. In contrast to Decision Tree expressions, each node may have an arbitrary number of sub nodes, which are ordered from "left" to "right." The processing logic is therefore different and can even be performed in three different modes.

The nodes of a search tree can, in principle, contain a condition and a result as well. If the condition evaluates to true at runtime, it depends on the processing mode whether the result is taken into account, and/or the sub nodes are processed from left to right. Consequently the condition of a node does not determine *which* sub node is processed, but rather *whether* the sub nodes are processed at all. The root node is somewhat special because it does not require an explicit condition definition. No condition corresponds to a condition that is always fulfilled for the root node.

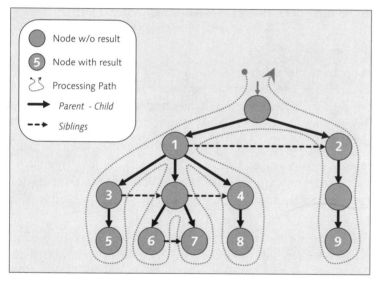

Figure 5.45 Search Tree Structure

Figure 5.45 shows the relationship among the nodes in a search tree. It also illustrates how the general processing path would look if all nodes were traversed.

The following three processing modes are currently available for the Search Tree expression:

▶ **First-Match-Mode**
The processing stops at the first matching node with an assigned result. Only "leaf" nodes with no further sub nodes should contain a result, because subsequent nodes would never be processed.

▶ **Multiple-Match-Mode**

The whole tree is traversed. If the condition of a node with assigned result evaluates to true, the result is added to a result table. All nodes may include a result in this mode.

▶ **Qualified-Match-Mode**

This mode is kind of an extension of the first-match-mode and allows all nodes of the tree to include a result. The processing of the tree in qualified-match-mode does not necessarily stop at the first matching node with an assigned result. If the node has sub nodes, the processing continues to check for a more qualified result in one of the corresponding sub trees. Sub nodes are more qualified than their common parent node, because more conditions need to be fulfilled to reach the sub nodes. In case the matching node is a leaf node without further sub nodes, the processing stops immediately because, by definition, there are no better qualified results possible.

To get an impression of how the different modes actually work, let us look at the example search tree in Figure 5.46. In this tree only some nodes have an assigned, numeric result. Supposed the conditions of the dark nodes were fulfilled and the conditions of the bright nodes were not fulfilled at runtime; the expression result would be the following:

▶ In first-match-mode the result would theoretically be "1" because the corresponding node is the first from top to bottom and left to right that matches *and* has a result. (The example is, however, not valid because only leaf-nodes can have a result in this mode.)

▶ In multiple-match-mode the result would include the values 1, 4, 2, 9 of all matching nodes that are traversed. The value 5 is not included even though the corresponding node condition would be fulfilled in principle. But because the parent node with value 3 does not match, the node with value 5 is not processed at all.

▶ In qualified-match-mode the result would be 4 because the node is more qualified than the first matching node with result 1. Before node 4 is processed, its left sibling nodes and sub nodes will be checked. But they either do not match or do not provide a result.

When no matching node with a result can be found at runtime, a processing exception occurs by default. For such cases, the expression can, however, be configured to return an initial result instead. Like other expressions, the Search Tree expression allows to switch the result type to actions. At runtime the IDs of all executed actions will then be collected into an actions table.

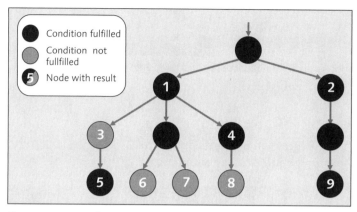

Figure 5.46 Search Tree—Processing Example

As you can see in Figure 5.47, the editor for the Search Tree expressions in the Workbench looks similar to the one for the Decision Tree expressions (see Section 5.5.9). The tree structure can be set up by means of a context menu that appears when you click on the right mouse button on a node entry. To each node, a condition and/or a result can be assigned. The conditions may consist of Boolean elements or expressions with Boolean result. Value range comparisons can directly be entered. Results must be compatible with the result data object of the expression. Result values can be entered by direct value input.

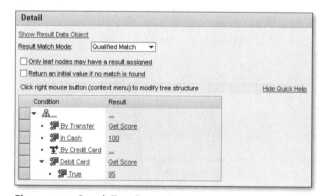

Figure 5.47 Search Tree Expression

Child nodes need to be created explicitly via the sub menu NODE OPERATIONS. Here new child or sibling nodes can be created, cut and pasted, or eventually be deleted.

Technical Attributes

If the display of technical attributes has been switched on in the user personalization, an additional entry NODE PROPERTIES is available in the context menu of the nodes. It provides information, such as an internally used node identifier and sequence number, which are primarily relevant from the API perspective.

Search Tree Expression API

The API for the Search Tree expression is covered by interface IF_FDT_SEARCH_TREE. In Table 5.44 all methods of the interface are summarized.

Method	Description
SET_TREE_PROPERTY	Defines general expression settings.
GET_ROOT_NODE	Returns the internal ID for the root node.
CREATE_NODE	Creates a new tree node with a condition and an optional result.
MOVE_NODE	Moves an existing node to another location within the search tree.
DELETE_NODE	Deletes a tree node.
SET_NODE_PROPERTY	Allows to set or change the condition and result of a node.
GET_CHILDREN	Provides the internal IDs of all child nodes for a parent node.
GET_TREE_STRUCTURE	Provides the tree structure by listing all branches of the tree.

Table 5.44 Methods of Interface IF_FDT_SEARCH_TREE

With method SET_TREE_PROPERTY some overall metadata can be set:

► With parameters IV_MULTIPLE_MATCH and IV_QUALIFIED_MATCH you can switch the processing mode from the default first-match-mode either to qualified-match-mode or alternatively to multiple-match-mode. The parameters must be used mutually exclusive.

► Parameter IV_EXECUTES_ACTION allows switching to an action result type.

► If IV_ALLOW_NO_MATCH is set to ABAP_TRUE no runtime error occurs if no matching node with result is traversed at runtime. Instead, the expression will return a default initial result value.

► The possibility of assigning results to all nodes can make a search tree quite compact. However, every search tree can be (re-)designed in a way so that only the bottom leaf nodes return results. To enforce such a tree structure, parameter IV_ONLY_LEAF_RESULT can be set to ABAP_TRUE.

The search tree structure can be built up node by node, similar to a decision tree. A new Search Tree expression implicitly contains a root node with an internal node ID. This node ID can be retrieved with method GET_ROOT_NODE.

With method SET_NODE_PROPERTY and the node ID, the condition and optionally a result can be set or changed for a node. Value range comparisons and constant result values can directly be specified with parameters IS_RANGE or IR_RESULT in respect.

In contrast to the Decision Tree expression, new nodes need to be created explicitly with method CREATE_NODE. To position the new node correctly in the tree structure, the internal IDs of the parent node and/or the "left," preceding sibling node need to be passed with the parameters IV_PARENT and IV_SIBLING. If no sibling node is specified, the node automatically becomes the sub node to the right of all existing sibling nodes. A condition and result for the new node can directly be specified like in method SET_NODE_PROPERTY. The internal ID of the new node is provided in parameter EV_NODE.

A node including all its subsequent nodes can be deleted from the search tree using method DELETE_NODE. Simply, the internal node ID needs to be passed. For convenience, it is also possible to move the position of an existing node within the search tree. Method MOVE_NODE allows you to specify a new sibling and/or parent node for an existing node.

The direct sub nodes of a node are also called child nodes and can be determined with method GET_CHILDREN. Method GET_TREE_STRUCTURE even provides the whole tree structure as a list of node assignments that correspond to the branches of the tree. Each entry of type S_TREE_STRUCTURE contains a parent and a child node ID together with a sequence number. The sequence number determines the order among sibling nodes from left to right.

5.5.18 Table Operation Expressions

A *Table Operation* expression can be used to perform a sole operation on a table data object. A wide range of operations to choose from is available. See Table 5.45. These can be divided into three categories:

▶ **Information retrieval**
  The table content is analyzed and a result is provided.

▶ **Data retrieval and aggregation**
  Specific parts of the table data are extracted or combined as expression result.

▶ **Modifications**

The table content is modified and the table itself is returned as result.

For almost all available operations, it is possible to define a set of conditions. Similar to the DB Lookup expression (see Section 5.5.7), the conditions are based on value range comparisons for table columns. The conditions will limit the scope of the chosen operation to selected rows. If no conditions are specified all table rows are selected.

Category	Operation	Result Type	Description
Information	Has at least	Boolean	Checks whether the table contains at least a specific number of selected rows.
	Has exactly	Boolean	Checks whether the table contains exactly a specific number of selected rows.
	Has not more than	Boolean	Checks whether the table contains not more than a specific number of selected rows.
	Count	Number	Returns the number of selected rows.
Data Retrieval	First row	Table line	Returns the first selected row.
	Last row	Table line	Returns the last selected row.
	All Lines	Table	Returns all selected rows
	Minimum	Column specific	Returns the minimum value of a specific column from the selected rows. It is only applicable for columns that contain amount, quantity, number, or timepoint values.
	Maximum	Column specific	Returns the maximum value of a specific column from the selected rows. It is only applicable for columns that contain amount, quantity, number, or timepoint values.
	Average	Column specific	Returns the average value of a specific column from the selected rows. It is only applicable for columns that contain amount, quantity, or number values.
	Total	Column specific	Sums up a total value for a specific column from the selected rows. It is only applicable for columns that contain amount, quantity, or number values.

Table 5.45 Table Operations

Category	Operation	Result Type	Description
Modification	Delete first	Table	Deletes the first selected row from the table.
	Delete last	Table	Deletes the last selected row from the table.
	Delete all lines	Table	Deletes all selected rows from the table.
	Sort	Table	Sorts the table rows according to a specific column sequence in ascending or descending order. The column sequence is limited to up to five columns. If no column sequence is specified, the table rows are sorted according to the sequence of table structure fields in ascending order.

Table 5.45 Table Operations (Cont.)

Figure 5.48 shows a typical definition of a Table Operation expression in the BRF-plus Workbench. First you select the desired operation, which will afterwards be reflected by a sentence below. In the sentence, you can select a table data object, enter operation specific data, and define the result data object of the expression. Having selected the table data object, you may also define conditions based on the table columns.

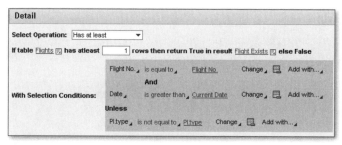

Figure 5.48 Table Operation Expression

The SORT operation differs from the other operations. Having selected the table data object, you cannot define any conditions. Instead, you may define a sorting sequence for up to five table columns. For each column, you can specify whether the values shall be sorted in ascending or descending order, see Figure 5.49.

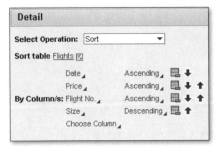

Figure 5.49 Table Operation Expression—Sort Operation

A sorting example is shown in Figure 5.50: A table with three columns is sorted first by the second column in ascending order and then by the first column in descending order.

C1	C2	C3		C1	C2	C3
X	1	5,00€		Z	1	1,20€
A	2	3,99€		Y	1	0,50€
Y	1	0,50€	C2 ascending	X	1	5,00€
Z	2	2,34€	C1 descending	Z	2	2,34€
Z	1	1,20€		A	2	3,99€

Figure 5.50 Table Operation Sort—Example

Table Operation Expression API

The API for the *Table Operation expression* type consists of interface IF_FDT_TABLE_OPERATION. Its methods are summarized in Table 5.46.

Method	Description
SET_TABLE	Sets the table data object for the operation.
SET_OPERATION	Sets the operation to perform on the table data object.
SET_CONDITION	Specifies conditions to select specific table lines for the operation.
SET_NUMBER	Sets a relevant row number for the operations HAS AT LEAST, HAS EXACTLY, HAS NOT MORE THAN.
SET_AGGREGATION_COLUMN	Specifies the column to aggregate for operations MINIMUM, MAXIMUM, AVERAGE and TOTAL.
SET_SORT_COLUMNS	Determines the sorting sequence for operation SORT.

Table 5.46 Methods of Interface IF_FDT_TABLE_OPERATION

First, the table data object for the operation needs to be specified with method SET_TABLE. The operation to perform can be set with method SET_OPERATION. The available operations are reflected by constants with the name pattern GC_OP_*. Accordingly, additional settings can be made.

▶ For the operations HAS AT LEAST, HAS EXACTLY, HAS NOT MORE THAN the relevant number of rows can be set with method SET_NUMBER. By default the relevant number of rows is 1.

▶ For the operations MINIMUM, MAXIMUM, AVERAGE and TOTAL, the column to aggregate can be specified with method SET_AGGREGATION_COLUMN.

▶ For the SORT operation up to five columns that determine the sorting sequence can be declared with method SET_SORT_COLUMNS. For each column, it can be specified whether the values will be sorted in ascending (default) or descending order.

▶ For all but the SORT operation a list of conditions can be defined with method SET_CONDITION. Each condition entry consists of a value range comparison for a specific column. The used table parameter is of structure type S_CONDITION and includes the same fields as structure S_RANGE of interface IF_FDT_RANGE (see also Table 5.19). The additional field COMPONENT refers the table structure element that is used for the comparison. For the OPTION field that defines the comparison operator, only the constant values GC_OPTION_* defined in interface IF_FDT_TALBE_OPERATION are valid.

Finally, the type of the result data object that is set for the expression must match to the result type of the chosen operation (see Table 5.45).

5.5.19 XSL Transformation Expressions

As the name indicates, this expression type performs an *XSL transformation* to derive a result value. Expressions of this type require at least one appropriate XSLT document in the system for that purpose. Such documents can be created with Transaction SE80 or XSLT_TOOL.

XSLT and XML

The abbreviation XSLT refers to *Extensible Stylesheet Language Transformations*, an XML-based language to transform XML documents into other XML documents. It uses a kind of pattern-matching engine on incoming XML data to assemble a new XML document as output. XML in turn refers to the *Extensible Markup Language*, which primarily describes how to encode documents in a specific, structured way.

The XSLT-document that shall be used for the transformation can be determined in two modes. Its ID/name is either statically set at design time of the expression, or it can be determined dynamically at runtime via a specific context parameter or nested expression.

An additional list of context parameters or nested expressions can be used as input for the XSL-transformation. In the XSLT-document, the underlying data objects can be referenced as equally named XML-elements. At runtime the respective content will be linked to those elements. Similarly, the name of the expression's result data object determines which parts of the XML-document that the transformation generates will be used as expression result.

Figure 5.51 illustrates the principle of operation. The expression shown as an example uses a context parameter INPUT as input for the transformation and a result data object RESULT for the output. The transformation that will be performed is determined by context parameter XSLT_ID. The XSLT-document that is used in the example checks only whether parameter INPUT contains the value "TEST_VALUE." It includes the value "RESULT_VALUE" for the RESULT data object in this case; otherwise, the result content remains empty.

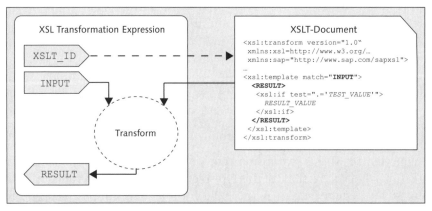

Figure 5.51 XSL Transformation Example

In the BRFplus Workbench, such an expression definition would look like in the screenshot in Figure 5.52. If the expression should instead use a statically defined transformation, you would need to click on the button USE DIRECT MODE and then enter the name of the desired transformation directly into an according input field. Additional input parameters for the transformation could easily be added into the table below.

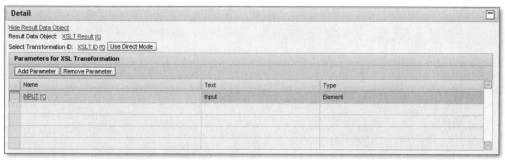

Figure 5.52 XSL Transformation Expression

XSL Transformation Expression API

The interface IF_FDT_XSL_TRANSFORMATION that represents the expression type contains only two methods, which are specified in Table 5.47.

Method	Description
SET_TRANSFORMATION	Specifies which XSLT-transformation will be used and how the transformation to use is determined.
SET_PARAMETERS	Defines a list of context parameters and expressions that will be used as input for the transformation.

Table 5.47 Methods of Interface IF_FDT_XSL_TRANSFORMATION

Method SET_TRANSFORMATION has two parameters that can only be used exclusively:

▸ Parameter IV_TRANSFORMATION refers directly to the name of an active transformation document in the system. The expression will use this statically declared transformation at runtime.

▸ Parameter IV_TRANSFORMATION_ID refers to a context parameter or expression that will determine the name of the transformation to use at runtime.

5.6   Actions

Actions define the interactive part of BRFplus. They are a special type of expressions that do not determine a result value but rather carry out changes, notifications, or other activities outside of BRFplus. Like normal expressions they may use context parameters and nested expressions as input to accomplish their work. Due to their task of manipulating data rather than retrieving data, actions may require database changes during processing. In this case, other pending database changes might also be committed. This should be kept in mind when calling a function that uses actions.

An action instance can always define an arbitrary number of follow-up actions so that a chain of actions will actually be executed at runtime. In the BRFplus Workbench, the additional actions can be maintained on a separate tab, as shown in Figure 5.53. The order of the follow-up actions may play a role because some action types allow changes on the context data, for example.

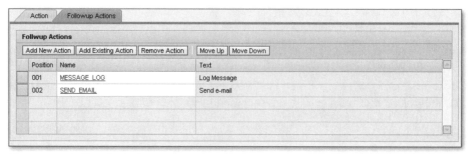

Figure 5.53 Follow-Up Actions

At runtime BRFplus collects the IDs of all executed actions into the standard table data object `ACTIONS` of application `FDT_SYSTEM`. If the object is part of a function result, it can be used for further analysis afterwards. For example, it is possible to check whether a specific action was triggered or not.

Table 5.48 lists all standard action types available with BRFplus in alphabetical order. The column "DB Commit" indicates whether the action type implicitly commits changes to the database. If not, this must be done explicitly when the function processing has finished.

Action Type	Description	DB Commit
Log Message	Writes a message into a specific application log.	no
Procedure Call	Calls either the static method of an ABAP class or a function module.	undefined
Send Email	Sends an email to a specific list of recipients.	yes
Start Workflow	Starts the execution of a workflow.	yes
Workflow Event	Triggers an event for a specific object to start or continue an according workflow.	yes

Table 5.48 Standard Action Types

5.6.1 Actions API

Each action type defines an ABAP interface that must extend the common interface IF_FDT_ACTION. It includes the interface IF_FDT_EXPRESSION so that actions are technically just a special kind of expressions. Consequently the attribute MV_EXPRESSION_TYPE_ID represents not only expression but also action types.

With the method SET_FOLLOWUP_ACTIONS of interface IF_FDT_ACTION the optional list of follow-up actions can be configured. It requires simply a list of corresponding action IDs.

The factory interface IF_FDT_FACTORY has no separate method for obtaining action objects. Instead, method GET_EXPRESSION can be reused to get or create also action instances. For action objects, the Boolean attribute MV_ACTION of the expression interface is set to ABAP_TRUE. It indicates that the object can be cast to interface IF_FDT_ACTION. But usually a specific action type is already expected when method GET_EXPRESSION is called, and the object is directly cast into the corresponding interface.

5.6.2 Log Message Action

Log Message actions can be used to add one or multiple messages to an application log. Application logs can be maintained in the system with Transaction SLG0. They are categorized by a LOG OBJECT and LOG SUB OBJECT. In the BRFplus Workbench, they can be entered into the according input fields (see Figure 5.54). In addition, individual logs can be associated with an external identifier so that they can easily be grouped, for example. This optional EXTERNAL IDENTIFICATION REFERENCE can be up to 100 characters long.

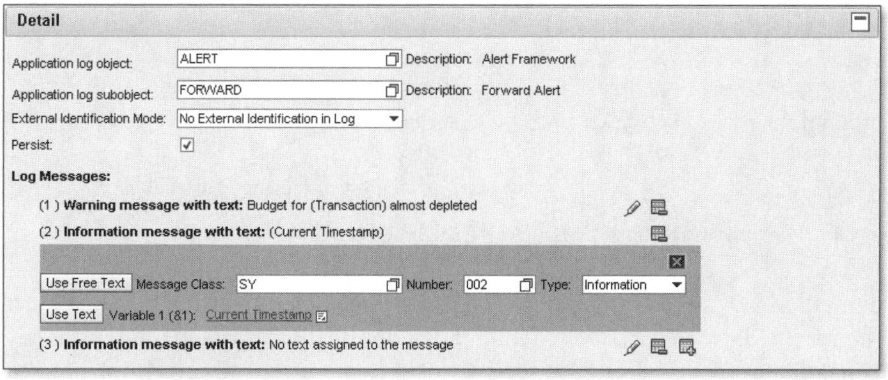

Figure 5.54 Log Message Action

By default, the log messages are kept only in memory for temporary usage. They can, however, also be persisted onto the database. In the UI the checkbox PERSIST needs to be marked accordingly.

The log object, sub object, and persistence settings can be preset by the corresponding default settings of the BRFplus application that the Log Message action belongs to. The application can even influence the changeability and visibility of these settings (see Section 3.4.2).

If an external log identifier is to be used, the EXTERNAL IDENTIFICATION MODE must be selected accordingly in the UI: The identifier can then either be set directly as text, or it can be determined at runtime by a referenced context parameter or expression.

The log messages that shall be written to the log can be entered as free text, or existing/predefined messages can be retrieved from a MESSAGE CLASS. Such messages are maintained with Transaction SE91 in the system. In the UI you can toggle between the two modes by clicking on the button USE FREE TEXT/USE PREDEFINED MESSAGE.

To each message, one of the standard message types—"Information," "Status," "Warning," "Error," "Abort," or "Exit"—can be assigned. If a message comprises placeholders (&1, &2, &3 and &4), they can be supplied by an according list of defined values, context parameters or expressions. In the UI you might need to press ⎡Enter⎤ for one of the message input fields to refresh the list of placeholders.

Log Message Action API

The Log Message action type uses the ABAP interface IF_FDT_ACTN_MESSAGE_LOG. Its methods are listed in Table 5.49.

Method	Description
SET_APPLICATION_LOG_OBJECT	Specifies the target log for the messages.
SET_PERSISTENCY_SETTINGS	Indicates whether the log messages shall be persisted.
SET_MESSAGES	Defines the list of messages to be logged.

Table 5.49 Methods of Interface IF_FDT_ACTN_MESSAGE_LOG

With method SET_APPLICATION_LOG_OBJECT the target log object and log sub object can be specified. An external log identifier can optionally be passed, either directly with parameter IV_EXTERNAL of type BALNREXT, or as a referenced object with parameter IV_EXTERNAL_ID.

If the log shall be persisted onto the database, the corresponding property can be set with method SET_PERSISTENCY_SETTINGS.

The messages that shall be added to the log can be defined with method SET_MES-SAGES. The line type of its importing table parameter TS_MESSAGE comprises the fields described in Table 5.50.

Fields	Description
SEQUENCE_NUMBER	Determines the order of the messages.
TEXT	Contains a message as plain text.
MSGID, MSGNO	Refer to a specific message that is predefined in a message class in the system. The two fields can be used instead of field TEXT.
MSGTY	Specifies the type of the message. The standard ABAP message types are supported: I — Information S — Status W — Warning E — Error A — Abort X — Exit
MSGV1_TXT, MSGV2_TXT, MSGV3_TXT, MSGV4_TXT	Contain values for corresponding placeholders &n in the message, with n = 1, ..., 4.
MSGV1, MSGV2, MSGV3, MSGV4	Refer to context parameters or expressions that provide values for corresponding placeholders &n in the message. They can be used instead of the respective fields MSGVn_TXT with n = 1, ..., 4.

Table 5.50 Fields of Log Messages

5.6.3 Procedure Call Actions

The *Procedure Call action* type is almost identical to the Procedure Call expression type, which is described in Section 5.5.14. The only difference is that no explicit result value can be returned with the result data object. The action type is, therefore, destined to perform some activities outside of BRFplus. However, context parameters can still be changed by a procedure call action if exporting or changing parameters are used.

Procedure Call Action API

Because the Procedure Call action type is an update of the former Static Method Call action type, the interface IF_FDT_ACTN_STATIC_METHOD is still used. The interface is identical to interface IF_FDT_STATIC_METHOD of the corresponding expression type (see Section 5.5.14, subsection "Procedure Call Expression API"), and therefore is not explained here again.

5.6.4 Send Email Action

With this action type you may send a specific text via email to an arbitrary list of recipients. The recipients can be specified as a string of email addresses that need to be separated by semicolons (;). Furthermore, it is possible to define a list of context parameters and expressions that dynamically provide additional email addresses at runtime.

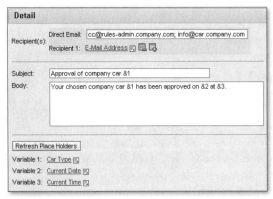

Figure 5.55 Send Email Action

The SUBJECT and BODY of the email consist of plain text that may include placeholders for dynamic content. The placeholders have the format &n with n being a number in the range from 1 to 8. For each placeholder, a context parameter or expression can be assigned that determines the value to insert at runtime. In the UI the button REFRESH PLACE HOLDERS needs to be clicked on to get the list of actually used placeholders.

> **Application Server Configuration**
>
> For sending emails the application server needs to be appropriately configured. This includes mainly the SAPconnect administration with Transaction SCOT. Further details and prerequisites are explained in SAP note 455140.

Send Email Action API

The interface for Send Email actions is `IF_FDT_ACTN_EMAIL`. The methods used in this interface are listed in Table 5.51. A static list of recipients or rather their email addresses can be specified with method `SET_RECIPIENTS`. Expressions or context parameters that shall determine recipients at runtime may be set with the importing parameter `ITS_RECIPIENT_PARAMETER` of method `SET_PARAMETER`.

The subject text and body text of the email can be defined with the corresponding methods `SET_SUBJECT` and `SET_BODY`. If these texts contain placeholders (&n, n = 1, ..., 8), a corresponding list of context parameters or expressions can be configured with the importing parameter `ITS_MESSAGE_PARAMETER` of method `SET_PARAMETER`. The position of the parameter entries correspond to the placeholder number n.

Method	Description
SET_RECIPIENTS	Defines the recipients of the email as a static list of email addresses.
SET_SUBJECT	Defines the subject of the email as plain text.
SET_BODY	Sets the email content as plain text.
SET_PARAMETERS	Two lists of parameters for variable content can be set: One determines an additional set of recipients, the other is used to fill-in values for placeholders in the message of the email.

Table 5.51 Methods of Interface IF_FDT_ACTN_EMAIL

5.6.5 Start Workflow Actions

Actions of this type allow you to start a specific workflow in the system. The actual execution of the workflow will be performed asynchronously.

Workflows and Tasks

A workflow can shortly be summarized to be a sequence or even mashup of tasks, which can either be executed automatically or require the involvement of dedicated persons. Workflows are usually defined with Transaction SWDD, the *Workflow Builder*. Workflow tasks can be regarded as single step workflows. They can be maintained separately with Transaction PFTC.

A Start Workflow action first requires the ID of an existing workflow or task definition. By default the chosen workflow will be immediately started in the background, when the action is processed. However, it is possible to specify a delay so that the workflow is not started until a specific period of time has elapsed. Meanwhile, some follow-up actions can be executed.

Figure 5.56 gives an impression of how a Start Workflow action may be defined in the BRFplus Workbench.

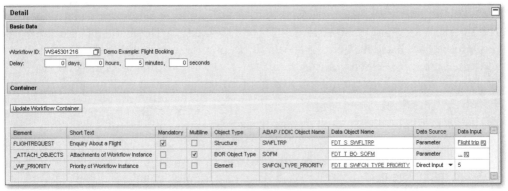

Figure 5.56 Start Workflow Action

Committing Changes

BRFplus never commits database changes itself during function processing. However, the workflow does! You should keep this in mind if you want to roll-back changes that the BRF-plus function may have triggered elsewhere.

Workflow Container

Workflows incorporate a container that consists of a collection of data elements. The container is used to exchange data along the processed task chain. For container elements that are marked with an import indicator, it is possible to pass values when the workflow is started. Some elements may even be marked to be mandatory. This is typically the case for the key fields of an associated business object.

Business Objects (BOR)

Similar to ABAP classes, business objects are entities that encapsulate data (attributes), methods, and events. Because the objects are stored in a *business object repository*, they are also referred to as BOR-objects. The maintenance of such object types can be carried out with the *business object builder*, Transaction SWO1.

In the BRFplus Workbench, the importing elements of the workflow container are displayed or refreshed after the entered WORKFLOW ID has been confirmed by pressing [Enter]. Alternatively, you can click the button UPDATE WORKFLOW CONTAINER for that purpose.

The importing elements can be mapped to defined values, context parameters or expressions. BRFplus automatically generates new data objects that match to the types of the corresponding container elements. If these data objects are added to the function or ruleset context, they can directly be used for the mapping. Alternatively, expressions can be created that use the generated data objects as result data object.

In the UI, the workflow container mapping is defined with a table that comprises the following columns:

▶ ELEMENT
The name of the container element.

▶ MANDATORY
Indicates whether a mapping of the element is required.

▶ MULTILINE
Indicates whether the element allows multiple lines of data and therefore corresponds to a table type.

▶ OBJECT TYPE
Shows the basic type of the container element. This can be for example "Element," "Structure," "Table," "BOR Object," or "ABAP Class." Only elements of type "ESI service object" are not supported.

▶ ABAP/DDIC OBJECT NAME
Shows the actual data type name of the element.

▶ DATA OBJECT NAME
Contains the name of the accordingly generated BRFplus data object.

▶ DATA SOURCE
Defines how the container element is mapped. For simple types it is possible to directly enter a value, whereas complex types can only be mapped to context parameters or expressions.

▶ DATA INPUT
This column contains the actual mapping, which consists of either a directly entered simple value or the referenced data or expression object. In the latter case, it is possible to choose the link menu entry GET EXPRESSION FOR DIRECT DATA INPUT, which may be useful especially for multiline/table type container elements. It generates a Decision Table expression with result columns that match to the table line type. The data to map can be directly entered into the result columns there.

Key Structures

The BRFplus data objects that are generated to map BOR-objects, classes, or XML messages of the workflow container are usually structures. They encompass key fields that are suitable to access an according object instance. The objects may, however, also be accessed by internal keys of the following structure types:

- Structure `SIBFLPORB` for BOR-objects
- Structure `SWF_LPORB` for classes and XML messages

The *Start Workflow* action therefore allows mapping to data objects that are bound to these corresponding DDIC structures.

Agents

If the entered WORKFLOW ID refers to a single task only, a list of "agents" that shall be addressed to execute the task can be assigned. Agents can be selected users or other entities of the organizational management such as positions, jobs, roles and organizational units. Transaction PPOS can be used to display the organizational plan.

Agents for the Start Workflow action can either be listed statically or determined at runtime by an appropriate context parameter or expression. The used context or result data object needs to be of a table or structure type and must be compatible to the DDIC structure `SWRAGENT`. It is also possible to mix both kinds of agent definitions, the static and the dynamic. At runtime both sources will then be connected. Figure 5.57 shows such an example.

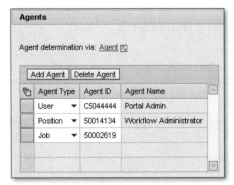

Figure 5.57 Start Workflow Action—Agents

Agent Assignment Settings

You can maintain the agent assignment settings for a specific task in Transaction PFTC under the menu entry ADDITIONAL DATA • AGENT ASSIGNMENT • MAINTAIN. The button ATTRIBUTES... leads to general assignment settings. Only if the task is set up as GENERAL TASK any agents may be used.

You should be aware that tasks usually limit the agent assignment to a specific list of allowed agents. In the UI the search help for the AGENT ID may therefore provide only selected results or even no results. Ineligible agents will result in an error when the action is checked.

Start Workflow Action API

The relevant interface IF_FDT_ACTN_START_WORKFLOW does not only offer methods to set or get the different properties. As listed in Table 5.52, it also contains some convenience methods to adapt to workflow changes or to retrieve some general information.

Method	Description
SET_WORKFLOW_ID	Sets the workflow or task that shall be started.
CHECK_WORKFLOW_EXISTENCE	Indicates whether the passed ID refers to an existing workflow or task instance.
GET_ALLOWED_WORKFLOW_TYPES	Returns a list of supported workflow types.
SET_DELAY	Optionally defines a delay for the starting of the workflow.
CALCULATE_DELAY_IN_SEC	Converts and sums up a number of days, hours, minutes, and seconds into a corresponding number of seconds.
CALCULATE_DELAY_IN_DHMS	Converts a number of seconds into a corresponding number of days, hours, minutes, and seconds.
SET_CONTAINER	Defines a mapping for workflow container elements.
UPDATE_CONTAINER	Updates an existing container mapping by generating data objects that match to the workflow container elements.
GET_VALUE_DI_EXPR	Gets or generates a Decision Table expression for a single container element mapping.
CHECK_WORKFLOW_FOR_ACTUALITY	Checks whether referenced workflow was altered after the last activation of the action.
GET_CONTAINER_INSTANCE	Returns the workflow container for a specific workflow ID.
SET_AGENTS	In case the set workflow ID refers to a single task only, this method specifies the agents that may handle the task.
GET_ALLOWED_AGENT_TYPES	Returns a list of supported agent types.
GET_AGENT_TYPE_TEXT	Returns short text descriptions for a specific list of agent types.

Table 5.52 Methods of Interface IF_FDT_ACTN_START_WORKFLOW

The workflow or task that shall be started can be specified with method SET_WORK-FLOW_ID. A delay in seconds can optionally be set with method SET_DELAY. With the methods CALCULATE_DELAY_* it is possible to split the delay into according numbers of days, hours, minutes and seconds or vice versa.

If the container of the set workflow includes mandatory elements, an adequate container mapping needs to be defined with method SET_CONTAINER. The container setting is otherwise optional. The structure of the passed mapping table comprises the fields listed in Table 5.53.

Field	Description
SEQUENCE_NR	Defines the order of the elements.
NAME	Contains the name of the workflow container element to map.
VALUE_TYPE	References the BRFplus data object that matches to the container element type.
VALUE	Maps a value directly to the container element.
VALUE_ID	Maps a data object or expression to the container element. This may again be the data object defined in VALUE_TYPE if it is part of the context.
VALUE_DI_EXPR	Retains a reference to an expression that was explicitly generated for direct input. This may currently be the ID of a decision table. Usually, this field is either empty or contains the same value as VALUE_ID.

Table 5.53 Fields of Structure IF_FDT_ACTN_START_WORKFLOW=>S_CONTAINER

For field VALUE_TYPE the container mapping requires data objects that match the container elements. Such data objects are automatically generated when method UPDATE_CONTAINER is called. It is therefore recommended that you call this method first and then retrieve a template of the container mapping with method GET_CON-TAINER. The individual entries of the mapping template can be completed and eventually be set with method SET_CONTAINER.

Method CHECK_WORKFLOW_FOR_ACTUALITY allows for checking whether the used workflow was altered after the action has been activated. In such a case it might be required to adjust the action, especially the container mapping, accordingly.

For the starting of a single workflow task, the agents that shall be addressed for its execution can be specified with method SET_AGENTS. Parameter IV_AGENT_ID refers to a context parameter or expression that provides one or multiple entries of DDIC type SWRAGENT. Table parameter ITS_AGENT can be used to specify a constant set of agents. Its structure type S_AGENT comprises the fields listed in Table 5.54.

Field	Description
SEQUENCE_NR	Defines the order of the entries.
OTYPE	Contains the agent type and corresponds to field SWRAGENT-OTYPE.
REALO	Contains the agent type specific agent ID and corresponds to field SWRAGENT-OBJID.
OTYPE_TEXT	Optional agent type description, can be retrieved with method GET_AGENT_TYPE_TEXT.
REALO_TEXT	Optional agent ID description.

Table 5.54 Fields of Structure IF_FDT_ACTN_START_WORKFLOW=>S_AGENT

5.6.6 Workflow Event Actions

Workflow Event actions allow you to start or continue an active workflow by triggering the event of a connected object. As for Start Workflow actions, a data container that consists of the event parameters can be mapped to transfer according information at runtime.

In general, two different types of objects may currently trigger a workflow event:

▶ BOR objects that have been created with the Business Object Builder, Transaction SWO1.

▶ ABAP classes that implement interface IF_WORKFLOW.

In the BRFplus Workbench, the object type is referred to as OBJECT CATEGORY in the section EVENT PROPERTIES (see also Figure 5.58). The triggering object and event name can be specified below.

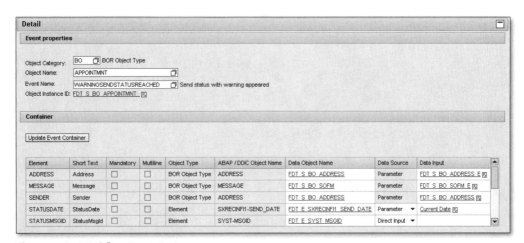

Figure 5.58 Workflow Event Action

The actual event object instance that triggers the event can be determined only at runtime via an according context parameter or expression result. The link GET EXPRESSION FOR DIRECT DATA INPUT of the OBJECT INSTANCE ID automatically generates a decision table expression with a matching result column for that purpose:

▶ For BOR-objects, the OBJECT INSTANCE ID can be set by means of a structure that consists of the object's key attributes. Alternatively, the ID can be passed by an element that is derived from DDIC-type `SIBFBORIID`.

▶ For ABAP class objects, the ID can be passed using a element that is compatible to DDIC-type `SIBFINSTID`.

Pressing `Enter` on the EVENT NAME input field or clicking on the button UPDATE EVENT CONTAINER will update the list of event parameters that can be mapped in the CONTAINER section. The mapping is defined the same way as it is done for the workflow container of Start Workflow actions (see Section 5.6.5).

Workflow Event Action API

The interface for Workflow Event actions is `IF_FDT_ACTN_RAISE_EVENT`. The methods used in this interface are listed in Table 5.55.

Method	Description
SET_EVENT_PROPERTIES	Configures the event to trigger.
CREATE_EVENT_VALUE_TYPE	Creates and sets a data object that matches to the type of the required event object identifier.
GET_EVENT_VALUE_DI_EXPR	Generates a decision table expression that can be used to determine the event object instance.
CHECK_EVENT	Checks whether a specific event exists.
SET_CONTAINER	Defines a mapping for event container elements.
UPDATE_CONTAINER	Updates an existing container mapping by generating data objects that match to the event container elements.
GET_VALUE_DI_EXPR	Gets or generates a decision table expression for a single container element mapping.

Table 5.55 Methods of Interface IF_FDT_RAISE_EVENT

With method `SET_EVENT_PROPERTIES` the event that shall be triggered can be configured. A structure of type `S_EVENT_PROPERTIES` needs to be passed. It comprises the fields in Table 5.56.

Field	Description
OBJECT_CAT	Specifies the event object category, typically BO for BOR-objects and CL for ABAP class objects. All valid values are defined in domain SIBFCATID.
OBJECT_TYPE	Refers to the name of the used event object.
NAME	Refers to the name of the event that shall be triggered.
VALUE	Sets a static event object identifier.
VALUE_ID	Specifies a context parameter or expression that determines the event object identifier at runtime.
VALUE_TYPE	References a data object that matches to type of the event object identifier.
VALUE_DI_EXPR	Retains a reference to an expression that was explicitly generated for the object identifier. Usually, this field is either empty or contains the same value as VALUE_ID.

Table 5.56 Fields of Structure IF_FDT_RAISE_EVENT=>S_EVENT_PROPERTIES

If no data object is available for field VALUE_TYPE, it can be automatically generated and set with method CREATE_EVENT_VALUE_TYPE. A matching decision table expression can be generated with method GET_EVENT_VALUE_DI_EXPR for the fields VALUE_ID and VALUE_DI_EXPR in respect. The static method CHECK_EVENT is only a utility that helps to determine whether a specific event actually exists.

If the container of the event includes mandatory elements, an adequate container mapping needs to be defined with method SET_CONTAINER. The container setting is otherwise optional. The structure S_CONTAINER of the passed mapping table is identical to the one in interface IF_FDT_ACTN_START_WORKFLOW and therefore also comprises the fields in Table 5.53. As for a Start Workflow action, it is recommended that you call method UPDATE_CONTAINER first and retrieve a still incomplete template afterwards with method GET_CONTAINER.

BRFplus is rich in tools that can be accessed from the Workbench. Some of them, like the simulation tool, can be relevant for all users. However, most of the tools are intended for administrative tasks and address expert users.

6 Tools and Administration

BRFplus provides a set of supportive tools that is accessible via the TOOLS menu at the very top of the Workbench. Each tool can be considered to be an independent application. Once started, the tool navigates away from the Workbench. However, the TOOLS menu remains within the different tools so that it is possible to switch directly from one tool to another. Only the menu entry for the currently active tool is disabled.

To return to the Workbench, there is always the BACK TO WORKBENCH button at the bottom of the UI. In addition, the Workbench is regarded as a tool itself and becomes selectable in the TOOLS menu from other tools.

By default the TOOLS menu comprises only two entries: one for a simulation tool and one for the Workbench itself. When users switch to expert mode via the menu WORKBENCH • USER MODE, the setting SHOW TECHNICAL ASPECTS in the user personalization is activated by default. If the setting is active, the complete set of tools becomes available in the TOOLS menu, as illustrated in Figure 6.1.

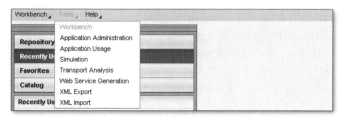

Figure 6.1 BRFplus Workbench—Tools Menu

All available tools in the Workbench are briefly summarized in Table 6.1.

Authorization

To access a specific tool, the user must have the required authorization. Authorization object `FDT_WORKB`, field `FDT_WB_ACT` is used for this purpose. Each tool corresponds to a specific numeric value for this field. The values are listed in the documentation for the field in Transaction SU21. Alternatively, they can be retrieved from domain `FDT_WORKBENCH_ACTIVITY` with Transaction SE11.

Tool	Description
Simulation	A function can be processed for testing and debugging purposes. Test data for the function context can be entered or imported. Besides the overall function result, intermediate processing steps and values also can be listed.
Application Administration	The tool helps optimize an application mainly by getting rid of objects or object versions that are no longer required.
Application Usage	Interrelationships among multiple applications can be detected and analyzed.
Transport Analysis	Transport requests with recorded BRFplus content can be analyzed and corrected, if required. The import of pending transports can be restarted.
Web Service Generation	A Web service that calls a specific BRFplus function can be generated.
XML Export	BRFplus objects can be exported into an XML file.
XML Import	BRFplus objects can be imported from an XML file.

Table 6.1 Tools in the BRFplus Workbench

Before the Workbench tools are described in more detail, it needs to be mentioned that some additional tools exist in the form of ABAP reports. These tools are not available in the BRFplus Workbench and can only be used in the SAP GUI. They are mainly designed as utilities for the SAP support and are not meant as a tool extension for the general public. Keep this in mind when you want to try them out. Since some of the tools allow for irreversible changes, including the danger of data loss, only users with an advanced set of technical and administrative skills should use them at their own risk. In any case, SAP will not to be held liable for any unwanted effects whatsoever that may arise when using those ABAP reports. Table 6.2 lists some rather uncritical reports that may provide useful information. Reports that are related to tools in the Workbench are mentioned in the following sections.

Report	Description
FDT_MASS_CHECK	Checks multiple objects for consistency.
FDT_OBJECT_DB_ENTRIES	Shows the database entries of saved objects.
FDT_SHOW_OBJ_REFERENCE_TREE	Shows the objects that are referenced by a specific object.
FDT_SHOW_OBJ_USAGE_TREE	Shows the objects that are using a specific object.

Table 6.2 Excerpt of Utility Reports

6.1 Simulation Tool

With the simulation tool, a function can be processed for testing or debugging purposes. Actually, only the last active version of the function and its referenced objects will be simulated. Inactive functions without an active version cannot be processed.

The tool can be invoked either from the TOOLS menu or also directly from the toolbar in the DETAIL section of the function UI, as depicted in Figure 6.2. In the first case, you need to select the function to process first. In the second case, the tool is displayed in a popup window and the current function is automatically preselected. You can switch to other functions with the button SELECT OTHER FUNCTION without leaving the tool.

Detail
Start Simulation
Show Traces
Generate Web Service
Properties
Signature
Assigned Rulesets
Code Generation
Mode:
Event Mode

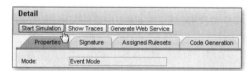

Figure 6.2 Simulation Tool—Invocation in the Function UI

In the section CONTEXT VALUES beneath the selected function, you can enter any test data for the context parameters of the function, as depicted in Figure 6.3.

Context Values
Import Test Data
Car CO² Emission:
129
Fuel Type:
Diesel
Diesel
Gross Price:
28,576.00
EUR
European Euro
Net Price:
25,400.00
EUR
European Euro

Figure 6.3 Simulation Tool—Context Values

Data for elements and structure fields can be entered into plain input fields. Figure 6.4 illustrates the data entry for table type parameters. First you have to add the desired number of table rows with button ADD ROW. Then you can enter the table content cell by cell by clicking on the contained links.

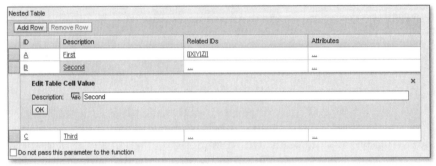

Figure 6.4 Simulation Tool — Table Context Parameters

It is also possible to enter data for deeply nested structures and tables. Nested structures and tables are represented by links for navigation. The current nesting path will be shown on top of the currently displayed data object, as Figure 6.5 illustrates. The nesting path consists of links that allow navigation back to the parent data objects.

Figure 6.5 Simulation Tool — Nested Context Parameters

The simulation will be triggered with the button RUN SIMULATION at the bottom of the screen. It can be run in two different modes that are selectable in the section SIMULATION MODE just above the button. If you are interested only in the function result, you can keep the option SHOW ONLY RESULT. When the alternative option SHOW ALSO RESULTS OF INTERMEDIATE STEPS is selected, single processing steps will be traced during the computation of the function result.

> **Code Generation**
>
> The simulation tool always processes the selected function in interpretation mode so that no code generation takes place. The last generated ABAP class for the function may therefore not reflect changes that have been simulated only.

After the function has been processed, the tool display switches to a RESULT view with the evaluated result at the top. When intermediate steps have been traced, they are shown underneath in the form of a tree structure. Figure 6.6 shows an example of such a result display.

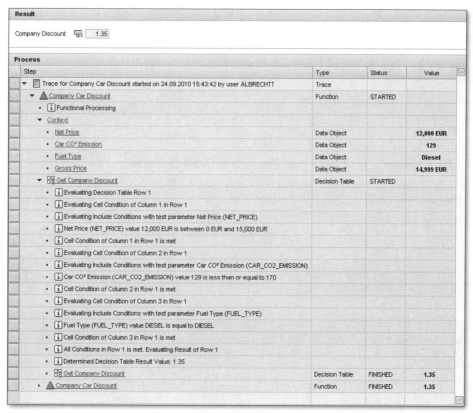

Figure 6.6 Simulation Tool — Result Display

The tree structure reflects the nesting of the actually processed objects and allows collapsing or expanding specific parts. The available information depends on the respective object types. For expressions, the determined intermediate results are always listed on the right-hand side in column VALUE.

Having run the simulation, you may now close the simulation tool. But if you want to configure another simulation setup you can click on the BACK button at the top of the result screen instead.

Mass Testing

The simulation tool can also be used for mass testing. It supports the import of test data for the context parameters from a Microsoft Excel sheet. In the upper right corner of the CONTEXT VALUES section, the button IMPORT TEST DATA needs to be clicked on for this purpose. However, for importing there is the limitation that table data objects are not supported. If table data objects are part of the function context the IMPORT button is disabled. When the button is clicked on, the section CONTEXT EXPORT/IMPORT that is depicted in Figure 6.7 appears.

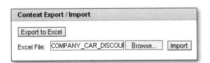

Figure 6.7 Simulation Tool—Excel Import

The Excel sheet that shall be imported needs to contain a column for each element of the function context. As a header line, the names of the elements have to be declared in the first row. For elements that are part of a structure, the structure name needs to be prepended with a - (dash) as a delimiter, for example STRUCTURE-ELEMENT. A compatible Excel template can easily be generated with the button EXPORT TO EXCEL.

In the Excel sheet the rows below the header line can be filled with test data. Figure 6.8 serves as a simple example.

	A	B	C	D
1	GROSS_PRICE	CAR_CO2_EMISSION	FUEL_TYPE	NET_PRICE
2	14000 EUR	180	Gas	13500 EUR
3	16000 EUR	156	Diesel	14400 EUR
4	21000 EUR	171	Gas	19999 EUR
5	25600 EUR	145	Diesel	24100 EUR

Figure 6.8 Simulation Tool—Excel Sheet

The format of the data must match the corresponding element type. Table 6.3 lists those formats and provides an example for each type. When you generate an Excel template, it has an additional HELP sheet that also provides the latest information about the formats.

Element Type	Pattern	Example
Text	*	Abc123
Number	###.###.###	123.456.789
Boolean	TRUE/FALSE	TRUE
Amount	###.###.### CURRENCY	123.456.789 USD
Quantity	###.###.### UNIT	123.456.789 M
Timepoint—Date	YYYYMMDD	20101231
Timepoint—Time	HHMMSS	100000
Timepoint—Date & Time	YYYYMMDD HHMMSS	20101231 100000
Timepoint—Timestamp	YYYYMMDDHHMMSS	20101231100000

Table 6.3 Simulation Tool—Data Type Format in Excel

The completed Excel sheet has to be saved into a file first. The file can then be selected for the field EXCEL FILE in the simulation tool with the help of the BROWSE... button. Clicking on the IMPORT button next to it will import all non-empty rows and present them as a table of individually selectable test data sets. This process is depicted in Figure 6.9.

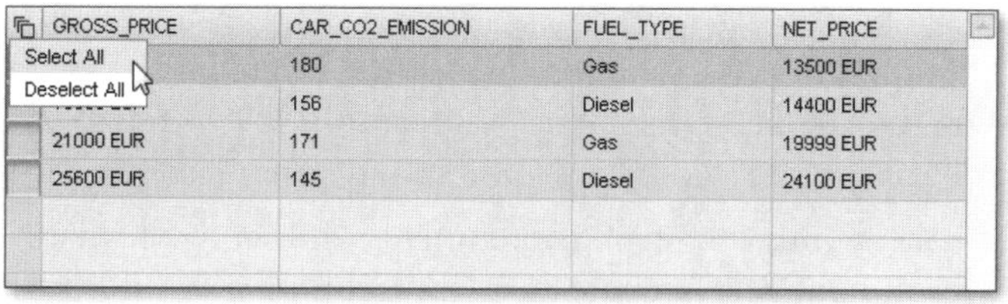

Figure 6.9 Simulation Tool—Test Data Selection

You can select a single row of test data in the table and run the simulation for the context values as usual by clicking on the button RUN FOR SELECTED TEST DATA. This is recommended in combination with the tracing of intermediate steps, if you need an in-depth analysis.

Another option is to select multiple test cases and click on the button EXPORT RESULT TO EXCEL. The function will then be processed for all selected rows of test data, one after another, and the results will be written into a file. To select all test cases at once, you can use the menu in the upper-left corner of the table display.

6.2   XML Export and Import

The XML export tool allows you to generate an XML file for selected objects or even a whole application. The file will contain all data that is required to recreate the last active versions of the objects. Previous versions or inactive versions cannot be exported with the tool. This can only be achieved via the API.

Together with the XML import tool it is possible to move or copy objects from one system to another, without using ABAP transports. Also, local objects can be transferred in this way.

The XML import will create the objects with their original UUIDs (Universally Unique Identifiers) in the target system in case they do not exist yet. If an object with the same UUID but different object type should be detected, the import will fail. However, such cases usually do not occur.

The application of the objects must already have been transferred or it needs to be contained in the imported XML file as well. The file content will always be imported into inactive object versions first. The versions can be activated only if also all referenced objects are available in the target system. For each object, the activation will, as usual, either replace the latest active version or add a new active version, depending on the individual versioning setting.

For the transformation into XML, two different schemas are supported: an internal and an external one. The schema defines the actual formatting of the XML document:

▶ The *internal schema* is used by default. The names of the resulting XML elements are rather technical and capitalized. Values are abbreviated when feasible.

▶ The *external schema* is intended to create XML documents with better readability. The names of the resulting XML elements look less technical and values are reflected by descriptive texts. However, the resulting XML document typically becomes larger.

With each new SAP NetWeaver release, enhancement package or even support package BRFplus objects may include additional attributes or other changes. If necessary, the XML schemas are adapted accordingly and receive a new version. The version number is stored within the XML documents to ensure a correct parsing of the content.

The XML schema version needs to be considered when objects shall be exchanged among systems of different SAP NetWeaver versions. By default objects are exported with the latest schema version supported by the system. BRFplus allows however exporting objects also with a lower version. This is necessary in case the object shall be transferred to a system of a lower NetWeaver version. The exported objects may however get downgraded in this process so that aspects of newer features get lost.

The highest schema version supported by the system is displayed in the import tool. The import of an XML file with a lower schema version is always possible. Properties that are not configured in the XML file will be supplied with default values in this case. For SAP NetWeaver 7.02, mainly versions beyond 1.07 are relevant.

The general concept of XML export and import has now been described. In the following two sub sections, the XML import and export tools in the Workbench are explained in detail.

6.2.1 XML Export Tool

The XML export tool needs to be run in the source system. It divides the exporting process into three major steps. At first the object to be exported needs to be selected by clicking on the button SELECT AN OBJECT. A dialog will appear where you can search and select the desired object.

Back on the main screen, the following export settings can be adjusted:

▶ INCLUDE REFERENCED OBJECTS
When marked, all referenced objects are exported into the same XML file as well. This might be required if the object is being transferred to a specific target system for the first time. Referenced objects that are contained in a separate application are, however, not included.

▶ INCLUDE SURROUNDING APPLICATION
When marked, the object's application is also exported into the same XML file. This is required if the object is being transferred to a specific target system for the first time.

▶ XML VERSION
Defines the schema version for the XML file. By default, the highest version is preselected. It should be lowered only if the target system is of an older release and does not support the latest version.

▶ XML SCHEMA
Allows choosing between two different XML formats.

If you want to export an entire application with all contained objects, you have to select the application for the OBJECT to export and mark the checkbox INCLUDE REFERENCED OBJECTS.

In the second step the XML file should be generated upon clicking on the button GENERATE XML FILE. All involved objects are checked once more and if no errors occur during the transformation into XML, a success message will be issued. Internally, the export is handled similar to recording onto a transport request. A generated transport request ID starting with $X1P will be displayed in the success message. This ID allows tracking of the exported object versions later on.

In the third and last step, the generated XML file can be downloaded and saved to the local system by clicking on the DOWNLOAD XML FILE button. This process is illustrated by Figure 6.10. A popup will appear where you can choose the desired location for the file.

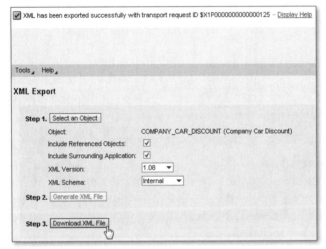

Figure 6.10 XML—Export Tool

An alternative to the tool in the Workbench is report FDT_XML_EXPORT. It provides basically the same functionality.

6.2.2 XML Import Tool

The XML import tool needs to be run in the target system. It requires first an XML file that contains the desired, previously exported BRFplus objects. The XML version of the file must be lower than or equal to the highest supported version, which is displayed just above the button UPLOAD FILE. In Figure 6.11 the highest supported XML version is 1.08.

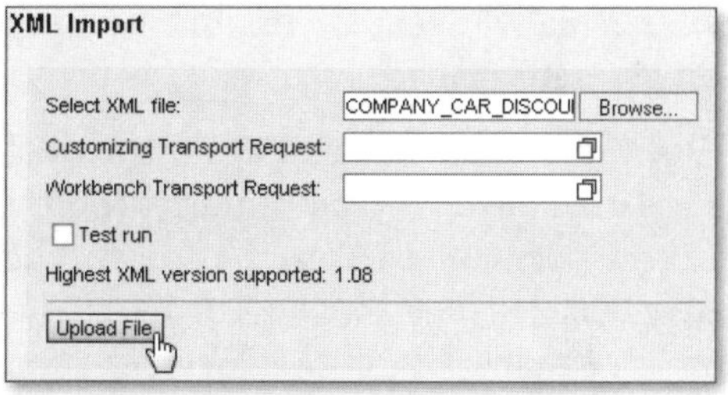

Figure 6.11 XML Import Tool

Depending on the system or client settings for change recording, a transport request may be required. When you import non-local customizing objects, you may have to provide a Customizing Transport Request. For non-local system objects, you may need to provide a Workbench Transport Request.

By ticking the checkbox Test run you can switch to a test mode so that the import will only be simulated. Otherwise, the imported object versions will be activated and saved. When you click on the button Upload File, the importing process is started. If all goes well, a success message will be issued.

The XML import is internally handled similar to import of a transport request. As for the XML export, an ID starting with $X2 for a virtual transport request will be generated and displayed in the success message. The ID allows tracking the origin of the imported object version.

An alternative to the tool in the Workbench is report FDT_XML_IMPORT. In addition to the standard XML import, it supports a "repair mode" to fix corrupted objects. This option should, however, be used with care.

6.2.3 Tracking of Imported Object Versions

When BRFplus objects are changed locally in the system, information about the user and the change timestamp are stored with the new version. If an object version has been imported by means of transport, the transport request is stored and can be used to track the origin of the new version. For object versions that have been imported from an XML document, it is also possible to determine the source.

For each exported XML document, a virtual transport request ID that starts with $X1P is generated. This request ID and also the current source system ID and client are stored as attributes in the root element of the XML document (see Table 6.4). In addition, a copy of the XML document is saved under the request ID in the database table FDT_XML_EXPORT. If the XML document was downgraded to fit to a lower XML schema, two XML documents are actually saved: the original one and the downgraded one that has been accordingly transformed.

When the XML document gets imported into the target system, again a virtual transport request ID that starts with $X2P is generated. For all imported object versions this ID is stored just like a normal transport request. Again, a copy of the XML document is saved: this time in database table FDT_XML_IMPORT. The ID, client, and transport request of the source system are extracted from the document and directly stored as additional information in the database table as well. If the XML document was upgraded to a higher XML schema version during the import, two XML documents are actually saved: the original one and the upgraded one that has been accordingly transformed.

To track an imported object, you have to determine the accordingly generated transport request ID first. For the latest version, this information is for example shown in the Workbench in the GENERAL section, ADDITIONAL INFORMATION tab, IMPORTED BY TRANSPORT field. Figure 6.12 illustrates such a case.

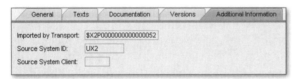

Figure 6.12 XML Import—Virtual Transport Request

Database table FDT_XML_IMPORT can be queried for this ID to find out the source system and client of the object version. In addition, the imported XML document can be retrieved. Report FDT_DEBUG_XML_EXPORT_IMPORT may be used for this purpose. On the source system, the original object can be analyzed. When the object has, for example, been downgraded during export to fit a lower XML schema version, the differences can be deduced.

6.2.4 XML Format

The XML documents created by BRFplus are well formed and valid. This actually means they are syntactically correct according to the XML 1.0 specification and they conform to a Document Type Definition (DTD). The DTD defines the XML elements and attributes used within the document. It also allows checking an XML document for consistency before it actually gets used. The DTD that is defined by BRFplus is stored in the system as a transformation object with the name FDT_APPEND_INTERNAL_DTD. All elements and attributes declared in the DTD are assigned to namespace `FDTNS`, which in turn refers to the URI `http://sap.com/fdt/transport`.

The root element of the XML document that encloses all other elements has the name `FDT`. It may look like the following example.

```
<FDTNS:FDT xmlns:FDTNS=http://sap.com/fdt/transport Client="000"
Date="20100106" BRFplusInitialVersion="1.08" BRFplusSchema="http://
sap.corp/fdt/Internal.xsd" BRFplusVersion="1.08" SAPRelease="702"
Server="aaa0000" SourceExportReqID="$X1P0000000000011083" SystemID="AAA"
Time="053827" User="ABC">
```

In addition to the namespace declaration, the root element incorporates several attributes that provide general information about the exported objects. These attributes are listed in Table 6.4 with a description of their individual content.

Attribute	Content
BRFplusInitialVersion	The highest currently supported schema version of the source system.
BRFplusVersion	The used schema version.
BRFplusSchema	The used schema: internal or external.
SourceExportReqID	A generated transport request ID for the export.
SystemID	ID of the source system.
Client	Client of the source system.
Server	Server name of the source system.
Date	Date of the document generation.
Time	Time of the document generation.
User	Name of the user who generated the document.
SAPRelease	The SAP release of the source system.

Table 6.4 XML Root Element—FDT

The schema referenced by attribute `BRFplusSchema` defines the syntax of the enclosed elements. The internal schema, which is used by default, uses capitalized element names and refers to abbreviated values. An element for this schema would typically look like:

```
<FDTNS:ELEMENT_TYPE>T</FDTNS:ELEMENT_TYPE>
```

The element names defined by the external schema are similar but use only partly upper case letters. Values are expanded into a readable format. With the external schema, the above element would look like:

```
<FDTNS:ElementType FixedValue="T">Text</FDTNS:ElementType>
```

In the following, the element names refer to the internal schema.

In the XML document, each exported object is reflected by an element inside the root element. Those elements are arranged in a specific order (the element names are given in brackets):

1. Application object (APPLICATION)

2. Data objects (DATA_OBJECT)

3. Expression types (EXPRESSION_TYPE)

4. Expressions (EXPRESSION)

5. Rulesets (RULESET)

6. Functions (FUNCTION)

7. Catalogs (CATALOG)

The properties that all objects have in common are bundled by an ADMIN_DATA element. The element is contained for each object and embeds further sub-elements. All other elements are specific to the object's type and sub type. Listing 6.1 concludes this section. It gives an example of what the ADMIN_DATA element and, similarly, other XML elements may actually look like:

```
<FDTNS:ADMIN_DATA>
  <FDTNS:APPLICATION_ID>0013212003FC02DB8AA7CB7F4D619AC2
    </FDTNS:APPLICATION_ID>
  <FDTNS:ID>0013212003FC02DB8AB782B628BD0157</FDTNS:ID>
  <FDTNS:NAME>EMPLOYEE_ID</FDTNS:NAME>
  <FDTNS:SYSTEM_OBJECT>X</FDTNS:SYSTEM_OBJECT>
  <FDTNS:CREATION_USER>ALF</FDTNS:CREATION_USER>
  <FDTNS:CREATION_TIMESTAMP>20070929112908
    </FDTNS:CREATION_TIMESTAMP>
  <FDTNS:CHANGE_USER>ALF</FDTNS:CHANGE_USER>
  <FDTNS:CHANGE_TIMESTAMP>20100717194229
  </FDTNS:CHANGE_TIMESTAMP>
  <FDTNS:VERSIONS>
    <FDTNS:item>
      <FDTNS:VERSION>000004</FDTNS:VERSION>
      <FDTNS:USER>ALF</FDTNS:USER>
      <FDTNS:TIMESTAMP>20100717194227</FDTNS:TIMESTAMP>
      <FDTNS:STATE>A</FDTNS:STATE>
      <FDTNS:TRREQUEST />
      <FDTNS:TRVERSION>000004</FDTNS:TRVERSION>
      <FDTNS:TRTIMESTAMP>20100717194227</FDTNS:TRTIMESTAMP>
      <FDTNS:TRSYSID>ABC</FDTNS:TRSYSID>
      <FDTNS:TRCLIENT />
```

```
      <FDTNS:OVERS_ID>001CC412326A02EC83EEACAF62D48002
        </FDTNS:OVERS_ID>
      <FDTNS:CUSTOMER_CHANGE />
      <FDTNS:VERSIONING />
    </FDTNS:item>
  </FDTNS:VERSIONS>
  <FDTNS:ACCESS_LEVEL>APPL</FDTNS:ACCESS_LEVEL>
  <FDTNS:LOCAL />
  <FDTNS:TEXT_DEPENDENCY_TYPE>1</FDTNS:TEXT_DEPENDENCY_TYPE>
  <FDTNS:TEXTS>
    <FDTNS:item>
      <FDTNS:LANGU />
      <FDTNS:TEXT>Employee ID</FDTNS:TEXT>
    </FDTNS:item>
  </FDTNS:TEXTS>
  <FDTNS:DOCUMENTATION_DEPENDENCY_TYPE>1
    </FDTNS:DOCUMENTATION_DEPENDENCY_TYPE>
  <FDTNS:DOCUMENTATIONS />
</FDTNS:ADMIN_DATA>
```

Listing 6.1 Admin Data XML Element—Example

6.2.5 XML Export and Import API

Interface IF_FDT_DATA_EXCHANGE defines the methods required to import and export BRFplus objects or even a complete application. An instance of this interface can be obtained with method GET_DATA_EXCHANGE of the factory interface IF_FDT_FAC-TORY. Only the three methods listed in Table 6.5 are of relevance.

Method	Description
EXPORT_XML	Exports individual objects and optionally all referenced objects as well into an XML document.
EXPORT_XML_APPLICATION	Exports an entire application with all contained objects into an XML document.
IMPORT_XML	Imports all objects from a valid XML document.

Table 6.5 Methods of Interface IF_FDT_DATA_EXCHANGE

With method EXPORT_XML_APPLICATION an entire application with all contained objects can be exported. The application is identified by the importing parameter IV_APPLICATION_ID. Method EXPORT_XML allows you to export individual objects of one application. The objects are listed in the table parameter ITS_OBJECT_ID. If the Boolean parameter IV_DEEP is set to true, all referenced objects within the application will also be included. Further parameters are the same in both methods and described in Table 6.6.

Parameter	Description
IV_SCHEMA	Type of the schema—internal or external—that shall be used.
IV_XML_VERSION	Version of the schema that shall be used.
IV_TIMESTAMP	The timestamp determines which active version of the object(s) shall be exported. By default, the latest active version is exported.
EO_DOM_TREE	Provides the generated XML document in the form of a document object model (DOM) tree.
EV_STRING	Provides the generated XML document as a text string.
ETS_FAILURE	Lists all objects that could not be exported.
ET_MESSAGE	Contains all messages that occur during the XML export.

Table 6.6 XML Export API—Common Parameters

In detail, the following steps are performed when objects are exported to XML:

1. It is checked whether the target XML schema version is valid and supported.

2. The XML root element with the namespace declaration and the general attributes is generated. Information about the installed software components is stored into additional XML elements.

3. The objects that shall be exported are sorted in the order they will appear in the XML document. At the same time, the existence of the objects for the specified timestamp is checked. All objects are checked for consistency.

4. According to their types, the objects are translated into an XML representation, one after another. For each object the method EXPORT_XML of interface IF_FDT_DATA_EXCHANGE_INTERNAL is called on the according ABAP object for this purpose.

5. If necessary, the resulting XML document is downgraded from the latest schema version to a given lower version.

6. If the external schema type has been requested, the XML document is transformed accordingly from the internal format.

7. An ID for a virtual transport request is generated and the XML document is stored under this ID into the database table FDT_XML_EXPORT.

If an error occurs in one of the above steps, the XML export is aborted.

The XML documents generated by the export methods can be imported with method IMPORT_XML. The import process can be fine-tuned in the following ways:

▶ The import of objects that are not yet present in the system can be forbidden. Parameter IV_CREATE must be set to true to allow the creation of objects.

▶ The import can be classified as an object repair. Objects that are normally not changeable according to the system settings can still be updated in this way. Parameter IV_IMPORT_TYPE must be set to the value of constant GC_XML_IMPORT_TYPE_REPAIR in this case.

▶ The import can be classified as a local copy. The imported objects are stored as local objects in this case. They must not exist as non-local objects yet and the application must be part of the import. When using this option you should remember that local objects cannot be referenced by non-local objects. Parameter IV_IMPORT_TYPE has to be set to the value of constant GC_XML_IMPORT_TYPE_LOCAL_COPY.

▶ After the new object versions are imported, they can directly be activated. The activation can be triggered with parameter IV_ACTIVATE.

▶ The import process can be simulated. If parameter IV_SIMULATE is set to true, the imported objects are not saved.

If automatic change recording is active in the system or client, a Workbench or respectively customizing transport request might be required to import non-local objects. The request can be provided with the parameters IV_WORKBENCH_TRREQUEST or IV_CUSTOMIZING_TRREQUEST. All parameters of method IMPORT_XML are summarized in Table 6.7.

Parameter	Description
IO_DOM_TREE	Contains the XML document to import in the form of a document object model (DOM) tree.
IV_STRING	Contains the XML document to import in the form of a text string. This parameter is used prior to parameter IO_DOM_TREE.
IV_CREATE	Only when set to true is the creation of the imported objects allowed if they do not exist yet.
IV_IMPORT_TYPE	Classifies whether a standard import, an object repair, or local object copy will be performed Allowed values are defined as constants with the name pattern GC_XML_IMPORT_TYPE_*.
IV_SIMULATE	When set to true the imported objects are not saved.
IV_ACTIVATE	When set to true the imported objects are activated.

Table 6.7 XML Import API—Parameters

Parameter	Description
IV_CUSTOMIZING_TRREQUEST	A customizing transport request that may be required when importing non-local customizing objects.
IV_WORKBENCH_TRREQUEST	A Workbench transport request that may be required when importing non-local system objects.
ETS_SUCCESS	Lists the successfully imported objects.
ETS_FAILURE	Lists the objects that could not be imported.
ET_MESSAGE	Contains all messages that occur during the XML import.

Table 6.7 XML Import API — Parameters (Cont.)

In detail, the following steps are performed when objects are imported from an XML document:

1. The XML root element is analyzed and it is checked whether the schema version is supported.

2. If necessary, the XML document is transformed from external to internal format.

3. If necessary, the XML document is transformed from the imported schema version to the latest schema version supported by the system.

4. The resulting XML document is validated against the DTD, which is stored as transformation object FDT_APPEND_INTERNAL_DTD in the system.

5. The object definitions in the XML document are extracted and according new inactive object versions are created. Objects that do not exist yet are created from scratch, if requested.

6. The imported object versions are checked for consistency.

7. If requested and possible, the imported object versions are activated.

8. The object changes are saved if the import shall not only be simulated. Also, an ID for a virtual transport request is generated and the XML document is stored under this ID into the database table FDT_XML_IMPORT.

If an error occurs in one of the above steps, the XML import is aborted.

6.3   Web Service Generation Tool

A BRFplus function can be regarded as a local interface to a business rule service. If the need arises to call such a service from external systems, you could manually develop a Web service that acts as a connector to the BRFplus function. The Web service generation tool allows you to create such a Web service without having to program a single line of code.

Prerequisites

For the creation of Web services, you require according authorizations. Starting with SAP NetWeaver 7.02, role SAP_BC_WEBSERVICE_ADMIN_TEC can, for example, be assigned to the current user. More details about the authorizations for Web services can be found in SAP note 1318883.

First, the tool creates a *Remote Function Call* module (RFC) in ABAP with an interface that matches the intended BRFplus function. The function context is mapped to importing parameters, whereas the result data object is mapped to an exporting parameter. Data dictionary types for the parameters are automatically generated, if required. The implementation of the RFC module maps the parameters to the function context and result, and eventually calls the function.

Second, a Web service definition that connects to the RFC module is generated. The Web service can be generated according to three different security profiles, from "low" to "basic" to "strong." The outcome is a *Web Service Description Language* (WSDL) document, which gets stored in the system. Transaction SOAMANAGER allows searching for the generated Web service and retrieving the corresponding WSDL file. Because this transaction is not part of BRFplus we will not go into details here.

Restrictions

Because RFC-modules do not support deeply nested structures and tables, the generation tool can be used only for BRFplus functions with flat context and result. Furthermore, the tool is only applicable to the last active version of a function. You should consider that the accordingly generated Web service and RFC module are only loosely coupled to the function. If the function is changed incompatibly, the Web service may not work correctly any more and may require manual adjustments.

The Web service generation tool can be invoked in the Workbench either from the Tools menu or in the function UI from the toolbar of the Detail section, as depicted in Figure 6.13. In the former case, you need to select the function for the Web service generation first. In the latter case, the tool is displayed in a popup window and the current function is automatically preselected. You can switch to other functions with the button Select Other Function without leaving the tool.

Figure 6.13 Web Service Generation Tool — Invocation

In the tool you need to declare a list of settings for the Web service generation. It starts with the declaration of a development package to which all generated objects will be assigned. To create local objects, you simply need to mark the checkbox Local Package so that the objects will be assigned to package $TMP.

For non-local objects, you need to specify the target package in the field Development Package. Because the generated objects are system objects, they usually need to be recorded onto a Workbench Request that can be entered into the according field. If the BRFplus function is a system object too, it will be recorded onto the same request as well. If the function is a customizing object it is possible to provide an additional Customizing Request in the appropriate field. The function will then be recorded onto that request.

For the generation of the RFC module, a target Function Group and a Function Module name have to be entered into the corresponding fields. If the specified function group does not exist yet, the flag Create Function Group needs to be marked to generate it. If the function context includes structures and tables, it may be necessary to generate matching DDIC types. For these types, a common prefix can be entered into the field Prefix for Generated Object. Besides expressing a relationship among the generated data types, the prefix may also avoid name clashes with other, existing data type definitions.

For the generation of the actual Web service definition, a unique Web Service Name needs to be specified. In the Web Service Text field, a short description can optionally be entered in addition. One of the three security profiles needs to be chosen in the field Web service Security Profile. It influences, for example, which authentication methods the Web service will support and accordingly restrict the access possibilities.

Having entered all required fields, you may finally click on the Generate button to start the Web service generation. If all goes well, a success message will be displayed. You can check the generated RFC with Transaction SE37 for example, and configure the new Web service with Transaction SOAMANAGER.

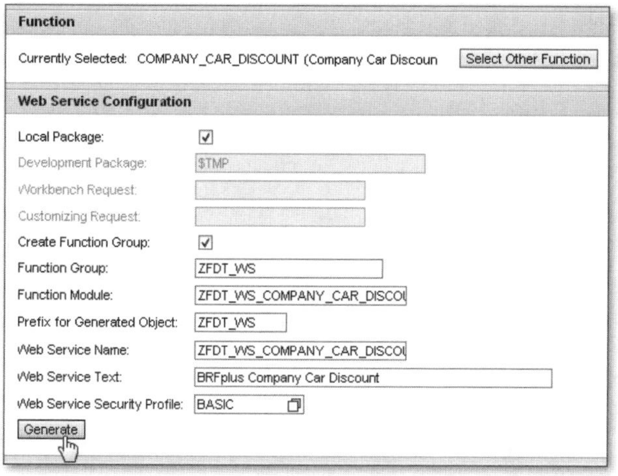

Figure 6.14 Web Service Generation Tool

Web Service Generation API

The API for the generation of Web services in BRFplus is encapsulated into class CL_FDT_WEB_SERVICE. With a single call to the public, static method GENERATE_FUNC_PROCESS_WEB_SERV, a new Web service can be generated for the currently active version of a specific BRFplus function. The importing parameters of the method correspond mainly to the input fields of the generation tool. They are listed in Table 6.8. If the Web service generation fails, according error messages are included into the exporting parameter ET_MESSAGE.

Parameter	Description
IV_ID	ID of the function
IV_PACKAGE_NAME	Name of the development package to which the generated objects will be assigned.
IV_TRREQUEST_WB	Transport request of type WORKBENCH. It is required in case the development package is not local and transportable.
IV_TRREQUEST_CUST	Transport request of type CUSTOMIZING. It is optional for non-local customizing functions.
IV_FUNC_GROUP_NAME	Name of the function group to which the generated function module will be assigned.
IV_CREATE_FUNC_GROUP	Flag that indicates whether the function group IV_FUNC_GROUP_NAME shall be created. It must be set to true if the function group does not exist yet.

Table 6.8 Web Service Generation API—Parameters

Parameter	Description
IV_FUNC_MODULE_NAME	Name for the RFC-enabled function module that will be generated.
IV_PREFIX	Prefix for the names of generated dictionary types (optional).
IV_WEB_SERVICE_NAME	Name of the Web service that will be generated.
IV_WEB_SERVICE_SHORT_TEXT	Short text description for the generated Web service.
IV_WS_SECURITY_PROFILE	Security profile used for the Web service generation. Possible default profiles are: ▶ PRF_DT_IF_SEC_LOW ▶ PRF_DT_IF_SEC_BASIC ▶ PRF_DT_IF_SEC_STRONG
ET_MESSAGE	Messages that give information about the generation process.

Table 6.8 Web Service Generation API—Parameters (Cont.)

If you only want to generate the RFC-enabled function module without a related Web service definition, you can use method GENERATE_RFC. The parameters of this method are a subset of the parameters of method GENERATE_FUNC_PROCESS_WEB_SERV.

6.4 Application Usage Tool

The application usage tool helps you find interrelationships among different BRF-plus applications. It aims at applications with objects that can be reused by other applications. Such objects have an access level that differs from "Same Application." If you want to change or even delete such a reusable object, you might have to consider existent references to that object. Conversely, you might want to find out which reusable objects of other applications are actually referenced by a specific application.

In the tool you first have to select the application you want to examine. You can directly enter the according application name in the field APPLICATION and press ⌐Enter⌐. Alternatively, you may trigger an application search dialog by clicking on the SELECT button. See Figure 6.15.

When the application is selected, you can decide what direction of usage you want to query in the section QUERY TYPE:

▶ If you keep the option GET APPLICATIONS USED BY THIS APPLICATION, you query for applications with reusable objects that are referenced by objects of the selected application.

▶ If you choose the option GET APPLICATIONS USING THIS APPLICATION, you query for applications with objects that are referencing reusable objects of the selected application.

Application Usage

| Application: * | COMPANY_CAR | Select | Description: Company Car | ID: 0014SEF41CBA02DDA88129B1B1AEC0C8 |

Query Type
Select which objects of other applications you're looking for.
◉ Get applications used by this application
○ Get applications using this application
☑ Display used objects

Query Scope
Select which version of the using objects is taken into account.
○ Latest version (default)
○ Version at timepoint   Date: Time: 00 00:00
◉ All versions

Specify further restrictions for the objects to query.
☑ Include local objects
☐ Restrict to component BC

Start Query   Max. Result Size: 200

Figure 6.15 Application Usage Tool — Options

With the checkbox DISPLAY USED OBJECTS you can request a detailed result list so that the used or respectively referencing objects of the found applications are included. Otherwise, only the related applications will be determined, which may improve the search speed.

In the QUERY SCOPE section you can fine-tune some query parameters. An important setting is the version option. Its impact is made clearer with the example illustrated in Figure 6.16: Application R contains a single, versioned object r that has three versions, two active and one inactive. They are referred to as r1, r2 and r3. Version r1 references an object a of application A, r2 references an object b of application B, and inactive version r3 references an object c of application C.

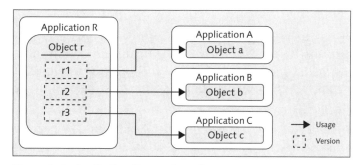

Figure 6.16 Application Usage — Example

Assume you have selected application R and you are searching for the used applications.

▶ If you are interested in the latest usages only, you can keep the LATEST VERSION option. Application C would be determined in our example because r3 is the latest version and references object c.

▶ If you are interested in the usage scenario at a specific point in time, you can choose option VERSION AT TIMEPOINT and enter a date and time. In this case only those references are taken into account that belong to an active object version that is valid at that point in time. This option makes sense if objects with multiple active versions are involved. By default, the current date and time is prefilled into the fields to query for the latest active versions. In our example, application B would be determined in this case because object b is referenced by the last active version r2. For an earlier timestamp version, r1 might be considered so that application A would be determined. If the timestamp were before the creation timestamp of object r, not surprisingly no application would be found.

▶ With the ALL VERSIONS option, the references of all object versions are taken into account. In the above example, the result list would therefore include applications A, B and C.

For the inverse search, let us assume application A of our example has been selected and the applications that are using application A are of interest. By default, application R would be determined only if option ALL VERSIONS would be selected.

Another setting that influences the result list is INCLUDE LOCAL OBJECTS. Local objects and consequently local applications can be excluded from the result list with the setting. It can, for example, be useful to ignore local testing applications. One should, however, remember that non-local objects can never use local objects. Eventually, it is possible to restrict the result list to applications of a specific application component. The application component can be entered if the RESTRICT TO COMPONENT checkbox is marked.

Before the query is started by clicking on the button START QUERY, you may consider changing the MAXIMUM RESULT SIZE entry on the right-hand side. It influences how many entries will be queried and displayed at once in the result list. If the checkbox DISPLAY USED OBJECTS is marked, it is possible to drill down to the individual used or using objects.

Figure 6.17 shows the result of a query that has retrieved the referenced objects of an application. In the example, several objects of the standard application FDT_SYS-TEM are referenced. In the first column of the result list, the found applications and objects are represented by a link. Clicking the link will open a popup where the respective object is directly displayed.

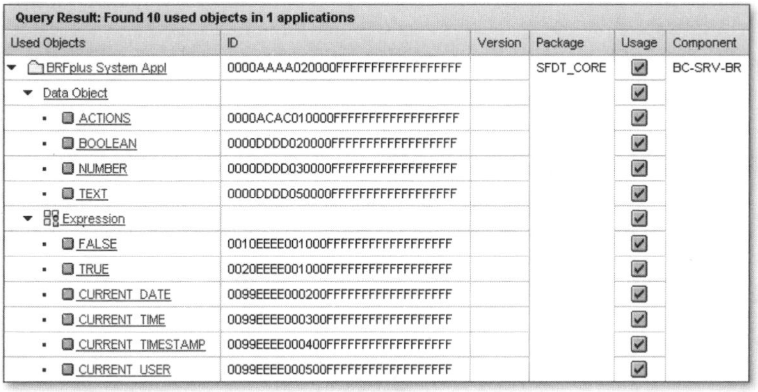

Used Objects	ID	Version	Package	Usage	Component
▼ ⌂ BRFplus System Appl	0000AAAA020000FFFFFFFFFFFFFFFF		SFDT_CORE	☑	BC-SRV-BR
▼ Data Object				☑	
• ☐ ACTIONS	0000ACAC010000FFFFFFFFFFFFFFFF			☑	
• ☐ BOOLEAN	0000DDDD020000FFFFFFFFFFFFFFFF			☑	
• ☐ NUMBER	0000DDDD030000FFFFFFFFFFFFFFFF			☑	
• ☐ TEXT	0000DDDD050000FFFFFFFFFFFFFFFF			☑	
▼ ⬚ Expression				☑	
• ☐ FALSE	0010EEEE001000FFFFFFFFFFFFFFFF			☑	
• ☐ TRUE	0020EEEE001000FFFFFFFFFFFFFFFF			☑	
• ☐ CURRENT_DATE	0099EEEE000200FFFFFFFFFFFFFFFF			☑	
• ☐ CURRENT_TIME	0099EEEE000300FFFFFFFFFFFFFFFF			☑	
• ☐ CURRENT_TIMESTAMP	0099EEEE000400FFFFFFFFFFFFFFFF			☑	
• ☐ CURRENT_USER	0099EEEE000500FFFFFFFFFFFFFFFF			☑	

Query Result: Found 10 used objects in 1 applications

Figure 6.17 Application Usage Tool—Result

For each object, the ID and the relevant version number are displayed. Furthermore, the development package and application component assigned to the respective applications are shown. For the query of used objects, an additional usage status is calculated in the column Usage. It allows you to check whether objects of an application might need adjustments. For example, if objects are used that are marked for deletion, the usage status will become a warning.

6.5 Application Administration Tool

The application administration tool allows the responsible user to optimize the application content. Its main purpose is currently to get rid of objects or object versions that are no longer used or required. In detail, the following operations are offered:

▶ DELETION OF UNUSED OBJECTS
Named objects that are not used by any other objects can be detected and deleted.

▶ DISCARDING OF OBJECT VERSIONS
Tries to trim versioned objects so that older versions that may not be required anymore are discarded.

▶ DELETION OF OBJECTS THAT ARE MARKED FOR DELETION
Tries to delete objects that have been marked for deletion for a specific period of time.

▶ CLEANUP THE DATABASE
Irrevocably removes deleted objects or discarded object versions from the database.

▶ REORGANIZE OBJECTS
Optimizes the database storage for objects that were created before enhancement package 2 of SAP NetWeaver 7.0. It can considerably reduce the number of unnamed Constant and Range expression objects, which have been required so far.

Loss of Data

This tool allows the irrevocable deletion of objects or object versions. The data retention time concept, which may help to restore unintentionally deleted objects, can be overridden. The authorizations for this tool should therefore be set accordingly.

The application administration tool can be invoked in the Workbench either from the TOOLS menu, or from the application UI via a button in the toolbar of the DETAIL section, as depicted in Figure 6.18. In the latter case, the application object must be shown in display mode or the button becomes disabled.

If the tool has been invoked from the TOOLS menu you first need to select the application that shall be administrated. When selected from the application UI, the tool is displayed in a popup window and the current application is automatically preselected.

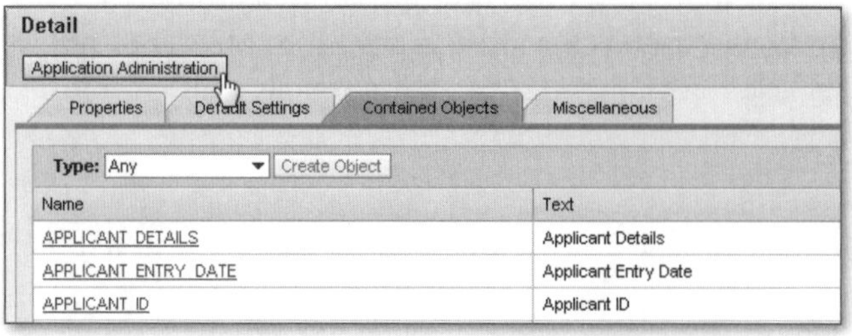

Figure 6.18 Application Administration Tool—Invocation

The name of the selected application is shown at the top of the tools UI. Below, you find the OPERATION dropdown from which you can select the operation you want to perform.

6.5.1 Deletion of Unused Objects

Objects that are not referenced by any other objects are often dispensable and can therefore be deleted. Their deletion not only frees up resources on the database or during transport; it also helps keep an application clear and more manageable.

Unnamed objects are inherently not reusable. If no reference from a parent object exists any longer, they are automatically deleted by a periodic background job. Named objects might, however, still exist for reuse purposes and therefore they can only be deleted manually.

The operation DELETE UNUSED OBJECTS determines all named but unused objects of the selected application and lists them as candidates for deletion. As Figure 6.19 illustrates the listed objects are ordered by object type and represented by links. Clicking on such a link will display the according object details in a popup window. Each object entry can individually be selected; multiple entries can be selected in the usual way by holding down ⎡Shift⎤ or ⎡Ctrl⎤. To delete the selected objects, you simply need to click on the button DELETE SELECTED OBJECTS at the bottom of the list.

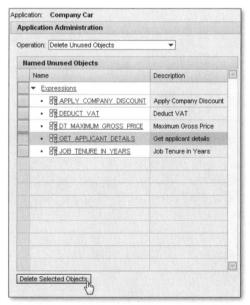

Figure 6.19 Application Administration Tool — Deletion of Unused Objects

After the deletion of unused objects, it is possible that new, unused objects may appear. This can happen if the deleted objects have referenced named objects that are not used elsewhere. Due to the deletion, the referenced objects become unused too.

6.5.2 Deletion of Marked Objects

Objects that are still referenced by other objects in the system cannot be deleted immediately. They can at first only be marked for deletion. This status ensures that no new usages can be created for such objects. It also indicates that an administrator is allowed to actually delete the objects as soon as this becomes possible. This is exactly the purpose of the operation DELETE OBJECTS MARKED FOR DELETION.

Transport

The status MARKED FOR DELETION is also of importance in the deletion of an object to be transported. In the target systems there might still exist references to the not yet deleted object. The import handling of BRFplus for transports detects existing usages for objects that shall be deleted. The objects will automatically be marked for deletion only in such cases.

Objects that have been marked for deletion can be deleted under the following circumstances:

▶ Previously referencing objects were changed in such a way that the references got lost. For versioned objects the referencing versions must have been discarded.

▶ Previously referencing objects were deleted.

▶ Referencing objects were marked for deletion and can be deleted too.

If the third case applies, a deletion might be possible only if all involved objects are deleted simultaneously.

When the operation DELETE OBJECTS MARKED FOR DELETION is selected in the tool, it checks first whether the selected application actually contains any objects that are marked for deletion. Only in this case will the button DELETE OBJECTS MARKED FOR DELETION, which can be seen in Figure 6.20, become enabled.

Figure 6.20 Application Administration Tool—Deletion of Marked Objects

The field DATA RETENTION PERIOD guarantees that other users have the chance to revoke the status MARKED FOR DELETION for an certain time span. Only objects that have been marked for deletion for more than the specified number of days are taken into account. If the default retention period is changed to zero days, all objects marked for deletion are considered for deletion.

The checkbox TEST MODE allows for simulation of the delete operation. A test run should always be taken into consideration to better estimate the influence of the retention period setting. The result of the operation is displayed in the form of a protocol. It can be closed by clicking on the BACK button at the top, as illustrated in Figure 6.21.

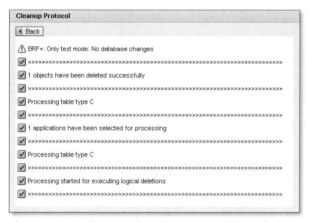

Figure 6.21 Application Administration Tool—Protocol

The deletion of objects that are marked for deletion can also be performed with the ABAP report FDT_DELETE. The report can be used not only in the scope of a single application: the selection screen of the report offers many more object selection options such as ranges of applications, storage types, and transport status. Similarly, the report FDT_MARK_FOR_DELETE allows you to mark multiple objects for deletion. The report can also perform the inverse operation and revoke the MARKED FOR DELETION status.

6.5.3   Discarding of Object Versions

Discarding of versions is mainly relevant for versioned BRFplus objects, or more precisely, for objects that have multiple active versions. The versioning setting for such objects may have been switched on for different purposes. It allows for example tracking of object changes.

Each time a versioned object is changed and activated in the Workbench, a new active version of the object is saved. The validity of a previously active version ends at that time. Versioned objects are implicitly time dependent with regard to rules processing. If a versioned object is processed for a specific timestamp in the past, the correspondingly valid object version will be evaluated.

Older versions of an object are typically dispensable after a reasonable period of time. They may, however, block the deletion of objects that are no longer required in recent versions. Such a scenario is shown in Figure 6.22. Two objects A and B are marked for deletion because they are not used by any current object version. Both objects shall be deleted together because object A has references to object B. An old, first version of object C still references object A and this fact precludes its deletion. At least the first version of object C needs to be discarded so that objects A and B can be deleted.

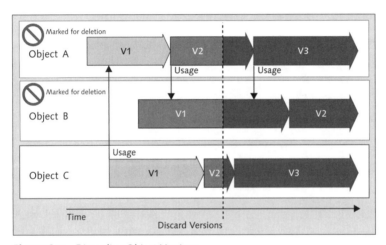

Figure 6.22 Discarding Object Versions

The operation DISCARD OLD OBJECT VERSIONS is performed on all objects of the selected application. It is based on a discarding timestamp:

▸ All object versions that cease prior to the given timestamp are discarded. Similar to deleted objects, discarded versions are treated as non-existent by BRFplus and can be removed from the database. In the example shown in Figure 6.22 the first versions of objects A and C are discarded.

▸ Object versions that overlap with the discarding timestamp will still be valid. They cannot be removed from the database. BRFplus will, however, consider these versions as existent only after the discarding timestamp. In Figure 6.22

this is the case for version 2 of object A, version 1 of object B, and version 2 of object C.

▶ Object versions that have been created after the discarding timestamp are not affected by the operation. In Figure 6.22 version 3 of object A, version 2 of object B and version 3 of object C will remain untouched.

The application administration tool allows you to enter the discarding timestamp in an indirect way with the field DATA RETENTION PERIOD. All object versions that are older than the specified number of days will be discarded. The discarding timestamp is consequently calculated as the current timestamp minus the specified number of days.

Application Administration

Operation: Discard Old Object Versions ▼

Data Retention Period (in Days): 90
Discard Versions

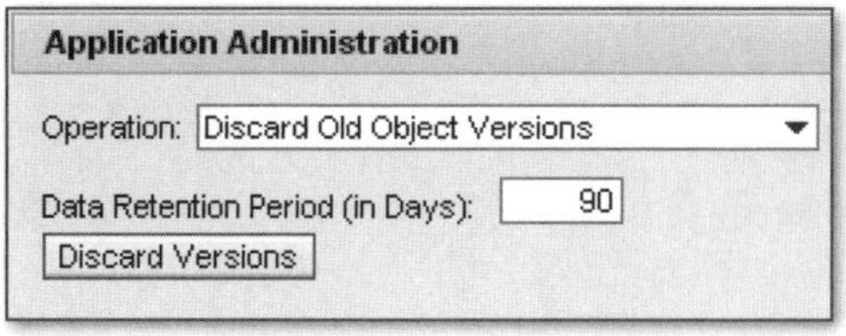

Figure 6.23 Application Administration Tool—Discarding Object Versions

Limitations

Discarding of object versions that might be referenced by objects of other applications could lead to inconsistencies. Therefore, the discarding of versions is supported only for objects that have the access level "Same Application."

The discarding of object versions can also be performed with the ABAP report `FDT_TRUNCATE_VERSIONING`. It basically provides the same functionality as the application administration tool in the Workbench.

6.5.4 Cleanup Database

Objects that have been deleted and object versions that have been discarded are not immediately removed from the database. Instead, they only get a deletion status and are usually treated as non-existent by BRFplus. With a special setting such "logically" deleted objects can, however, still be displayed in the Workbench. To do so, you need to mark the checkbox SHOW DELETED OBJECTS in the user personalization, on the REPOSITORY tab. Figure 6.24 demonstrates the display of a logically deleted object in the Workbench.

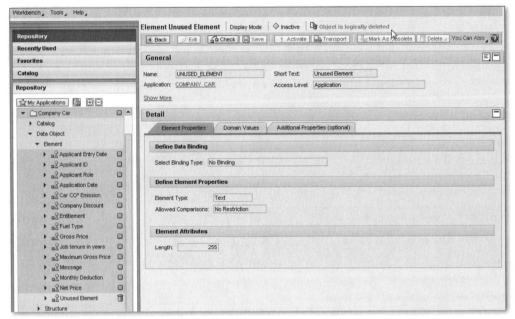

Figure 6.24 Display of Deleted Objects

After a retention time of 180 days, a background job will ultimately remove the objects or object versions from the database. With the operation CLEANUP DATABASE, the removal can be brought forward for objects of the selected application.

As illustrated in Figure 6.25 you can first select whether you want to remove deleted objects or only discarded object versions. The DATA RETENTION PERIOD determines which objects or versions are taken into account. They must have been deleted or discarded for more than the specified number of days. To remove all deleted objects or discarded versions, the DATA RETENTION PERIOD must be set to zero.

When you click on the REMOVE DELETED OBJECTS button, the cleanup of the database is triggered. If the checkbox TEST MODE is marked, the cleanup of the database will only be simulated. This simulation allows you to check how many objects or versions will be affected when the cleanup is run for real.

The removal of deleted objects from the database can also be performed with the ABAP report FDT_DELETE. In the report the process is referred to as "physical" deletion of objects. The report may be used not only in the scope of a single application: the selection screen offers many more object selection options such as ranges of applications, storage types, and transport status. Likewise, the ABAP report `FDT_TRUNCATE_PHYSICAL` can be used to remove discarded object versions to a larger extent.

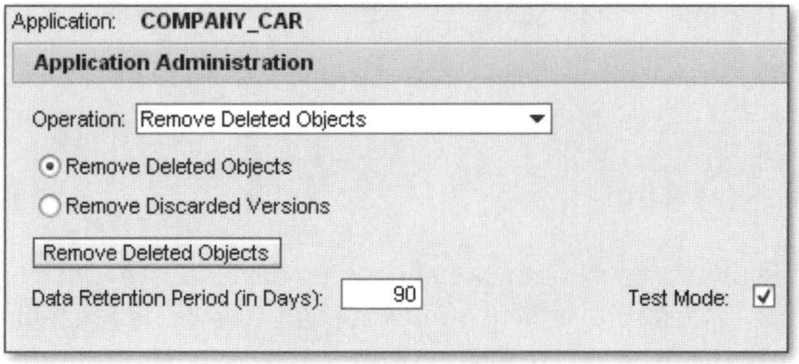

Figure 6.25 Application Administration Tool—Cleanup of Database

6.5.5   Reorganization of Objects

In SAP NetWeaver release 7.0, enhancement package 1, the definition of values and range comparisons required the creation of individual, unnamed objects of the corresponding expression types. For complex rules, this often meant that a huge number of objects were needed. This requirement noticeably reduced the performance of mass operations like transport.

Starting with enhancement package 2, values and value ranges are by default stored together with the using objects. Explicit Constant and Value Range expressions are required only for reuse purposes. Of course, the old storage format is still supported.

The operation REORGANIZE OBJECTS is intended for applications that stem from a former release. It can simply be triggered with the button REORGANIZE OBJECTS, as depicted in Figure 6.26. The operation will try to integrate all unnamed Constant and Value Range expression objects into their referencing parent objects. If feasible, the unnamed objects are deleted afterwards. The semantic definition of the parent objects will be preserved by the operation. All functions and rules will work as before. Only the method of data storage might have been changed afterwards.

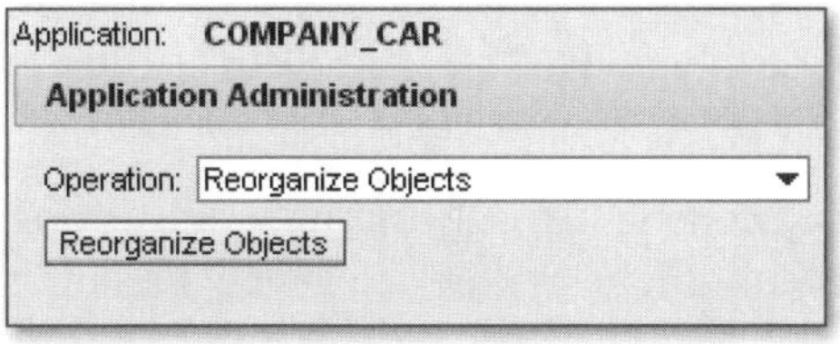

Figure 6.26 Application Administration Tool—Reorganization of Objects

Aftermath

The object reorganization may have an impact if objects of the application are accessed programmatically. The API for many expression types has, for example, been extended to support the direct storage of values and value ranges. Therefore, it might be necessary to adjust existent coding, which does not take the new storage concepts into account. SAP note 1305978 contains detailed information on this topic.

6.6 Transport Analysis Tool

BRFplus supports the SAP standard way of moving or copying development objects from one system to another via transports. The transport analysis tool will help in resolving problems that may occur in this respect. Before going into details of the tool, the transport process for BRFplus will be explained in more detail now.

6.6.1 Transport in Detail

For the transportation of BRFplus objects some prerequisites have to be considered. The objects—in our case especially the relevant BRFplus applications—must have been assigned to a non-local package. Master data objects are consequently never transportable. The transportability depends also on general system settings for client-dependent and cross-client objects. These settings are typically maintained with Transaction SCC4. With respect to BRFplus, the settings have impact for objects of storage type customizing or system. The transport of objects of either type may be allowed or forbidden. In the first case the recording of changed objects on a transport request can be enforced.

The transport request that shall be used for the recording of BRFplus objects must be of compatible type:

▸ Customizing objects are stored on client-dependent database tables of delivery class C. These objects can only be recorded on customizing requests. They are transported into client 000 of the target system and can be copied into other clients afterwards, using Transaction SCC1, for example.

▸ System objects are stored cross-client on database tables of delivery class S. These objects can only be recorded on Workbench requests. The recording on a transport tasks requires a compatible task type like "Development," "Correction," or "Repair."

The compatibility of transport requests may depend not only on the request type: additional settings, such as the target system, might also be relevant. The target system setting of the request must, for example, conform to the transport layer setting of the development package to which the objects are assigned.

Once recorded onto a transport request, the BRFplus objects leave a footprint in the piece list of the request. Because BRFplus objects are spread over multiple database tables, the piece list will contain key entries for each table and object. Customizing objects are stored under the object name FDT0000 (*FDT/BRFplus: Central Transport Object for C-Tables*), system objects under the object name FDT0001 (*FDT/BRFplus: Central Transport Object for S-Tables*).

When a BRFplus object is recorded onto a transport request, its application is automatically recorded too. System applications are recorded with an additional entry under the object name FDT0 (*FDT/BRFplus: System Application*). With this entry the application is registered as a "logical" object in the central object repository of the system (table TADIR). The registration avoids name clashes among the applications. It also ensures that the application can only be recorded in one transport request at a time.

When the release of a transport request is triggered, for example with Transaction SE09, a check routine of BRFplus is run on the piece list to ensure that the listed objects are ready for export. The check routine will test the following conditions:

- All listed objects must not currently be locked for other purposes. Objects are for example locked during editing in the Workbench.
- All listed objects must have been activated. There must not be an inactive object version.
- All listed objects must be consistent.
- All referenced objects must either be part of the same transport request or must have been transported before. This prerequisite shall help preventing invalid references in the target systems but it cannot guarantee consistency in all cases.
- The transport piece list must be consistent. For each object the required database table entries must be included, according to the object's type.

If one of the above conditions is not fulfilled, the transport release is cancelled, with according error messages. If the transport request is valid, the recorded objects are transferred into the target systems by the standard transport mechanisms. Database entries that are referenced by the piece list are copied to the according database tables in the target system. Deleted or rather non-existent database entries are removed in the target system too.

In each target system an importing routine of BRFplus will be triggered after the data transfer. If multiple transports have reached the target system, BRFplus can run the importing routine also for a combination of transports. Each new transport is therefore automatically registered in a so-called *import queue*. The importing routine will perform the following steps:

1. BRFplus analyzes all pending transports of the import queue that have not yet been fully imported. Transports that have interdependencies with the current transport are combined in the further steps.

2. The transported object versions have been stored under a special version number (zero). These versions are only needed for transport and not used elsewhere. Only now are the transported versions copied to a "real" inactive object version. The version number for the inactive version depends in each case on the existing object versions. (If the transported version has been copied already in a previous run of the importing routine, it is not copied again.)

3. The new inactive object versions are checked and if there is no error they are also activated. If an inconsistent new version is detected, the import of the transport fails, and error messages are added to the transport protocol.

4. Objects that have been deleted in the source system are now also deleted in the target system, if feasible. It can happen that objects that shall be deleted are still locally referenced. Those objects are only marked for deletion in this case.

5. If no errors have occurred so far, an asynchronous process is started to clean up the database. The cleanup affects only the objects that were deleted in the previous step. If their counterparts in the source system have already been removed from the database, the removal is now forwarded to the target system.

The progress of the import routine is reflected by status messages that are written to the current transport log. It is the main source of information in case a transport has failed. The overall status of the transport is summarized with a numeric return code at the end of the log. The log can be examined with Transaction SE09, for example.

If the importing routine could be executed without problems, the handled transport requests are deregistered from the import queue. The return code of the transport should be 0, or 4 in case of warnings. Erroneously imported requests remain on the import queue. The return code for such transports is normally 8 or 12. Return code 12 should be issued only for temporary problems, for example, because objects were locked. The importing routine will then automatically be retriggered after some time. Permanent errors are represented by return code 8.

In such a case, the importing routine will not be triggered again and the transport will be *pending*, unless a new, corrective transport with related objects reaches the system.

A common reason for failing transports is the dependency on objects that are missing in the target system. This concerns not only missing BRFplus objects. Application objects may require a certain ABAP class for application exits, data objects are often bound to DDIC types, Procedure Call expressions access ABAP classes or function modules as well, DB Lookup expressions depend on specific database tables, and message log actions refer to a specific log objects. This list of examples could easily be extended.

Dependencies on BRFplus objects are less critical than dependencies on other development objects. If objects of one BRFplus application reference objects of another application, it is of course advisable to transport the latter application entirely, before the first application, into any follow-up systems. However, when the referenced application is transported, any pending transports in the target systems with dependent BRFplus objects will automatically be detected and merged in the first step of the importing routine.

Dependencies of pending transports on transports with other development objects cannot be detected. Let us take for example a BRFplus application object that requires a certain ABAP class. If the application object is transported before the ABAP class, it cannot be activated in the target systems and the transport will fail. When the missing ABAP class is imported later with a separate transport, the importing routine for the failed transport is not retriggered automatically. The application object must either be transported again, or the importing routine needs to be triggered manually. The transport analysis tool can be used for this purpose.

6.6.2 Usage of the Tool

The transport analysis tool in the Workbench helps with detecting and solving transport-related problems. It can be used in the source system to avoid errors during the exporting phase. It can be used as well in the target systems for importing issues. To start the tool you need to select the corresponding menu entry in the Tools menu of the Workbench.

The tool is divided into three tabs that address consecutive transport issues. The first tab, Open Transports, allows you to explore transport requests that have not been release yet. It will help analyze or avoid problems with the release of transports in source systems. Figure 6.27 shows how the tab content may look. By default, any open transport request of the current user can be selected from the

REQUEST dropdown. Requests of a different user can be selected after entering the user's name into the USER field and pressing ⌈Enter⌋.

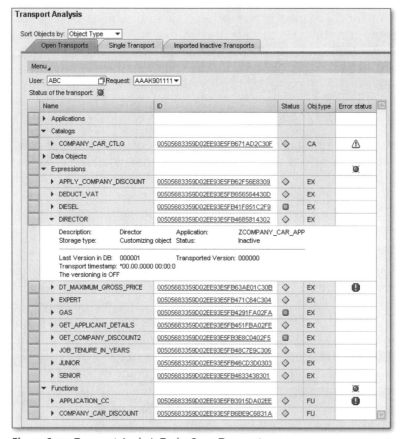

Figure 6.27 Transport Analysis Tool—Open Transports

Having chosen a request, an overall STATUS OF THE TRANSPORT with respect to BRFplus objects is displayed in the form of an icon. The status indicates whether the transport request is in principle ready to be released. The main area of the tab underneath is occupied by a table that lists all the recorded BRFplus objects. This object display is common to all tabs of the tool. With the dropdown SORT OBJECTS BY (above the tabs), the objects can be ordered by object type (default), by application or by storage type. For each recorded object the name, ID and type are displayed in according columns. When you drill down to a specific object you can access more information in a separate area below.

The Status column indicates whether the recorded objects are active or inactive. The listed objects are furthermore automatically checked for consistency. In case errors or warnings are detected for an object, the status is reflected by an icon in the column Error Status. Clicking on the icon will display the underlying messages.

In case there are objects that require adjustments, you can use the links in the ID-column to navigate to the corresponding objects and fix any errors. The selected objects will be displayed in a separate popup window. After closing the popup window the status display might not be up to date. You can refresh the objects table by selecting the menu entry Refresh in the Menu at the top of the tab.

If the transport is not ready for release, you may also try to perform some automatic adjustments. The menu entry Check and Correct in the Menu at the top of the tab can be used for this purpose. It will trigger the following actions on all recorded objects:

▶ Inactive objects will be activated, if feasible. Export errors due to inactive object versions should be prevented or respectively eliminated in this way. Erroneous objects can however not be corrected automatically.

▶ The objects are recorded once more onto the same transport request or eventually task. This action will ensure a complete piece list for the recorded objects. The piece list can usually only become inconsistent when it is edited manually.

The results of the automatic adjustments are displayed in a table of messages. With the Back button on top of the message table you can switch back to the transport display. If no inconsistencies concerning the transport release are left, the overall status for the transport will change to "green" afterwards.

The second tab, Single Transport, differs from the tab Open Transports primarily in the selection of the transport request. Any existing transport request, including released ones, can be entered in the field Transport Request. The tab shall facilitate the identification and analysis of the BRFplus objects that have been recorded on the given transport. They are listed in a table just as with the Open Transports tab, when you click on the button Get Transport Details.

The tab Imported Inactive Transports is relevant in the target systems of transports. It allows the selection of pending transports that have not yet been imported. For those transports, the importing routine may simply not have been triggered yet. But usually the importing routine was already executed and failed due to some permanent errors. The transported object versions remain inactive in this case.

If any pending transports are registered in the system, they can be selected in the INACTIVE IMPORTED TRANSPORT dropdown. As for the other tabs, the BRFplus objects of the selected transport are listed below in a table with according status information. You can now try to resolve any reported errors in the source system and transport the concerned objects again. If any referenced BRFplus objects are missing, you can simply transfer them with a new transport. The import of the new transport should automatically activate also the pending transport.

If development objects like ABAP classes are missing, you have to import them from the source system with an additional transport. Yet another option may be to repair erroneous BRFplus objects locally, if allowed by the system settings. In the latter two cases, you need to restart the importing routine for the pending transport manually. To do this, you simply need to select the menu entry RESTART IMPORT from the MENU at the top of the tab. Such a scenario is depicted in Figure 6.28. An alternative outside the Workbench is the ABAP report FDT_TRANS_Q_RESTART. When executed, the report will try to import all pending transports that are registered in the import queue.

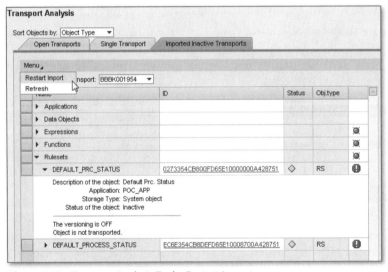

Figure 6.28 Transport Analysis Tool—Restart Import

This chapter presents some advanced topics in BRFplus and gives more detailed insight into concepts that have only been touched on earlier. Programming skills are essential to understand the content of this chapter.

7   Advanced

The first advanced topic is performance. This section lists the most important factors in the performance of BRFplus. It also presents some runtime measurements that are intended to give the reader an idea of the typical BRFplus performance in both, general and specific scenarios.

Tracing will be explained in detail in Section 7.2. This feature may be used for debugging purposes. It can, however, also be relevant in a productive environment where every rule processing needs to be recorded.

BRFplus can be extended for custom requirements in many ways. Application exits have already been mentioned and are now explained in Section 7.3. The definition of a custom formula function is described in depth to provide a common use case.

If the need arises to integrate the user interface for BRFplus objects into custom applications, you may have a look at Section 7.4. It gives an insight into the basic concepts of UI integration and provides a simple example.

7.1   Performance

The performance of business rule executions becomes a crucial factor when hundreds or thousands of rules have to be evaluated. To optimize the performance of rule processing in BRFplus, it is important to know which factors are most relevant in this respect. Not only can the way the API is used for calling a function make a big difference; the usage of certain expression types can heavily influence the runtime.

Performance measurements are highly dependent on available hardware, network capacity, and other processes that are running on the system. Absolute numbers of measurement are therefore less meaningful than a comparison of the relative deviations, which result from various approaches. At the end of this section, such figures are presented to give a general idea about the performance of BRFplus.

7.1.1 Performance Relevant Factors

BRFplus rules are in general executed by calling a function via the API. For maximum performance BRFplus uses generated ABAP code that is encapsulated into a class per function. The first call of a function in a session retrieves the appropriate class name and loads the class into the ABAP memory. Time-dependent processing in combination with the usage of versioned objects may require different classes for different time slots.

If no appropriate class exists yet, a new one will be generated automatically. Accessing a new or altered function the very first time may therefore cause a small but noticeable delay. The memory consumption of generated classes depends, of course, on the number and complexity of the included expressions. But typically less than 100 KB needs to be allocated. Despite the context data, usually almost no additional memory is required at runtime.

Once the generated class has been loaded into memory, the processing is delegated to a specific method of the class. For successive function calls during the session, no further database access is needed. Hence, the call of a BRFplus function in mass scenarios does not differ much from a standard ABAP method call. The factors that may further influence the processing speed are described in the following sections.

Calling a Function

BRFplus provides several options for calling a function. On a first level they can be distinguished as remote and local calls. You can generate RFC-enabled function modules and Web services that allow you to call a function from an external system. Local function calls can be implemented by using appropriate methods of the BRFplus API.

A remote call will always cause some overhead with respect to resources and runtime. Data has to be packaged, sent over a network with unknown traffic, and unpackaged again. Calling a remote function module asynchronously usually causes further delays. Web services are based on XML-related standards like SOAP, WSDL, and UDDI. Therefore, they typically require more memory and processing resources than remote function calls. The overhead for remote communication can be reduced significantly if it is possible to bundle multiple BRFplus function calls into one remote call.

If the function is called locally, there are two different approaches that mainly influence the performance:

▶ Method `IF_FDT_FUNCTION~PROCESS` can be called for an object instance of the corresponding function. This approach is easy to implement and understand. But it requires loading the function object and possibly also related data objects from the database. Thus, it performs worse than the second approach.

▶ The static method `CL_FDT_FUNCTION_PROSSESS=>PROCESS` can be called without instantiating any objects. Context data can be passed by reference variables. If the context data is formatted according to BRFplus specific data types, the rule processing can start with almost no delay.

These two approaches are described in detail in Section 5.1.4.

In summary, the different call types can roughly be ordered with respect to decreasing performance:

1. Local, static method call

2. Local method call on a function instance

3. Remote function call

4. Web service call

Execution Mode

As already mentioned, BRFplus by default executes generated ABAP code to determine a function result. In specific situations, it can, however, be necessary to switch into an interpretation mode. The interpretation of rules is a magnitude slower than the execution of generated code. You can expect a performance decrease of a factor of 50 to 500.

In general, the interpretation mode can be regarded as a fallback that is used when the execution of generated code is not possible. It can, for example, happen that a new or altered function (including all used objects) is being processed the very first time, but the function is locked by another process or session at the same time. The generation of a new or respectively updated class is not possible in this case, so the function can only be evaluated in interpretation mode.

Further reasons for switching to the interpretation mode are:

▶ Usage of the technical trace

▶ Usage of the dynamic expression type

▶ Usage of custom action or expression types that do not support code generation

Tracing

The activation of tracing always leads to a decrease in performance because the trace data needs to be extracted, collected, and saved to the database on top of the regular processing. When recorded traces need to be analyzed instantly after the function processing, an additional conversion to an XML document is typically required. Mainly for performance reasons BRFplus provides two trace types for different use cases. Details are provided in Section 7.2.

The lean trace is integrated into the code generation of BRFplus. It will have as little impact on performance as possible, by recording a minimum of required data. Saving lean traces to the database will always cause additional delays. However, the API allows some optimizations in this respect:

▶ Multiple traces can be buffered in memory before they are saved together with only one access to the database.

▶ The saving can be delegated to an update task, which is only executed by a final commitment of changes.

▶ Skipping of authorization checks avoids further delays.

The request for a technical trace will switch the rule processing into interpretation mode. Because the interpretation of rules causes a substantial increase in runtime, the technical trace is not suitable for performance critical use cases.

Loop and Table Operation Expressions

Loop and the Table Operation expressions are an uncertainty factor with respect to performance. For both, the number of actually processed steps is usually not fixed but is determined only at runtime. For loops that are conditionally repeated, it must be ensured that the processing ends after a finite number of iterations. For performance-critical use cases, a maximum number of allowed iterations should be modeled.

The impact on performance can be even less predictable when loops are nested into each other. The number of overall iterations can then easily run into the millions. If such a definition cannot be avoided, it is recommended that you embed only lightweight expressions of little complexity. DB Lookup expressions should, for example, never be evaluated within a Loop expression.

DB Lookup Expressions

The use of DB Lookup expressions typically slows down the rules processing, because the database access is a costly operation with respect to runtime. A database access performed by BRFplus does, however, not differ from an access that is manually programmed in ABAP. Therefore, the standard means for performance optimizations with respect to database tables apply. Just a few are listed here:

▸ The data selection should be based on key columns of the table.

▸ An additional table index may support the data selection otherwise.

▸ Tables can be buffered to allow faster data access in successive selections.

A business user lacks the knowledge to assess the performance implications of a database lookup expression. It is therefore recommended that a technical expert be involved in the expression definition. It might sometimes even be a better alternative to use a procedure call expression with optimized ABAP code.

Procedure Call Expressions

Procedure Call expressions (and actions) facilitate the usage of ABAP methods and function modules during rule processing. They are often used to retrieve additional, processing relevant data on demand. The action type allows triggering arbitrary processes and tasks.

At runtime BRFplus performs only a mapping of data object values to the parameters of the called method or function module. Hence the performance depends solely on the respective implementation of the procedure.

Actions

Actions are often not designed for mass data scenarios. They typically call the API of an additional service, which might not be optimized for high performance scenarios. For example, the standard action types that trigger a workflow perform even a database commit. Thus, if actions are to be included into the rules processing, it is advisable to check their individual performance first.

Currency and Unit Conversion

Amount and quantity data objects store a numeric value with respect to a currency or unit value at runtime. The values may either be set externally in the function context or determined by expressions. Rule definitions, which compare amount or quantity elements against static values or elements of the same type, can have an increasing impact on performance.

A typical comparison of that type is the following:

```
If Income is greater than 1000.00 EUR Then <do something>.
```

When the currencies of two compared amounts differ at runtime, one amount needs to be converted into the currency of the other amount. In the above comparison the *Income* element might, for example, have the value `1250.00 USD`.

The used conversion services have to look up exchange rates that are located on buffered customizing tables. Also, additional conversion logic needs to be executed. For a single or only few conversions, the effect on performance is negligible. However, in principle, it is possible that one function call may trigger hundreds or thousands of amount comparisons. The time spend on currency conversions can become a measurable factor in such cases. Quantity conversions should be regarded in a similar way.

For best performance, you may try to avoid amount and quantity values. If you expect that currencies and units do not differ at runtime, you can simply use elements of type number.

Number and Complexity of Rules

The more rules and expressions need to be evaluated for a function, the more the processing runtime increases. The complexity of the involved expressions will also individually influence their respective processing time. However, compared to the other factors mentioned so far, the number of rules or the complexity of expressions is far less relevant. Whether a decision table contains, for example, 10 or 100 table lines is almost negligible. With code generation, the value comparisons are translated into native ABAP statements, which can be processed extremely fast.

Parallel Processing

Parallel processing is not a feature of BRFplus itself, but rather a general programming option. BRFplus is, however, prepared to be used in parallel. The approach may be considered for processing large data volumes that can be split into separate chunks.

In ABAP the parallel processing can be implemented by distributing a task over several work processes. This can be achieved with a special variant of asynchronous RFCs. An appropriate, RFC-enabled function module has to be called in the following way:

```
CALL FUNCTION STARTING NEW TASK DESTINATION IN GROUP.
```

Parallel processing causes some overhead at first. It usually requires preparation of the data that is to be distributed. The starting and synchronization of multiple processes also causes some delay. Depending on the underlying hardware, a parallel execution of BRFplus rules may, however significantly increase the overall performance.

7.1.2 Performance Measurements

To get a better impression of the impact that performance relevant factors might typically have, we will now present some runtime measurements. The function in Chapter 2 will be used for this purpose.

All measurements have been carried out in a controlled environment with the following hardware and software:

- 4 CPUs of type AMD Opteron 852
- 16 GB of RAM
- Operating System: SUSE Linux Enterprise Server 10 SP2 (x86_64)
- Database: MaxDB 7.7.04.032
- SAP NetWeaver 7.0 with enhancement package 2 SP4

The precision of the measurements has been limited to 10 microseconds. A runtime of 10 microseconds per call would mean that a function could be processed 100,000 times per second, or 6,000,000 times per minute.

The first measurements compare the runtime for different ways of calling a function.

Comparison of Function Calls

Four different scenarios to call a function have been measured:

- Local, static method call
- Local, static method call with lean trace
- Local method call on a function instance
- Remote call with an RFC-enabled function module

For each scenario the function has been repeatedly called for a different number of times. In each call different data has been passed to the function. The measured total runtime for all calls is presented in Table 7.1. From the numbers, one can easily deduce that static function calls are by far the fastest ones. Even when using lean trace, the runtime is better than using an instance-based or remote invocation.

Call Type	1 Call (ms)	10 Calls (ms)	100 Calls (ms)	1,000 Calls (ms)	10,000 Calls (ms)
Static	0.78	1.39	7.26	46.37	484.65
Static, Trace	1.21	3.07	22.83	151.58	1500.76
Instance	8.88	13.28	40.68	354.52	3425.81
RFC	13.47	24.24	133.42	1118.43	11406.82

Table 7.1 Performance Measurements—Total Runtime per Call Type

Figure 7.1 presents the measured runtime for 1 to 100 calls in a graphical overview. It makes it obvious that the runtime is not increasing linearly for only a few calls. The first call always causes some overhead for the loading of classes, buffers, and other initialization work. Consecutive calls in the same session are thus noticeably faster.

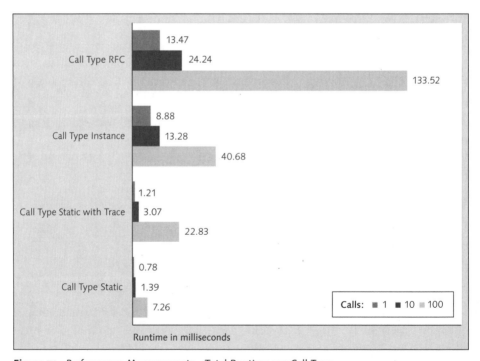

Figure 7.1 Performance Measurements—Total Runtime per Call Type

For mass data scenarios, the average runtime per function call is usually of more interest. The rounded numbers are shown in Table 7.2. With an increasing number of calls, the average runtimes converge to the optimal runtime in each scenario. The slight deviations for RFCs between 100 and 10,000 calls might be caused by measurement inaccuracies. Looking at the average runtime for static method calls, we see that the function is finally processed within only 50 microseconds. This means that the rules can be evaluated about 20,000 times per second.

Call Type	1 Call (ms)	10 Calls (ms)	100 Calls (ms)	1,000 Calls (ms)	10,000 Calls (ms)
Static	0.78	0.14	0.07	0.05	0.05
Static, Trace	1.21	0.31	0.23	0.16	0.15
Instance	8.88	1.33	0.41	0.36	0.35
RFC	13.47	2.43	1.34	1.12	1.14

Table 7.2 Performance Measurements—Average Runtime per Call Type

The diagram in Figure 7.2 illustrates the declining average runtime for the different call types. It reflects that the overhead of the first calls is weighted less and less. For a better comparison, the vertical axis of the diagram uses a logarithmic scale. The diagram thus demonstrates very clearly that the magnitude of runtime difference for the four scenarios is stable.

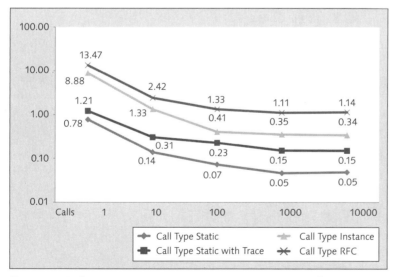

Figure 7.2 Performance Measurements—Average Runtime per Call Type

Knowing how BRFplus performs in general, it might also be interesting to see a comparison with an alternative technology.

BRFplus versus Database Selection

An alternative to the evaluation of primitive BRFplus rules is typically the selection of (customizing) data from a database table. The main advantage of database tables is that they can store an almost unlimited number of data entries. This disadvantage is that database selections are typically hardcoded with a native SELECT statement in ABAP. The statement also offers only limited functionality and flexibility compared to the expressiveness of BRFplus. With regard to performance, the main question is, however, how well a BRFplus function call can compete against a native ABAP statement.

For the comparison two—probably well known—database tables have been selected:

▸ The T100 table stores messages that can programmatically be accessed with the ABAP statement MESSAGE. Single lines of the table are buffered in memory. A selection therefore does not necessarily have to access the database but can retrieve the requested data from the buffer. For details you may inspect the table definition with Transaction SE11.

▸ Table SFLIGHT is available in all NetWeaver installations and used mostly for demonstration purposes. This table is not buffered, so a database access is always required for data selections.

For the runtime measurements, the buffers of the T100 table have been prefilled so that all data selections requests could be satisfied without real database access. For each of the two tables, 10,000 successive database selections were triggered. The average selection of a buffered T100 table record took about 0.068 milliseconds and the average selection of a non-buffered SFLIGHT record about 0.416 milliseconds.

As Figure 7.3 depicts, not only is the measured runtime of the BRFplus function example less than the runtime of the unbuffered database access: with only 0.048 milliseconds, it can even outperform a buffered database selection with about 30% less processing time.

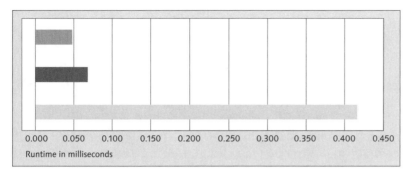

Figure 7.3 Performance Measurements—BRFplus Versus Database Selection

7.2 Tracing

BRFplus has the capability to trace the processing of a function. Tracing allows you to investigate how the outcome of a function is determined with respect to the passed context parameter values. For each single processing step, information is recorded into a trace log.

Because tracing may have quite an impact on the performance of the rules evaluation, there are two flavors of traces available: the *technical trace* and the *lean trace*:

▶ The technical trace is primarily intended for debugging purposes. It records the full processing details for all concerned objects. Requesting the technical trace will switch the rules processing to interpretation mode. This switch may noticeably slow down the evaluation speed, compared to the use of generated code.

▶ The lean trace is integrated into the generated code for a BRFplus function. It addresses the need to keep a record of all executions of a function during productive usage. The lean trace may be used, for example, for legal requirements, if it must be possible to prove an evaluated result at a later point in time. The lean trace can also fulfill explanatory requirements. It can, for example, be utilized to make the determination of a rule result comprehensible for the users.

Tracing needs to be requested programmatically by the application that is calling a function. As explained in Section 5.1 the BRFplus API offers different ways to call a function. However, the methods share the same parameters with respect to tracing. So in general the following kind of ABAP code needs to be executed:

```
CALL METHOD lo_function->process
  EXPORTING
    io_context   = lo_context
    iv_trace_mode = if_fdt_constants=>gc_trace_mode_lean "Mode
  IMPORTING
```

```
eo_result     = lo_result
eo_trace      = lo_trace.    "Request trace
```

Listing 7.1 Requesting Tracing

To activate tracing, the exporting parameter EO_TRACE of type IF_FDT_TRACE needs to be requested. The trace mode can be specified with the optional importing parameter IV_TRACE_MODE. By default a technical trace will be performed. For other trace modes, there are constant definitions GC_TRACE_MODE* in interface IF_FDT_CONSTANTS that can be used. For example, a lean trace can be requested by passing the value of constant GC_TRACE_MODE_LEAN. There are some defined trace modes that should not be used because they are no longer supported:

▶ GC_TRACE_MODE_TRANSIENT

▶ GC_TRACE_MODE_DB_EXT_COMMIT

▶ GC_TRACE_MODE_DB_INT_COMMIT

The differences between lean and technical traces can best be illustrated with a very simple example scenario. We use a function with a single context parameter, which will hold a number between 1 and 7 for the respective day of the week. The Case expression depicted in Figure 7.4 is used as top expression by the function. It transforms the incoming context parameter into a corresponding domain value. If the function were called with the number 3, the outcome would be WED for Wednesday.

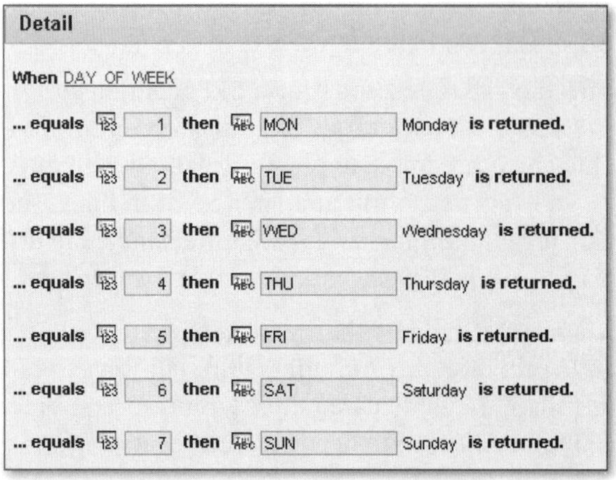

Figure 7.4 Tracing—Case Expression Example

The following two sections will refer to the example scenario described above.

7.2.1 Technical Trace

A technical trace can be activated for the processing of a function simply by requesting the exporting parameter `EO_TRACE` of type `IF_FDT_TRACE`. Importing parameter `IV_TRACE_MODE` may only optionally be set to the value of constant `GC_TRACE_MODE_TECHNICAL` in interface `IF_FDT_CONSTANTS`.

The reference variable, which is passed to parameter `EO_TRACE`, can be reused to process multiple functions in succession. It may also happen that a processed Procedure Call expression again invokes a BRFplus function and forwards the trace instance. In both cases, more than one function is recorded with the same trace instance.

The technical trace can be recorded only in interpretation mode, which is slow compared to the execution of generated ABAP code. The usage of the technical trace in productive scenarios is therefore not recommended. BRFplus itself leverages the technical trace, for example, for the simulation tool in the Workbench.

Technical traces are only buffered in memory and cannot be persisted to the database. The recorded information is stored as a list of log entries in an XML-like format.

With the information provided in the trace log, it is in principle possible to understand how the according function result has been determined. All processed objects are included with their ID, type, name, and version. The executed steps are described in a textual manner. In contrast to the lean trace, all processing steps are actually recorded, even those that do not yield a result or are not significant for a decision.

XML Document

The trace log can be converted into an XML document that brings the recorded steps into a hierarchical structure. Therefore, the XML document reflects not only the processing order but also the relationship among the objects. Figure 7.5 is intended to give you a first impression of what XML documents generated out of a technical trace log may look like. It shows the tracing result for the function in our example scenario (Figure 7.4).

```
- <FDT FormulaDerivationToolVersion="1.0">
  - <FUNCTION ID="00505683359D02DE95C7AB8DED020F6C" LogId="00505683359D02DE96DB694289245E1C" Name="DAY_OF_THE_WEEK"
    RecordingTimeStamp="20100804080042.6775250" Server="aserver" TraceVersion="1.01" User="ABC">
    <StartProcessingTimeStamp>20100804080035</StartProcessingTimeStamp>
    <TEXT ProcessingTimeStamp="20100804080035" RecordingTimeStamp="20100804080042.6830540" Server="aserver" Time="080042"
      User="ABC">Functional Processing</TEXT>
    <CONTEXT DataObjectID="00505683359D02DE838C2443A32888EC" DataObjectName="DAY_OF_WEEK"
      ProcessingTimeStamp="20100804080035" RecordingTimeStamp="20100804080042.6915400" Server="aserver" Time="080042"
      User="ABC">3</CONTEXT>
  - <EXPRESSION ID="00505683359D02DE838A0C25554F9041" LogId="00505683359D02DE96DB694289245E1C" Name="DAY_OF_WEEK"
    RecordingTimeStamp="20100804080042.6931370" Server="aserver" TraceVersion="1.01" User="ABC">
    <StartProcessingTimeStamp>20100804080035</StartProcessingTimeStamp>
    <TEXT ProcessingTimeStamp="20100804080035" RecordingTimeStamp="20100804080042.7443270" Server="aserver" Time="080042"
      User="ABC">Evaluating When-Condition 1</TEXT>
    <TEXT ProcessingTimeStamp="20100804080035" RecordingTimeStamp="20100804080042.7512530" Server="aserver" Time="080042"
      User="ABC">3 is not equal to 1</TEXT>
    <TEXT ProcessingTimeStamp="20100804080035" RecordingTimeStamp="20100804080042.7545750" Server="aserver" Time="080042"
      User="ABC">When-Condition is not met</TEXT>
    <TEXT ProcessingTimeStamp="20100804080035" RecordingTimeStamp="20100804080042.7545751" Server="aserver" Time="080042"
      User="ABC">Evaluating When-Condition 2</TEXT>
    <TEXT ProcessingTimeStamp="20100804080035" RecordingTimeStamp="20100804080042.7553470" Server="aserver" Time="080042"
      User="ABC">3 is not equal to 2</TEXT>
    <TEXT ProcessingTimeStamp="20100804080035" RecordingTimeStamp="20100804080042.7553471" Server="aserver" Time="080042"
      User="ABC">When-Condition is not met</TEXT>
    <TEXT ProcessingTimeStamp="20100804080035" RecordingTimeStamp="20100804080042.7553472" Server="aserver" Time="080042"
      User="ABC">Evaluating When-Condition 3</TEXT>
    <TEXT ProcessingTimeStamp="20100804080035" RecordingTimeStamp="20100804080042.7617010" Server="aserver" Time="080042"
      User="ABC">3 is equal to 3</TEXT>
    <TEXT ProcessingTimeStamp="20100804080035" RecordingTimeStamp="20100804080042.7633470" Server="aserver" Time="080042"
      User="ABC">When-Condition is met</TEXT>
    <TEXT ProcessingTimeStamp="20100804080035" RecordingTimeStamp="20100804080042.7650050" Server="aserver" Time="080042"
      User="ABC">Determined Result Value: 3</TEXT>
    <RESULT DataObjectID="00505683359D02DE838C18FF106808B7" DataObjectName="DAY" ProcessingTimeStamp="20100804080035"
      RecordingTimeStamp="20100804080042.7656640" Server="aserver" Time="080042" User="ABC">WED</RESULT>
    <EndProcessingTimeStamp>20100804080035</EndProcessingTimeStamp>
  </EXPRESSION>
  <RESULT DataObjectID="00505683359D02DE838C18FF106808B7" DataObjectName="DAY" ProcessingTimeStamp="20100804080035"
    RecordingTimeStamp="20100804080042.7791670" Server="aserver" Time="080042" User="ABC">WED</RESULT>
  <EndProcessingTimeStamp>20100804080035</EndProcessingTimeStamp>
  </FUNCTION>
</FDT>
```

Figure 7.5 Technical Trace—XML Document Example

The root element of the XML documents is <FDT>. Embedded are <FUNCTION> elements for the traced functions. Each <FUNCTION> element probably nests multiple <CONTEXT> elements to describe the initial context state. Traced rulesets are expressed by nested <RULESET> elements. These may include a list of <RULESET_ VARIABLES> elements first, which introduce ruleset-specific, temporary context parameters.

All processed expressions are reflected by an according <EXPRESSION> element. They typically contain multiple <TEXT> elements that describe the atomic processing steps in a textual way. Thus, the content of <TEXT> elements is specific to the processed expression or object type. The outcome of an expression or function is encapsulated by a <RESULT> element, which contains the result value. Additional elements are briefly described in Table 7.3. It summarizes all XML elements for the technical trace.

XML Element	Description
`<FDT>`	The root element of the document.
`<FUNCTION>`	Represents the processed function. It encapsulates all related elements.
`<CONTEXT>`	Represents a single context parameters of the function. It contains the current parameter value.
`<CONTEXT_UPDATE>`	Represents the update of a context parameter. It contains the new parameter value.
`<RULESET>`	Represents a triggered ruleset.
`<RULESET_VARIABLES>`	Represents a single ruleset variable. It contains the current value of the variable.
`<EXPRESSION>`	Represents a processed expression. It encapsulates elements for all processed nested steps.
`<RESULT>`	Represents the result of a function or expression and contains the according value.
`<TEXT>`	Describes a processing step in a textual way.
`<INFO>`	May add additional information or hints for a processed object. It is seldom used.
`<EXCEPTION>`	Represents processing errors and contains information for the cause.
`<StartProcessingTimeStamp>`	Contains the date and time when processing of an object has started.
`<EndProcessingTimeStamp>`	Contains the date and time when processing of an object has ended.
`<IterationIndex>`	Contains the current iteration number of a Loop expression.

Table 7.3 Technical Trace—XML Elements

The number of attribute types that may occur within the XML elements is limited. Some of the attributes may be used by several, if not all XML elements. For example, the `RecordingTimeStamp` attribute, which contains the processing time, is relevant for all elements. The `TraceVersion` attribute should be considered when parsing the document. It refers to the format of the XML document, which might need adaptations for future developments. Table 7.4 gives an overview of the currently used attributes.

Attribute	Description
ID	Unique identifier of the processed object
Name	Name of the processed object
RecordingTimeStamp	Time when the processing step has been recorded with a precision of microseconds
Time	Time when the processing step has been performed with a precision of seconds
User	Name of the system user who has triggered the function processing
Server	Name of the server on which the function has been processed
LogId	Unique identifier that is automatically assigned to the trace
TraceVersion	Version of the tracing format
DataObjectID	Unique identifier of a related data object
DataObjectName	Name of the related data object in attribute DataObjectID

Table 7.4 Technical Trace—XML Element Attributes

Trace API

The API for technical traces is encapsulated in interface IF_FDT_TRACE. Only two methods of the interface are actually still relevant. The READ method can be used to retrieve logged trace data in its raw format. Its optional importing parameters of range type allow the selection of specific traces and/or log entries. Only log entries that match to the given value ranges are taken into account for reading. Table 7.5 summarizes the parameters of the method.

Parameter	Description
ITR_TIMESTAMP	Range of trace recording timestamps
ITR_USER	Range of trace creation users
ITR_FUNCTION_ID	Range of traced functions
EV_TRACE	The selected log entries, concatenated into a text string
ETS_TRACE	A list of single log entries that match to the selection criteria
IV_MEMORY_ONLY	Obsolete

Table 7.5 Parameters of Method IF_FDT_TRACE~READ

More relevant than the raw trace log is the XML document that can be generated out of it. An extra method, READ_HIERARCHY, exists for this purpose. It internally calls the READ method and therefore shares the same importing parameters. The output of the method is an XML document that is formatted according to the description in the previous section. The document can be requested either as a text string with exporting parameter EV_TRACE or in the form of a document object model of type IF_IXML_DOCUMENT with parameter EO_TRACE_DOCUMENT.

The rest of the methods and attributes of interface IF_FDT_TRACE are relevant for lean traces only because technical traces cannot be stored onto the database. Nevertheless we will mention that attribute MV_UUID is used to store a unique identifier for the last recorded traces. The identifier is also assigned to all log entries that have been recorded.

Table 7.6 lists all the methods of interface IF_FDT_TRACE. We can now conclude the explanation of the technical trace and continue on to the lean trace. The lean trace shares some concepts of the technical trace but is more sophisticated.

Method	Description
READ	Selects all or specific recorded log entries.
READ_HIERARCHY	Generates an XML document that describes the trace in a hierarchical way.
SET_TRACE_DB_TABLE	Defines a custom database table for storing recorded traces; only relevant for lean traces.
GET_TRACE_DB_TABLE	Returns the currently set database table for storing traces; only relevant for lean traces.
DELETE	Obsolete

Table 7.6 Methods of Interface IF_FDT_TRACE

7.2.2 Lean Trace

The term "lean" refers primarily to a minimized tracing volume and only a small reduction of performance during the function processing. The lean trace needs to tackle the challenge of fulfilling two contradictory demands. On the one hand, it must gather enough information to make the function processing reproducible. On the other hand, it must keep a high processing speed for permanent usage. Both demands can be met only if the following concepts and prerequisites are considered:

▶ **Versioning**
All processed objects must be versioned. This allows retrieval of the exact definition of the objects for a given timestamp. Object details like the name, texts, and the complete content do not have to be stored within the trace. They can be determined any time solely by the object ID and processing timestamp.

▶ **Code Generation**
The lean tracing is integrated into the code generation for BRFplus functions. A

specially enhanced ABAP code is actually generated if the lean trace is requested. It is up to the individual object types whether they allow code generation at all and whether they support code generation for lean tracing in particular. Almost all standard BRFplus object types support lean tracing. An exception is the dynamic expression type, which does not allow code generation at all.

▶ **Minimized Data**
Information that is not relevant for the determination of a result value is not traced. The processing steps that do not yield a result can typically be reconstructed from the object definitions. For a Case expression like the one in Figure 7.4, it is, for example, only relevant to know which branch matched to the given case parameter at runtime. All previous branches have obviously not matched. Even though the previous branches must have been evaluated, it is not required to trace them.

▶ **Buffering**
For performance reasons, the lean trace does not immediately write the recorded information to the database. The trace log for a processed function is at first only buffered in memory with an assigned unique identifier. The logs of multiple function executions can be collected in this manner and saved together to the database afterwards. The saving needs to be explicitly triggered by the calling application. For some use cases, saving might not be required at all. To output a temporary explanation, it could, for example, be sufficient to evaluate the trace log in memory directly after the according function has been processed.

▶ **XML Conversion**
The data that is recorded by the lean trace provides only the required minimum of information. It is stored in a format that is not easy to read. The lean trace data can therefore be parsed and converted into an XML document. The document is enriched with more details that are retrieved from the processed object versions. With the XML document customers are able to generate their own lean trace format. An explanatory description in the form of a XHTML document could for example be created using a suitable XSL transformation.

If lean tracing is to be activated upon processing a function, the parameter IV_ TRACE_MODE has to be set accordingly. Listing 7.2 gives an example. The lean trace can be requested in two modes, which are reflected in two corresponding constant definitions in interface IF_FDT_CONSTANTS:

▶ GC_TRACE_MODE_LEAN
The function processing will be traced in lean mode, if possible. If a required code generation cannot be performed, the function will nevertheless be processed in interpretation mode without tracing.

▶ GC_TRACE_MODE_LEAN_REQUIRED
The function processing will fail with an exception if lean tracing cannot be performed. Such an error primarily occurs when a required code generation is not possible. This may, for example, temporarily be the case, if a used object is currently locked by another system process. If the top expression of the function does not support code generation (as is the case for dynamic expressions), the processing will always fail.

The trace instance that is provided in exporting parameter EO_TRACE after the function processing implements the general tracing interface IF_FDT_TRACE. It must be cast to type IF_FDT_LEAN_TRACE to access the lean trace-specific API. This is also demonstrated in Listing 7.2.

```
DATA: lo_trace TYPE REF TO if_fdt_trace,
      lo_lean_trace TYPE REF_TO if_fdt_lean_trace.
CALL METHOD lo_function->process
  EXPORTING
    io_context   = lo_context
    iv_trace_mode = if_fdt_constants->gc_trace_mode_lean "Mode
  IMPORTING
    eo_result    = lo_result
    eo_trace     = lo_trace.   "Request trace
lo_lean_trace ?= lo_trace.
```

Listing 7.2 Requesting Lean Trace

Usually an initial reference variable is passed to the parameter EO_TRACE so that a new trace instance can be automatically created. An existing lean trace instance can, however, be reused to record the processing of multiple functions. The according reference variable simply needs to be passed again to parameter EO_TRACE in subsequent function calls.

Multiple traces are automatically stored in a trace instance if a traced function calls any sub functions. This may happen if, for example, a Function Call expression is used or if a Procedure Call expressions executes ABAP coding that again calls a BRFplus function.

In the Workbench you can display and analyze lean traces that have been saved to the standard database table FDT_TRACE_0100. (Saving of traces is explained in section titled "Lean Trace API" below.) The option SHOW TECHNICAL ASPECTS needs to be marked in the user personalization for that purpose. When you open a traced function in the UI, you can then simply click on the button SHOW TRACES in the toolbar of the DETAIL section, as depicted by Figure 7.6.

Figure 7.6 Invocation of the Lean Trace Display

In a popup window all traces that are currently stored in the database for the function will be listed in a table, as Figure 7.7 illustrates. You can drill down to the recorded steps for each trace. The according entries are presented in a hierarchical way that reflects the processing order. The displayed information is based on the enriched XML document that can be generated out of the raw tracing data. For more detailed information, the definition of the processed objects can be displayed by clicking on the respective links in the NAME column. The displayed object version corresponds to the processing timestamp of the traced function.

Lean traces of other functions may be displayed by expanding the SEARCH OPTIONS tray. Here you may enter search criteria for the processing time and user but not for specific functions. Clicking on the SEARCH button will update the table display with all respectively found traces.

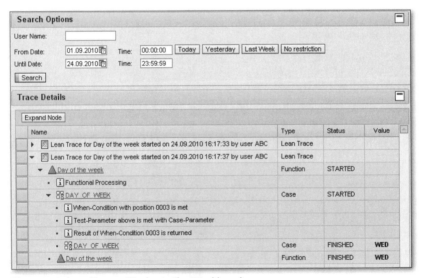

Figure 7.7 Lean Trace—Display in the Workbench

Lean Trace API

The API for lean traces is encapsulated in interface IF_FDT_LEAN_TRACE. An instance of the interface for a new trace can be requested upon processing a function. This has already been explained. If existing lean traces will be loaded from the database, it is also possible to create an initial instance. The factory method GET_TRACE of interface IF_FDT_FACTORY has to be used for this purpose like in Listing 7.3.

```
DATA: lo_factory TYPE REF TO if_fdt_factory,
      lo_lean_trace TYPE REF TO if_fdt_lean_trace.
lo_factory = cl_fdt_factory=>get_instance( ).
lo_lean_trace ?= lo_factory->get_trace( iv_trace_mode =
  if_fdt_constants=>gc_trace_mode_lean ).
```

Listing 7.3 Retrieval of an Initial Trace Instance

The lean trace interface provides some attributes that primarily buffer the trace data of new traces. The attributes are listed in Table 7.7. Details about the trace data are explained in section titled "Recorded Data" below.

Attribute	Description
MV_UUID	A universal identifier for the last recorded trace.
MS_HEADER	Header information for the last recorded trace.
MT_HEADER	A list of header information for all traces that have been recorded. It is only relevant when multiple traces have been recorded or are loaded with the same instance.
MTS_RECORD	The logged data that has been recorded by all traces.

Table 7.7 Attributes of Interface IF_FDT_LEAN_TRACE

BRFplus provides the authorization object FDT_TRACE for activities that can be performed on lean traces. The object has four different fields to adjust the authorizations:

▶ FDT_ACT: the activity that shall be performed.

▶ FDT_APPL: the application of the traced function

▶ FDT_FUNC: the traced function

▶ FDT_EXT_ID: an external identifier that has been assigned to the trace

Three different activities can be distinguished. They are reflected by constant definitions in interface IF_FDT_CONSTANTS:

▶ GC_ACTIVITY_DISPLAY
Corresponds to reading lean traces from the database.

▶ GC_ACTIVITY_CREATE
Corresponds to saving lean traces to the database.

▶ GC_ACTIVITY_DELETE
Corresponds to deleting lean traces from the database.

An explicit authorization check can be performed with method AUTHORITY_CHECK of interface IF_FDT_LEAN_TRACE. Its importing parameters correspond to the four fields of the authorization object FDT_TRACE. The method result consists simply of a Boolean returning parameter RV_PASSED. It is true if the requested authorization is granted.

The authorization checks can also be performed implicitly when calling one of the methods READ, SAVE, and DELETE. These methods correspond to the activities mentioned above. They share the common importing parameter IV_AUTH_CHECK. If the parameter is set to true, the methods will fail if the according authorization check is not passed.

Table 7.8 briefly summarizes the methods provided by interface IF_FDT_LEAN_TRACE.

Method	Description
AUTHORITY_CHECK	Checks the user's authorization for different actions on the lean trace.
READ	Reads specific traces from the database.
SAVE	Saves all buffered traces to the database.
DELETE	Deletes specific traces from the database.
PARSE	Parses specific traces and converts them into an XML document.
CLEAR_MEMORY	Clears all trace data that is buffered in memory.
MERGE	Merges data of another trace instance.

Table 7.8 Methods of Interface IF_FDT_LEAN_TRACE

Method SAVE will try to save all currently buffered trace data to the database. Lean traces are by default stored in database table FDT_TRACE_0100. You can, however, imagine that the table size would grow rapidly if all lean traces were permanently stored in the same database table. Traces that are older than five days are therefore automatically removed. To keep the trace data for a longer period, customers can clone table FDT_TRACE_0100 and set their own table as the storage target. Method SET_TRACE_DB_TABLE of interface IF_FDT_TRACE has to be called for that purpose.

Each trace will be stored with a unique identifier that has been automatically generated. With importing parameter IV_EXTERNAL_ID of method SAVE an additional, arbitrary identifier can be assigned. It is not necessarily unique and will be shared by all traces that are saved together. The parameter allows for example grouping of multiple traces according to custom needs.

With parameter `IV_UPDATE_TASK` the saving can be delegated to an update task. The update task is technically a special function module that is executed only when the ABAP `COMMIT` statement is executed. Without the update task, the `SAVE` method does *not* commit any database changes itself. All parameters of method `SAVE` are summarized in Table 7.9.

With the method `READ` one or multiple lean traces can be retrieved from the database. If the traces to read are not stored in the default table `FDT_TRACE_0100`, the source table has to be set accordingly with method `SET_TRACE_DB_TABLE` before. Traces that have just been recorded in memory with the trace instance are considered by the method too. With parameter `IV_MEMORY_ONLY` it is possible to extract a subset of the traces that are buffered in memory.

Parameter	Description
IV_AUTH_CHECK	Indicates whether an implicit authorization check shall be performed before saving.
IV_EXTERNAL_ID	Assigns an arbitrary external identifier to the saved traces.
IV_UPDATE_TASK	Indicates whether saving shall be postponed and executed in an update task.
ET_SAVE_OK	Headers of the traces that were successfully saved.
ET_SAVE_FAILED	Headers of the traces that could not be saved, e.g.. due to missing authorization.

Table 7.9 Parameters of Method IF_FDT_LEAN_TRACE~SAVE

Most importing parameters of the `READ` method are of range type. They represent search criteria for the traces to read. Only traces that match to the defined value ranges will be taken into account. The full list of method parameters is described in Table 7.10.

Parameter	Description
IV_AUTH_CHECK	Indicates whether an implicit authorization check shall be performed before reading.
ITR_TRACE_UUID	Range of trace IDs
ITR_USER	Range of trace creation users
ITR_FUNCTION_ID	Range of traced functions
ITR_EXTERNAL_ID	Range of external identifiers
ITR_TRACE_REF_UUID	Range of parent trace IDs
ITR_TRACE_START	Range of trace starting timestamps
ITR_TRACE_END	Range of trace ending timestamps

Table 7.10 Parameters of Method IF_FDT_LEAN_TRACE~READ

Parameter	Description
IV_DEEP	Indicates whether sub traces shall be included.
IV_MEMORY_ONLY	Indicates whether traces shall only be read from memory.
ET_TRACE_HEADER	Provides the header information of the successfully read traces.
ETS_TRACE_RECORD	Provides the recorded data of the successfully read traces.

Table 7.10 Parameters of Method IF_FDT_LEAN_TRACE~READ (Cont.)

Method DELETE can be used to delete saved traces from the database. The parameters of the method are a mixture of the parameters in the methods READ and SAVE. Like method READ it has importing parameters of type range to select the traces that shall be deleted. As for method SAVE an implicit authorization check can be requested and the deletion can be transferred to an update task. Exporting parameter ET_DELETE_OK will contain the header data of the traces that could successfully be deleted. Conversely, exporting parameter ET_DELETE_FAILED will contain the header data of the traces that could not be deleted.

With method PARSE the recorded trace data can be converted into an XML document. It is possible to select multiple traces and combine them into one document. For a detailed description of the document's format and its contained XML elements, you can advance to the section titled "XML Documents" below.

The PARSE method implicitly calls the READ method to obtain the trace data to parse. The method therefore shares the same range type parameters to select the desired traces. Also, the implicit authorization check for reading traces can be requested with parameter IV_AUTH_CHECK. The generated XML document can be taken over in two formats. Parameter EV_TRACE contains the document in the form of a text string. Parameter EO_TRACE_DOCUMENT provides a document object model (DOM) of type IF_IXML_DOCUMENT.

The trace data that is buffered by one trace instance can be merged into the buffer of another trace instance with method MERGE. The method basically copies the data of the table attributes MT_HEADER and MTS_RECORD from the trace instance in parameter IO_TRACE to the current instance.

The traces of the instance IO_TRACE can also be merged as sub traces of the latest trace in the current instance. The latest trace is defined by the identifier in attribute MV_UUID. Method parameter IV_AS_CHILD needs to be set to "true" in this case, and a parent object of the latest trace needs to be specified with parameter IV_PARENT_ID. The parent object is the processed object that has called the functions of the merged traces. Note that it is not checked whether the parent object ID is a valid one.

Method CLEAR_MEMORY can be used to free the buffers of a trace instance. The instance can therefore be reused multiple times. When traces are, for example, saved and/or parsed directly after the recording, the logged data is probably not required any more.

Recorded Data

The lean trace result consists technically of two parts: a header with some overall information and a set of log entries for the recorded processing steps. Both are reflected by structure types S_HEADER and S_RECORD in interface IF_FDT_LEAN_TRACE. The header fields are self-explanatory and thus briefly summarized in Table 7.11.

Field	Description
TRACE_UUID	A unique identifier for the trace that is automatically generated.
TRACE_FCT_ID	The ID of the processed function.
TRACE_PROC_TIME	The requested processing timestamp. It determines the object versions to be processed.
TRACE_EXT_ID	An optional, external identifier. Traces may e.g. be grouped by sharing the same external identifier.
TRACE_REF_ID	The ID of a parent trace in case multiple function calls are nested.
TRACE_START	Timestamp when the function call is started.
TRACE_END	Timestamp when the function call has ended.
TRACE_USER	The system name of the user that triggered the function call.
TRACE_VERSION	Version of the lean trace format.

Table 7.11 Lean Trace—Structure IF_FDT_LEAN_TRACE=>S_HEADER

The fields of structure S_RECORD that are listed in Table 7.12 require some more explanation. Let us begin with the first field, TRACE_UUID, which allows identification of the log entries that have been recorded for a specific trace. It contains the unique identifier that has been assigned to the trace in the header.

The sequence number SEQNR of the recorded steps is unique within a trace. It always starts with 1 for the processed function object. For each subsequently processed object, a new entry is created with an incremented sequence number.

The currently processed object is referred to by its unique identifier in field ID. For values and ranges that are not objects but rather embedded parts of an object, the ID field remains initial (zero). The object they belong to is identified by the field PARENT_ID in these cases.

The field `PARENT_ID` refers generally to the parent object that has triggered the processing of the current object. The field reflects the usage hierarchy of the objects involved in the function processing. It can be utilized to reconstruct a stack level for the recorded log entries.

The value of the `POSITION` field depends on the type of the parent object. It specifies the usage of the current object by the parent object more precisely. If an object is, for example, evaluated inside the cell of a Decision Table expression, the `POSITION` field will refer to the table cell with row and column number.

The result value that is determined by the processed object is stored in the field `VALUE`. For constants and ranges, the value is not required because it can be retrieved from the according object definition. Values are converted into a binary format of type `XSTRING`. This universal format allows you to persist also structured and table type data in an elegant way.

Field	Description
TRACE_UUID	The unique identifier of the trace to which the record entry belongs.
SEQNR	A sequence number that reflects the order in which the entries have been recorded.
ID	ID of the processed object. For constants and ranges the ID is initial.
PARENT_ID	ID of the parent object that is processed. The field allows reconstructing the hierarchy of nested objects.
POSITION	Indicates the usage of the processed object within the parent object.
VALUE	The result value of the processed object, converted into a binary format (type XSTRING).

Table 7.12 Lean Trace—Structure IF_FDT_LEAN_TRACE=>S_RECORD

Figure 7.8 shows a screenshot of recorded log entries for our example scenario with the Case expression given in the introduction to Section 7.2.

SEQNR [X(4)]	ID [X(16)]	PARENT_ID [X(16)]	POSITION [C(50)]	VALUE [XString]
00000001	00505683359D02DE95C7AB8DED020F6C	00000000000000000000000000000000	Function	
00000002	00505683359D02DE838C2443A32888EC	00505683359D02DE95C7AB8DED020F6C	Context	FF0602010102800034313033(
00000003	00000000000000000000000000000000	00505683359D02DE838A0C25554F9041	TestParam_0003	
00000004	00505683359D02DE838A0C25554F9041	00505683359D02DE95C7AB8DED020F6C	Expression	FF0602010102800034313033(

Figure 7.8 Lean Trace—Recorded Data Example

Because the field for the trace ID contains the same value for all entries, the according column is not included in Figure 7.8. Even though the trace is quite small, it nevertheless illustrates a recurring pattern:

1. The first entry refers always to the processed function. The function itself does not yield any result value.

2. The context passed to the function is traced next. For each data object of the function context, a separate entry with the ID and value is recorded. The parent object is the function and the position or rather usage in the function is the "Context." In Figure 7.8 there is only one data object in the context.

3. The Case expression is processed next, but before the result can be recorded, some intermediate information needs to be traced. For the Case expression, this information is the matching test parameter. Previous, non-matching test parameters are neglected. In our example the third test parameter matches. Because the test parameter is a value that is part of the Case expression, it has no object ID of its own. The Case expression is recorded as the parent object. The value of the test parameter does not have to be traced because it can be retrieved from the definition of the Case expression, if required.

4. The top expression of a function is always recorded in the last entry. It has the function as parent object and provides the final result value.

The data that is actually recorded depends primarily on the processed object types. Information that can be reconstructed from the object definitions is typically not traced. Many entries are therefore recorded only under certain conditions. Included values or Constant expressions are never traced. The according values can always be retrieved from the respective object definitions. Table 7.13 lists the traced information together with the corresponding value for the POSITION field in the records.

Object Type	Position	Traced Information
Function	Function	Processed function
	Context	Each data object in the context
	Expression	Top expression
Ruleset	Rs	Processed ruleset
	PsPrecond	Ruleset precondition object
	RsInit_<pos>	Expression initializing ruleset variable at position <pos>
	Rule_<pos>	Rule within ruleset at position <pos>

Table 7.13 Lean Trace—Recorded Data

Object Type	Position	Traced Information
Rule	RPrecond_<pos>	Rule precondition at position <pos>
	RCond	Rule condition, if it is not a value range
	RTActn	Single action, performed if rule condition is true (outdated)
	RFActn	Single action, performed if rule condition is false (outdated)
	ExtActn_<pos>	Action processed at position <pos>. Might also refer to an expression or data object in case of a context value assignment.
Boolean Expression	Operand_<pos>	Operand at position <pos>; only for referenced expressions
Case Expression	CaseParam	Case parameter, if it is not a constant
	TestParam_<pos>	Test parameter that matches to the case parameter
	ReturnParam	Evaluated result, only for referenced objects
	OtherParam	Evaluated result for test parameter others, only for referenced objects
Decision Table Expression	CondCell_<row>_<col>	Condition in table row <row>, column <col>, which is either *not* fulfilled or uses another object
	ResultCell_<row>_<col>	Evaluated result in table row <row>, column <col>.
Decision Tree Expression	CondNode_<ID>	Condition for tree node with identifier <ID>; only for referenced expressions
	ResultNode_<ID>	Evaluated result of tree node with identifier <ID>
Formula Expression	Token_<pos>	Expression used within the formula at position <pos>
Loop Expression	FETab	Table that is looped over in mode "For each entry in …", if it is not in the context.
	LpPass_<num>_LpCond	Condition that terminates the loop in iteration <num>; only for loop modes "While … do" and "Do … until."
	FpPass_<num>_Rule_<pos>	Rule evaluated within the loop in iteration <num> at position <pos>
	FpPass_<num>_LpExit_<pos>	Exit condition in iteration <num> at position <pos>, only if it is true.
	FpPass_<num>_LpContinue_<pos>	Continue condition in iteration <num> at position <pos>, only if it is true.

Table 7.13 Lean Trace—Recorded Data (Cont.)

Object Type	Position	Traced Information
Procedure Call Expression	`StaticMethod`	Triggered method or function
Search Tree Expression	`NodeCond_<ID>`	Condition for tree node with identifier `<ID>`; only for referenced expressions.
	`NodeResult_<ID>`	Evaluated result of tree node with identifier `<ID>`
Value Range (Expression)	`_#SR`	For included value ranges, the postfix `_#SR` is appended to the respective position value, e.g., `CondCell_1_1_#SR`.
	`TestParam`	Test parameter, only for referenced objects.
	`Range_<pos>_L`	Low value of range at position `<pos>`, only for referenced objects.
	`Range_<pos>_H`	High value of range at position `<pos>`, only for referenced objects.
Others		The resulting value is traced without internal details.

Table 7.13 Lean Trace—Recorded Data (Cont.)

With the `PARSE` method of the lean trace API, it is possible to read recorded trace data from the database or memory, and generate an XML document out of it. The format of the XML is described in the following section.

XML Documents

The content of the XML document, which can be generated with the lean trace API, primarily consists of elements that correspond to the processed objects. The nesting of the XML elements reflects the processing order. All element names are associated with the namespace prefix `FDTNS`. It refers to the namespace `http://sap.com/fdt/trace`. The root element in the document is `FDT`, which also introduces the mentioned namespace. Figure 7.9 shows an XML document example.

Like the recorded trace data, the XML document starts with a description of the processed function. The corresponding `<FUNCTION>` element nests elements for the start and the end time of the processing. Multiple `<CONTEXT>` elements are typically also embedded, one for each context parameter. They have the initially passed value as content. The `<FUNCTION>` element will also contain an `<EXPRESSION>` element for a processed top expression or `<RULESET>` elements for all triggered rulesets. A `<RESULT>` element finally encapsulates the processing result of the function.

```
- <FDTNS:FDT xmlns:FDTNS="http://sap.com/fdt/trace">
  - <FDTNS:FUNCTION Name="DAY_OF_THE_WEEK" ID="00505683359D02DE95C7AB8DED020F6C" VERSION="000002"
    TraceUUID="00505683359D02DE95C8A399B7FED67F" TraceVersion="1.00" User="ABC" ProcessingTimeStamp="20100729115537">
    <FDTNS:START_PROCESSING_TIMESTAMP>20100729115537.5569910</FDTNS:START_PROCESSING_TIMESTAMP>
    <FDTNS:TEXT>Functional Processing</FDTNS:TEXT>
    <FDTNS:CONTEXT DataObjectID="00505683359D02DE838C2443A32888EC" DataObjectName="DAY_OF_WEEK" DataObjectType="DO"
      Version="000002">3</FDTNS:CONTEXT>
    - <FDTNS:EXPRESSION Name="DAY_OF_WEEK" ID="00505683359D02DE838A0C25554F9041" VERSION="000002" ExpressionType="EXTY_CASE">
      <FDTNS:START_PROCESSING_TIMESTAMP>20100729115537</FDTNS:START_PROCESSING_TIMESTAMP>
      - <FDTNS:CASE_PARAMETER>
        <FDTNS:CONTEXT DataObjectID="00505683359D02DE838C2443A32888EC" DataObjectName="DAY_OF_WEEK" DataObjectType="DO"
          Version="000002">3</FDTNS:CONTEXT>
      </FDTNS:CASE_PARAMETER>
      - <FDTNS:WHEN_BRANCH Position="0003">
        <FDTNS:TEXT>When-Condition with position 0003 is met</FDTNS:TEXT>
        - <FDTNS:TEST_PARAMETER>
          <FDTNS:VALUE DataObjectType="N">3</FDTNS:VALUE>
        </FDTNS:TEST_PARAMETER>
        <FDTNS:TEXT>Test-Parameter above is met with Case-Parameter</FDTNS:TEXT>
        - <FDTNS:RETURN_PARAMETER>
          <FDTNS:VALUE DataObjectType="T">WED</FDTNS:VALUE>
        </FDTNS:RETURN_PARAMETER>
        <FDTNS:TEXT>Result of When-Condition 0003 is returned</FDTNS:TEXT>
      </FDTNS:WHEN_BRANCH>
      <FDTNS:RESULT DataObjectID="00505683359D02DE838C18FF106808B7" DataObjectName="DAY" DataObjectType="DO"
        Version="000002">WED</FDTNS:RESULT>
      <FDTNS:END_PROCESSING_TIMESTAMP>20100729115537</FDTNS:END_PROCESSING_TIMESTAMP>
    </FDTNS:EXPRESSION>
    <FDTNS:RESULT DataObjectID="00505683359D02DE838C18FF106808B7" DataObjectName="DAY" DataObjectType="DO"
      Version="000002">WED</FDTNS:RESULT>
    <FDTNS:END_PROCESSING_TIMESTAMP>20100729115540.4695460</FDTNS:END_PROCESSING_TIMESTAMP>
  </FDTNS:FUNCTION>
</FDTNS:FDT>
```

Figure 7.9 Lean Trace—XML Document Example

The XML elements mentioned so far can be regarded as general elements. Except for the function element, they may in principle be nested by all other elements. The <RESULT> element reflects, for example, not only the function result but also intermediate results of expressions. Yet another general element is the <TEXT> element. It contains some descriptive text that may optionally be used for the explanation of the trace. Table 7.14 lists all the general XML elements.

XML Element	Attributes	Content
<FUNCTION>	Name, ID, Version, TraceUUID, TraceVersion, User, ProcessingTimeStamp	Nested elements
<START_PROCESSING_ TIMESTAMP>		Timestamp
<END_PROCESSING_ TIMESTAMP>		Timestamp
<CONTEXT>	DataObjectID, DataObjectName, DataObjectType, Version	Value of the context parameter
<EXPRESSION>	Name, ID, Version, ExpressionType	Nested elements, <RESULT> element
<RESULT>	DataObjectId, DataObjectName, DataObjectType, Version	Result value
<TEXT>		Descriptive text

Table 7.14 Lean Trace XML—General Elements

The processing of rulesets is represented by the XML elements listed in Table 7.15. Each triggered ruleset is introduced by an according `<RULESET>` element. The rules of the ruleset that have actually been evaluated are described by `<RULE>` elements. Such elements are not limited to rulesets only. They can also be nested by certain other elements, for example, within Loop expressions.

XML Element	Attributes	Content
`<RULESET>`		Nested elements
`<RULESET_PRECONDITION>`		Nested `<EXPRESSION>` element
`<RULESET_INITIALIZATION>`		Nested `<INITIALIZATION_EXPRESSION>` and `<RULESET_VARIABLE>` elements
`<INITIALIZATION_EXPRESSION>`	Position	Nested `<EXPRESSION>` element
`<RULESET_VARIABLE>`	Position	Nested `<CONTEXT>` element
`<EXIT_CONDITION>`	Position	Nested `<EXPRESSION>` element
`<RULE>`	Position	Nested `<RULE_PRECONDITION>` and `<RULE_CONDITION>` elements
`<RULE_PRECONDITION>`		Nested elements
`<RULE_CONDITION>`		Nested elements
`<TRUE_ACTION>`		Nested `<EXPRESSION>` or context change element
`<FALSE_ACTION>`		Nested `<EXPRESSION>` or context change element
`<CONTEXT_CHANGE>`	ChangeMode	Target of context change

Table 7.15 Lean Trace XML — Elements for Rulesets and Rules

Traced expressions are principally introduced by an `<EXPRESSION>` element. Its `ExpressionType` attribute refers to the respective type. The element may include additional, expression type specific elements. These XML elements are listed in Table 7.16. The last element inside an `<EXPRESSION>` element is always a `<RESULT>` element. It contains the determined result value of the expression.

The representation of expressions in the XML has two exceptions:

▶ Constant values are directly embedded, no matter whether they are implied or referenced as separate Constant expressions.

▶ Value range definitions are also often implied by expressions. In such cases, the value-range-specific XML elements are surrounded by a `<RANGE>` element rather than an `<EXPRESSION>` element.

Expression Type	XML Element	Attributes	Content
Boolean	`<OPERATION>`	`OperationID, Invert`	Boolean operation
	`<OPERAND>`	`Position, Invert, Operand`	Operand content or nested element
Case	`<CASE_PARAMETER>`		Case parameter content or nested elements
	`<WHEN_BRANCH>`	`Position`	Nested elements: `<TEST_ PARAMETER>`, `<RETURN_ PARAMETER>`
	`<TEST_PARAMETER>`		Test parameter content or nested element
	`<RETURN_ PARAMETER>`		Returned value or nested element
Decision Table	`<TABLE_PROPERTY>`		Match Mode
	`<ROW>`	`RowNo`	Nested `<CELL>` elements
	`<CELL>`	`ColNo, IsResult`	Cell content or nested `<EXPRESSION>` element
Decision Tree	`<NODE>`	`Node, IsResult`	Nested elements
Formula	`<TOKEN>`	`TokenType`	Nested `<ARGUMENT>` elements
	`<ARGUMENT>`		Content or nested elements
Loop	`<LOOP_PROPERTY>`	`LoopMode`	Nested elements
	`<FOR_EACH_TABLE>`		Nested elements: `<CONTEXT>`, `<EXPRESSION>`
	`<FOR_EACH_ CONDITION>`	`Position`	Nested `<RANGE>` elements
	`<LOOP_CONDITION>`		Nested elements
	`<LOOP_PASS>`	`Index`	Nested elements: `<RULE>`, `<EXIT_CONDITION>`, `<CONTINUE_CONDITION>`
	`<EXIT_CONDITION>`	`Position`	Nested elements
	`<CONTINUE_ CONDITION>`	`Position`	Nested elements
Procedure Call	`<STATIC_METHOD>`	`Class, Method`	Nested elements

Table 7.16 Lean Trace XML—Expression Type-Specific Elements

Expression Type	XML Element	Attributes	Content
Search Tree	`<TREE_PROPERTY>`		Match Mode
	`<NODE>`	Node	Nested elements: `<NODE_CONDITION>`, `<NODE_RESULT>`
	`<NODE_CONDITION>`		Condition content or nested element
	`<NODE_RESULT>`		Result content or nested `<EXPRESSION>` element
Value Range (embedded)	`<RANGE>`		Nested elements: `<TEST_PARAMETER>`, `<RANGE_ENTRY>`
Value Range	`<TEST_PARAMETER>`		Content or nested element for test parameter
	`<RANGE_ENTRY>`	Position, Option, Sign	Nested elements: `<LOW>`, `<HIGH>`
	`<LOW>`		Content or nested element for low value of range
	`<HIGH>`		Content or nested element for high value of range

Table 7.16 Lean Trace XML—Expression Type-Specific Elements (Cont.)

Due to its hierarchical structure, the XML document for lean traces should make it easy to understand how the corresponding functions have been processed. As a custom extension, the document may be transformed and/or enriched with further details from the processed object versions.

7.3   Extending BRFplus

BRFplus inherently incorporates many possibilities for adapting business rules to custom needs. However, there is always a limit to the functional scope that standard implementations can cover. To overcome such unavoidable boundaries, BRFplus supports the integration of custom behavior at specific places of various depth and complexity:

▶ The *Procedure Call* expression and action types can be used to program almost any logic with ABAP. For details, see Section 5.5.14.

▶ Application exits allow many ways to influence the maintenance and behavior of objects. Section 7.3.1 gives a deeper insight into this concept.

▶ Related to application exits is the creation of additional functions for Formula expressions. Section 7.3.2 will give an in-depth example of such an enhancement.

7.3.1 Application Exits

Application exits are programmatic enhancements that will be executed at specific events for specific purposes. For example, they allow restricting the access to objects using a more finely granular authorization check mechanism than the standard one. The validity of data entered for a specific expression may need to be cross-checked against some external data sources. Or you may simply want to be notified if an object is saved so that some dependent adaptations can be triggered.

Application exits are technically based on an ABAP class that implements the special interface IF_FDT_APPLICATION_SETTINGS. They are typically used and valid only within the scope of a single BRFplus application. Per application, one such class can be assigned in the field APPLICATION EXIT CLASS on the PROPERTIES tab of the application UI, as shown in Figure 7.10. The counterpart in the application API is the method SET_SETTINGS_CLASS of interface IF_FDT_APPLICATION.

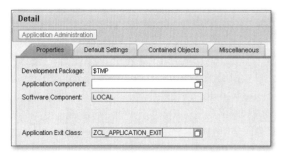

Figure 7.10 Application Exit Class

Interface IF_FDT_APPLICATION_SETTINGS defines a set of static methods: the actual "exits" that can be implemented. For each method, a corresponding Boolean attribute GV_<EXIT> exists. Implemented exit methods will be called by the BRFplus framework only if the corresponding attribute has been set to "true." It is therefore recommended that you define a class constructor that sets the attributes for all implemented exits accordingly. Application exits that are not used do not require an (empty) implementation.

Once an application exit method is called, the currently executed coding leaves the realm of BRFplus. It is therefore the responsibility of the programmer to avoid and handle any kind of runtime errors. If a severe error occurs, only exceptions of type CX_FDT_SYSTEM are allowed and handled by the framework. In such a case, the triggering event may be aborted with an error message, or the exception may simply be ignored for application exits that have the characteristic of a notification.

A CX_FDT_SYSTEM exception will also be raised automatically if BRFplus detects recursive calls to an exit method. It would, for example, not be a good idea to change the object passed to a change notification exit again because doing so would cause yet another call of the same exit.

Table 7.17 lists the currently available application exits. In the following section we will look into the details of each exit. Only the calendar exit is left out because it is not supported in the SAP NetWeaver release 7.0.

Application Exit	Description
Authorization Check	This exit allows enhancing or even completely replacing the standard authorization checks of BRFplus.
Check	Additional consistency checks can be implemented for BRFplus objects, which will also affect the possibility of activation.
Activation	The activation of objects can explicitly be prevented.
Change Notification	A notification is triggered whenever an object of the application is changed.
Save Notification	A notification is triggered whenever an object of the application is saved.
Element Values	Dynamic value lists can be retrieved for elements.
Formula Functions	The standard list of formula functions can be restricted or custom defined functions can be added.
Changeability	Adjusts the changeability of customizing objects.
Calendar	Sets a specific calendar. Not supported in SAP NetWeaver 7.0.

Table 7.17 Application Exits

Authorization Check Exit

Authorization checks are performed when method AUTHORITY_CHECK of interface IF_FDT_TRANSACTION is called for a BRFplus object. This is, for example, the case when an object is accessed or manipulated in the BRFplus Workbench. The standard check is based on authorization object FDT_OBJECT that takes the object's application, the object type, and the performed activity into account. The authorization object has the corresponding fields FDT_APPL, FDT_OBJTYP and FDT_ACT. The technical values for the activity types "Display," "Create," "Change," "Activate," and

"Delete" are defined as constants with the name pattern GC_ACTIVITY_* in interface IF_FDT_CONSTANTS.

Sub Activities

With Service Pack 5 of SAP NetWeaver 7.0, Enhancement Package 2 an additional parameter, IS_SUB_ACTIVITY, can be passed to method AUTHORITY_CHECK. It allows more refined checks in the application exit. Currently the sub category is filled if a new object is created as a copy of another object. The constant value GC_SUB_ACTIVITY_COPY of interface IF_FDT_CONSTANTS and the ID of the copied object are then set in parameter IS_SUB_ACTIVITY.

The importing parameters of method AUTHORITY_CHECK are simply forwarded to the equally named exit method. The exit method is invoked before the standard authorization check is performed. This allows the exit to decide whether the standard checks shall be skipped or be evaluated in addition. All parameters of the authorization check exit are listed and described in Table 7.18.

Parameter	Description
IV_ID	ID of the accessed object
IV_ACTIVITY	The activity that shall be performed
IS_SUB_ACTIVITY	Defines an additional activity that is part of the main activity.
IV_DEEP	Authorization needs to be checked deeply, including all referenced objects.
EV_PASSED	Indicates whether authorization has been granted.
ES_MESSAGE	Defines an optional, explanatory message that will be stored in the global variable SYST.
EV_SKIP_CHECK	Indicates whether the standard authorization checks shall be skipped for the passed object.
EV_SKIP_REFERENCED	Indicates whether the standard authorization checks shall be skipped for referenced objects. This is only relevant if parameter IV_DEEP is "true."

Table 7.18 Authorization Check Exit—Parameters

Check Exit

BRFplus objects are checked for consistency when method CHECK of interface IF_FDT_TRANSACTION is called. Only consistent objects can be activated to ensure that they can actually be processed. Inconsistent objects may, however, still be saved in an inactive state.

The check exit allows the implementation of additional checks, for example, due to relations to some external data. Method CHECK of the exit class is therefore called after the standard checks have been performed, and only if the standard checks have successfully been passed. The result of the custom checks can be a list of information messages, warning messages, and error messages. If error messages are issued, the check fails and the object cannot be activated.

Because the check messages will also be displayed in the BRFplus Workbench, they are intended to refer to properties of the current object. Users defining the object should be able to correct the properties in case the checks fail. Checks that are not related to object properties or that are of a temporary nature should instead be implemented in the activation exit.

The signature of the check exit is briefly summarized in Table 7.19.

Parameter	Description
IV_ID	ID of the object to be checked
IV_OBJECT_TYPE	Type of the object to be checked
ET_MESSAGE	Messages that are issued by the additional checks

Table 7.19 Check Exit—Parameters

Activation Exit

An active BRFplus object must be ready for processing in general. This is normally ensured by standard checks on the object's properties. With the activation exit it is, however, possible to explicitly veto only the activation of an object that has been successfully checked already. For example, the object might be used by other objects and shall not be activated incompatibly in this respect. For authorization-related vetoes the authorization check exit described above should preferably be used and be implemented for the ACTIVATE activity.

The method to be implemented for the activation exit is ACTIVATION_VETO. Its signature, which is listed in Table 7.20, is similar to the one for the check exit; however, it allows you to veto the activation without a specific message.

Parameter	Description
IV_ID	ID of the object to be activated.
IV_OBJECT_TYPE	Type of the object to be activated.
EV_VETO	Prohibits the activation of the object, if set to "true."
ET_MESSAGE	Messages that can be issued in case the activation is vetoed.

Table 7.20 Activation Exit—Parameters

Change Notification Exit

The change notification exit is called whenever a property of an object is changed. The exit cannot prohibit a change but only react to it. If you want to adapt settings of other BRFplus objects, you should take into account that those objects might not be changeable, for example, due to locking interferences.

When an object is reset to its last saved state, multiple settings may be discarded at once. This kind of change can be treated specially. The exit method CHANGE_NOTI-FICATION provides the Boolean parameter IV_CHANGES_DISCARDED for that reason. Its complete signature is summarized in Table 7.21.

Parameter	Description
IV_ID	ID of the object that was changed.
IV_OBJECT_TYPE	Type of the object that was changed.
IV_CHANGES_DISCARDED	Indicates whether changes to the last saved version have been discarded.

Table 7.21 Change Notification Exit—Parameters

Save Notification Exit

The save notification exit is called whenever an object was saved to the database, no matter whether it is active or inactive. The exit cannot prohibit saving but only react to it. The object itself must not be altered in this exit. Instead, specific settings should be enforced upon checking or activation. As for the change notification exit you cannot rely on changing or saving other BRFplus objects because they might be locked externally.

The method that needs to be implemented for the save notification exit is reasonably named SAVE_NOTIFICATION. Its simple signature is listed in Table 7.22.

Parameter	Description
IV_ID	ID of the object that was saved.
IV_OBJECT_TYPE	Type of the object that was saved.

Table 7.22 Save Notification Exit—Parameters

Element Values Exit

BRFplus data elements may include a static list of valid values with corresponding descriptions. The element values exit allows dynamically retrieval of a list of valid values for a specific element. The values may be selected from a database table, for example. The exit is not intended for elements that are bound to a data dictionary type. Those elements automatically derive the value list from a respective domain or reference table.

The exit method GET_ELEMENT_VALUES is called in various situations for three different purposes:

▶ To find out whether the element actually has a non-empty value list.
▶ To retrieve specific entries of the value list only.
▶ To retrieve the complete value list.

For performance reasons, the implementation should collect only the kind of information that is actually needed. This can be achieved by checking which exporting parameters are actually requested, using the ABAP statement IS REQUESTED.

The exit method will be called for all data elements of an application with the respective ID in parameter IV_ID. Only if the exit is applicable to the current element must the exporting parameter EV_APPLICABLE be set to true and the requested information be retrieved.

If parameter EV_NO_CHECKLIST is requested, it should be set to true when the value list is currently empty. Actual values need to be retrieved only in case parameter ET_VALUE is requested. The optional importing parameters ITR_VALUE and ITR_TEXT need to be considered then. They might be filled with range selections if only specific entries of the value list are of interest. This is the case, when, for example, the existence of a given value is checked. Parameter ITR_VALUE contains only a single entry in this case.

The returned value list must only contain entries that match to the provided range selections. It is not filtered automatically by BRFplus, to avoid unnecessary memory and runtime consumption. If the value list is for example retrieved from a database table, the filtering can easily be included into an SQL SELECT statement.

If the element is versioned, the optional importing parameter IV_TIMESTAMP might need to be considered, but only if it is actually supplied. The value list can then be retrieved in a time-dependent way. In contrast, parameter IV_LANGU should always be taken into account for the retrieval of short texts in the value list. The complete list of parameters is summarized in Table 7.23.

Parameter	Description
IV_ID	ID of a data element.
IV_LANUG	Language requested for the texts in the value list.
IV_TIMESTAMP	Optional timestamp for version dependent elements.
ITR_VALUE	Optional range selection for values.
ITR_TEXT	Optional range selection for texts.
IO_SELECTION	Is intended to provide additional context for the value list determination. It is, however, currently not supplied with sensible data.
EV_APPLICABLE	Indicates whether the application exit is applicable for the provided element.
EV_NO_CHECKLIST	Indicates whether a value list is available or not.
ET_VALUE	Must contain the requested value list. Only specific value list entries may be requested if parameters ITR_VALUE or ITR_TEXT are not empty.

Table 7.23 Element Values Exit—Parameters

Formula Functions Exit

Formula expressions normally have access to a standard set of formula functions. The functions are grouped into various categories, as shown in Figure 7.11. With the formula functions exit, it is possible to adapt the list of available functions and categories within an application in general or only for specific expressions. The exit method GET_FORMULA_FUNCTIONALS cannot only filter out standard functions. It may also add custom defined functions and categories. More details on custom defined functions are given in Section 7.3.2.

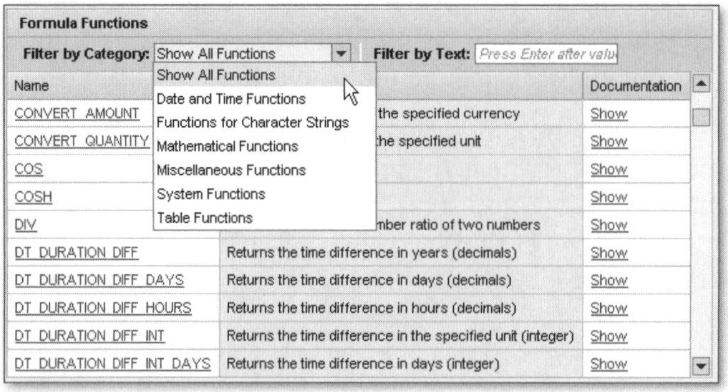

Figure 7.11 Formula Function Categories

In importing parameter IV_ID the currently accessed Formula expression is passed to the application exit. This allows the exit to react only on specific expression instances. Furthermore, two lists of standard functions and categories are passed in the changing parameters CT_FUNCTIONAL_DEFINITION and CT_FUNCTIONAL_CATEGORY respectively. They can easily be adapted to the desired needs. Changes must, however, be made in a consistent way. For example, if you want to remove a category, you should also remove or reassign all functions of that category.

The function category entries are of structure type S_FUNCTIONAL_CATEG of interface IF_FDT_FORMULA. As listed in Table 7.24 the structure comprises a category key value, a descriptive text, and an optional key value of a parent category. The parent category is required only if the categories shall be hierarchically ordered.

Field	Description
CATEGORY	A unique key value for the category
DESCRIPTION	Descriptive text for the category
PARENT	Optional key value of a parent category

Table 7.24 Structure IF_FDT_FORMULA~S_FUNCTIONAL_CATEGORY

The entries for functions have the structure type, S_FUNCTIONAL_DEF. As listed in Table 7.25 the structure includes fields to assign a category and a unique identifier, called "token." Because formula functions are implemented in static class methods, the names of the class and method also need to be specified.

Field	Description
CATEGORY	Key value of a category to which the function shall be assigned
TOKEN	A unique function key
CLASS	Name of the class implementing the function
METHOD	Name of the static method implementing the function
TYPE	Currently not required

Table 7.25 Structure IF_FDT_FORMULA~S_FUNCTIONAL_DEF

For more information on new, custom defined formula functions, you can proceed to Section 7.3.2.

Changeability Exit

The changeability of BRFplus customizing objects follows the general client settings for client-dependent data by default. For special use cases, it might be desirable to deviate from these settings. The changeability exit allows for overruling of the standard changeability of customizing objects for a whole BRFplus application. Also, the automatic recording of changes onto transport requests can be enabled or disabled.

A typical requirement is the ability to change transportable customizing objects in a productive system, which is usually not allowed. The standard process is that customizing objects are adjusted only in a customizing development system and then transported into the productive system.

> **Pitfalls**
>
> When transportable customizing objects become editable in the productive system, those changes may get lost with the next transport from a customizing system or client copy. To prohibit editing of critical objects it is also recommended that you implement the authorization check exit accordingly.

The exit method GET_CHANGEABILITY comprises the parameters listed in Table 7.26. If a customizing object is to be changed, the method is called with the UUID of the object's application. The two parameters CV_CHANGEABLE for the changeability in general and CH_CHANGE_RECORDING for the change recording can be modified individually. If the application is not changeable by system default, error messages are provided in parameter CT_MESSAGE. They should be removed or replaced if the changeability is changed. Conversely, it is recommended that you add some sensible error messages in case the changeability is disabled by the exit implementation.

Parameter	Description
IV_APPLICATION_ID	Provides the ID of the concerned BRFplus application.
CV_CHANGEABLE	Allows overruling of the general changeability for objects of the application.
CV_CHANGE_RECORDING	Allows overruling of the change recording for objects of the application.
CT_MESSAGE	Allows overruling of messages in connection with the changeability settings.

Table 7.26 Changeability Exit—Parameters

Possible use cases of the changeability exit are presented in Chapter 8.

7.3.2 Custom Formula Functions

Internally, the Formula expression type uses the separate formula builder component of package S_FORMULA_BUILDER. The formula builder itself provides a basic set of commonly used, built-in functions. With its open architecture, the formula builder also allows you to add custom defined functions. BRFplus delivers some additional functions already in the standard. By means of the formula functions exit, BRFplus allows you to attach further functions to all or only specific Formula expressions of an application.

The creation of a new custom function will now be explained step by step, following an example. The example function will remove trailing zeros from a decimal number. For example, for the number 123.456078900 the result would be 123.4560789.

Formula Function Class

Formula functions are technically implemented in static class methods. Class CL_FOEV_BUILTINS contains the basic functions implemented by the formula builder. The functions defined by BRFplus are contained in the classes CL_FDT_FORMULA, CL_FDT_FORMULA_SYS_FUNCTION and partly also in class CL_FDT_DATE_TIME.

As is the case for date- and time-related functions in BRFplus, it can make sense to reuse an existing class for the definition of formula functions. In general it is recommended that you collect formula functions into a separate class. In our example, depicted in Figure 7.12, we create the class ZCL_MY_FORMULA_FUNCTIONS with the class builder, Transaction SE24.

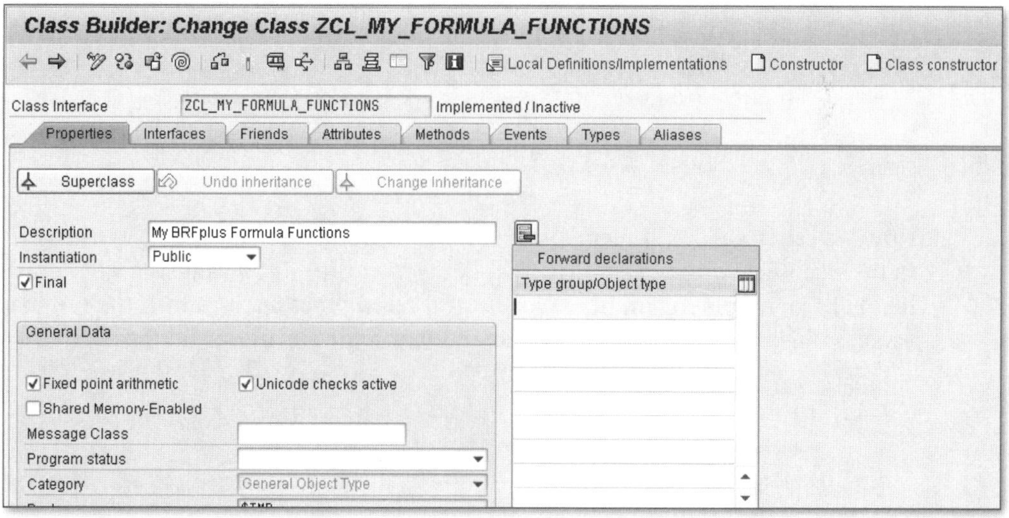

Figure 7.12 Custom Formula Function—Class

On the METHODS tab we enter a new public, static method REMOVE_TRAILING_ZEROS as shown in Figure 7.13. For the method, we define an importing parameter IV_VALUE for the incoming value and a returning parameter RV_VALUE for the result. Formula function methods may also have multiple importing parameters, and instead of the returning parameter, you could also use an exporting parameter for the result.

Figure 7.13 Custom Formula Function — Method

As parameter type we use the reasonably generic type STRING. In general it is recommended that you choose the type as generic as possible so that the function can be used for a wide range of inputs. You must not use types from a type pool, and for Boolean results either the data type BOOLEAN or SEU_BOOL should be used. Figure 7.14 illustrates the settings in our example.

Parameter	Type	P..	O.	Typing ...	Associated Type	Default value	Description
IV_VALUE	Importin	☐	☐	Type	STRING		Incoming value
RV_VALUE	Returnin	☑	☐	Type	STRING		Value without trailing zeros
		☐	☐	Type			

Method parameters: REMOVE_TRAILING_ZEROS

Figure 7.14 Custom Formula Function — Parameters

Now we can write the implementation for the formula function, as in Listing 7.4. In the example we do not explicitly check whether the passed value is a valid number. For a non-numeric input, we could add coding that might return the original value or raise a CX_FDT_PROCESSING exception to indicate an invalid formula.

```
METHOD remove_trailing_zeros.
  DATA: lv_i    TYPE i,  "Index
        lv_sub  TYPE i,  "Substring
        lv_c    TYPE c LENGTH 1. "Char

  CHECK iv_value IS NOT INITIAL. "Quick pre-check >>>

  rv_value = iv_value.
```

```
  CONDENSE rv_value.
  lv_i = strlen( rv_value ) - 1.
  WHILE lv_i >= 0.
    lv_c = rv_value+lv_i(1).
    IF lv_sub = 0 AND lv_c NA '0.'. "No trailing zero?
      lv_sub = lv_i + 1. "Set substring
    ELSEIF lv_c EQ '.'. "Decimal point found?
      IF lv_sub = 0. "Only trailing zero so far?
        lv_sub = lv_i. "Set substring, excluding decimal point
      ENDIF.
      EXIT.
    ENDIF.
    lv_i = lv_i - 1.
  ENDWHILE.

  IF lv_i >= 0. "Decimal point found?
    rv_value = rv_value(lv_sub).
  ENDIF.
ENDMETHOD.
```

Listing 7.4 Custom Formula Function—Implementation

The formula function can and should be documented by means of the standard documentation feature for class methods. On the one hand, there is the short DESCRIPTION text that can be maintained directly in the table on the METHODS tab. On the other hand, a detailed SAPscript document can be maintained. The document is accessible via a toolbar button as shown in Figure 7.15, by pressing F9 or by choosing the menu entry GOTO • DOCUMENTATION • TO COMPONENT.

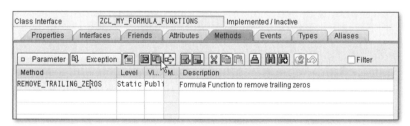

Figure 7.15 Custom Formula Function—Description

In display mode, the documentation could look like Figure 7.16 for our example. Both, the method description text and the deposited SAPscript document are or can be displayed in the Formula expression UI later on.

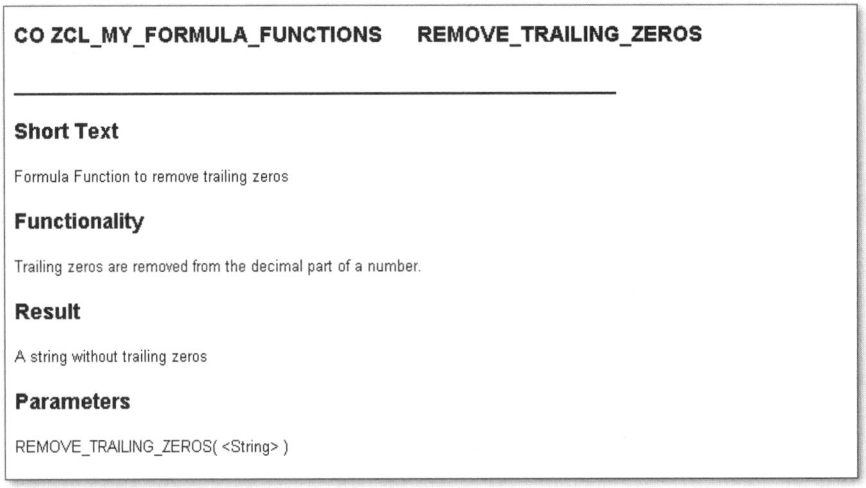

CO ZCL_MY_FORMULA_FUNCTIONS	REMOVE_TRAILING_ZEROS

Short Text

Formula Function to remove trailing zeros

Functionality

Trailing zeros are removed from the decimal part of a number.

Result

A string without trailing zeros

Parameters

REMOVE_TRAILING_ZEROS(<String>)

Figure 7.16   Custom Formula Function — Documentation

Application Exit Class

In the next step the implemented formula function must be made available for the desired BRFplus application. For that purpose, an application exit class is required as described in Section 7.3.1, subsection "Formula Functions Exit."

Usually each application gets its own, separate application exit class. To keep our example simple, we will reuse our class ZCL_MY_FORMULA_FUNCTIONS. The class will not only contain the formula function definition but also include the application exit implementation. As depicted in Figure 7.17, we simply add the interface IF_FDT_APPLICATION_SETTINGS on the INTERFACES tab for that purpose. On the METH-ODS tab, the corresponding interface methods will be listed afterwards.

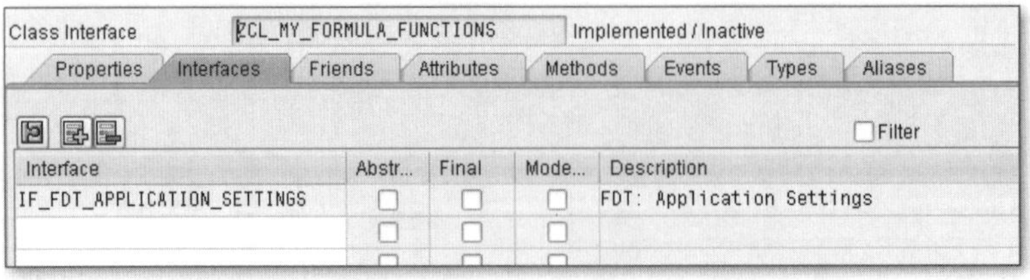

Class Interface	ZCL_MY_FORMULA_FUNCTIONS		Implemented / Inactive			
Properties	Interfaces	Friends	Attributes	Methods	Events	Types	Aliases

Interface	Abstr...	Final	Mode...	Description
IF_FDT_APPLICATION_SETTINGS	☐	☐	☐	FDT: Application Settings
	☐	☐	☐	

Figure 7.17   Custom Formula Function — Application Exit Interface

The implementation of interface method GET_FORMULA_FUNCTIONALS needs to append an entry to parameter CT_FUNCTIONAL_DEFINITION for the new function.

The entry must point to the method created in the previous step. In the Listing 7.5 example, a new category MY_FUNCTIONS is also created for the function.

```
METHOD if_fdt_application_settings~get_formula_functionals.
  DATA: ls_func_def   TYPE if_fdt_formula=>s_functional_def,
        ls_func_categ TYPE if_fdt_formula=>s_functional_categ.

  ls_func_categ-category    = 'MY_FUNCTIONS'.
  ls_func_categ-description = 'My Functions'.
  APPEND ls_func_categ TO ct_functional_category.

  ls_func_def-category = 'MY_FUNCTIONS'.
  ls_func_def-token    = 'REMOVE_TRAILING_ZEROS'.
  ls_func_def-class    = 'ZCL_MY_FORMULA_FUNCTIONS'.
  ls_func_def-method   = 'REMOVE_TRAILING_ZEROS'.
  APPEND ls_func_def TO ct_functional_definition.
ENDMETHOD.
```

Listing 7.5 Custom Formula Function—Application Exit

You must not forget that exit methods are evaluated only at runtime when the according exit attributes are set to "true." We therefore create a class constructor, as shown in Listing 7.6. In the implementation of the class constructor, a single line of code accomplishes the task of switching on the exit method for our formula function.

```
METHOD class_constructor.
  if_fdt_application_settings~gv_get_formula_functionals =
    abap_true.
ENDMETHOD.
```

Listing 7.6 Custom Formula Function—Class Constructor

Eventually we only need to activate the class changes to complete the programmatic part of the formula function example.

Testing

Testing of the new formula function requires an application that uses the developed application exit class. In the BRFplus Workbench the class name simply needs to be entered into the according field of a new or existing application object. Figure 7.18 shows the setting for our example.

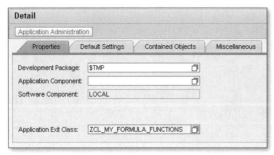

Figure 7.18 Custom Formula Function—Application Setting

After the application setting is saved, all Formula expressions of that application will offer the additional function in the UI. In our example, the new formula function REMOVE_TRAILING_ZEROS will be listed either within all functions or under the new category "My Functions."

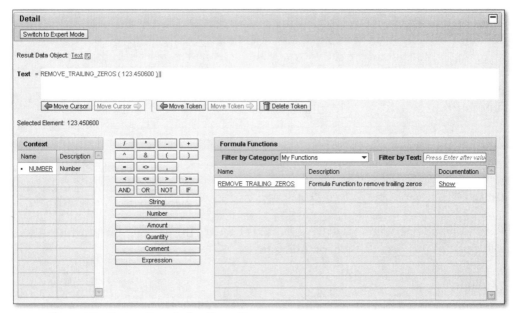

Figure 7.19 Custom Formula Function—UI

To test the runtime behavior of the new formula function, it is easiest to create an expression example, as shown in Figure 7.19, and to assign it to a function object that works in functional mode. With the simulation tool for function processing, the outcome can then be analyzed. Figure 7.20 contains a screenshot of such a simulation run.

Figure 7.20 Custom Formula Function—Simulation

7.4   User Interface Integration

The user interface that BRFplus provides for displaying and editing objects in the Workbench can be integrated into custom user interfaces. The integration is based on standard concepts of the Web Dynpro for ABAP technology. A basic knowledge of this UI technology is a prerequisite to following the subsequent descriptions.

BRFplus provides an API for its Web Dynpro related functionality. The API is based on a set of classes and (Web Dynpro) interfaces, which have the common name pattern FDT_WD_*. In Table 7.27 you will find an overview of the types that are relevant for this chapter.

Class/Interface	Description
FDT_IWD_OBJECT_MANAGER	Web Dynpro interface that encapsulates an object manager component.
IF_FDT_WD_TYPES	Defines BRFplus specific types that are used within the API.
IF_FDT_WD_STATE	Reflects the editing state of an object.
CL_FDT_WD_SERVICES	Provides a set of services for convenience.
CX_FDT_WD	Super class of all UI related exceptions.
CL_FDT_WD_FACTORY	A factory class for UI related objects.
IF_FDT_WD_COMPONENT_FACTORY	Provides methods to instantiate Web Dynpro components.
IF_FDT_WD_UI_MODE	Represents a display mode for the UI.
IF_FDT_WD_CONFIGURATION	Encapsulates a set of display settings as part of the UI mode.
IF_FDT_WD_OBJM_CONFIGURATION	Encapsulates object manager specific display settings.

Table 7.27 Classes and Interfaces of the UI-Related BRFplus API

For easier understanding, the UI integration is explained through the creation of a simple Web Dynpro application. The display of a BRFplus function in the resulting application should look like Figure 7.21.

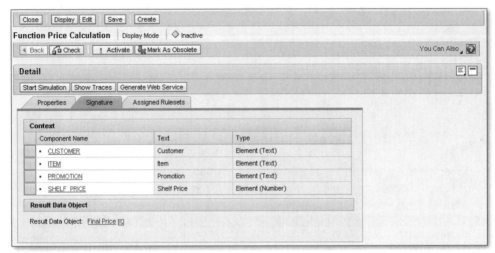

Figure 7.21   Example Application

In our example we create a local Web Dynpro component ZEMBED_BRFPLUS_UI. The ABAP Workbench (Transaction SE80) has to be used for that purpose. The component and its contained window and view can be freely named. Figure 7.22 serves as an example.

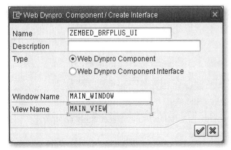

Figure 7.22   Creation of Web Dynpro Component

7.4.1   Object Manager

BRFplus displays objects with help of a Web Dynpro component that is referred to as "object manager." The component implements the Web Dynpro interface

FDT_IWD_OBJECT_MANAGER. It defines a window that can be embedded into custom Web Dynpro views. The window encapsulates the editor for BRFplus objects.

The methods of the interface allow controlling of the editor. It can, for example, show an object in display or edit mode, save a currently edited object, and trigger the creation of new objects. The complete list of methods is shown in Table 7.28.

Method	Description
SET_UI_MODE	Allows setting of various display settings.
DISPLAY	Shows a specific object in display mode.
EDIT	Shows a specific object in edit mode.
SAVE_CURRENT_OBJECT	Saves the currently displayed object.
SAVE_OBJECTS	Saves multiple objects that have been edited.
DELETE	Deletes the currently displayed object.
CLOSE	Closes the editor. It is a precondition to display or edit another object.
IS_OBJECT_DISPLAYED	Indicates whether an object is currently displayed.
GET_DISPLAYED_OBJECT	Returns the currently displayed object together with the display state and timestamp.
GET_SIZE_OF_OBJECT_STACK	Returns the number of memorized objects.
IS_UNSAVED_OBJECT_EXISTING	Indicates whether a changed object has not been saved yet. Currently only the displayed object is regarded.
MAINTAIN_OBJECT_IN_WIZARD	Shows only the basic properties of an object in a "wizard"-like UI.
UPDATE_WIZARD_OBJECT	Applies changes in the wizard UI to the object.
SAVE_WIZARD_OBJECT	Saves changes performed in the wizard UI.

Table 7.28 Methods of the Web Dynpro Interface FDT_IWD_OBJECT_MANAGER

Apart from the window and methods, the interface defines a set of events that may be triggered by user actions. The complete set of events is listed in Table 7.29.

Event	Description
STATE_CHANGE	The state of the current object was changed, for example, through activation.
STATE_CHANGE_CANCEL	Changing the object state has been cancelled by the user.
NAVIGATE_TO_OBJECT	The user has navigated to another object.
ASSIGNED_TO_CATALOG	The current object has been assigned to a catalog.
PLUG_EXEC_FAILED	Change oft he UI has failed, for example, when navigating to another object.

Table 7.29 Events of Web Dynpro interface FDT_IWD_OBJECT_MANAGER

To use the object manager, an according component usage for this interface type has to be defined. In our example, we give the component usage the name FDT_ OBJECT_MANAGER, as illustrated in Figure 7.23.

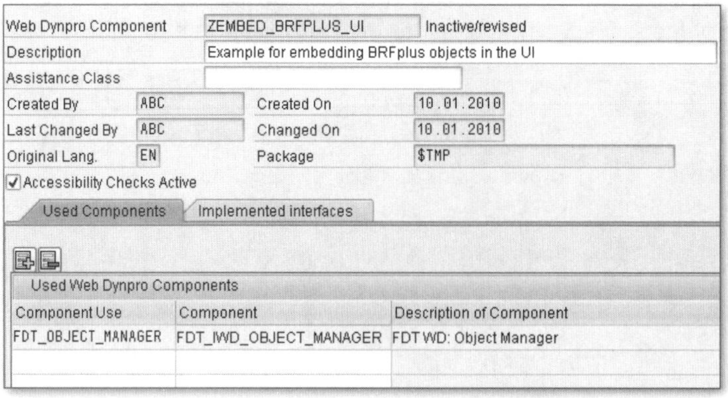

Web Dynpro Component	ZEMBED_BRFPLUS_UI	Inactive/revised	
Description	Example for embedding BRFplus objects in the UI		
Assistance Class			
Created By	ABC	Created On	10.01.2010
Last Changed By	ABC	Changed On	10.01.2010
Original Lang.	EN	Package	$TMP
☑ Accessibility Checks Active			

Used Components	Implemented interfaces

Used Web Dynpro Components		
Component Use	Component	Description of Component
FDT_OBJECT_MANAGER	FDT_IWD_OBJECT_MANAGER	FDT WD: Object Manager

Figure 7.23 Component Usage for the Object Manager Interface

Each controller of the Web Dynpro component that shall access the used component or its interface has to define additional, controller-specific usages on its Prop- erties tab. For the component controller, this may look like Figure 7.24.

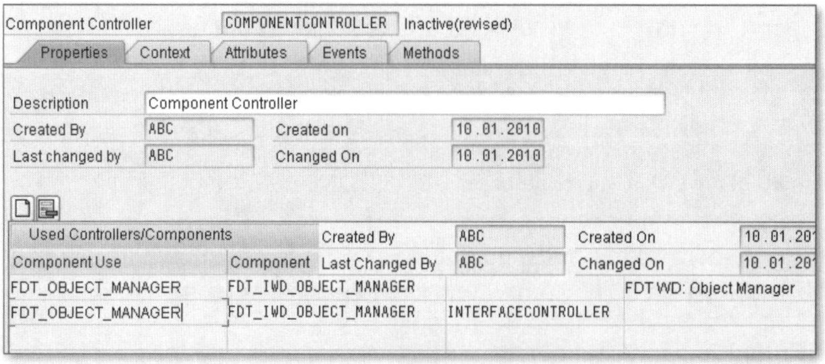

Component Controller	COMPONENTCONTROLLER	Inactive(revised)

Properties	Context	Attributes	Events	Methods

Description	Component Controller		
Created By	ABC	Created on	10.01.2010
Last changed by	ABC	Changed On	10.01.2010

Used Controllers/Components		Created By	ABC	Created On	10.01.201
Component Use	Component	Last Changed By	ABC	Changed On	10.01.201
FDT_OBJECT_MANAGER	FDT_IWD_OBJECT_MANAGER			FDT WD: Object Manager	
FDT_OBJECT_MANAGER	FDT_IWD_OBJECT_MANAGER	INTERFACECONTROLLER			

Figure 7.24 Controller Usages

At runtime, an instance of the used component has to be instantiated. This is typi- cally done in method wdDoInit of the component controller. BRFplus provides a factory class for the instantiation of an appropriate object manager component. The usage of the according API is demonstrated by Listing 7.7.

```
DATA: lo_fdt_wd_component_factory TYPE REF TO
        if_fdt_wd_component_factory,
```

```
    lo_fdt_object_manager_usage TYPE REF TO
        if_wd_component_usage.
"Create an instance of the object manager
lo_fdt_object_manager_usage =
  wd_this->wd_cpuse_fdt_object_manager( ).
lo_fdt_wd_component_factory ?=
  cl_fdt_wd_factory=>get_instance( ).
lo_fdt_wd_component_factory->create_object_manager_comp(
  lo_fdt_object_manager_usage ).
```

Listing 7.7 Instantiation of Object Manager Component

7.4.2 Embedding the UI

In the view MAIN_VIEW of our Web Dynpro component, we need to access the interface of the object manager later. As for the component controller we have to define a corresponding usage on the PROPERTIES tab of the view controller (see also Figure 7.24). Afterwards, we switch to the LAYOUT tab to define a basic UI, as depicted in Figure 7.25.

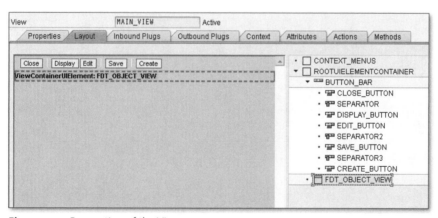

Figure 7.25 Preparation of the View

Most important is the definition of a ViewContainerUIElement that shall embed the object manager UI. In our example, we name it FDT_OBJECT_VIEW. Because we will need to trigger some actions later, we already define a toolbar on top of the view with a list of buttons:

▶ A CLOSE button to close the object manager display

▶ A DISPLAY button to show an object in display mode

▶ An EDIT button to show an object in edit mode

389

▸ A SAVE button to save the currently displayed object

▸ A CREATE button to allow the creation of new objects

To actually embed the object manager UI, we need to switch to the controller of our MAIN_WINDOW. On the WINDOW tab we can drill down to our ViewContainerUIElement FDT_OBJECT_VIEW and embed the MAIN_WINDOW of the object manager interface via a context menu. The selection process is illustrated in Figure 7.26.

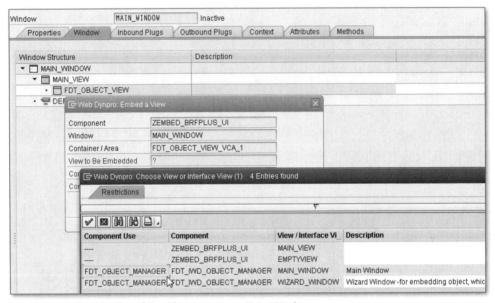

Figure 7.26 Selection of the Object Manager Main Window

The window and view structure should look like Figure 7.27.

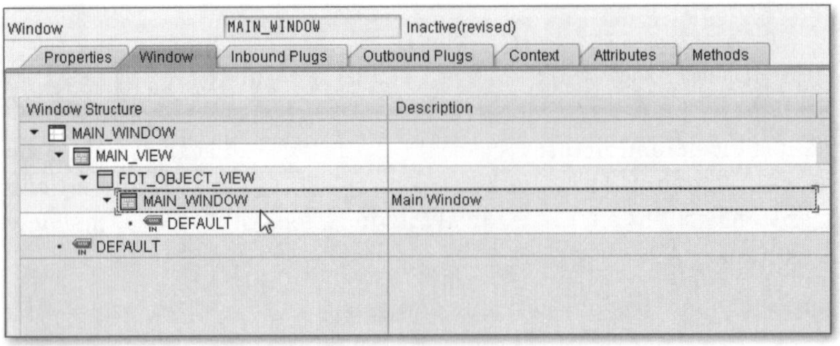

Figure 7.27 Window Structure with Embedded Object Manager Window

The embedded object manager component is now ready for use. To actually display an object, we require only a small additional piece of coding. In the MAIN_VIEW controller, we create a new action for the DISPLAY button. We must not forget to assign the action to the onAction property of the button in the LAYOUT tab. Web Dynpro automatically creates an event handler method for the action. To trigger the display of a BRFplus object we implement the method as in Listing 7.8.

```
DATA: lx_fdt_wd TYPE REF TO cx_fdt_wd.
TRY.
  "Display the BRFplus object
  wd_this->wd_cpifc_fdt_object_manager( )->display( iv_id =
    '00505683359D02DE97FAB4E171B5054E' ).
 CATCH cx_fdt_wd INTO lx_fdt_wd.
  cl_fdt_wd_service=>report_exception(
    EXPORTING
      io_message_manager = wd_this->wd_get_api(
        )->get_message_manager( )
      ix_wd_exception = lx_fdt_wd ).
ENDTRY.
```

Listing 7.8 Displaying an Object with the Object Manager

The coding basically calls the DISPLAY method of the object manager interface. For simplicity, we pass a static object ID to parameter IV_ID in our example. Of course, it needs to be adapted to an existing object ID.

To be able to close the object display later on, we create and assign another action to the CLOSE button. The implementation of the event handler is similar to the previous one. It may look like Listing 7.9.

```
DATA: lx_fdt_wd TYPE REF TO cx_fdt_wd.
TRY.
  "Close the object manager display
  wd_this->wd_cpifc_fdt_object_manager( )->close( ).
 CATCH cx_fdt_wd INTO lx_fdt_wd.
  cl_fdt_wd_service=>report_exception(
    EXPORTING
      io_message_manager = wd_this->wd_get_api(
        )->get_message_manager( )
      ix_wd_exception = lx_fdt_wd ).
ENDTRY.
```

Listing 7.9 Closing the Object Manager

When an object is displayed by the object manager and you want to display another object, you have to close the object manager first. This is also the case when you want to toggle between display and edit mode, after having accomplished Section 7.4.4.

Enforced Closing

The close method of the object manager will not necessarily close the display of the current object. If the object is shown in edit mode and has been changed, a loss-of-data dialog needs to be confirmed by the user. To avoid such a dialog, the close method provides the optional parameter IV_FORCE. When set to true, the object manager always closes with the risk of losing unsaved data. However, closing the object manager also frees up any reserved resources and unlocks edited objects. It is therefore recommended that you enforce the closing before the application gets terminated. The wdDoExit method of the component controller is usually a good place for an according implementation.

To test our example, we need to create a Web Dynpro application that triggers the display of the MAIN_WINDOW of our component. The properties of the application should look like Figure 7.28.

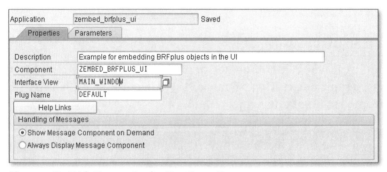

Figure 7.28 Web Dynpro Application Properties

The saved example application can now be tested for the first time.

7.4.3 Object Manager Configuration

The object manager provides, by default, an object toolbar. It is the same toolbar that is available in the BRFplus Workbench. It allows the user to switch between display and edit modes and to perform all kinds of transactional state changes to the object. It is, however, possible to hide individual buttons or even the entire toolbar. With the interface of the object manager it is then still possible to trigger selected actions in a controlled way. For details, see Section 7.4.4.

The configuration of the object manager is connected to the definition of a "UI mode." In the BRFplus Workbench you can, for example, choose between a standard and an expert user mode in the personalization dialog (menu entry WORK-BENCH • PERSONALIZE...). The UI mode is technically implemented by a class that implements interface IF_FDT_WD_UI_MODE. BRFplus uses class CL_FDT_WD_UI_SIM-PLE_MODE by default. The easiest way to implement your own UI mode is to create a class that extends the default class and overwrites only certain interface methods. As an example, we create such a class with the name ZCL_EXAMPLE_UI_MODE, as illustrated in Figure 7.29.

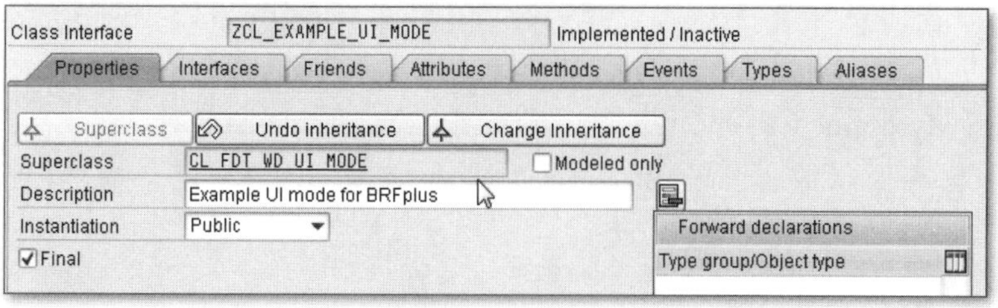

Figure 7.29   Creation of a UI Mode Class

The UI mode class is basically a wrapper for the actual configuration. Method GET_CONFIGURATION of interface IF_FDT_WD_UI_MODE has to return the real configuration in the form of an object that implements interface IF_FDT_WD_CONFIGURATION. In our example class, we redefine method GET_CONFIGURATION and implement it as in Listing 7.10.

```
"Get default implementation
ro_configuration = super->if_fdt_wd_ui_mode~get_configuration( ).
"Hide edit-, delete- and transport-button
ro_configuration->if_fdt_wd_objm_configuration~
  set_toolbar_button_visible(
    iv_button_name = :
if_fdt_wd_objm_configuration=>gc_toolbar_button_delete
    iv_is_visible = abap_false ),
if_fdt_wd_objm_configuration=>gc_toolbar_button_save
    iv_is_visible = abap_false ),
if_fdt_wd_objm_configuration=>gc_toolbar_button_chg_dspl
    iv_is_visible = abap_false ).
  "Do not show general data section
ro_configuration->if_fdt_wd_objm_configuration~
  set_general_data_visible( abap_false ).
```

Listing 7.10 Configuring the Object Manager

In the listing we first get the default configuration that is provided by the super class CL_FDT_WD_UI_SIMPLE_MODE. The object manager-specific configuration is altered afterwards with methods that are defined by interface IF_FDT_WD_OBJM_CONFIGURATION:

▸ With method SET_TOOLBAR_BUTTON_VISIBLE the DELETE, SAVE, and DISPLAY/EDIT buttons of the object toolbar are set to invisible. (With method SET_TOOLBAR_VISIBLE the whole toolbar could in principle be set to invisible).

▸ With method SET_GENERAL_DATA_VISIBLE the complete GENERAL data section of displayed objects is set to invisible.

With the above coding, our class ZCL_EXAMPLE_UI_MODE is ready to be used and needs only to be activated.

To apply the newly defined UI mode to the object manager, we have to adapt the coding of the wdDoInit method in the component controller of our Web Dynpro component. It needs to look like Listing 7.11.

```
DATA: lo_fdt_wd_component_factory TYPE REF TO
        if_fdt_wd_component_factory,
      lo_fdt_object_manager_usage TYPE REF TO
        if_wd_component_usage,
      lo_fdt_wd_ui_mode TYPE REF TO if_fdt_wd_ui_mode.
"Create an instance of the object manager
lo_fdt_object_manager_usage =
  wd_this->wd_cpuse_fdt_object_manager( ).
lo_fdt_wd_component_factory ?=
  cl_fdt_wd_factory=>get_instance( ).
lo_fdt_wd_component_factory->create_object_manager_comp(
  lo_fdt_object_manager_usage ).
"Apply a custom UI mode
CREATE OBJECT lo_fdt_wd_ui_mode TYPE zcl_example_ui_mode.
wd_this->wd_cpifc_fdt_object_manager( )->set_ui_mode(
        lo_fdt_wd_ui_mode ).
```

Listing 7.11 Applying a Custom UI Mode to the Object Manager

The additional coding creates an instance of our UI mode class ZCL_EXAMPLE_UI_MODE and forwards it to method SET_UI_MODE of the object manager. If you run our example application again, the new configuration settings should take effect.

7.4.4 Object Changes and Events

With the changed configuration settings, a user can no longer switch the object manager into edit mode via the standard toolbar. It is, however, still possible to trigger the edit mode programmatically. In our example Web Dynpro component, we therefore create just another action in the MAIN_VIEW view and assign it to the

EDIT button. The implementation of the action event handler is almost identical to Listing 7.8. You only have to replace the call of the object manager's DISPLAY method with a call of its EDIT method.

Similarly, you can create a new action for the SAVE button. The implementation of the event handler is almost identical to Listing 7.9. You only have to replace the call of the object manager's CLOSE method with a call of its SAVE_CURRENT_OBJECT method. For transportable objects, you might have to pass a valid transport request with parameter IV_TRANSPORT_REQUEST, if change recording is activate. If a required transport request is missing, the method call will cause an exception. To keep our example simple, we do not support change recording.

For the creation of a new BRFplus object, one simply has to call the CREATE method of the object manager interface. The method will trigger an object creation dialog, where the user can choose from the available object types. To limit the selectable object types, an optional importing parameter IT_OBJECT_TYPE can be used. For our example, we define an action for the CREATE button and implement the event handler according to Listing 7.12. With this coding, the object creation dialog will allow only the creation of new Decision Table expressions.

```
DATA: lt_object_type TYPE
        if_fdt_wd_types=>t_object_type_extended,
      ls_object_type LIKE LINE OF lt_object_type,
      lx_fdt_wd TYPE REF TO cx_fdt_wd.
"Define allowed object types (decision table)
ls_object_type-type =
   if_fdt_constants=>gc_object_type_expression.
ls_object_type-subtype =
   if_fdt_constants=>gc_exty_decision_table.
APPEND ls_object_type TO lt_object_type.
TRY.
  "Close the object manager display
  wd_this->wd_cpifc_fdt_object_manager( )->create(
    it_object_type = lt_object_type ).
 CATCH cx_fdt_wd INTO lx_fdt_wd.
  cl_fdt_wd_service=>report_exception(
    EXPORTING
      io_message_manager = wd_this->wd_get_api(
        )->get_message_manager( )
      ix_wd_exception = lx_fdt_wd ).
ENDTRY.
```

Listing 7.12 Creation of a New Object with the Object Manager

When the creation dialog is opened, the user may still decide to abort the creation process. With the events listed in Table 7.29, the object manager can inform the using Web Dynpro component of such user decisions or interactions in general.

In our example component, we will register onto the STATE_CHANGE event. This event is always triggered when the state of the currently displayed object has changed. On the METHODS tab of the component controller, we therefore define a new method with the name HDL_FDT_OBJECT_STATE_CHANGE. The METHOD TYPE has to be changed to "Event Handler." For the EVENT, CONTROLLER, and COMPONENT USAGE settings, the STATE_CHANGE event of the object manager has to be chosen. The associated dialog is illustrated in Figure 7.30.

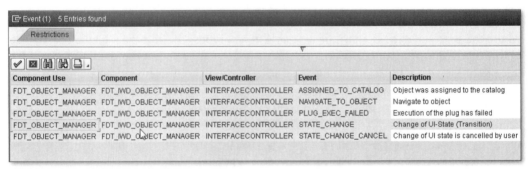

Figure 7.30 Object Manager Events

The final method definition should look like Figure 7.31.

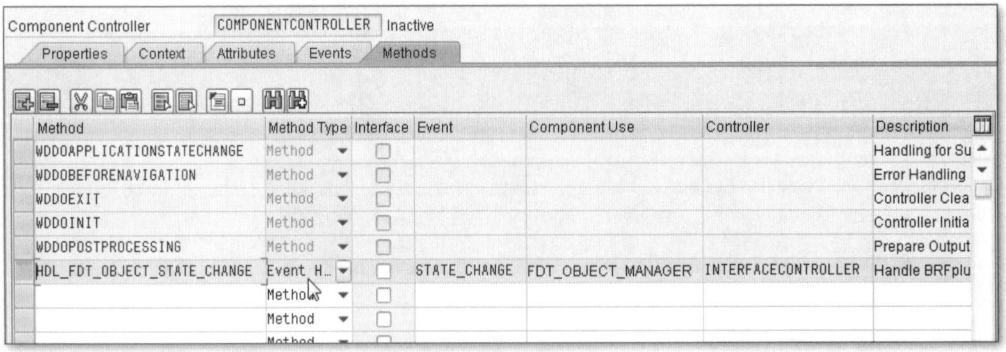

Method	Method Type	Interface	Event	Component Use	Controller	Description
WDDOAPPLICATIONSTATECHANGE	Method	☐				Handling for Su
WDDOBEFORENAVIGATION	Method	☐				Error Handling
WDDOEXIT	Method	☐				Controller Clea
WDDOINIT	Method	☐				Controller Initia
WDDOPOSTPROCESSING	Method	☐				Prepare Output
HDL_FDT_OBJECT_STATE_CHANGE	Event H…	☐	STATE_CHANGE	FDT_OBJECT_MANAGER	INTERFACECONTROLLER	Handle BRFplu
	Method	☐				
	Method	☐				
	Method					

Component Controller | COMPONENTCONTROLLER | Inactive

Properties | Context | Attributes | Events | Methods

Figure 7.31 Event Handler for the STATE_CHANGE Event

The event provides the importing parameter IV_TRANSITION, which determines the type of the performed state transition. The possible transitions are listed as constants GC_TRANSITION_* in interface IF_FDT_WD_STATE. As an example, we output an information message, in the case that a displayed object gets closed. For simplicity, we output a static, non-translatable message text only. Listing 7.13 provides the according implementation.

```
IF iv_transition EQ if_fdt_wd_state=>gc_transition_close.
  wd_this->wd_get_api( )->get_message_manager( )->report_message(
    message_text = 'Object has been closed'
    message_type = if_wd_message_manager=>co_type_standard ).
ENDIF.
```

Listing 7.13 State Change Event Handler

At this point, the basic concepts of the integration of the object manager have been explained. The provided example can easily be extended to experiment with features that have not explicitly been mentioned. Specific usage scenarios may require an additional method or event. However, a detailed description of more sophisticated usages is not within the scope of this book.

This chapter introduces the deployment scenarios in BRFplus projects. Each scenario is discussed in terms of its advantages and implications. Technical insight into the SAP change and transport management is a prerequisite to understanding the explanations in this chapter.

8   Deployment

In a proof of concept (POC) the focus is usually on the visible aspects of BRFplus, such as the user interface and the possibility of enhancing specific requirements. Often, performance is also a critical factor. Only rarely are questions of deployment discussed at this stage, although there are many options, and decisions can have long-lasting implications for the project. The reason is that the initiators of the POC first want to have the buy-in of the business experts. Deployment options are a highly technical topic that is, in many cases, discussed only after the project decision has been made. Details are then worked out by the implementation team. This chapter shall help you identify the deployment options and the implications involved with each option. The deployment is closely related to the well established three-system landscape in the SAP customer base. Therefore, the chapter starts with common explanations about the Change and Transport System (see Section 8.1) to develop several local (see Section 8.2) and remote (see Section 8.3) scenarios for how BRFplus may be used.

8.1   Change and Transport System

BRFplus is connected to the toolset for software logistics for ABAP applications, which is called the Change and Transport System (CTS). The CTS standardizes and automates the distribution of software artifacts in complex system landscapes. It helps organize development projects by recording changes in customizing and repository data, and transporting these changes between SAP systems in the landscape. BRFplus fully integrates with the CTS so, depending on the storage type and client settings, changes of BRFplus artifacts have to be recorded in transport requests.

In the creation process of a BRFplus application, a storage type has to be selected. BRFplus provides three different storage types that define how the application and its contained objects behave with respect to the CTS.

▶ **System Data (S)**
System data is cross-client. The database tables used to save the data do not have a client key field. Changes affect all clients of an SAP system. Consequently, the transport of changes into another system does affect all clients of this system as well. The package is a mandatory attribute of system applications. The changeability of BRFplus objects in system applications is derived from the changeability of the package that is assigned to the application. If a local package is assigned, transport is not supported.

▶ **Customizing Data (C)**
Customizing data is client-dependent. The database tables that store the data have a client key field. Changes to customizing data in one client have no effect on other clients. The changeability of BRFplus objects in customizing data applications depends on client-specific system settings, which are maintained with Transaction SCC4. The import of changes into transport target systems happens in client 000. From there, they may be distributed into other clients with Transaction SCC1.

▶ **Application Data (A)**
In contrast to customizing and system data, application data is not part of the configuration of the software. Application data is split up into master data (such as customers, products, materials) and movement data (such as line items, documents). Application data is always client-specific. The CTS does not manage changes to application data and the CTS cannot be used to transport changes into other clients or systems. There is no technical restriction on changeability. Application data may be copied between clients and systems with help of the XML exchange features of BRFplus.

System data cannot refer to customizing or application data because both may not be available in all the clients of the system. Customizing data cannot refer to application data because application data cannot be transported. Consequently, references in customizing data would become invalid when transporting. The same argument applies to the usage of local objects by non-local objects, which is not supported. Figure 8.1 shows in a table which references per storage type are possible.

using \ used	System Data	Customizing Data	Application Data
System Data	OK	not OK	not OK
Customizing Data	Ok	OK	not OK
Application Data	OK	OK	OK

Figure 8.1 Allowed References per Data Type

More information about the transport and how BRFplus is connected to the CTS can be found in Section 6.6. Information about XML data exchange in BRFplus can be found in Section 6.2.

8.2   Local Scenarios

Local scenarios have in common that changes are distributed with the CTS so that calls for business rules evaluation can be done locally. Usually, overall business rules performance depends very much on the performance related to accessing the data that the rules operate on. Therefore, local execution provides big performance advantages.

In the simplest case, all BRFplus artifacts are created in the development system and recorded in change requests. Customizing data is recorded in customizing requests, while system data requires Workbench requests. Releasing the requests allows for transfer of the data to the quality assurance system. After import into the quality assurance system, automatic and manual tests can be performed to check whether any linked changes are missing. They may, for example, still bei pending in unreleased change requests. When testing is successful, the change requests with the data are transported into the production system. BRFplus does not require a downtime for the import. It supports updates into a system on the fly.

Figure 8.2 illustrates how changes are distributed in a three-system landscape. SAP's recommendation for customizing and system data is to change it only in the development system and to update the quality assurance system and the production system only by transport requests. The objects are locked for changes in those systems (indicated in Figure 8.2 with the lock icon). This ensures that originals of all objects reside in the development system and changes to the other systems happen in a controlled way. Changes can be tested first in the quality assurance system before using them productively.

Development projects may also require more than one development and quality assurance system, depending on their size. To ensure consistency, the same principles as in the three-system landscape apply. The concept of changing objects at the original location also prevents unintentional, parallel work on the same object. BRFplus system data enforces the originality concept by locking the objects in a Workbench request. When locked, the object cannot be recorded into other transport requests.

Business rules do not behave differently compared to any other customizing or repository objects. This has the advantage that system administrators do not need to learn new concepts. They may not even know about the usage of BRFplus. There is also no need for additional hardware. BRFplus does not require new servers, nor is new sizing for the existing servers necessary.

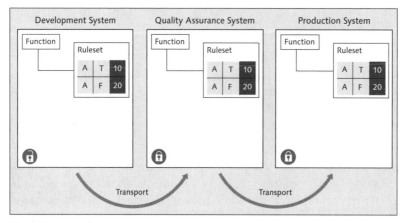

Figure 8.2 Local Scenario in a Three-System Landscape

Another advantage is the depth of integration into processes and applications. Changes in BRFplus can be recorded together with other changes in one transport request. Processes and applications that embed the business rules may also have customizing and repository objects that are linked and updated synchronously.

8.2.1 Application Exit for Object Changeability

In production systems, customizing data is typically protected against changes by restrictive client settings. Customers do not want the production system to be changed with respect to configuration or repository data. However, business users may request a level of agility that cannot be met by the transport. Examples are business rules that need to use master data that is only available in the production system, or there may be a need for emergency changes in the productive system directly.

For those scenarios BRFplus provides an application exit that allows bypassing client checks, and changing BRFplus customizing objects in the production system directly. Section 7.3.1 explains how the exit must be implemented. Each object that shall be changeable in the production system must be known at the time of implementation of the exit. It is very important to limit the changeability in the production system to only a very few selected objects. Ideally, these are only objects that cannot introduce errors that could stop the productive processes from working. Therefore, the exit may additionally be combined with appropriate authorization checks.

If such an application exit is used, a mechanism must be established to apply the changes from the production system in the development system as well. Otherwise, the development system would become outdated and transports from the development system would reverse the changes in the production system. This situation would result in unpredictable system behavior. The distribution of changes from the production system into other systems may be done in one of the following ways:

▶ By inspection of the production system and manual update of the development system

▶ By ABAP code, inspecting the objects opened for changes, and applying the changes in the development system (communication by RFC)

▶ By XML export and import for all objects that are changeable in the productive system (may also be automated with RFC communication)

▶ By transport of copies from the production system into the development system

Figure 8.3 illustrates a three-system landscape where a decision table is changed in the production system. All other objects are locked so that changes are not possible. Through the alignment path, changes are updated in the development system.

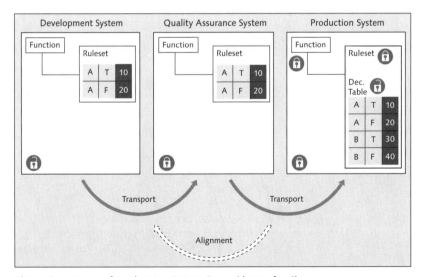

Figure 8.3 Usage of Application Exit to Open Objects for Changes

8.2.2 Combination of Objects with Different Storage Types

There are scenarios where the business rules as transported into the production system may need to be extended by more than just a few lines in a decision table. BRFplus provides the ability to assign rulesets of different storage types to one function. Figure 8.4 illustrates this concept. In the development system, a function and a ruleset have been created as customizing data. It is not required to create the function and the ruleset in the same application. Function and data objects may even be created in a system application. The only prerequisite is that access level settings of function and data objects allow the usage from another application. For more information concerning access levels see Section 4.3.5.

Consequently, in the production system, it is possible to create a ruleset as application data and attach it to the function to add more business rules logic locally. The sequence of the ruleset processing can be defined with help of the ruleset priority attribute. Ruleset preconditions can be used to dynamically include or exclude all rules of a ruleset. An application data ruleset with priority 1 would always be processed first if the customizing ruleset has priority 2. With a precondition, it could be defined that ruleset 2 is executed only if the result has not yet been determined by the application data ruleset. In such a scenario, the customizing ruleset implements the default rules, whereas the application data ruleset contains the exceptions. More information about how to use the ruleset can be found in Section 5.3.

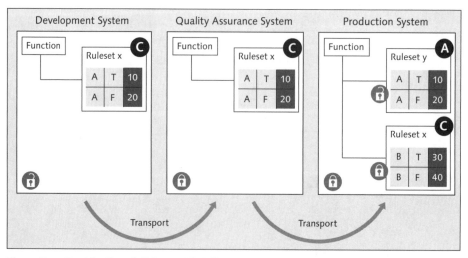

Figure 8.4 Combination of Objects with Different Storage Types

8.2.3 Creation of Objects with the API

The use of the BRFplus API to create objects in any system on demand can be an alternative to the transport or manual creation of objects. In this scenario, illustrated in Figure 8.5, ABAP code is transported but not BRFplus objects. At specific events, such as the first usage of a specific process, the ABAP code creates all relevant artifacts in BRFplus. The creation of BRFplus rules may, for example, be triggered by the maintenance of other data outside of BRFplus. Of course, it is also possible to combine BRFplus objects being created by the API with objects being created and changed manually in the system. The ABAP code may create, for example, a function and data objects as well as a ruleset with some basic rules. When business experts want to refine the logic, they can access and change them in the BRFplus UI.

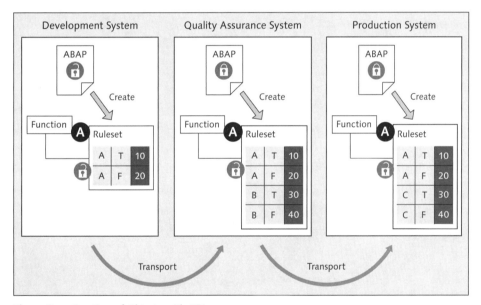

Figure 8.5 Creation of Objects with API

8.3 Remote Scenarios

Remote scenarios are characterized by the fact that rules modeling and execution take place in remote systems. The invocation can be performed with remote function calls (RFC) or Web service calls. BRFplus provides a tool for the creation of both, as described in Section 6.3.

There can even be the need to invoke rules from multiple systems but critical data is only available on one of them. In such a case, the remote call helps to avoid data copying and data transfer steps between the systems. Rules may also be invoked from non-ABAP systems where a local call is technically not possible.

Sometimes none of those reasons is present but still it can be a good practice to run BRFplus on a separate server. The system landscape shown in Figure 8.6 consists of two system tracks, one for the business rules and one for the business applications and processes. Both have their own transport strategy with a three-system landscape. From the production system of the business processes, remote calls for rules invocation happen to the production system of the business rules.

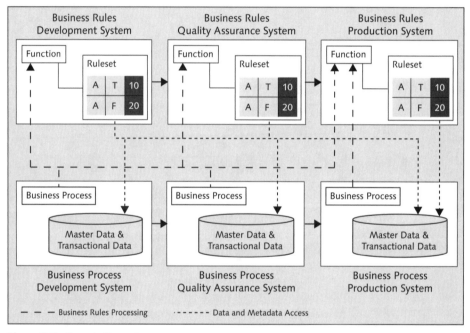

Figure 8.6 Remote Scenario

Separating the business rules in this way allows for more flexible handling of changes of business rules. For example, transports can be imported with a greater frequency into the production system for business rules than into the production system for the business processes. The production system for business rules may even be open for changes to customizing. In addition, the options to test the business rules are improved. For example, it is now easy to connect a business process in the quality assurance system to the business rules from the production system.

Business rules in the development systems can also be built based on metadata from the production system of the business process.

A prerequisite to modeling rules with reference to data of a remote system is the implementation of application exits. Data objects may be created according to metadata in the business process systems. However, value helps and value checks will not work without the implementation of the application exit "element values" as described in Section 7.3.1. The code in the exit must not select data locally. Instead, it has to call into the respective business process system.

The procedure described in this chapter offers a methodology for dealing with business rules and estimating costs in a project. The approach is based on an iterative concept for business rules with technical and functional experts working cooperatively.

9   Methodology

The focus of the previous chapters was on rules modeling and technical aspects. Still missing from this book is the methodology that can be applied to gather requirements and transform them into productive business rules. This chapter provides such a methodology, along with guidelines for good practice for the organization of a business rules project, the activities in a business rules project, and cost estimation. Business rules projects impose challenges that should not be faced with conventional software development methodologies alone.

For better illustration of the concepts, a simplified real world example is used. The example deals with student grant programs in the context of SAP Grants Management for Grantor.

9.1   Classic Approach to Software Development

Many rules projects are planned following a linear and sequential development process, such as the waterfall model illustrated in Figure 9.1. This is especially true when project participants are not very familiar with the business rules approach. Progress is seen as flowing steadily downward through various phases such as Requirements Specification, Design, Implementation, Test and Maintenance.

Each phase has a set of deliverables to be completed before the next phase can be started. The specification must be completed as a prerequisite to starting the design phase. When the design has been completed and accepted, the implementation is started, and so on. The waterfall model is a popular model mainly because it allows for departmentalization and managerial control, especially with respect to schedules and responsibilities. An assumption underlying this model is that bugs and design problems are cheaper to fix in terms of time and money the earlier they are identified.

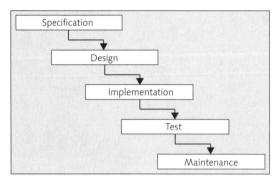

Figure 9.1 Waterfall Model

In many rules projects, the involved stakeholders cannot define all the requirements beforehand. Instead, functional teams come up with a set of documents that they think describe the business logic to the best of their knowledge. However, the requirements are frequently incomplete or even contradictory. It is often impossible to identify these gaps and contradictions in the early stages because the requirements come from different teams, such as different functional groups, system engineers, and administrators. The requirements often reflect the background of the teams and focus on different aspects of the new or improved system. Business needs to operate are naturally different from system needs to operate. The traditional approach, based on a thin initial scoping, forces project management to provide an inflated estimate to ensure that risk is appropriately covered.

The magnitude of written information generated during the process of requirements gathering often cannot be conceived and analyzed by human beings. Stakeholders may not even understand the capabilities of the involved components and systems, which may lead to incorrect assumptions — assumptions that are reflected in the requirements they put forward. Finally, stakeholders keep learning from conflicts and discussions in order to overcome such erroneous assumptions. Learning often leads to very valuable input, which in turn leads to the improvement of processes and systems. However, not all involved parties can foresee how a system is supposed to work prior to running prototypes or the first stages of implementation. Only in rare cases can requirements and limitations be entirely known before implementation starts.

9.2   Classification of System Building Blocks

A good approach to overcoming the problems inherent in the waterfall model is to classify the building blocks of the system to be implemented with respect to their change frequency. Such a classification is shown in Figure 9.2.

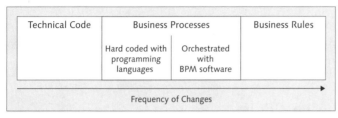

Figure 9.2 Classification of System Building Blocks

Technical code refers to all parts of the system that are of little relevance to business users, such as the operating system or the database. Usually, decisions about such matters are long lasting and based on availability of expertise of the IT department.

Business processes can be hard coded with a programming language such as ABAP or Java, or composed with Business Process Management (BPM) software. Hard coded processes are incorporated into the products of standard software vendors for business applications. But customers may decide to implement custom processes without the help of BPM software because program code provides the greatest flexibility.

BPM software provides tools and services for faster process implementation and better process control, especially for less complex processes. Consequently, those business processes allow for better involvement of business users because they provide a graphical overview of sequence and steps, which makes it easier to understand the process. Moreover, BPM software eases the change in processes.

Business rules are implemented with a Business Rule Management System (BRMS). They are the most dynamic building block, with specifics changing all the time because of regulations, policies, competition, market changes, or simply a desire to implement new strategies. Pricing rules are a good example: they require adaptations multiple times a month compared with the order-to-cash process, which remains unchanged for years. Therefore, flexibility should be brought into a process with business rule services (also called decision services) to increase control over the process and the capacity for change. This practice allows for a stable process even when decision-making is constantly changing and evolving.

Any business logic implemented not with business rules but with program code excludes the functional departments because it is not possible for them to determine where the logic is implemented. This lack of transparency creates a need to discuss and write down assumptions about system behavior and desired changes as specifications. In contrast, visibility of business logic leads to better insight on the part of the business experts who are responsible for the process. Usually they have best knowledge about how the decisions and processes should evolve to achieve better business results. Instead of the abstractions of a specification document, they work better when dealing with business rules and defining concrete changes to these rules, within a set of existing processes.

9.3   Model for Business Rules

The advantage of the business rules approach is that functional and technical experts can meet in the same environment, which facilitates communication and reduces the likelihood of misunderstandings and errors, especially when compared to the process of implementing and testing code changes. Making business logic visible to business experts consequently reduces the time and costs needed to communicate, discuss, and implement changes. Business rules must be managed in a different way. Therefore, business rules are often not designed on the waterfall model because the waterfall approach does not provide the required responsiveness. Instead, the rules are designed on a modified model with iterative and agile elements.

The modified model should reflect the frequency of changes of the involved building blocks. Consequently, business rules should be separated from the rest of the system (for which the waterfall model may still be used). Business processes call into the BRMS using stable business rules services. The logic implemented with the business rules often requires more agility and flexibility compared to business process changes. An agile approach that also includes iterations is essential. Figure 9.3 shows a modified model that illustrates how business processes and business rules relate to each other. While the business processes are implemented in the phases of the waterfall approach, the business rules phases, from sketch and draft to the versions, explicitly include iteration. The model, with its distinct processes, is based on well defined connection points.

Changes to business rules usually do not end with the completion of the implementation project. Business rules are evolutionary, with business experts having the responsibility for refining them incrementally and continuously. Release live cycles and related processes should not impose constraints and boundaries on business rules refinement. Therefore, the ultimate goal of a rules project is the enabling of more frequent change and the empowering of business users to conduct the changes.

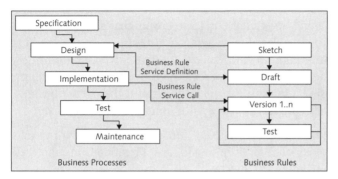

Figure 9.3 Modified Model—Separation of Business Rules from Business Processes

9.4 Action Plan

Based on the model for business rules, an action plan for a rules project can be created. The action plan should consist of the steps shown in Figure 9.4. The diagram not only lists the steps but brings them into an order. The bars indicate the time typically spent on each task. Depending on the complexity of the project, a multiplier for the time may need to be applied.

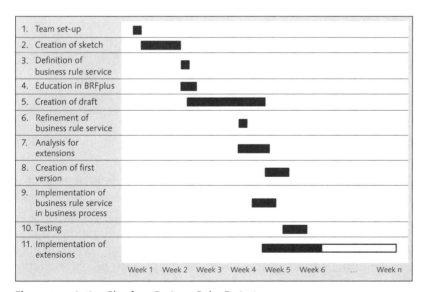

Figure 9.4 Action Plan for a Business Rules Project

9.4.1 Team Setup

Strong involvement of functional experts in the development of requirements and business rules is critical to the success of the solution. An ideal team for a rules project consists of technical and functional experts to ensure that all critical aspects from both perspectives are considered. This will not only increase the function team's level of comfort with the product; it will also decrease overall costs as they become responsible for a significant portion of the design work. Functional experts are responsible for the business logic in the rules and also for the overall business processes. They are the ones who have to accept the solution for the go-live.

Technical experts are supporters. They guide the functional experts with respect to the use of new technologies such as BRFplus and in implementation processes. Ideally the technical team includes an expert with BRFplus experience. This expert can also be an external consultant. The responsibilities of the technical team are platform and technology decisions. During the project they need to make sure that requirements, in terms of data quality and integrity, are met. Nevertheless, functional users demand maximum freedom and flexibility. However, a BRMS is a part of a solution landscape that it needs to connect to and integrate with. This makes it necessary to work well with data that already exists, such as master data records (students, student programs, etc.) or customizing (funding types, course groups, etc.). Only technical experts can decide where in the processes to implement the call into the BRMS and how to do it (e.g. locally or remote, single or bundled calls, with or without trace). They need to consider as well how changes in business rules can happen in a controlled environment including test strategies. Finally, they need to create transparency about cost drivers, such as number and costs of systems, costs for administration, costs for interfacing, and costs for custom development.

Ideally, a team for a rules project consists of a core team with only a few (two to six) people and an extended team. The core team works through the action plan. Whenever needed, experts from the extended team are included.

9.4.2 Creation of Sketch

The sketch is a first collection of the requirements to be implemented with business rules. At first, unstructured text documents, spreadsheet documents or drawings are usually used. At this stage, it is not yet clear how the business rules fit into the process or how the entities the rules operate on will be represented in the system. Often, functional experts also list various requirements that cannot or should not be transferred to business rules. This happens especially when the project team does not yet have experience with the business rules approach. It is also likely that several requirements are omitted. Figure 9.5 shows an extract from a sketch document.

1 Education Costs	
1.01 Tuition and Compulsory Fees	1. Obtain name of school and program from the application 2. Obtain tuition and fees from the program information module or student 3. Prorate tuition fees based on course load (caution: some schools have different rules) 4. Deduct partial waiver from prorated amount 5. The total of the two are subject to the $25,000 limit **Additional Notes** Tuition and fees should be two different fields as the calculation rules are different Designation tables store 100% course load in cost tables, hence proration. Out of province schools always asses 100% tuition, no matter the course load Automatically override the fees specified on application if needed, e.g. too high or low when compared with standard values Compulsory fee: Action (100% taken into consideration)
1.02 Books and Supplies	1. Obtain name of school and program from the application 2. Obtain books and supplies from program information module or student 3. Subject to the $3,000 annual limit **Additional Notes** Books and supplies: If program information module does not return data take data on form $500 computer costs + books and supplies cannot exceed $3000 limit Book and supplies are pro-rated based on course load

Figure 9.5 Example of a Sketch

9.4.3 Definition of Business Rule Service

The sketch delivers a good overview of the required business rules and educates the technical experts on the business rules and the business process. It is an important input for the design phase of the business processes. The business process has to be prepared to trigger the evaluation of business rules. Consequently, decisions are needed as to when and where in the business process to call into BRFplus and what data to hand over. This goal of the business rules service definition phase is mainly driven by the technical experts.

The service definition not only defines the purpose of the call: it also includes the signature, which consists of the parameters passed into the business rule service and the parameters returned. The signature can be derived from the data required by the business rules. At this stage, it is often not decided which data is passed into the service, and which data is retrieved additionally in the business rules. Parameters need to be described with semantic information such as description and documentation, and technical information such as binding to the data dictionary, field type and length and allowed field values. The business rule service definition corresponds to a BRFplus function.

Business Rule Service Definition

- ▶ Name
- ▶ Description
- ▶ Documentation
- ▶ Input parameters (context)
  Data objects (elements, structures, tables)
  Bindings to data dictionary
- ▶ Output parameters (result)
  Data objects (elements, structures, tables)
  Bindings to data dictionary

Figure 9.6 shows an example of a business rule service definition. All relevant information is available so that it can be easily created in BRFplus as a function.

Business Rule Service:	Calculate Fees
Description:	Calculate Tuition and Compulsory Fees
Documentation:	Calculate of tuition and compulsory fees based on program information, course load, waiver. Limit of $25,000. Changes are directly applied to the context.

Parameters (Context)

Name	Description	Documentation	Data Type	DDIC Data Element
NAME_OF_SCHOOL	Name of School	Form field 702	Text	ABC_SCHOOL
NAME_OF_PROGRAM	Name of Program	Form field 703	Text	ABC_PROGRAM
STIPEND	Stipend	Form field 1307	Amount	ABC_STIPEND
TUITION	Tuition	Read with FM ABC_1	Amount	ABC_TUITION
FEES	Fees	Read with FM ABC_2	Amount	ABC_FEES
COURSE_LOAD	Course Load	Form field 709, 0..1	Number, no digits	/CUS/CLOAD
PRORATION_INDICATOR	Proration Indicator		Boolean, true/false	BOOLE_D
...				

Figure 9.6 Example of a Business Rule Service Definition

Sometimes it is not clear at this stage how many business rules services are needed. Usually, it is a good idea to have a distinct purpose for each business rules service and not to bundle many tasks into one service. However, there are also good examples of when bundling can make sense. For instance, take form processing, where data validation, defaulting of missing fields, as well as calculation of read only fields may be done in one step. The ability to assign rulesets to functions allows the separation of different tasks into different rulesets. One ruleset with highest priority may do the data validation, another takes over the field defaulting, and a third ruleset with lowest priority performs the calculation steps. The last ruleset will get a precondition so that calculation is done only when checks have been passed successfully.

After defining the purpose of the business rule service and its parameters, a team needs to analyze where in the process flow the call will be best placed. It also needs to specify exactly how the call is to be done: there are various ways of calling into BRFplus. Aspects to look for are performance, availability of data in the ABAP memory, the chance of bundling of calls, and technical commit behavior. The findings are input for the design and implementation of new or changed business processes as shown in Figure 9.3.

A growing number of SAP standard applications provide out-of-the-box integration with BRFplus. The native integration allows business rules to be written for a set of integrated BRFplus functions. There is no need to design and create a function as a business rule service and plug it into a process. In this case, the step involving service definition can be omitted.

9.4.4 Education in BRFplus

The business rules documentation in the sketch is often disorganized, inconsistent, and lacking in the finer details required for operational usage. But the time comes when it is necessary to document the business rules in a more structured way that is closer to BRFplus. A prerequisite is, of course, the availability of knowledge regarding the important concepts and artifacts in BRFplus.

Good practice is to take one or two straightforward functions and demonstrate their implementation in the BRFplus Workbench to the functional team. Important artifacts they should know are rulesets, rules, decision tables, and formulas. The education should not be complete but rather should focus on only a few concepts and artifacts. Various features in BRFplus should never become relevant to functional experts. Other features can be introduced as soon as they become relevant. This is true, for example, when more technical expressions such as Database Lookup or Procedure Call are needed to enrich the context with data that is not provided as part of the context. The technical experts need good knowledge of BRFplus to support and guide the functional users in such cases.

9.4.5 Creation of Draft

On the way from the sketch to the draft, business rules are further refined and more details are worked out. They have to be transferred into a more structured format that is based on the business rule service definition as well as BRFplus artifacts such as rules, decision tables, and formulas. The better the draft is structured and the more it follows BRFplus concepts, the more easily the business rules can be moved into BRFplus later.

Decision tables are an excellent format because it is possible to upload them from Microsoft Excel into BRFplus. Furthermore, decision tables are very powerful in terms of visualization. Grouping business rules into a single table provides a compact and structured overview. This overview facilitates error prevention with respect to consistency and completeness. Figure 9.7 illustrates with an example how text rules can be structured in a decision table. The decision table is easy to read and to enhance. Functional users tend to work extensively with decision tables as soon as they understand how they work.

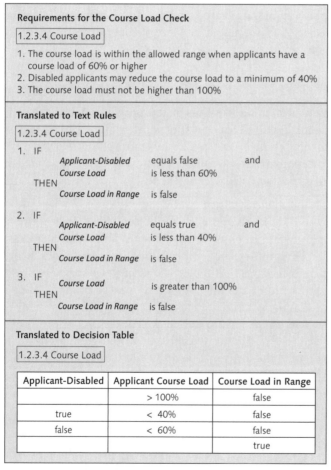

Figure 9.7 Comparison of Sketch Requirements with Text Rules and Decision Table

Figure 9.8 shows how rules can be structured. Restructuring the plain English text from the sketch into a more usable format imposes new questions and forces the experts to rethink the assumptions and requirements stated in the sketch. Consequently, gaps and contradictions become transparent and the quality of the business rules increases. The task of structuring is often seen as the most complex and time consuming part of a business rules project. Discussions among the functional teams about unclear, missing, and contradicting requirements may lead to several iterations until the draft can be completed.

Ruleset:	CALCULATE_FEES
Description:	Calculate Tuition and Compulsory Fees
Documentation:	Calculate of tuition and compulsory fees based on program information, course load, waiver. Limit of $25,000 . Changes are directly applied to the context.
Assigned to Function:	CALCULATE_FEES
Precondition:	IF *Tuition* is not equal to 0 or *Fees* is not equal to 0
Ruleset Variables:	

Name	Description	Documentation	Data Type	DDIC Type
COURSE_LOAD_IN_RANGE	Course Load in Range	Allowed Course Load	Boolean, true/false	

Rules:

#	Description	IF (Condition)	Then (Action)	Else (Action)	Comment
1	Course load check	Course Load in Range (DecTab expression) is false	Message: "Course load is out of range" (Message Log action)		
2	Obtain tuition and fees from PIM		Update Tuition, Fees from Load PIM (Call Procedure expression)		PIM = program information module, FM PIM_READ
3	Prorate tuition based on course load	Proration Indicator is false	Update Tuition from Tuition * Course Load (Formula expression)		
4	Cap fees	Fees > $1500	Set Fees to $1500 Message: "Fees capped at $1500" (Message Log action)		
5	...	...	...	...	...

Figure 9.8 Example of a Draft—Ruleset with Rules

The sketch, as an initial documentation of the business rules, is simply a starting point to get people familiar with the topic. However, the step is critical in framing the project goals and it is unlikely that one would save time by skipping directly to the structured step. Starting with structured documents can work well only for teams that are experienced with BRFplus.

Recommendations

- ▶ Create a spreadsheet document with several worksheets per business rules service
- ▶ List all parameters on one worksheet
- ▶ Whenever referring to data in the rules, use the parameter names/description from the parameters worksheet
- ▶ Explain at least the following concepts to the functional experts: decision tables, formulas, rules, rulesets
- ▶ Create one worksheet per ruleset: a ruleset worksheet should contain all rules
- ▶ Insert any expressions for which the content fits into a spreadsheet cell into the ruleset worksheet
- ▶ Create separate worksheets for action and expression types that do not fit into the ruleset worksheet; give them a name to be used in the ruleset worksheet
- ▶ Use decision tables whenever possible
- ▶ Create one worksheet per decision table
- ▶ Name the decision tables and use the names in the rules
- ▶ Create one worksheet for all open issues

9.4.6   Refinement of Business Rule Service

Functional experts should not be limited to what has been defined in the previous phase in which the business rule service was defined. The business rules may require access to additional information as a prerequisite to implementing the logic. The draft helps to identify missing parameters. Technical expertise is required to make the data available. There are two options: One is to add the missing parameters into the business rule service definition (the function signature). Alternatively, ruleset variables with initialization expressions may be added. Ruleset variables do not require any business process program code to be changed. Business users should not need to deal with data retrieval and necessary technical expressions, such as database lookup or Procedure Call expressions.

9.4.7   Analysis for Extensions

Another important aspect of the draft is the identification of required extensions to BRFplus. These extensions can be extensions to the expressiveness of BRFplus, additional checks, or better user interfaces. Several extensions can be done free of modifications:

- ▶ Custom action and expression types
- ▶ Custom formula functions
- ▶ Application exits

You can find more information about extensions in Section 7.3.

Extensions are necessary because of additional required features. In addition, depending on the degree of involvement of non-technical users in the business rules maintenance, it can be a good idea to invest in optimized user interfaces. Database lookup or Procedure Call expressions both have user interfaces that non-technical users are hardly able to work with. A separate UI with limited functional scope may be easier for them to use. In any case, the availability of the business logic as business rules in BRFplus facilitates discussion between functional and technical experts. Ultimately, the goal is to empower business users to make changes to future versions of the rules without the help of technical experts. As a result, new development requests for customization and simplification may arise.

The change infrastructure can be a source of additional requirements. These requirements relate to the decisions regarding where business rules should be changed, whether they should be transported between systems, and by whom they should be changed and released. Functional users may feel comfortable changing and testing business rules. However, business processes that depend on the rules may be disrupted when users lacking technical expertise and problem awareness perform changes without oversight. Therefore, business rules used in critical processes should be checked by technical experts, too, and be released only by them.

Another method for preventing disruption is the preparation of business rules artifacts by technical experts. Often, functional experts are not authorized to change functions, data objects, and rulesets. Instead, those users may change only a predefined set of expressions, such as decision tables or formulas. This approach ensures that the basic logic in the ruleset will not be changed, only the parameters. The changeable objects can be collected in catalogs for a better overview. The responsibility of the technical teams is to enable business change for functional users. They need to make sure that system requirements in terms of data integrity, stability and consistency are met.

Usually, customers follow a waterfall approach when implementing extensions for BRFplus. The technical team has the responsibility for specifying and designing extensions. For the implementation of extensions, solid knowledge of BRFplus and the BRFplus API is needed, in particular for the implementation of exits or custom action and expression types. If this knowledge is not available, external consultants need to be included. Finally, careful attention needs to be paid to which procedures should be done in BRFplus and which ones are better suited to pre or post processing in ABAP.

9.4.8 Creation of First Version

The better the structured information gathered in the draft is, the more easily it can be transferred into BRFplus. First, the BRFplus function and all the context parameters have to be created. Then the rulesets are created and assigned to the function. Perhaps additional variables and initialization expressions are needed. The rules from the draft can now be created in BRFplus. Ideally, decision tables have been used that can now be uploaded into BRFplus with little or no modification required. For other action and expression types, additional information is required, such as the names of function modules or log objects. This information, as well as the creation of ruleset variables, has to be provided by the technical experts. In the end, all rules content is checked and activated. Then it is possible to perform tests with the rules.

In some cases, the first version of the business rules cannot be completed without custom development. Several aspects of extensibility can still be added at a later point in time. However, extensions to the expressiveness of BRFplus, such as custom formula functions or actions, may be required to complete the first version. Sometimes it is an option to move such requirements to an ABAP method or a function module and use it from the rules with Procedure Call expressions. As soon as the development of such extensions is completed, those Procedure Call expressions may be replaced.

9.4.9 Implementation of Business Rule Service in Business Process

Several SAP standard applications are tightly integrated into BRFplus. In this case, the business rule service definition does not need to be designed and implemented: it is already part of prepared processes. Often in such applications, only the rules have to be defined in BRFplus. Sometimes there are even samples and templates available in form of pre-delivered customizing.

For applications that have no native integration, the implementation of the business rule service into the business process can start as soon as the business rule service definition has been completed. Technical questions with respect to extensions and breakup of tasks into business rules and ABAP code are answered. Adding more parameters usually takes very little effort and can be done on demand by the functional experts.

A completed version of the business rules is not even required. It can be sufficient to assign a dummy ruleset to the function. This ruleset does not contain any logic, except for setting a default result value. This ensures that the business process with the call into BRFplus can be implemented and tested.

9.4.10 Testing

At least one executable version of the business rules has to be created in BRFplus and connected to the business process. This is the prerequisite for service tests, also called module tests. Module tests entail testing the business rule service disconnected from the business processes. A first test may be done in the BRFplus Workbench with the simulation tool. It is possible to capture test data in an Excel sheet and upload it as input for the simulation. Ideally, module tests are set up also for tests of future versions. Whenever a new version is created, the test cases are executed against them to make sure that the business rules do still return the expected results and that errors have not been introduced accidentally. Once the tests are successful, end to end tests, also called integration tests, are conducted. Integration tests span across business processes and business rules.

9.5 Effort Estimation

An important decision to make at an early stage is who is going to deliver the design. As soon as a technical expert with good BRFplus knowledge is involved, rules projects can be implemented very smoothly. Such an expert can also be an external consultant. Ideally, there are technically savvy functional users involved. The BRFplus expert can form a team with another technical expert to address questions related to how BRFplus is embedded into system landscape and processes. One BRFplus expert should be able to derive the draft with two to three functional experts over a period of four to six weeks. Of course, effort depends greatly on the size and the complexity of the business as well as on clarity of functional and technical requirements, or the number of rules and expressions needed.

The Following Numbers Give an Indication of the Effort to be Expected:

Low complexity

▶ Requirements are for the most part clear

▶ Number of rules and expressions does not exceed 30

▶ Four experts need about two weeks to complete the draft

Medium complexity

▶ Some unclear requirements

▶ Number of rules and expressions does not exceed 100

▶ Four experts need about four weeks to complete the draft

High complexity

- ► Mostly unclear requirements
- ► Number of rules and expressions does exceed 100
- ► Four experts need about six weeks to complete the draft

In case a team has to implement several business rule services, subsequent services can be implemented more efficiently compared to the first one. A reduction of 20–30% of time needed is a realistic assumption. Very experienced BRFplus users will need very little time to enter the rules into BRFplus. The alignment concerning requirements will then take nearly all the remaining time.

The biggest challenge to the approach outlined in this chapter is that one cannot easily provide a good effort estimation until the draft is available. Only the draft can make required and optional investments transparent, which may be needed to optimally embed BRFplus into the customer landscape. Table 9.1 contains a list of extensions that are frequently implemented in customer projects. Of course, the list is not comprehensive. Depending on the specific customer situation, the efforts can deviate substantially. The effort numbers shown in Table 9.1 assume clear requirements.

Extension	Effort
Implementation of a custom expression or action type	From 10 to 50 person days
Embedding BRFplus expression UIs into custom UI	Up to 10 person days
Implementation of an exit method	Up to 10 person days
Creation of a transaction to call the BRFplus UI with predefined configuration	Up to 5 person days
Creation of a formula function	Up to 5 person days
Remote call of rule evaluation	Up to 5 person days
Remote access to metadata and value help (maintaining rules against remote data)	From 30 to 100 person days
Test framework for automated testing	Up to 30 person days

Table 9.1 Effort Estimation for Development of Extensions

Good effort estimations for the extensions are possible only for BRFplus experts who have experience from several projects. However, the learning curve for the business rules approach with BRFplus is very good. It is quite likely that the same team will need significantly less time for a subsequent rules project because extensions and knowledge can be reused.

A   Formula Functions

The following table contains all formula functions currently available for formula expressions in the BRFplus Workbench.

Category	Function	Description
Mathematical	ABS	Absolute value
	ARCCOS	Arcosine
	ARCSIN	Arcsine
	ARCTAN	Arctangent
	COS	Cosine
	COSH	Hyperbolic Cosine
	DIV	Division without fraction
	EXP	Exponential function for basis e
	FRAC	Fraction of a number
	LOG	Natural logarithm
	LOG10	Logarithm for basis 10
	MOD	Modulo division
	SIGN	Sign: -1, 1 or 0
	SIN	Sine
	SINH	Hyperbolic Sine
	SQRT	Square root
	TAN	Tangent
	TANH	Hyperbolic Tangent
	TONUMBER	Extracts the number from an amount, quantity or string
	TRUNC	Integer part of a number
Character Strings	CONCATENATE	Concatenates two strings
	CONDENSE	Trims of leading and trailing blanks
	EDIT_DISTANCE	Measures the difference among two strings using the "Levenshtein distance" metric
	STRING_LENGTH	Returns the number of characters in a string

Table A.1   Formula Functions

Category	Function	Description
	STRING_SIMILARITY	Measures the similarity of two string
	SUBSTRING	Extracts a part of a string
	TOUPPER	Converts characters of a string to upper case
Miscellaneous	CONVERT_AMOUNT	Converts an amount into a specific currency
	CONVERT_QUANTITY	Converts a quantity into a specific unit
	GET_CURRENCY	Extracts the currency from an amount as text
	GET_UNIT	Extracts the unit from a quantity as text
	IS_INITIAL	Checks if the provided value is initial
	MAX	Returns the maximum of two values
	MIN	Returns the minimum of two values
	ROUND	Rounds a value to a specific number of decimals
	TO_AMOUNT	Combines a number and a currency into an amount value
	TO_QUANTITY	Combines a number and a unit into a quantity value
Table	TABLE_AVG_AMOUNT	Calculates the average of an amount table column
	TABLE_AVG_NUMBER	Calculates the average of a number table column
	TABLE_AVG_QUANTITY	Calculates the average of a quantity table column
	TABLE_MAX_AMOUNT	Calculates the maximum of an amount table columns
	TABLE_MAX_NUMBER	Calculates the maximum of a number table column
	TABLE_MAX_QUANTITY	Calculates the maximum of a quantity table column
	TABLE_MAX_TIMEPOINT	Calculates the maximum of a timepoint table column
	TABLE_MIN_AMOUNT	Calculates the minimum of an amount table columns
	TABLE_MIN_NUMBER	Calculates the minimum of a number table column

Table A.1 Formula Functions (Cont.)

Category	Function	Description
	TABLE_MIN_QUANTITY	Calculates the minimum of a quantity table column
	TABLE_MIN_TIMEPOINT	Calculates the minimum of a timepoint table column
	TABLE_ROW_COUNT	Returns the number of rows of a table
	TABLE_SUM_AMOUNT	Calculates the sum of an amount table column
	TABLE_SUM_NUMBER	Calculates the sum of a number table column
	TABLE_SUM_QUANTITY	Calculates the sum of a quantity table column
Date & Time	DT_DURATION_DIFF	Time difference in a specific unit, including fraction
	DT_DURATION_DIFF_ SECONDS	Time difference in seconds, including fraction
	DT_DURATION_DIFF_ MINUTES	Time difference in minutes, including fraction
	DT_DURATION_DIFF_HOURS	Time difference in hours, including fraction
	DT_DURATION_DIFF_DAYS	Time difference in days, including fraction
	DT_DURATION_DIFF_WEEKS	Time difference in weeks, including fraction
	DT_DURATION_DIFF_MONTHS	Time difference in months, including fraction
	DT_DURATION_DIFF_ QUARTERS	Time difference in quarters, including fraction
	DT_DURATION_DIFF_YEARS	Time difference in years, including fraction
	DT_DURATION_DIFF_INT	Time difference in a specific unit, without fraction
	DT_DURATION_DIFF_INT_ SECONDS	Time difference in whole seconds, without fraction
	DT_DURATION_DIFF_INT_ YEARS	Time difference in whole minutes, without fraction
	DT_DURATION_DIFF_INT_ HOURS	Time difference whole hours, without fraction

Table A.1 Formula Functions (Cont.)

Category	Function	Description
	`DT_DURATION_DIFF_INT_DAYS`	Time difference in whole days, without fraction
	`DT_DURATION_DIFF_INT_WEEKS`	Time difference in whole weeks, without fraction
	`DT_DURATION_DIFF_INT_MONTHS`	Time difference in whole months, without fraction
	`DT_DURATION_DIFF_INT_QUARTERS`	Time difference in whole quarters, without fraction
	`DT_ADD_SECONDS`	Adds seconds to a timepoint
	`DT_ADD_MINUTES`	Adds minutes to a timepoint
	`DT_ADD_HOURS`	Adds hours to a timepoint
	`DT_ADD_DAYS`	Adds days to a timepoint
	`DT_ADD_WEEKS`	Adds weeks to a timepoint
	`DT_ADD_MONTHS`	Adds months to a timepoint
	`DT_ADD_QUARTERS`	Adds quarters to a timepoint
	`DT_ADD_YEARS`	Adds years to a timepoint
	`DT_SUBTRACT_SECONDS`	Subtracts seconds from a timepoint
	`DT_SUBTRACT_MINUTES`	Subtracts seconds from a timepoint
	`DT_SUBTRACT_HOURS`	Subtracts minutes from a timepoint
	`DT_SUBTRACT_DAYS`	Subtracts days from a timepoint
	`DT_SUBTRACT_WEEKS`	Subtracts weeks from a timepoint
	`DT_SUBTRACT_MONTHS`	Subtracts months from a timepoint
	`DT_SUBTRACT_QUARTERS`	Subtracts quarters from a timepoint
	`DT_SUBTRACT_YEARS`	Subtracts years from a timepoint
	`DT_PART_SECONDS`	Extracts the seconds from a timepoint
	`DT_PART_MINUTES`	Extracts the minutes from a timepoint
	`DT_PART_HOURS`	Extracts the hours from a timepoint
	`DT_PART_TIME`	Extracts the time part from a timepoint
	`DT_PART_DAYS`	Extracts the day from a timepoint
	`DT_PART_WEEKS`	Extracts the week of the year from a timepoint
	`DT_PART_MONTHS`	Extracts the month from a timepoint
	`DT_PART_QUARTERS`	Extracts the quarter of the year from a timepoint

Table A.1 Formula Functions (Cont.)

Category	Function	Description
	`DT_PART_YEARS`	Extracts the year from a timepoint
	`DT_PART_DATE`	Extracts the date part from a timepoint
	`DT_ROUND_TO_FIRST`	Rounds a timepoint to the beginning of a specified time unit
	`DT_ROUND_TO_MIDDLE`	Rounds a timepoint to the middle of a specified time unit
	`DT_ROUND_TO_LAST`	Rounds a timepoint to the end of a specified time unit
	`DT_GET_CURRENT_DATE`	Returns the current date
	`DT_GET_CURRENT_TIME`	Returns the current time
	`DT_GET_CURRENT_DT`	Returns the current date and time
	`DT_CET_CURRENT_UTC`	Returns the current UTC timestamp
	`DT_GET_CURRENT_DT_OFFSET_UTC`	Returns the current date and time with offset to UTC
	`DT_GET_DAY_OF_WEEK`	Returns the day of the week for a timepoint as number
	`DT_GET_DAY_OF_YEAR`	Returns the day of the year for a timepoint as number
	`DT_GET_FIRST_DAY_OF_WEEK`	Returns first day of the week according to the used calendar
	`D.T_IS_LEAP_YEAR`	Checks if a specific year is a leap year
	`DT_IS_NULL`	Checks if a timepoint is initial (01.01.0001)
	`DT_IS_VALID`	Checks if a timepoint is valid
	`DT_MAX`	Returns the maximum of two timepoints
	`DT_MIN`	Returns the minimum of two timepoints
	`DT_IS_ACTIVE`	Checks if a timepoint is active with respect to working days in the current calendar
	`DT_PREVIOUS_ACTIVE`	Returns the previous active timepoint with respect to working days the current calendar
	`DT_NEXT_ACTIVE`	Returns the next active timepoint with respect to working days in the current calendar

Table A.1 Formula Functions (Cont.)

Category	Function	Description
System	SYS_INFO_SYSTEM_ID	Returns the name of the system
	SYS_INFO_CLIENT_ID	Returns the current system client
	SYS_INFO_USER_NAME	Returns the name of the current user
	SYS_INFO_LANGUAGE	Returns the current system language key
	SYS_INFO_CURRENT_DATE	Returns the current system timepoint
	SYS_INFO_LOCAL_DATE	Returns the local date for the current user
	SYS_INFO_LOCAL_TIME	Returns the local time for the current user
	SYS_INFO_CALENDAR_DAY	Returns the current day with respect to the system calendar
	SYS_INFO_TIME_ZONE	Returns the system time zone
	SYS_INFO_TIME_ZONE_DIFF	Returns the difference of the system time zone to UTC in seconds
	SYS_INFO_DAYLIGHT_SAVING	Checks for active daylight savings time in the system
	SYS_INFO_SAP_RELEASE	Returns the SAP release name
	SYS_INFO_HOST	Returns the application server identifier
	SYS_INFO_DB_SYSTEM	Returns the name of the database system
	SYS_INFO_OPERATING_ SYS	Returns the operating system name of the server

Table A.1 Formula Functions (Cont.)

B   The Authors

Carsten Ziegler is the inventor, chief product owner, and architect of Business Rules Framework plus (BRFplus) at SAP. He joined SAP in 2001 working in multiple roles including developer, development architect, and project manager for numerous projects in the area of technical tools and frameworks and analytics applications. Since 2006 he has driven SAP's business rules strategy and he is responsible for the BRFplus architecture and development as well as its adoption within in SAP's applications. Carsten is also a key contributor to defining SAP's overall business process strategy for SAP's business suite and successfully prepared the acquisition of Yasu in 2007. He has a track record of guiding many large-scale projects, in terms of both setting up and using business rules and business process management technology. Drawing upon his extensive experience, he provides global business rules expertise supporting sales, consulting, development, and solution management. Carsten holds a diploma in Business Administration at ...

Thomas Albrecht is a senior software developer in the Business Rule Framework plus (BRFplus) team. After completing his studies with a master's degree in computer science, he joined SAP in 2003. He started working in and driving several development projects in the ERP Travel Management department with focus on architecture and user interfaces. In 2008 he delved into the area of BRFplus and quickly became a key member of the development team.

Index

Program
FDT-TEMPLATE-FUNCTION-PROCESS

Presents the most important ABAP statements comprehensively

Covers key object-oriented programming concepts

Step-by-step techniques to develop a working ABAP application

2nd, revised, and updated edition for ABAP 7.0

Günther Färber, Julia Kirchner

ABAP Basics

In this newly revised and updated book, you will become acquainted with the most important and commonly used ABAP commands and terminology. Updated for ABAP version 7.0, you will find all of the typical tasks and issues that a programmer faces within the fast-paced SAP environment, which will enable you to write your own ABAP application.

approx. 508 pp., 2. edition, 59,95 Euro / US$ 59.95
ISBN 978-1-59229-369-8, Nov 2010

>> www.sap-press.com

 **booksonline**

Your SAP Library is just a click away

1. Search 🔍

2. Buy 🛒

3. Read ≡

Try now!

www.sap-press.com

✓ Easy and intuitive navigation
✓ Bookmarking
✓ Searching within the full text of all our books
✓ 24/7 access
✓ Printing capability

Galileo Press

Interested in reading more?

Please visit our Web site for all
new book releases from SAP PRESS.

www.sap-press.com